# Rio Grande do Sul
# and Brazilian Regionalism
# 1882–1930

Joseph L. Love

D1445458

Stanford University Press, Stanford, California   1971

Sources of photographs and illustrations:
1, 6, 7, 10, 13, Editôra Globo; 2, 11, Olavo Dutra;
3, 8, Sinval Saldanha; 4, 9, 12, Biblioteca Nacional;
5, Arthur Ferreira Filho.


Stanford University Press, Stanford, California
© 1971 by the Board of Trustees of the
Leland Stanford Junior University
Printed in the United States of America
ISBN 0-8047-0759-6
LC 71-130829

*For My Parents*

# Contents

*Eight pages of pictures follow page 160*

# Preface

If the genius of the Brazilian political elite has been to preserve the unity of an immense and underdeveloped nation, it is nonetheless true that regional cleavage is one of the constant themes of Brazilian history. Politics in any era is inexplicable without reference to the economic, social, and political configurations of the various regions or states. This study deals with a single state, Rio Grande do Sul, and its role in national politics during Brazil's Old Republic (1889–1930), a period in which a loose federal system and the absence of national political parties made the states exceptionally important. The work is divided into two parts: the first emphasizes internal developments in Rio Grande from 1882 to 1908, and the second deals with Riograndenses in national politics between 1909 and 1930. Part One, however, necessarily treats national developments to some degree, just as Part Two makes reference to changes within the state.

The Old (or First) Republic has not received adequate attention in the historiography of Brazil. Most Brazilian historians have preferred to concentrate on the colonial and Imperial eras; Brazilian social scientists have written most extensively about the contemporary period, with 1930 as the standard point of departure. This book, therefore, is a contribution to the literature on a relatively neglected era. It also attempts to fill another gap—the lack of "intermediate range" studies between those that are national in scope and those that focus on specific communities. By intermediate range study, I do not mean state or regional history as such, but rather the type of work for which national and local developments are essential elements in the story. This book is not a state history in the usual sense, just as it is not a history of the Old Republic; it is a study of the "internal" and "external" dynamics of Rio Grande do Sul in the Brazilian federation. In it I attempt to show the complex ways in which modernization was related to centralization and decentralization, and I indicate the initiatives undertaken by the states as well as the federal government. Yet this is not primarily a story of "success"; it deals with the failures of the political elite as well as its achievements.

Rio Grande's role in the national arena is, of course, hardly the whole story of Brazilian politics in this era. My perspective has been a limited one, and I have reduced the political dynamics of other states to the minimum required for the coherence of the narrative. However, Robert M. Levine, John D. Wirth, and I are currently at work on a multi-volume study of regionalism and elite politics that will correct the single-state perspective of this book.

In some ways scholarship is a lonely journey, but every investigator who completes a lengthy study owes a debt of gratitude to scores of persons and institutions. My own obligations are extensive. Research for this book was initiated with funds from the Foreign Area Fellowship Program, which provided me support from the second year of graduate study through the Ph.D., including 14 months' residence in Brazil in 1964–65. Two additional grants by the Social Science Research Council and the Center for International Comparative Studies of the University of Illinois allowed me to return to Brazil for three months in 1968 to complete my field work. I am also grateful to the Research Board of the University of Illinois for funds for research assistance on campus. The opinions expressed herein are of course my own, and do not necessarily reflect the views of any organization that supported me.

Among the persons who helped me write this book, I wish to thank the following teachers and colleagues who criticized the manuscript in whole or in part at some stage of its development: Lewis Hanke, who was my dissertation director at Columbia University; and Francisco de Assis Barbosa, J. G. Bell, Robert Conrad, Raymundo Faoro, Richard Graham, Octavio Ianni, Robert M. Levine, Dwight C. Miner, Thomas E. Skidmore, Mauricio Solaún, Peter H. Smith, Walter Spalding, and John D. Wirth. I alone, of course, am responsible for the errors and weaknesses that remain. Others whose aid I gratefully acknowledge are Alzira Vargas do Amaral Peixoto; Euclides Aranha Netto; Zilda Galhardo de Araújo; Joaquina, Lídia, and Lydia Assis Brasil; James Bier; Dario de Bittencourt; the late George C. A. Boehrer; Ralph della Cava; Sérgio da Costa Franco; Tomás Duarte; Arthur Ferreira Filho; José Bonifácio Flôres da Cunha; Ludlow Flower; Roberto Piragibe da Fonseca; Othelo Laurent; Juan J. Linz; B. E. Mnookin; Adoaldo Queiroz; José Honório Rodrigues; the late Sinval Saldanha; Paulo Brossard de Souza Pinto; Stanley J. Stein; James L. Taylor; Carlos Torres Gonçalves; Moysés Vellinho; Pedro Leite Villas Boas; and my research assistants, Catherine Cortés, Janet Crist, and Rubens Estrella. To the dozens of other people who helped me in one way or another, I offer thanks collectively.

Personnel of the following institutions were especially helpful: the Biblioteca da Assembléia dos Representantes do Estado do Rio Grande do Sul; the Biblioteca Pública do Estado; the Departamento Estadual de Estatística; the Federação das Associações Rurais do Estado; and the Instituto Histórico e Geográfico do Rio Grande do Sul (all in Pôrto Alegre); and the Arquivo do Ministério da Guerra; the Arquivo Nacional; the Biblioteca Nacional; the Casa de Rui Barbosa; the Instituto Brasileiro de Geografia e Estatística; and the Instituto Histórico e Geográfico Brasileiro (all in Rio de Janeiro).

To the following persons and institutions, I extend my thanks for help in obtaining pictures: Olavo Dutra, Arthur Ferreira Filho, Sinval Saldanha, the Biblioteca Nacional, and Editôra Globo.

Thanks finally to Marcia, who encouraged me from initial enthusiasm to final completion.

J.L.L.

*Urbana, Illinois*
*Fall 1970*

# Explanatory Note

"Elite" is a word that appears frequently in the following pages, and an elaboration of the term is in order here. Defining an elite, social scientists have warned, presents numerous conceptual and practical problems. The pitfalls seem greater, however, in attempting to determine elites in "modern," politically pluralistic societies than in defining elites in "traditional," more highly stratified cultures. Not many would argue against the use of "political elite" in connection with the Old Republic, when only 2 to 6 per cent of the population voted, and a small group made the decisions on government personnel and policies. As I use the term, the elite includes the executive committees of the state parties, governors, members of the federal government at the cabinet level and above, congressional leaders, and regional military commanders. The "power" of the elite is defined as its ability to choose candidates for public office at state and national levels without consulting the voting public. The members of the political elite belonged to a broader socioeconomic elite, whose interests they defended in government. "Elites" in the plural refers to the various state components of the national political elite.

Another important term is "legitimacy," by which I mean the acceptance of the prevailing political system by those who participated in it by means of the vote. Legitimacy figures in the definition of "regionalism," which is introduced at the beginning of Part Two. The regions of Rio Grande do Sul and of the nation will be clear in context. The north in this study refers to the states from Bahia northward. The northeast, a less inclusive term, applies to the contiguous coastal states from Sergipe to Piauí. The south refers to the states from Espírito Santo southward.

Anyone who writes about Brazil for readers of English must come to grips with problems of usage, since Portuguese and English practices differ on many points. I have followed the Brazilian system of referring to important historical personages in second and later references by the names most commonly given them in the scholarly literature. Thus, Artur Bernardes is Bernardes, whereas Hermes da Fonseca is Hermes. I have adopted modern Portuguese orthography in the text but have kept the original spelling in the older works cited in the notes. Some names in the notes have more than one spelling, depending on the date of publication of the works in which they appear.

Rendering Portuguese terms into English presents other difficulties. In this book a state *presidente* is a governor, but an *intendente* is an intendant, rather than a mayor, since his area of jurisdiction (the *município*) was more like a county than a city. I have retained the Portuguese to designate inhabitants of the states: Paulista, Mineiro, Bahiano, Fluminense, and Carioca, refer, respectively, to persons from São Paulo, Minas Gerais, Bahia, the State of Rio de Janeiro, and the city of Rio de Janeiro (the federal capital in the period under study). Inhabitants of Rio Grande do Sul are Riograndenses or Gaúchos; the terms are interchangeable. Where I use the word gaúcho (pronounced ga-oo'-shoo) without a capital G, I refer specifically to the cowboy of Rio Grande do Sul, whose name was ultimately applied to all natives of the state. Some usage is more or less arbitrary. I have chosen the Spanish spelling for a few words, e.g., *caudillo* (Port., caudilho), because the Spanish form is more familiar to readers of English and because Brazilians usually use the term with the Spanish-American model in mind.

Statistics offer still other problems. The collection and ordering of statistics between 1872 and 1930 had many shortcomings, some of which are mentioned in the notes. Population figures are especially troublesome; in 1960 the Instituto Brasileiro de Estatística e Geografia (IBGE) published retrospective estimates of the national population back to 1851 (see *Anuário estatístico do Brasil—1960: Ano XXI* [Rio, 1960], p. 21), and these figures are often at variance with contemporary estimates. The global results of the 1890 census stand up better than do those for 1872 and 1920. The 1872 count under-estimated the population of Brazil by one million, and the 1920 census overestimated it by three million. In 1920 the count was off by 12 per cent, and from that year to the end of the Old Republic, contemporary estimates consistently overstated the population. Unfortunately, the IBGE's retrospective data are not broken down by state and município, so the researcher must declare his reservations and make do with the contemporary figures. By and large, in comparing state populations, I have been concerned with relative rather than absolute magnitudes; hopefully, the relative positions accorded the states are more reliable.

A final note on Brazilian currency: The monetary unit in the Old Republic was the *milréis*, written 1$000; budgetary figures, however, were more often expressed in *contos*. A conto equalled 1,000 milréis, and was expressed 1:000$000. Where appropriate, I have given the value of a sum in contemporary (or "current") dollars.

# PART ONE

# The Rise of Castilhismo

# CHAPTER ONE

# The Structure of Gaúcho Society

W HEN the revolution of 1930 ended the Old Republic and brought Getúlio Vargas to power, several "provisional corps" of gaúchos from the estâncias of Rio Grande do Sul entered Rio de Janeiro with their chief. Although Vargas came from Rio Grande by train, many of the gaúchos made the trek on horseback, and rode into the national capital with a mixture of contempt and admiration for urban splendor. Reaching the center of the city, they hitched their mounts to the famous obelisk on the Avenida Rio Branco. To many of the capital's inhabitants, this "desecration" of a symbol of European culture seemed ominous. Hadn't the literary and social critic Sílvio Romero declared that Rio Grande do Sul was governed by "semi-barbarous souls created by a pastoral system"? Was this act a foretaste of what a barbaric horde from "a foreign body in the Brazilian federation" (as another writer put it) had in store for the refined inhabitants of the "real" Brazil?[1]

Many, probably most, Brazilians living north of Rio Grande do Sul thought of that state as a flat, endless pampa populated by roaming cowboys—the original meaning of *gaúchos*—who looked to an *estancieiro* for their livelihood and to a *caudillo* for political leadership. Indeed, to other Brazilians the Gaúchos were not "Brazilian" at all, but Spanish-American: their lands were like the pampa of Argentina, and their caudillos were men like Juan Manuel Rosas, Argentina's rough-riding dictator from 1829 to 1852. Even after the Vargas cycle had closed with the President's dramatic suicide in 1954, *Anhembi*, a leading intellectual journal of São Paulo, found it convenient to explain Vargas's career in regionalist terms. Caudillismo, it asserted, had entered Brazil through Rio Grande do Sul; its first practitioner had been José Gomes Pinheiro Machado, the crass, scheming, "barbarian" boss of the senate in the middle years of the Old Republic, and Vargas had simply taken up the torch from Pinheiro.[2] That the myth of Gaúcho foreignness was still alive as late as the 1960's is attested to by the publication of Moysés Vellinho's *Capitania d'El-Rei*, which eloquently argues that Riograndense history and regional culture are deeply Brazilian and are alien to their Platine counterparts.[3]

Still, it would be wrong to assume that all the qualities attributed to the Gaúchos by their fellow Brazilians are unflattering. The Mineiro historian and sociologist Francisco Oliveira Viana found the Riograndenses brave and egalitarian, men who were "warriors by education and inclination"; and the proposition that "every Gaúcho is a soldier" was widely accepted by Oliveira Viana's contemporaries.[4] Most of these generalizations were directed at the gaúcho (cowboy), but by extension referred to the inhabitants of Rio Grande in general. This is true, for instance, of Euclides da Cunha's famous saga, *Os Sertões*, which stressed the gaúcho's romantic, happy-go-lucky character: "He goes through life adventurous, jovial, eloquent of speech, valiant and swaggering; he looks on labor as a diversion which affords him the sport of stampedes; lord of the distances is he, as he rides the broad level-lying pasture lands. . . . He is a conquering hero, merry and bold."[5] Interestingly enough, the debate on the nature of Gaúcho character has focused almost exclusively on one of the subcultures of Rio Grande, the pastoral complex, a way of life that only a minority of Riograndenses follow today. This chapter will sketch the three basic subcultures, and trace the role of each up to the 1880's in economics, social relations, and politics.

First, however, a word about the geography of Rio Grande do Sul, so often misunderstood by Brazilians from other states. Rio Grande, which measures some 478 miles from its easternmost to its westernmost point, and almost the same distance from north to south, is larger than two South American republics, Ecuador and Uruguay, even though it occupies only a little more than 3 per cent of the territory of Brazil. Contiguous to Argentina and Uruguay, it lies well below the tropics (falling between 27° S and 34° S), but far from being the endless pampa, or grass-covered plain, that Cunha and others imagined, Rio Grande—including the ranching region—is in the main hilly. The state is divided into two hydrographic basins by the Cochilha Grande, a series of hills that begins in the coastal range where Rio Grande meets the state of Santa Catarina, moves west and slightly north beyond the Jacuí River, and then turns sharply south, skirting the Vacacaí River to pass into Uruguay near the frontier town of Livramento. To the west of the Cochilha Grande, the Quaraí, Ibicuí, and Ijuí rivers flow into the Uruguay, and ultimately into the River Plate estuary. To the east of the divide, the Caí and Vacacaí empty into the Jacuí, which flows eastward into the lagoon called the Lagoa dos Patos, as does the Camaquã River farther south. Separating southeastern Rio Grande do Sul from the Republic of Uruguay is the Jaguarão River, which flows into the Lagoa Mirim.

Physiographically geographers have distinguished as many as six regions in Rio Grande do Sul, but culturally and economically a division into three regions is commonly accepted, and this convention will be adopted here.[6] These areas are the Litoral, the Campanha, and the Cima da Serra (or simply the Serra). The Litoral, smallest of the regions, consists of the coastal strip and the alluvial areas washed by the Lagoa dos Patos and the Lagoa Mirim; it extends from Tôrres in the north to Santa Vitória do Palmar in the south, and includes the Jacuí Valley as far west as Cachoeira. An area of relatively poor soil, the Litoral has nonetheless historically been the most densely populated of the three regions, as the locus of exports, intrastate commerce, and industry. In the twentieth century the region's main agricultural activity has been the cultivation of rice along the Lagoa dos Patos and its tributary rivers, especially the Jacuí. Pôrto Alegre, the state capital and a city of almost a million inhabitants, is Brazil's third or fourth most important manufacturing center. It is served by one of the most navigable river systems in Brazil, but is inaccessible to large ocean-going vessels because of the shallowness of the Lagoa dos Patos. Thanks to dredging in this century, however, these ships today can cross the bar of Rio Grande and dock at Pelotas, the state's second-largest city.

The Campanha, the second region, is the area south of the east-west line cut by the Jacuí and Ibicuí rivers, from the Litoral to the confluence of the Uruguay and Ibicuí. Hilly uplands between the Vacacaí and the Lagoa dos Patos cover more than a third of the Campanha, but gently rolling hills called *cochilhas*—a term referring to the hills themselves as well as to groups of hills—spread across a far greater area, and are a typical physical feature in much of the Serra as well. Between the uplands of the Campanha and the Cochilha Grande lies a lowland, extending from the Uruguayan border to the central depression in the Jacuí Valley. The Campanha landscape alternates a semiarid vegetation with a wide variety of shades of green. The umbu tree thrives in the Campanha, as it does in the adjacent republics of the Plate.

Here in the southwestern part of Rio Grande is the ranching country that gives the state its image elsewhere in Brazil. Although the soil could be used for agriculture, pastoral activities dominate everywhere except in the Campanha's northern and eastern fringes. In the eighteenth century the first inhabitants of the region carved it up into huge ranching estates—*estâncias* (or *fazendas*)—which still predominate. During the Old Republic (1889–1930), the high degree of concentration of land ownership in the state was due primarily to the existence of latifundia in the Campanha. Towns in the Campanha are few and widely separated by sparsely settled grazing lands; compared to the urban centers of the Serra and the Litoral, the towns of the Campanha are sleepy and relatively static in population.

The Cima da Serra, the third region, comprises the area extending north and west of Pôrto Alegre to the Uruguay River and bounded on the south by the Ibicuí-Jacuí line. Its red soil (including both *terra vermelha* and *terra roxa*) is richer than those of the other regions. As the Cima da Serra's name indicates, the region is a high plateau; its altitude, varying from about 325 feet to more than 3,000 feet above sea level, makes it the coolest region in the state. Forests cover about half the region, with the tall, flat-coned pinheiro the most distinctive tree. *Campos* (rolling grasslands) account for the remainder, except in the far west. There lies the valley of the Uruguay River, where the soil changes from red to brown and semiarid vegetation appears, including tall cacti. For historical purposes the Serra may be divided into three subregions: the Colonial Zone, the Central Plateau, and the Missões (missions) District.

The first of these subdivisions, the Colonial Zone, constitutes the eastern portion of the region, which was populated by German and

Italian *colonos* engaging in mixed farming in the nineteenth century; since then, their descendants and other non-Iberian immigrants have pushed family-sized holdings westward and northward toward the Uruguay Valley, (though not without resistance from the large landowners, who have kept the small farms largely confined to the forested areas). In the north-central part of the Serra, the colonos cleared the forests and planted wheat, transforming the district into one of Brazil's major granaries by 1940. Unlike the wooded sections, the campos of the Serra were occupied in the eighteenth and nineteenth centuries by estancieiros. The Central Plateau was originally settled by woodsmen and ranchers moving south from São Paulo. The Missões District, whose name derives from the famous Jesuit settlements established in the seventeenth century to convert the Guarani Indians, was claimed for Brazil in the 1750's as ranchers moved north from the Campanha and west from the Central Plateau. As the last region to be occupied, the Serra was isolated from the commercial axis of the Litoral, and was denied cheap transportation to centers of consumption and distribution until the railroad cut across the region in the early twentieth century.

Each of the three regions—Litoral, Serra, and Campanha—was penetrated in the colonial era, but the Serra, the last to be permanently settled, was the site of the state's first experiment in Iberian civilization. The Society of Jesus entered Rio Grande when its members forded the Uruguay from the Guarani settlements of Paraguay and Misiones (now part of Argentina) in 1619. Despite the virtual destruction of the Riograndense missions by slave-hunting *bandeirantes* from São Paulo between 1636 and 1638, the Jesuits returned to the east bank of the Uruguay in 1687, founding or refounding a total of seven missions, the Sete Povos.

Until the late seventeenth century, this area and the rest of Rio Grande formed the frontier of the Spanish Empire; Portuguese America ended at Laguna, a hamlet on the coast of southern Santa Catarina. In 1680, however, the Portuguese took a bold step to extend their New World empire southward, pushing down to the eastern bank of the River Plate to found Colônia do Sacramento, which they defiantly planted across the estuary from Buenos Aires. For the next 150 years the territory between Laguna and the mouth of the Plate was the scene of continual warfare as first Spain and Portugal and later Argentina and Brazil fought over the limits of their domains. Since Colônia staked out the southernmost limit of Portugal's claim, it had to be defended, and the coastline of Rio Grande do Sul was traversed almost incidentally as a line of supply for the outpost on the Plate. Colônia was destroyed four times by the Spaniards and rebuilt three times by the Portuguese; with the Treaty of San Ildefonso in 1777, it definitively passed into Spanish hands.

Partly because of the need to supply Colônia and partly because of the need for pastures to raise cattle, horses, and mules for the gold and diamond fields of Minas Gerais, Portuguese and Brazilian soldiers and frontiersmen occupied the Litoral and the Central Plateau in the first half of the eighteenth century. An overland route connected Laguna and northern Rio Grande as early as 1725. In 1736 a bandeirante named Cristóvão Pereira opened another route from the interior of Santa Catarina down to the bar of Rio Grande, laying the groundwork for a more conventional military expedition the following year, led by Brig. Gen. José da Silva Paes. At the bar of Rio Grande Silva Paes founded a fortified town, which he called São Pedro do Rio Grande do Sul; the hinterland behind the town was given the same name. In 1742 a group of Azorian settlers founded Pôrto dos Casais (which later became Pôrto Alegre) on the Guaíba estuary. To the west Portuguese-speaking settlers founded Rio Pardo on the Jacuí, and by mid-century Portuguese and Brazilian pioneers were even pushing into the Missões District. The Spanish Jesuits resisted this invasion, though Spain had officially ceded to Portugal the territory east of the Uruguay River in 1750. A Guarani chieftain named Sepé Tiaraju (popularly known as Saint Sepé) led a valiant fight on behalf of the Jesuits until his death in 1756. But he was unable to stop the Portuguese penetration of the Missões District, which continued even after the territory reverted to Spain in 1777.

Meanwhile the Spaniards took the offensive along the coast. Pedro de Ceballos, the governor of Buenos Aires, sailed northward from the Plate and put the fortified town of Rio Grande under Spanish rule in 1763. The Spaniards also attacked Rio Pardo, thereby threatening the Portuguese invaders of the Missões District from the rear. But Spanish power was overextended, as Portuguese claims in the Plate had been 50 years before, and in 1776 Spain lost its foothold in the port town of Rio Grande. The Treaty of San Ildefonso in the following year returned the Litoral region to Portugal; the Missões District, over which the Portuguese had de facto control after the mid-eighteenth century, was incorporated into Rio Grande by the Treaty of Badajoz in 1801. Rio Grande do Sul was declared a captaincy-general in 1807 and became a province of the Kingdom of Brazil in 1821, one year before national independence.

With the Litoral and the Missões District secured by the end of the eighteenth century, the only remaining territorial issue was the line at which the Banda Oriental (roughly today's Uruguay) would be divided from Rio Grande. In the absence of good natural boundaries, the border between Rio Grande and its southern neighbor remained undefined until the middle of the nineteenth century. In the meantime, Luso-Brazilian estâncias began to penetrate the Campanha more rapidly because of the rise of a new industry in Rio Grande: the production of dried, salted (jerked) beef, known in southern Brazil and the Plate as *charque*. This low-grade meat, which could be transported over long distances with a minimum of spoilage, provided the economic impetus for an expansion of the Riograndense estâncias south of the Jacuí. By-products included cowhides and tallow. In these same years, the Serra economy was stagnating because the mining industry of Minas, on which the Serranos were economically dependent, was in decline; furthermore, the Serranos had to transport their chief products, livestock and pack animals, overland, making a slow and laborious trek to the Sorocaba fair in São Paulo. The estâncias of the Campanha by contrast had access to relatively low-cost water transportation via the bar of Rio Grande. In the early nineteenth century, the Campanha estancieiros pushed their holdings westward and southward into what became the northwest corner of Uruguay; and many Portuguese-speaking Brazilians continued to settle beyond the frontier line at the Quaraí River, even after Uruguay became an independent state in 1828.

Life was hard on the southern frontier, where settlers found themselves embroiled in constant struggles with both Spanish-speaking settlers and nomadic Indians. In order to attract immigrants, the Portuguese government made land grants of two, three, or more leagues, sometimes amounting to hundreds of square miles.[7] Thus the latifundium was created with the earliest settlement of the region.

Ranching entered Rio Grande with the seventeenth-century Jesuit missions. In the early eighteenth century, Spanish Jesuits, once again in possession of the Missões District, brought cattle into the campos of the Central Plateau. Frequent skirmishes between Spanish Jesuits and Portuguese frontiersmen in the thinly populated area dispersed the herds, and wild cattle strayed across the Serra into the Campanha during the eighteenth century. Ranching, accordingly, seemed an almost preordained activity for the Portuguese as they began making a serious bid for the lands beyond the coast around 1750. Yet there were other economic pursuits as well. The Jesuits had grown yerba mate on a commercial basis, but the Portuguese conquerors of the Missões District did not, having neither the disciplined Indian labor force nor the free access to the entrepôt of Buenos Aires that had made the cultivation of mate profitable. Instead, wheat became the chief competitor to cattle and charque in the colonial era. Azorian settlers introduced wheat farming in the Litoral in the mid-eighteenth century, and for a time wheat was Rio Grande do Sul's main export, reaching a maximum in 1813.

With the development of a charque industry at the freshwater port of Pelotas, however, cattle ranching soon challenged the preeminence of farming. *Charqueadas* (charque processing plants) were introduced in the Pelotas area following the 1777 drought in Ceará, until then the main source of charque for Brazil's coastal cities. By the beginning of the nineteenth century, Rio Grande was facing stiff competition in the Brazilian market from the Banda Oriental and Buenos Aires, whose ranchers could sell charque in Rio de Janeiro more cheaply than the Gaúchos because of superior pasturage and cheaper (coastal) transportation. Nevertheless, Rio Grande was able to reign supreme in the charque markets of coastal Brazil in the early national period, thanks to a series of revolutions that convulsed the Plate region between 1810 and 1830. Cattle ranching consequently expanded and eclipsed farming. Wheat production declined sharply after the peak year of 1813, and wheat all but disappeared as an export crop within a decade, in part because of a rust that attacked the grain, but more importantly, because of the greater profitability of ranching. Coupled with rising cattle prices was the fact that in a colony with a short supply of manpower, wheat farming was labor-intensive compared to stock raising. In 1801 it was estimated that an estância with 10,000 head of cattle required only a foreman and ten peons.[8]

Latifundium owners dominated Gaúcho society in the eighteenth and early nineteenth centuries, as they dominated society in other parts of Brazil. In Rio Grande as in the tropical zones the owners of the big estates, faced with a scarcity of labor, began importing African slaves. In 1803 there were only some 500 landowners in Rio Grande do Sul, though most of the Campanha was theoretically occupied.[9] Slaves were important as ranch hands and as workers in the charqueadas, but slavery never established an iron grip on Rio Grande as it did farther north in the sugar- and coffee-producing areas. For one thing, mounted gaúchos could escape to freedom with relative ease. For another, frequent border wars helped disorganize the regime of slavery. Rio Grande consequently tended to develop the patron-peon relationship of the Plate countries rather than the master-slave system of plantation Brazil. Yet Negroes and mulattoes formed an important component of the labor force, especially in the early years, and they still accounted for almost 30 per cent of the state's population in 1890.[10]

The first 150 years of estância life were the great age of the gaúcho, whose name in due course became a synonym for Riograndense. By the late nineteenth century, his colorful dress included a broad-brimmed hat; a bandana (lenço) around his neck; tall leather boots with accordion pleats at the ankles; huge jangling spurs, called chilenas; full, heavy trousers (bombachas) to protect his legs from the scrub; and a woolen poncho to protect him against the vicissitudes of the weather, especially the dry winter wind known as the minuano.* Almost part of his person was his horse, the pingo, on which he spent most of his waking hours. Attached to the saddle was a lasso, and perhaps also a set of boleadeiras, three leather-covered stones connected by rawhide thongs, which, when expertly thrown at game and runaway livestock, could bring them down by entangling their feet. The gaúcho rarely carried a pistol but was never without his dagger-like knife, the facão, an all-purpose instrument for slaughtering, skinning, eating, and fighting. Like his Platine counterpart, the Riograndense gaúcho lived largely on a diet of beef, which he cooked

---

* Bombachas replaced the more primitive chiripá, a piece of cloth about five feet long that was tucked between the legs and hooked onto the front part of the belt. The gaúcho's boots were also a fairly recent development. Typically in the early nineteenth century he wore only leather leggings and went unshod.

by reflected heat on spits or knives stuck upright in the ground; his open-air feast was called a *churrasco*. With his beef he took his *chimarrão*, a concoction of boiling water and mate, which he sipped through a silver straw (*bomba*) from an embossed hollow gourd (*cuia*). This meal he often finished off with a *fumo crioulo*, a hand-rolled cigarette.[11]

Roaming across the Campanha astride a well-groomed steed, his dark poncho draped around his shoulders, the gaúcho cut a noble and romantic figure. In fact, however, his life was hard and his horizons limited. He acknowledged four "races" of men—Gaúchos, Bahianos, Gringos, and Castelhanos. The first term included all the native Portuguese-speaking inhabitants of Rio Grande. The second (literally natives of Bahia) referred to all Brazilians living north of Rio Grande, with the occasional exception of inhabitants of the southern states of Santa Catarina and São Paulo; the term Bahianos contained an element of scorn, since such "greenhorns" usually were poor horsemen by gaúcho standards. Gringo referred to non-Iberian foreigners in general, and to Italian colonists in particular. The last term, Castelhanos (Castilians), applied to the Spanish-speaking inhabitants of the lands beyond the Argentine and Uruguayan frontiers. The undefined borders made the Castelhanos the gaúcho's traditional enemies; he was accustomed both to carrying out raids on their side of the frontier and to repelling their raids on his side.

By the year of Brazilian independence (1822) the ranching complex had triumphed over agriculture, but two years later a new element entered Rio Grande that would eventually set off the Serra from the rest of the state. Pedro I, the first ruler of independent Brazil, encouraged German immigration in an effort to populate the area with farmers who would defend their homeland against attacks from the Plate. In 1824 the first German colonos settled at São Leopoldo, 20 miles north of Pôrto Alegre. Over the next 34 years, some 8,000 German immigrants entered the province, bringing the total German-Brazilian population to more than 20,000 by 1859. Unlike their Portuguese-speaking neighbors, the Germans engaged in mixed farming on family-sized plots. Although the immigrants were given homestead sites and some initial aid by the Brazilian government, their lot was far from easy. Many were too poor to establish farms of the sort they had known in Germany. In addition, corrupt local officials often harassed and exploited the colonists, sometimes even demanding sexual access to the settlers' wives and daughters.[12] In 1859 immigration was officially, though temporarily, discouraged by the Prussian government.

In the first decade of independence, Rio Grande was the only area of Brazil with a true cultural frontier, i.e., one in which a well-established Brazilian population faced equally well-rooted and distinct peoples just across the border. Flanked by Spanish-speaking neighbors to the west and to the south, the Riograndenses grew accustomed to the threat and the reality of border warfare. Frontier estâncias necessarily formed close ties with nearby military posts, in part because the estancieiros supplied provisions to the garrisons. Many ranching families also sent sons into regular military service. Before the Spanish occupation of the Port of Rio Grande in 1763–76, most of the battles had taken place in the Banda Oriental; but in the nineteenth century Rio Grande do Sul and its Platine neighbors all suffered foreign invasion. During the Imperial era, Rio Grande was involved in four major wars—the Cisplatine campaign (1817–28), the Farroupilha Revolution (1835–45), the Platine campaigns of 1849–52, and the Paraguayan War (1864–70).

Of these struggles the most momentous locally was the Farroupilha Revolution, a Gaúcho civil war that almost separated Rio Grande from the Brazilian Empire.[13] (The word Farroupilha, "ragamuffin," was originally a term of derision applied to members of the Riograndense Liberal Party who demanded decentralization of Imperial authority; later the name became a badge of honor.) For ten years the Gaúcho rebels (Farrapos) held out against the Empire, as the defenders of an independent state. Initially they had had no such intentions, but had demanded only that the Additional Act of 1834, providing for significant decentralization, be put into effect with dispatch. The act had created provincial legislatures in Brazil, and the first Gaúcho assembly met in Pôrto Alegre in April 1835. Grievances leading to the outbreak of hostilities centered around burdensome "export" duties that made it impossible for Riograndense charque to compete with the prices offered in Rio by the charque producers of an economically expanding Plate. Abandoning the hope of satisfactory redress within the Empire, the Gaúchos began a struggle for independence on September 20, 1835. Led by a frontier soldier and estancieiro named Bento Gonçalves, the Farrapos quickly took possession of Pôrto Alegre. In June 1836 they were driven from the capital and fell back on the town of Piratini in the Campanha, where in November they proclaimed a republic with Gonçalves as its provisional president. Thenceforth Imperial troops dominated the province's eastern hydrographic basin, a position that gave them a major strategic advantage. By and large, the Litoral remained loyal to Rio de Janeiro, and the sparsely populated Serra counted for little. Soldier-estancieiros of the Campanha directed and sustained the revolt; ranchers of the Campanha and some of the charque producers of Pelotas (with economic links to the Campanha) bore the cost of the rebel campaign.[14]

The rebels were far from united in their attitudes toward the Spanish-speaking republics of the Plate. Some of them dreamed of a state that would include the Argentine provinces of Entre Rios and Corrientes, plus Uruguay and Rio Grande do Sul. Others, among them Gonçalves, continued to hope for some sort of federal relationship with Brazil.[15]

Though the Farrapos were never able to recapture Pôrto Alegre, they continued the war in the Campanha. With the assistance of a number of foreign adventurers, notably Giuseppe Garibaldi, they even seized the offensive in 1839 by moving up the coast to Santa Catarina, where another (albeit ephemeral) republic was declared. The northward advance was rapidly turned back, and after 1839 the rebels were permanently on the defensive. Three years later the Barão de Caxias arrived as governor and commander-in-chief of Imperial troops in Rio Grande do Sul. In 1843, the same year the Farrapos finally got around to drafting a constitution, Caxias brought the war into the Campanha, taking Caçapava, Bagé, and Alegrete.* Exhausted and defeated, the Gaúcho rebels accepted Caxias's generous peace terms in February 1845. Officers in the republican army were even allowed to reenter the Imperial forces with the ranks they had held in the rebel organization. To satisfy the insurgents' economic de-

---

* The constitution was republican in form but far from radical in content: it tolerated slavery, established Catholicism as the official religion, and required elections that were indirect and based on a narrowly limited suffrage. In all these provisions the charter resembled the Imperial constitution of 1824.

mands, the national government had already imposed a 25 per cent import duty on Platine charque, and by the end of the war Gaúcho sales were booming.*

From a national perspective the ten-year campaign was only one of a number of regional revolts—although one of the most serious— that threatened to divide the Brazilian Empire into several independent states. But from a Riograndense perspective, the Farroupilha Revolution was something more than simply a regionalist uprising. Gaúchos remembered the struggle as a great popular campaign, and radicals of a later generation would stress the republicanism and federalist aspirations of the Farroupilha movement rather than its separatist aspect.

The wisdom of General Caxias's leniency in pacifying Rio Grande was demonstrated in 1852, when three-quarters of the Brazilian troops he led against the Argentine dictator Rosas were Gaúchos. In the Paraguayan War, the bloodiest of Brazil's foreign conflicts, Rio Grande supplied some 34,000 soldiers, or more than a quarter of the total number of troops mobilized by Brazil.[16] In both cases the leading position of the Gaúchos was accounted for partly by their proximity to the theaters of combat, but also by their active participation in the affairs of the Plate basin. Rio Grande's leaders had now proved their loyalty to Brazil and its Imperial government: commanders who had revolted in 1835, e.g., Davi Canabarro, João Antônio da Silveira, and Antônio da Silva Neto, served with loyalty and ability in Paraguay 30 years later.

Since Rio Grande was Brazil's first line of defense against enemies and potential enemies in the Plate, it was only natural that more troops would be stationed there than in any other province, even after the demobilization following the Paraguayan campaign. In 1879, over 4,000 of Brazil's 14,871 troops were billeted in Rio Grande do Sul. Ten years later, in the last year of the Empire, the total number of Brazilians under arms had fallen slightly (13,152), but Rio Grande's proportion remained the same.[17] Thus, between a quarter

---

* Gaúcho prosperity in the mid-1840's was probably due more to political and economic troubles in the Plate than to the effectiveness of an Imperial tariff. The Rosas government interfered continuously in Uruguayan politics from 1839 to 1851, and an Anglo-French blockade interrupted the commerce of Buenos Aires from 1845 to 1848.

and a third of the nation's active military forces were garrisoned in its southernmost province. The myth of a Gaúcho penchant for military life was supported not only by the number of troops stationed in Rio Grande, but also by the number of high-ranking officers born there. At the end of the Empire, more officers holding the rank of brigadier general and above were from Rio Grande than from any other province.[18]

In the last two decades of Imperial rule (1870–89), important changes took place in Rio Grande's economic and social structure. The same factors that transformed the Argentine pampa—technological innovations, foreign investment, and immigration—had a similar impact on Rio Grande do Sul, though later and in a more attenuated fashion. As we shall see in the following chapter, these changes also had major political consequences.

Wire fencing began to spread across the campos of the Campanha and the Serra after 1870, and barbed wire followed in the 1880's. The *frigorífico* (frozen-beef plant), which transformed ranching in Argentina in the late nineteenth century, was not introduced into Rio Grande until the end of the First World War, but charque production was becoming big business; by the last decade of the Empire, some 300,000 head of cattle were slaughtered yearly in Pelotas alone. In the 1880's charque had only one other major competitor in the province's foreign and interprovincial exports, namely cowhides.[19] New breeds of cattle had begun to enter Rio Grande in the 1870's, and though they did not have as great an effect on production as they had in Argentina, the pastoral economy remained dominant.

Two developments had increased Rio Grande's sales: a reduction in time-in-transit, which made spoilage of charque less of a problem, and a decrease in freight costs. Steamships and railroads were responsible for these changes. In the early 1870's steamers were already plying the Lagoa dos Patos and its tributaries as far as 192 miles up the Jacuí, and 336 miles up the Uruguay from Barra do Quaraí. Steam-powered vessels connected Montevideo with the Port of Rio Grande, and two sailings per month linked Rio de Janeiro with Rio Grande. By 1890 a monthly ocean-going steamer provided access to the ports of northern Brazil and Europe. Instead of two ships per month to Rio, there were now five. From Pôrto Alegre, ships traversed the major tributaries of the Jacuí as often as three times a day. Between 1859 and 1883 the number of ships crossing the bar at Rio Grande more than doubled.[20]

The province's first rail line began operations in 1874, running the short distance between Pôrto Alegre and the largest German colony, São Leopoldo. A stretch of track connected the Taquari River with Rio Pardo and Cachoeira in 1883, and two years later the line was pushed westward to Santa Maria, in the heart of the province. In 1884 a railway was opened between Rio Grande and Bagé, the commercial center of the Campanha. Lines in the west were also opened, connecting the frontier towns of Uruguaiana and Itaqui along the Uruguay River. In a single decade (1889–98), as Sérgio da Costa Franco has noted, some 445 miles of rail lines were opened, compared to only 27 in the preceding decade.[21] By 1889, the last year of the Empire, daily trains connected Rio Grande with Bagé, and Barra do Quaraí with Itaqui. Two trains per day linked Nôvo Hamburgo (north of São Leopoldo) with the capital.[22]

Though the extension of the railroad westward clearly promoted internal trade in the province, as long as the east-west line remained uncompleted, the Barra do Quaraí–Itaqui line simply reinforced the economic ties of the western frontier towns with the Plate. By 1890 a Uruguayan railroad just across the Quaraí River at Bella Unión linked Itaqui and Uruguaiana with Montevideo, and another spur of the same trunk reached the border at Quaraí in 1891. Moreover, a line was completed a year later between Montevideo and Rivera,[23] a town separated from Livramento on the Brazilian side by a single street. The western and southwestern frontier regions, therefore, continued to look south for their commercial interests. In such a situation, contraband trade was bound to flourish. Not that smuggling was anything new in the area; it had been carried on since the earliest attempts to define the limits between Portuguese and Spanish America. But with the rapid economic growth of the Plate and Rio Grande, smuggling grew to "phenomenal proportions."[24] Contraband traffic continued to preoccupy the frontier police into the twentieth century, though the problem tended to diminish as Rio Grande achieved a higher degree of economic integration.

However loosely integrated the provincial economy was at the end of the Imperial era, the province's links with the rest of Brazil were strong. In interprovincial exports, Rio Grande do Sul was second (by value) among the constituent units of the Empire in 1885–86. It is worth noting that Rio Grande's exports went chiefly to other parts of Brazil, as they had previously;[25] even the goods sent from the Missões District and the Campanha to the River Plate were mostly re-exported to Brazil's coastal cities.

The changing economy of Rio Grande was accompanied by a partial transformation of Gaúcho society. Between 1872 and 1890 the province's population doubled, from 447,000 to 897,000 inhabitants. The increase came partly from immigration; in all, some 60,000 immigrants, most of them from Germany and Italy, settled in the province between 1874 and 1889. In 1891, the peak immigration year for the century, 20,739 immigrants entered Rio Grande do Sul.[26]

Most of the non-Iberian settlers continued to flock to the traditional colono area, the eastern flank of the Serra, where they settled on plots granted them by the government. Their mixed farming helped balance pastoral activities in other parts of the province, just as socially the small farm provided a counterweight to the traditional latifundium, which was entrenched in the southern half of the province and in the campos of the Serra. Only in contiguous Santa Catarina was a similar pattern of immigrant farms introduced.

As the earliest arrivals, the German colonists had settled near the markets of Pôrto Alegre and the navigable rivers that afforded access to the capital and the other towns of the Litoral. Initially locating in São Leopoldo and along the northern side of the Jacuí, the German colonos spread into adjacent areas 50 years before the first group of Italians arrived from the Po Valley. The Italians were forced to settle farther to the north and west, notably around Alfredo Chaves and Caxias do Sul. Both groups cultivated their traditional Old World crops, the Germans rye and potatoes, the Italians grapes. To be sure, there were difficult adjustments. Arriving without capital, the early immigrants were forced to adopt *caboclo* (native backwoods) techniques of slash-and-burn agriculture in order to get through the bleak initial years.[27] For all this, however, enough European techniques survived to constitute a sizeable advance over the caboclo agriculture of adjoining areas.

The Germans more than the Italians tended to create an island of homeland culture in the midst of a Luso-Brazilian society. One of the odd developments of German colonization was a millenarian movement called the Muckers, a sect composed entirely of Germans and German-Brazilians who revolted against the government in 1874 and were destroyed the same year by the Brazilian army. Though the hypothesis has yet to be explored in detail, it seems likely that the movement appeared at this time partly because of the socioeconomic changes beginning to affect traditional and isolated peasant culture in the German area as well as Gaúcho society as a whole.*

As the German and Italian colonos moved westward, they provided a link between the Serra and the Litoral. Even so, most of the Serra remained undeveloped in the 1880's. Arsène Isabelle, a French traveler in the region in the 1830's, had noted that the Serra was poor and underpopulated compared with the rest of the province; another observer in the same period, Nicholas Dreys, wrote that in the Missões District Guarani was still the most widely spoken language.[28] The economic expansion of the 1870's and 1880's affected the Central Plateau least, and Serra inhabitants felt so neglected by the provincial government that twice the município council of Cruz Alta called for the creation of a new province in the Serra. In 1884 the council charged that its inhabitants suffered "complete abandonment: We do not have a bridge, a highway, [or] any public works." Indeed, the council complained, the government of the province had never even sent a high official to visit the region, and the Pôrtoalegrenses thought the Serra was inhabited only by wild Indians.[29]

Despite the backwardness of the central Serra, the deterioration of Old World agricultural techniques in the German and Italian colonies, and the lag between Rio Grande and Argentina in developing a modern cattle industry, the province compared favorably with the rest of late-nineteenth-century Brazil in social development, judging by the few indexes collected at the time. In 1872 Rio Grande do Sul

---

* Steamships were plying the Rio dos Sinos linking São Leopoldo with Pôrto Alegre; immigration was beginning to accelerate; and most significantly, the railroad reached São Leopoldo in 1871. The leader of the Muckers, Jacobina Maurer, had predicted the line would never be used and even tried to prevent its operation. Ironically, the railroad soon contributed to her demise, for troops were sent via rail from Pôrto Alegre to put down the revolt. Ambrósio Schupp, *Os Muckers* (Pôrto Alegre, n.d.), *passim.* Another important source is Leopoldo Petry, *O episódio do Ferrabraz (Os mucker): Documentos para o estudo da história dos "mucker" do Ferrabraz* (2d ed., São Leopoldo, Rio Grande do Sul, 1966). It is possible that the crisis between secular and religious authority in Brazil's Religious Question (1872–75) and, more remotely, the German Kulturkampf (also beginning in 1872) helped create a climate of exaltation.

was third among the provinces in the rate of literacy (21.9 per cent for all ages), and by 1890 it had climbed to first place. In the last count of slaves in Brazil (1887), Rio Grande stood thirteenth among the provinces with only 8,442, though it ranked fifth in total population. Significantly, according to the last município-by-município figures (for 1872), the majority of the slaves were located in the southern Litoral and the Campanha; after the provincial capital, Pelotas was second and Bagé third in the number of slaves.[30]

The chief use of slaves in Rio Grande in the last half of the nineteenth century was in the charque industry, the main economic activity of Pelotas. By the mid-1870's, however, slave labor was becoming increasingly uneconomical. The slaves of Pelotas had to be clothed and fed year round, whereas the free workers of Argentina and Uruguay could be laid off or fired during the long slack season between slaughters, and the labor force could be adjusted to meet the demand for charque. Slave labor was also qualitatively inferior to the free labor in the Plate.[31] Following abolition in 1888, the charque industry was the only economic activity in Rio Grande that faced a major readjustment.

Pelotas, Rio Grande's second-largest urban community, was a município of only 41,591 inhabitants in 1890, and the population of Pôrto Alegre, the capital, had reached only 52,421. Urban development had not kept apace of the general population growth of the state: though Rio Grande doubled its population between 1872 and 1890, the município of the capital (including its rural areas) increased by only 19 per cent. Nonetheless, the dull village of twelve to fifteen thousand persons that Isabelle described in the 1830's had acquired many of the characteristics of civilization by the late 1880's. In Isabelle's time, the women of Pôrto Alegre, unlike those of Montevideo or Buenos Aires, were kept in Moorish seclusion; by the 1880's they were attending masked balls during Carnival season and going to operas staged by foreign troupes in the Teatro São Pedro. (Electric lighting, introduced in 1887, played a role here, making it safer for escorted ladies to be out on the streets at night.) Spanish zarzuelas (operettas) were performed in the city, and horse races were held at the "Jockey Club Pôrtoalegrense." Bullfights were another popular attraction; one grande corrida tauromáquica in 1891 featured "two new artistes from Buenos Aires."[32] To be sure, these expanded opportunities for entertainment were not accompanied by any sustained effort to supply basic public works, such as sewers, on which a modern city depends; and the urban progress of the 1880's was not followed by equivalent advances in the next two decades.

Coincidental with the economic and demographic changes in the province was the establishment of political hegemony by the Liberal Party of Rio Grande do Sul. Until 1872 the two Imperial parties, the Liberals and Conservatives, had been roughly balanced in the province; but in that year the Liberal Party gained control of the provincial assembly, and it remained the dominant force in Rio Grande thereafter, under the leadership of Gaspar Silveira Martins. The Conservatives continued to alternate with the Liberals in national elections, but principally because the Rio-appointed governor could manipulate the electoral machinery on behalf of his party.

Six Gaúchos, all of them Liberals, played prominent roles in national politics after the Paraguayan War: Manuel Luís Osório, Gaspar Silveira Martins, the Visconde de Pelotas, João Francisco Diana, Francisco Antunes Maciel, and the Barão de Mauá.* The two most important were the party's successive leaders, Osório and Silveira Martins. Both of these men were estancieiros in the Campanha; both owned estates in Uruguay; and though separated by a generation, both served in the Sinimbu cabinet of 1878. But there all similarities ended.

Osório, one of Brazil's great military heroes, was above all a professional soldier. Proud, patrician in bearing if not in origin, dark and handsome, correct, reserved, respectful to his superiors, he entered politics through military assignments and was able to organize political tickets through his great prestige as a soldier; he had neither the time nor the inclination for day-to-day political maneuvering.

Manuel Luís Osório was born in 1808 in the Litoral of Rio Grande, where his father owned a modest estância.[33] Entering military service at fifteen with almost no formal education, he fought to keep the Banda Oriental in the Brazilian Empire as the Cisplatine Province. As a loyalist in the Farroupilha Revolution, he distinguished himself in Caxias's eyes, and in 1845 he entered politics as a deputy to the provincial assembly. In the 1840's and 1850's his military service

* All were ministers in the last years of the Empire save Mauá, who was better known as a financier than a politician.

brought him to the Uruguayan and Argentine frontiers in the capacity of military strategist, diplomat, and explorer. He served in the campaign that overthrew the Argentine dictator Rosas in 1852, coordinating Brazilian military efforts with Justo José Urquiza, the caudillo of Entre Rios. In 1859 he was promoted to brigadier general.

In the 1850's Osório first began to take a serious interest in politics as such, building a political base for himself on the western and southern frontiers. Even before the period of non-ideological politics called the Era of Conciliation drew to a close in Brazil, revived Liberal and Conservative parties began to emerge across the country, and Osório helped found a new Liberal Party in Rio Grande in 1860. The organization quickly divided into two factions; after 1862 he was a leader of the wing called the Historical Liberals.* Osório might have played a more sustained role in politics if the tumult in the Plate (for which Brazil was partly responsible) had not required that he devote himself almost exclusively to military affairs between 1864 and 1870. After leading the Brazilian force that occupied Montevideo in 1864, he returned to Gaúcho soil to repel an invading army from Paraguay that had overrun São Borja, Itaqui, and Uruguaiana. He subsequently held a series of important commands, and was wounded at the Battle of Tuiuti in Paraguay. He was promoted to field marshal in 1865 and raised to the nobility the following year as the Barão (subsequently Marquês) de Herval. After his retirement, he was promoted to marshal of the army, Brazil's highest military rank, and was elected to life tenure in the Brazilian senate. He served as minister of war in the cabinet of the Visconde de Sinimbu. As a war hero, Osório was second only to Caxias in prestige; as Caxias was the paladin of the Conservatives, so was Osório the champion of the Liberals. His death in 1879 deprived the Empire of one of its greatest generals, and Rio Grande do Sul of a major political figure.

Gaspar Silveira Martins was a politician of a different stripe. Born into the elite, he was voluble where Osório was laconic, rebellious and aggressive where the Marshal was disciplined and correct, and eager for popular acclaim where Osório was aloof from the crowd. In short, Silveira Martins was the stereotype of the Gaúcho caudillo. Tall, barrel-chested, and corpulent, with a flowing beard, he gazed at the

---

* The Progressive Liberals, led by the Barão de Pôrto Alegre, meanwhile formed links with the Conservatives at provincial and national levels.

world through round spectacles perched atop a Roman nose. His booming voice and quick mind impressed all who knew him. Like Pedro I, he was liberal by conviction—passionately so—but authoritarian by temperament. Of his sway over his fellows, one contemporary wrote: "He did not know how to speak softly. When he left a room where he had been talking, the echo of his voice seemed to remain for a time in the air. . . . He was a man who could fascinate the masses, a leader of men, a true caudillo."[34] So commanding was his presence that Joaquim Nabuco, himself one of the leading parliamentary figures of the late Empire, considered Silveira Martins "almost a force of nature—sudden and irresistible, natural and insensitive, like a cloudburst or a cyclone."[35]

Gaspar Silveira Martins, who became the undisputed head of the Gaúcho Liberal Party after Osório's death, was born in 1834 in the município of Bagé, on the Uruguayan border. His father's estate extended into the neighboring republic, and had been the site of a historic meeting between the founders of independent Uruguay, Juan Antonio Lavalleja and José Fructuoso Rivera. Though Silveira Martins was baptized in Melo, Uruguay, his parents "Brazilianized" him by sending him to northern and central Brazil for his education— São Luís and Rio de Janeiro for secondary school, Recife for law school. After a stint as a lawyer and a judge in the Imperial capital, he returned to Rio Grande just as the traditional party labels were being revived, and won election to the provincial assembly in 1861, at the age of twenty-six.

The resignation of the Liberal cabinet of Zacarias de Góes e Vasconcelos and the upsurge of ideological reformism in 1868 had a considerable effect on the Liberal Party of Rio Grande do Sul. Silveira Martins played a pivotal role in merging the two wings of the party (divided since 1861) into a Radical Liberal Party that reflected the national reformist mood. In 1868 he founded a newspaper in Pôrto Alegre called *A Reforma*, a name given several other newspapers by leftward-moving Liberals in other provinces. Silveira Martins did not hesitate to attack the Emperor by name. In a speech in Rio in 1869— a year of fiery Liberal manifestoes—he declared that "the ignorance, the demoralization, the bankruptcy, the hatred of foreigners, and the discrediting of everything and everyone are the dire results of 25 years of government by D. Pedro II."[36]

Three years later, at the age of thirty-eight, the Gaúcho leader entered the chamber of deputies, where he delivered a memorable maiden speech in December 1872. The Visconde de Taunay, who witnessed the event, later wrote that the address was a "veritable explosion, a kind of lashing of a furious pampa wind entering through all the windows and doors . . . infusing in all astonishment, almost terror."[37] Silveira Martins' angry voice boomed away at the Conservative cabinet for two hours, exposing fraud, incompetence, and corruption eloquently and in detail. He denied that the government had any mandate from the Brazilian people: "You, representatives of the nation?" he scornfully asked. "You're nothing more than illustrious nobodies." A few weeks later, he made the same point in writing: "The government is everything, the parliament nothing, and the people less than nothing."[38] Thanks to such sweeping denunciations, he soon became the hero of young Brazilians with republican aspirations, to whom he was known as the Tribune.[39] His program was drawn largely from the celebrated Radical Liberal Manifesto of 1869, which demanded direct elections, ministerial responsibility, decentralization of authority, full religious liberty, and emancipation of the slaves.

By 1878 the Tribune had moderated his criticism of the Imperial system sufficiently to enter the Liberal government of the Visconde de Sinimbu as minister of the treasury, but he resigned the following year when the rest of the cabinet refused to endorse his plan to allow non-Catholics to vote. (About half the German-speaking population of Rio Grande was Protestant.) In 1880 he entered the senate.

In the Imperial era politicians could serve simultaneously in the provincial and national legislatures, and the Tribune had taken control of the provincial assembly in 1872, the same year he entered parliament. One renegade Liberal charged that after 1872 nothing was done without his approval in the assembly.[40] Upon Osório's death in 1879, Silveira Martins became the undisputed leader of a powerful and increasingly disciplined organization. "The Riograndense Liberal Party moves like a regiment of Frederick [the Great]," he once declared.[41]

Like political battles elsewhere in Imperial Brazil, those of Rio Grande do Sul were fought on a narrow social plane. In the 1889 elections (for a parliament that never sat), only some 12,000 Gaúchos voted—less than 2 per cent of the province's population. Moreover, as in the other provinces, fraud, intimidation, and violence were widespread at election time.[42] In the last years of the Empire, however, the Liberals were clearly the majority party in Rio Grande do Sul. The Conservatives could periodically take charge of the provincial executive and the Gaúcho delegation in parliament as the control of the national government changed; but the Liberals dominated the National Guard in Rio Grande do Sul, along with the provincial legislature and most of the município governments. Within Rio Grande, the Conservatives plainly could not contest the power of Silveira Martins. But a new generation of politicians, in a new party, was ready to try.

# CHAPTER TWO

# From Agitation to Consolidation

Stimulated by the leftward shift of the Liberal Party in 1869 and the appearance of the Third French Republic the following year, Brazilian radicals founded a Republican Party in Rio de Janeiro in December 1870. In the following decade, Republican organizational advances were largely confined to the national capital and São Paulo Province. A Republican Club was founded in Pôrto Alegre as early as 1878, but it was not until the 1880's, when a number of young professionals returned to Rio Grande after completing their studies elsewhere in Brazil,[1] that systematic agitation began on a province-wide basis.*

In February 1882 the Gaúcho Republicans held their first convention, formally organizing the Partido Republicano Riograndense (PRR). At the founding meeting they endorsed the Republican manifesto promulgated in Rio de Janeiro in 1870, and this document, whose salient feature was federalism, remained their basic program until the end of the Empire; the founders of the PRR required all local Republican clubs to pledge themselves to its principles. The

---

* Since the Gaúcho movement got a late start, it is not surprising that its leaders were ten to fifteen years younger than their counterparts in São Paulo and Rio. The Gaúcho Republicans were a close-knit group, linked not only by age but also by education and, in the case of the more prominent ones, by family business interests (ranching) as well. Walter Spalding lists 46 Gaúcho Republicans in his article "Propaganda e propagandistas republicanos no Rio Grande do Sul," *Revista do Museu Júlio de Castilhos*, I, 1 (Jan. 1952), 57–136. Of the 37 whose birthdates he gives, just over half were born in the decade 1855–64; of 17 whose preparatory schooling he identifies, two-thirds studied in the provincial capital; and of the 30 whose professional education is given, almost two-thirds attended the Law School at São Paulo.

Gaúchos eagerly took up the cry of 1870, "Centralization-Dismember-ment; Decentralization-Unity," a slogan that was later carried on the masthead of the party newspaper, *A Federação* (The Federation); some even went so far as to suggest the separation of their province from the rest of Brazil if a federal republic were not introduced.*

Federalism was not the only ideological feature adopted in 1882. The Gaúchos' position on slavery and their affinity for the philosophy of Auguste Comte were also present from the beginning. The issue of slavery did not divide the Gaúcho party as it had earlier divided the Paulista Republicans. At the 1882 convention the Riograndenses followed the Paulista practice of begging the question, declaring that each province should deal with the matter in its own way; but after 1884 the Gaúchos remained fairly consistent in condemning slavery in their own province. *A Federação* denounced the institution re-peatedly. Most of the leading Gaúcho Republicans were members of anti-slavery societies in their home municípios (though many aboli-tionists were not Republicans). In any case, the Gaúchos could clearly afford to take a more radical stand on this important issue than the Paulistas. For one thing, their province had far fewer slaves than São Paulo—some 8,000 compared to 107,000 in 1887.[2] For another, their organization had been formed a decade later than that of the Paul-istas, in an era when abolition had become much more popular.

The Riograndenses' interest in Comtian positivism, a school of philosophy in vogue in the early 1880's, also set the PRR off from Paulista and Carioca models, though Comte had sympathizers scat-tered throughout the country. Positivism tinged Gaúcho Republican-ism from the outset: Comte's motto "order and progress" was adopted by the PRR at the founding session.[3]

In October 1882 the Gaúcho Republicans entered the electoral arena on a province-wide basis for the first time, offering six candi-dates for the provincial assembly. None was elected, but enthusiasm remained high. It was not long before the question of a party news-paper, first raised at the founding convention, was considered more thoroughly. The project was approved at a PRR congress in 1883,

---

* *Convenção republicana de 23 de fevereiro* (Pôrto Alegre, 1882), p. 61. In raising the either-or issue of separation or federation, the Gaúchos harked back to the demand of the Farroupilha rebels: they cited the Farrapos episode as evidence that Rio Grande do Sul had stronger Republican traditions than any other province, despite greater organizational advances elsewhere.

and the first copies of *A Federação* rolled off the presses on New Year's Day the following year. Republicans continued to hold province-wide congresses, to form local clubs (20 by March 1884), and to run for public office. Joaquim Francisco Assis Brasil, one of the most talented of the Gaúcho Republicans, won election to the provincial assembly in 1884, two years after his graduation from law school.

The remarkable progress of the PRR in the face of the political domination of the Liberal Party and Silveira Martins was in large part due to the efforts of a group of lawyers who had pledged themselves to creating a Brazilian republic during their student days at the São Paulo Law School. In addition to Assis Brasil, this group included Júlio de Castilhos, José Gomes Pinheiro Machado, and Antônio Augusto Borges de Medeiros. All four of these men had graduated between 1878 and 1885, and all came from ranching families;[4] three of them would govern Rio Grande and the fourth, Pinheiro Machado, was to become the state's foremost representative in the federal senate. In the early years of the Gaúcho movement, Assis Brasil and his brother-in-law Castilhos were the most prominent figures. Assis, born in 1857 the heir to extensive properties in the Campanha, had made a mark for himself as a fiery young orator in law school. At São Paulo he had helped found the Student Republican Club (Clube Acadêmico Republicano), which he used as a forum for his vehement denunciations of monarchism, centralism, and Catholicism. Something of a Jacobin at the time, he believed that Republicans should do battle for their cause "even if it [was] necessary to spill a sea of blood."[5] With Castilhos and a third Gaúcho, he edited a student magazine, *Evolução* (Evolution), which condemned Imperial institutions as archaic and reactionary. Wealthy, handsome, and an excellent speaker, he rapidly achieved a following in his native land, and his election to the provincial assembly in 1884 seemed to presage the most distinguished career of his generation of Riograndenses.

Assis Brasil's close friend and brother-in-law had a different set of gifts. Júlio de Castilhos, born in the Serra in 1860, was neither as handsome, nor as wealthy, nor as able a speaker as Assis. Castilhos' forte was journalism, a talent he exercised first in law school and then, after his graduation, as a Republican propagandist. In 1885 he became the editor of *A Federação*. He was not just a brilliant writer, however; even in law school he showed qualities of leadership that brought him election to the presidency of the Student Republican Club. After he returned to Rio Grande he figured prominently in the deliberations of Republican organizers there. Unlike Assis Brasil, Castilhos did not become more moderate as he matured; but this rigidity did not prevent him from becoming governor and political boss of Rio Grande—and the most powerful Gaúcho politician of his day.

Pinheiro Machado, the son of a Paulista who had become both an important rancher in Rio Grande and a member of the Imperial parliament, was a native of the Missões District. Nine years older than Castilhos and five years ahead of him at São Paulo, Pinheiro had interrupted his studies at the age of fifteen to participate in the Brazilian campaign against Paraguay. At São Paulo Law School he had been an indifferent student and a minor figure in the Student Republican Club; but whatever his shortcomings his political ability soon become clear, and this ability was to make him one of the most powerful men in the federal senate and a "kingmaker" in presidential politics. Other Riograndense Republicans at São Paulo included Vitorino Monteiro, a future senator and interim governor, and a half-dozen future congressmen.

Among the other leading Republican propagandists in Rio Grande were three physicians, each of whom played an important role in the PRR in the Republican era. Carlos Barbosa Gonçalves, a collateral descendant of the Farrapo leader Bento Gonçalves, became governor of the state and later senator; Fernando Abbott became acting governor and minister to Argentina; and Ramiro Barcelos became a senator and diplomat. These men too were estancieiros. Barcelos, the most important of the three in the years before the Republic, was a distant cousin of Borges de Medeiros and came from the same município in central Rio Grande (Cachoeira). After earning a medical degree in Rio de Janeiro, he began a promising political career, serving as a Liberal deputy in the provincial assembly from 1878 to 1882. He became a Republican in 1882, and later collaborated with Castilhos in editing *A Federação*. Barcelos had a talent for satire and liked to sign his articles with the pseudonym Amaro Juvenal, which he later used for his famous poem *Antônio Chimango*.

Throughout the 1880's the young Republican propagandists crisscrossed Rio Grande, forming clubs, distributing propaganda, and presenting candidates in provincial and national elections; yet their role in bringing about the fall of the Empire was limited to two issues that only indirectly undermined support for Imperial institutions. These were the Military Question and the Question of the Municipal Councils. The first issue, by far the more important of the two, was by no means limited to Rio Grande do Sul. Nevertheless, the Gaúcho role was significant, for through the Gaúchos leading officers were brought into the fray, and their associations with Republicans, if not their republican sentiments, were strengthened. The Military Question arose in 1883 when Lt. Col. Antônio da Sena Madureira became the spokesman for a military group opposed to a plan for compulsory retirement insurance for officers, a seemingly minor complaint that obscured the larger issue of military subordination to a civilian government. In 1884 Sena Madureira was disciplined for insubordination in another incident. The issue was raised more forcefully in 1886, when another lieutenant colonel, Ernesto da Cunha Matos, publicly criticized the minister of war, and was subjected to a brief confinement. In the senate, a Riograndense marshal, Correa da Câmara (the Visconde de Pelotas) passionately defended Cunha Matos, insisting that the whole question of "military honor" was at stake. The intervention of Pelotas was a serious matter for the Conservative government: not only had he been a hero of the Paraguayan campaign and minister of war, he was the Liberals' chief authority on military affairs.

Hardly had the Cunha Matos incident died down when Sena Madureira spoke out again. In August 1886 A Federação printed a letter from the lieutenant colonel, now in charge of a school for advanced military training in Rio Grande, in which he defended himself against the charges of Franco de Sá, the minister who had disciplined him in 1884. The matter lay dormant for almost six weeks. Then, at the end of September, Júlio de Castilhos made a sensational announcement in his newspaper: Marshal Manuel Deodoro da Fonseca, one of the most important figures in the Brazilian army and acting governor of Rio Grande do Sul, would resign as Commander of Arms of the local Military Region if Sena Madureira were punished. A vain and politically naive man (who was to overthrow the Empire three years later), Deodoro may have been goaded into some of his rasher statements by the fulsome praise *A Federação* heaped on him. To Deodoro's statement Castilhos added his own: the question, he wrote, involved not only the honor of Sena Madureira, "but also that of the national army," the banner Pelotas had raised in connection with the Cunha Matos incident. The controversy was kept alive when the Republican newspaper, in a later number, denied that "military discipline consists of absolute passive obedience."[6] By October letters and manifestoes from officers garrisoned across the province were appearing in *A Federação*, and similar rumblings were being heard in Rio de Janeiro. It came as no surprise when Pelotas took up the cry of his brother officers in the senate, since the Conservatives still ruled. Ultimately the Conservative government, led by the Barão de Cotegipe, had to resign over the matter—"with scratches on its dignity," as Cotegipe conceded.[7]

In Rio Grande, meanwhile, a group of military personnel, ranging in rank from cadet to marshal, signed a protest on behalf of the offended military instructor Sena Madureira. Among these men were a number of officers who were to have political dealings with the Riograndense Republicans at various times over the next 40 years.* An official censure of Sena Madureira was canceled in 1887; yet just as the Madureira donnybrook was being smoothed over, prominent officers in Rio de Janeiro formed a Military Club, which though ostensibly a social organization made the defense of military interests a major concern—as it does to this day. Deodoro, who along with Pelotas had been a leading figure in the Military Question, was elected the first president of the club.

Castilhos could well congratulate himself. He had widened the breach between military officers and Imperial ministers, and in the process he, Ramiro Barcelos, and Assis Brasil had become good friends of Deodoro. In November 1886 a committee of officers from the Pôrto Alegre garrison had presented Castilhos an engraved plaque, honoring him for his "unsurpassable patriotism in the defense of the sacred rights of the military class in the *Affaire Madurei-*

---

* They included Júlio Falcão da Frota and Domingos Barreto Leite, both governors of Rio Grande do Sul in the opening years of the Republic; João Cesar Sampaio and Tomás Thompson Flores, defenders of the Castilhos government during the Gaúcho civil war of 1893–95; and Clodoaldo da Fonseca, Cipriano da Costa Ferreira, and Carlos Frederico Mesquita, future commanders of the Rio Grande Military Region. The manifesto appeared in the October 22 issue of *A Federação*.

*ra."* Castilhos was later to demonstrate this same skill in dealing with the military time and again.

Though the Question of the Município Councils, or the Motion of São Borja, had less of an impact on national affairs, it represented another taste of moral victory for the impatient Republicans in Rio Grande do Sul. In January 1888 the council of the município of São Borja (bordering the Uruguay River) passed a resolution calling for a poll of local governments to determine whether there should be a third reign after the death of Pedro II. The motion, introduced in the council by a Republican, Aparício Mariense, was published in *A Federação* on January 11. Castilhos made the demand a cause, as he had done in the case of the Military Question, and gloated at the moral bankruptcy of the Imperial government when the São Borja council was dismissed and charges were brought against its members. Elsewhere in Brazil, militant Republicans took up the cry for a national plebiscite.

In the closing years of the Empire the PRR began a shift toward tighter organization, a process that continued into the first three years of the Republic. The Gaúcho Republicans increasingly came under the domination of the editor of the party organ, Júlio de Castilhos, a man who had the special quality of inspiring fanaticism in his followers and hatred among his opponents. Indeed, the personality and ideology of Castilhos bear so heavily on later developments in the history of Rio Grande do Sul as to merit an extended comment here.

A man of small stature, Castilhos nevertheless impressed his contemporaries with his power to command. One German observer who had met him wrote: "He is a small, thick-set man with an energetic appearance, dark intelligent eyes, a tanned complexion and close-cropped hair. Whoever has once encountered him knows that he has an iron will—a rare phenomenon in Brazil."[8] Assis Brasil made a similar assessment in a statement written five years after his brother-in-law's death. Comparing Castilhos to Silveira Martins, he asserted: "He did not have the same brilliant qualities in the degree as the Tribune of the Empire; but he made up for that in balanced judgment and tenacity, both in his studies and in his actions, and—what is most important for success—he consistently concealed, through troubles and triumphs, that well-controlled ambition to govern and command, without which no man comes to power except in rare situations. . . . Castilhos had still another quality that prepared him for the leading role he played in politics: it was that mysterious gift of making converts, of bending the wills of other men to his, of inspiring confidence and obedience."[9]

Júlio de Castilhos was born in the south-central part of the Serra in 1860. His father was an estancieiro, and through his mother he was related to the aristocratic families of the Campanha. In spite of the family's wealth in land and livestock, the Serra was still a backward and isolated area in the 1860's, and high freight costs deprived the family of most luxuries.[10] Júlio, one of nine children, had a difficult boyhood: he was only eleven when his father died, and he stuttered badly as a boy. A school friend recalled how young Castilhos' classmates howled with laughter at his first recitation at the Colégio Wellington. "On the written examinations he always got the best mark. On the oral quizzes, though, a disaster took place. After failing on his first try, he never succeeded in articulating one word [correctly]."[11] Castilhos had still another painful boyhood experience: a case of smallpox that almost cost him his life, and that left his face deeply pitted. Without trying to probe the complex personality of this talented and troubled man, we can at least speculate that the frequency with which such terms of derision as "ridiculous," "laughable," and "absurd" appear in his mature writings may be related to his childhood traumas.

Unlike Silveira Martins, Castilhos got all his primary and secondary schooling in Rio Grande before proceeding to law school at São Paulo, where he edited two student publications and became a Republican militant. Graduating in 1881, Castilhos returned to Rio Grande to open a law practice in Pôrto Alegre; however, he concentrated most of his exceptional energy on politics and journalism. He married a well-to-do girl from Pelotas in 1883. Castilhos was never more than a mediocre orator, though he did manage to overcome his childhood stuttering. Political writing was his strong point, and he made a province-wide reputation for himself as the editor of *A Federação*. His journalism was combative, at times fiercely so, and was often bitterly ironical. He attacked the two monarchical parties as corrupt, spent, and—worst of all—lacking in ideologically grounded principles. In 1888, for example, he ran a series of articles in *A*

*Federação* entitled "Political Janus," comparing Silveira Martins' ideals and programs in 1868–77 with his clearly more accommodating stand in the late 1880's.[12]

Júlio de Castilhos was intolerant of other points of view, even within the Republican fold, but he knew enough to bide his time rather than try to enforce a premature orthodoxy on his fellows. Still, as he put it, he believed "only in definitive victories," and once his machine was consolidated, he acted on that principle, asserting: "We must always show or prove that in Rio Grande, the Republican establishment is monolithic [*inteiriça*] and does not accept the least compromise."[13] His ability to inspire devotion and loyalty, his incorruptibility in financial matters, and his willingness to sacrifice his health and fortune for his cause were positive aspects of a personality that, except toward his family and a few close followers, seems to have had little warmth. Castilhos had almost no esteem for Brazilian politicians whom he could not control. In private correspondence he once referred to Lauro Müller, minister-designate of transportation, as the "sinister Lauro," to President Prudente de Morais as a "cretin," to President-elect Campos Sales as "frivolous or foolish," and to José Joaquim (J. J.) Seabra, future governor of Bahia, as an "imbecile."[14]

Like many of his generation, Castilhos was a perfervid disciple of Auguste Comte. Comtian positivism had begun to penetrate Brazilian thought in the 1860's, and had a considerable number of adherents in Brazil's professional schools by the time Castilhos arrived in São Paulo. Positivism appealed to students and professionals (especially those in the pure and applied sciences) much as Saint-Simonianism had appealed to French intellectuals in the 1830's; it was also like the Saint-Simonianism of the earlier day in developing two distinct but related traditions—one with the complete trappings of a religion, the other a more diffuse tradition based on secular philosophical writings.

French philosophical currents had long had a great attraction for Brazilian intellectuals, and Comte's universal system easily displaced the French eclecticism of the second quarter of the nineteenth century. Comte's vision of historical development (borrowed in part from Saint-Simon, his former employer) was roughly consonant with the evolutionary theory that set the tenor of the times. In positivism

Brazilians discovered, or imagined they discovered, an explanation for Brazilian backwardness, scientific arguments against slavery, and a program for national development.* Nor were Brazilians unique in their enthusiasm for Comte's doctrines. In other Latin American countries, especially Mexico, Comtian positivism was in vogue in the latter years of the nineteenth century. Throughout Latin America positivism appealed to conservative modernizers, who wanted the benefits of material progress without sacrificing the social hierarchy: Comte seemed to offer a blueprint for development without social mobilization.

Without making a detailed analysis of the tedious and voluminous writings of the French philosopher, we should note the principles of positivism that are relevant to events in Rio Grande do Sul. Comte believed historical and social phenomena could be reduced to a set of scientific laws, and it was he who coined the term sociology. He saw history as developing through three great epistemological stages: the theological, the metaphysical, and the positive. In the final phase, all social as well as physical phenomena would be fully explained by scientific laws. For Comte, the upheavals in Europe from 1789 to 1848 were indications of the decline of the second stage and of the imminence of the positive epoch ("sociocracy"). This final stage, however, would have to be ushered in by a republican dictatorship. Comte, who knew and condemned the chaos of revolution, placed great emphasis on order; indeed, he defined progress as "the development of order." He therefore proposed the training of a class of positivist "priests" to counsel and guide heads of state in the transition period. Once established, the dictator was to leave to the priests the ideological preparation for the "sociocratic" era, to which end they were to be assured absolute freedom from government interference in the "spiritual" realm. This feature of ideological permissiveness linked Comte to the liberalism of his day, despite certain obvious nonliberal aspects of his philosophy, such as government protection of the proletariat.[15]

Castilhos took from Comte a belief in a republican and dictatorial form of government: he embraced Comte's faith in rule by the con-

---

* I suspect that Comte's emphasis on the family as the fundamental unit of social organization (as opposed to the individual) also appealed to a conservative streak in Brazilian youth.

servative classes and fervently championed order as the basis of social progress. "To conserve while progressing" became Castilhos' motto; on numerous occasions he reaffirmed his theoretical debt to Comte. Castilhos can be correctly viewed as a conservative, but his interest in the progressive elements of positivism was not sheer cant; Comte's social philosophy provided Castilhos and his generation with a paternalistic and highly rationalist version of nineteenth-century liberalism. In particular, Castilhos and other positivists adopted the philosopher's defense of individual liberties, his condemnation of slavery, and his demands for separation of church and state, universal elementary education, and state intervention to protect industrial workers.

In political affairs Castilhos faithfully adhered to Comte's precepts on governmental organization and conduct. In insisting on a balanced budget, an executive that could rule by plebiscite, a legislature whose powers were limited to approving income and outlay, and a strict separation of spiritual and temporal powers (as defined by Comte), Castilhos drew heavily on *Appel aux conservateurs*, the work by Comte he studied most thoroughly.[16]

Though not a member of the Positivist Apostolate founded by Miguel Lemos in Rio de Janeiro, Castilhos respected "orthodox" Comtism, the Religion of Humanity. In fact, since members of the Positivist Church could not participate in politics, even to the extent of voting, Castilhos was excluded by definition; yet in his later years he made it rather clear that he was not a Catholic, at the same time hinting at a deep sympathy with the religious variety of positivism.[17]

Castilhos never hid his positivist convictions in politics, but it was to be some time yet before he tried to convert his doctrines into an official creed for his party. Meanwhile, as one of the most visible Republicans in his capacity as the hard-hitting editor of *A Federação*, he began to exert more and more influence in an organization that initially prided itself on having no single leader, in sharp contrast to the Gaúcho Liberal Party. In 1885 he was elected president of the Republican Party congress, but declined to accept the honor. Running for parliament in the same electoral district as Silveira Martins, Castilhos was overwhelmingly defeated time after time, but he continued to insist that the Empire could not survive the death of Pedro II, whose malady Castilhos privately diagnosed as "idiocy resulting from cerebral anemia."[18] Despite his unshakable faith in the imminent end of the Empire, the young Gaúcho assumed that upon the Emperor's death Imperial courtiers would attempt to continue the monarchy by crowning Princess Isabel Empress. Brooding on this possibility, which he considered akin to a coup d'état, Castilhos was pondering revolutionary action by 1887.[19] Similar thinking on the part of other PRR leaders led to a conspiratorial meeting at Castilhos' ranch (in the município now called Júlio de Castilhos) in March 1889. At this historic meeting, attended by Assis Brasil, Pinheiro Machado, and other Republican notables from various parts of the province, Castilhos was made de facto leader of the PRR (at least on a temporary basis),[20] and the participants formally committed themselves to revolutionary action to prevent a third reign.

It was perhaps inevitable that the Gaúcho Republicans, facing a party whose organization, according to its leader, could be compared to a regiment of Frederick the Great, would have to counter with an organization built along parallel lines. The meeting was significant from another viewpoint as well, namely, that a small elite made the basic decision about both the future party leadership and the future thrust of party action, ignoring the tradition of making such policy decisions at a party congress. Castilhos had clearly established his preeminence by March 1889 (the very fact that the meeting took place at his estância was an indication of the prestige he now enjoyed), but he was still far from exercising the iron rule he would establish later.*

In the end, when the Imperial regime came crashing down with a pronunciamento and a few troop maneuvers on November 15, 1889, Republican politicians played only a modest role in the coup.[21] Indeed, only three Republican propagandists participated directly.† The more radical Republicans were purposely excluded; Silva Jardim, for instance, who had earlier tried to interest the military in a

---

* Even at the national constituent assembly in 1890, the Gaúcho delegation tried to pretend that the party had no chief. Two short years later such fictions were to be abandoned.

† Quintino Bocaiuva, Aristides Lobo, and Francisco Glicério Cerqueira Leite. A few other Republican leaders in São Paulo were informed of the conspiracy and were prepared for action. See George C. A. Boehrer, *Da Monarquia à República: História do Partido Republicano do Brasil (1870–1889)*, tr. Berenice Xavier ([Rio], n.d.), p. 286.

conspiracy, was not informed about the plotting in November 1889. Castilhos and Assis Brasil were better informed about Silva Jardim's schemes than about the plans of the men who executed the successful coup: though the two Gaúchos expected the life of the Empire to be a matter of months, they were caught unaware by the proclamation of the Republic. They were not strangers, however, to the leader of the new revolutionary government, Deodoro da Fonseca, who had had frequent contact with Castilhos during the critical days of the Military Question. Two months before the coup, in September, Deodoro had expressed his admiration for Castilhos, Assis Brasil, and Barcelos, publicly declaring that if he had been in Rio Grande in August, he would have voted for the three in the elections for the Imperial chamber—even though he was a member of the Conservative Party.[22]

But in the month following the coup d'état, it was another Gaúcho politician active in the Military Question controversy who was on Deodoro's mind—Gaspar Silveira Martins. Over the past three years the leader of the Riograndense Liberals had tried to take a compromise position on the Question: on the one hand, he had successfully moved a resolution through the senate that suspended disciplinary measures against the offending officers; on the other he had flatly rejected the notion of a military conspiracy against the Empire when his colleague from Rio Grande, the Visconde de Pelotas, mentioned the possibility.[23] Deodoro considered Silveira Martins an enemy, not because of the Gaúcho's lack of attention to military demands, but because of his public attacks on the hypersensitive Marshal while Deodoro was acting governor of Rio Grande do Sul in 1886.

In July 1889 Silveira Martins himself had been appointed governor of Rio Grande, but at the beginning of November he turned his office over to the lieutenant governor in order to resume his seat in the senate. At the time of Deodoro's coup, the Tribune was returning to the capital by sea. During the crisis the Prime Minister (the Visconde de Ouro Preto) recommended to the Emperor that Silveira Martins be allowed to form a new cabinet, as the man best qualified to deal with the situation. Given the enmity between Deodoro and Silveira Martins, the suggestion, if adopted, would probably have strengthened Deodoro's resolve to topple the Empire as well as the incumbent administration. In any case, the Tribune was immediately detained when his ship docked in Santa Catarina, then sent under guard to Rio. A month later, on the suspicion that the Gaúcho was involved in a plot to restore the Empire, Deodoro sent him into exile.

The detention and exile of the Liberal leader was precisely the stroke of luck the Riograndense Republicans had been waiting for: the Liberals, however well regimented they might be, had temporarily lost their Frederick. Even *A Federação* had admitted earlier in 1889 that "the Liberal Party has an incontestable electoral majority."[24] In the last Imperial election in Rio Grande, in August 1889, the Liberals had trounced both the Conservatives and the Republicans, electing six deputies in six contests. In the same year 25 Liberals and 11 Conservatives took their seats in the provincial legislature; the Republicans were not represented. As noted earlier, the Liberals under Silveira Martins managed to dominate the provincial assembly even when the Conservatives controlled the Rio-appointed executive. In controlling the legislature, as well as most of the município councils, the Liberals were able to manipulate local patronage.

Despite their electoral inferiority, the Republicans had reason for encouragement in the late 1880's. True enough, they were easily defeated in the national parliamentary elections of 1889: Castilhos, for instance, lost by a margin of four-and-a-half to one against his Liberal opponent. Yet in the same contest Republicans pulled ahead of the Conservatives for the first time, placing second in five of the six races; Assis Brasil even came within 300 votes of winning (out of some 2,100 cast). Conservative strength was clearly on the wane, and in the previous July, Francisco da Silva Tavares, a leading Conservative deputy in the provincial assembly and member of one of the most powerful clans in the province, had announced his conversion to republicanism and resigned his mandate. This dramatic action was in part motivated by a desire to strike a blow at the Liberal Party, which had thrown Conservative appointees out of office with unprecedented alacrity a month earlier. Lesser Conservative leaders across the state, including another deputy, José Gabriel da Silva Lima, soon joined Tavares in his realignment.*

---

* The Conservatives' propensity to ally with Republicans is observable in other southern provinces in 1888–89. The entente was undoubtedly influenced by abolition—especially in the provinces with large numbers of slaves—but it has yet to be adequately explained.

The November coup produced a similar purge of Gaúcho Liberals from posts of authority. Though Deodoro made a Liberal, Pelotas, the governor of Rio Grande do Sul, he named Júlio de Castilhos secretary of state, a post that allowed the young politician to pass on most officeholders. At state and local levels Liberal appointees were turned out en masse. *Delegados* (local police officers) were fired, as were commanders of units of the National Guard.

The Liberal organ, *A Reforma*, asserted four days after Deodoro's coup that "the Liberal Party constitutes the majority in the province; it is a [political] force, and as such it ought to be respected." The next day, November 20, Castilhos replied in *A Federação*, indicating what the Liberals could expect from the Republicans. The best thing for the Liberals, he counseled, was to repent of their monarchism and leave governing the Republic to Republicans. Accompanying this message was a barely disguised threat about what would happen if the Liberals did otherwise: "We cannot say which would be greater: our tolerance of today or the irrepressible anger with which we will punish [monarchist] criminals *whomever they may be*." Castilhos insisted on a monopoly of power for the PRR; on 25 November he wrote, "In this supreme moment, there is only room for one party—the party of the consolidation of the Republic." He and his cohorts were on guard against restoration movements, and *A Federação* soon began accusing the Liberals of Sebastianism. This was a millenarian cult still active in rural Brazil, based on a belief that Sebastian I (a sixteenth-century king of Portugal) would miraculously deliver his country from the Spaniards and usher in a golden age, despite his death in a battle against the Moors in 1578. By analogy, the Liberals were superstitious and reactionary monarchists.*

Castilhos was not only a master of invective; he also knew how to use power. He immediately began to set up units of a Military Brigade,† which in effect replaced the old National Guard. Its commander, a regular army colonel on leave for this assignment throughout the Old Republic, was chosen for his loyalty to the Republican

---

* Four days after the proclamation of the Republic, PRR leaders were preparing for the contingency of a counterrevolution. Pinheiro Machado had a thousand men ready for action in the Serra. Pinheiro to Aparício Mariense, São Luís (RGS), Nov. 19, 1889, Archive of Aparício Mariense (copy), library of Walter Spalding.

† Initially called the Civil Guard, it received the name Military Brigade (still in use) on October 15, 1892.

Party of Rio Grande do Sul. Sooner or later Castilhos' highly partisan policies were bound to clash with the moderation of Governor Pelotas. It took Pelotas only three months to find he could not work with the sectarian Historical Republicans, as those who had labored for the advent of the Republic before November 1889 were now known. Pelotas, according to his own account, had tried to carry out a policy of conciliation toward the ex-monarchists; however, in his words, the Republican leaders wanted "to distinguish between victors and vanquished" in order to persecute their enemies.[25] Disputes over policy and patronage led Castilhos to submit his resignation, and other members of his organization quickly followed suit. Soon after, Pelotas submitted his own resignation to Deodoro.

In the meantime the PRR was having troubles with Deodoro's provisional government at the national level. One of the party's militants, a positivist named Demétrio Ribeiro, had been appointed minister of agriculture under the Republican regime. An estancieiro and teacher of mathematics, Ribeiro was a highly principled but ineffectual member of Deodoro's first cabinet;[26] he had resigned his post a week before Castilhos' withdrawal from the Pelotas government in Rio Grande. In both cases the principal issue was the national government's decision to undertake a controversial monetary policy.*

Castilhos made it clear that the breach was a limited one, and Deodoro on his part offered the young Gaúcho the governorship of Rio Grande do Sul. Castilhos declined the appointment but recommended Gen. Júlio Falcão da Frota, who was appointed in February 1890. When a new crisis between state and national governments came in May—this time over patronage in a key federal post in Rio Grande involving banks of issue—Frota and his aides resigned together, at the instigation of Castilhos. Again Castilhos assured Deodoro that the issue on which the Gaúcho Republicans resigned was specific and limited in its implications.

A third military governor was then appointed, Gen. Cândido Costa. While the state was awaiting his arrival from Rio de Janeiro, Francisco Silva Tavares (the Conservative-turned-Republican) temporar-

---

* The issue that so troubled PRR leaders was a law of January 17, 1890, creating banks that could issue currency backed by federal bonds instead of gold reserves. These banks were also given privileges that had important implications for patronage. It is possible that the Positivist Apostolate's condemnation of the program influenced Ribeiro and Castilhos.

ily took over the state executive. Almost immediately he faced yet another crisis. On May 13, the anniversary of the abolition of Brazilian slavery in 1888, the Republican Party held a commemorative demonstration in Pôrto Alegre. But Tavares's police, deciding that the demonstration was degenerating into a riot, fired into the crowd; they killed one participant and seriously wounded several others, among them a Republican firebrand named João Barros Cassal, and political passion reached a new level of intensity. PRR leaders in collusion with military officers overthrew Tavares before his interim term expired. With Castilhos' entry into the government of General Costa the persecution of ex-monarchists began anew. The situation grew so tense that Pelotas feared a state-wide civil war.[27] In June he joined with others to form the National Union, in opposition to the PRR. The new party counted among its members the Tavares family and the followers of Silveira Martins; it supported the Republic but proposed a parliamentary rather than a presidential form of government.

Meanwhile Castilhos had made a decision that caused some prominent members of his own party to go over to the opposition: he had agreed to support Deodoro for president when the constituent assembly met in Rio to formally organize the Republic, in return for the lieutenant-governorship.[28] At the end of May Castilhos went to Rio de Janeiro for consultations with Deodoro, and on July 10 *A Federação* abruptly endorsed the Marshal's candidacy for president, thereby flouting the democratic procedures by which the PRR still theoretically operated. Three veteran propagandists now bolted the party: Barros Cassal, Demétrio Ribeiro, and Antão de Faria. The last two had already been nominated by the PRR for the constituent assembly elections in September; both were elected. The National Union abstained in this important contest, which determined the 16 deputies and three senators Rio Grande sent to the constituent assembly. And with good reason: local election boards (the key level of authority under Republican electoral regulations) were uniformly controlled by Castilhistas. *A Reforma* did not even wait until the election to pronounce it "a ridiculous farce."

On the whole, the PRR delegates who went to the constituent assembly in Rio in November were quite young in comparison with the delgates of other states. Castilhos was only thirty, and Borges de Medeiros, who later succeeded Castilhos as party boss, was only twenty-seven. Most of the Riograndenses took orders from Castilhos.* He was named by his delegation to the Committee of Twenty-One, a group composed of representatives of each state and from the Federal District, charged with making the final revision of a constitutional draft to be sent to the plenum. As leader of the Riograndenses, Castilhos fought for a radical interpretation of federalism. His chief objectives were to secure a strict demarcation of federal and state revenues, avoiding double taxation; and the right of the states to charter banks of issue, to establish civil, criminal, and commercial codes, to regulate and tax mines, and to control lands in the public domain. In addition, the Gaúcho chief championed a unicameral legislature, direct election of the president and vice president, suffrage for illiterates, and both "freedom of education" and "freedom of profession" (meaning, respectively, no government participation in higher education and no regulation of professions through licensing). Though the second group of proposals was clearly influenced by positivism, the record of the constituent assembly debates offers no evidence that Castilhos attempted to saddle a Comtian political system on Brazil as a whole.†

The federal constitution that emerged from the assembly on February 24, 1891, bore the stamp of liberal rather than positivist theories, but the Gaúchos managed to achieve some of their objectives. Castilhos won approval of his proposal for direct presidential and vice presidential elections, which had been rejected by the Committee of Twenty-One but was adopted in the plenary session. But his proposal to reserve residual taxing powers for the states and to prohibit double taxation lost in the assembly by a vote of 123 to 103. Nor were he and his Riograndense colleagues able to incorporate unicameralism or suffrage for illiterates into the constitution. As for the "freedoms" issue, the decision was left to the discretion of the states.

The assembly, obedient to the wishes of the provisional govern-

---

* Though Castilhos clearly led the Gaúcho deputation, Barcelos and Assis Brasil did most of the speaking, for oratory was not one of the party chief's strong points. Some of the delegates scarcely opened their mouths in the constituent assembly; Pinheiro Machado uttered a single sentence during the lengthy debates and Borges de Medeiros did not speak at all.

† This was not true of Demétrio Ribeiro. The former minister of agriculture, now at odds with Castilhos, presented the full-blown Comtian model in the assembly on behalf of the Positivist Apostolate; he was politely ignored by the other delegates. See Camara dos Deputados, *Annaes do congresso constituinte da Republica* (2d ed., rev., Rio, 1924–26), I, 477–507.

ment, decided to elect the first constitutional president immediately after the signing of Brazil's new charter, and Castilhos delivered as many votes as he could for Deodoro, who easily won. Yet six of the 19 Gaúchos, among them Assis Brasil, voted for Prudente de Morais (of São Paulo), the assembly's presiding officer.

Castilhos returned to Rio Grande in March to prepare for the election of a state constituent assembly, as required by the federal constitution. On March 16 General Costa resigned as governor, giving Castilhos the opportunity to run the government as lieutenant governor and thereby to control the election. In fact, Castilhos himself quickly resigned, but was careful to see that authority was consigned to an unswerving Castilhista, Fernando Abbott. Despite a measure of fraud and intimidation at the polls, the election of May 5, 1891, was the freest state-wide contest during the whole of the Old Republic. The Castilhista candidates averaged about 28,800 votes each, those of the Federal Republican Party (successor to the National Union) 17,350. The opposition's strength lay predominantly in the Campanha, and its candidates received absolute majorities in Bagé and Alegrete; the PRR won in a majority of municípios in each of the state's three regions, but triumphed by the heaviest margin in the Serra. But even with a sizeable minority vote and a probable majority in a number of municípios, none of the candidates of the anti-Castilhos coalition were recognized as members of the state constituent assembly. This PRR monopoly on the 32-seat legislature was both a radical departure from the biparty representation in the provincial assembly of the Empire and a foretaste of the Castilhista style.

The May elections differed from those of Imperial times in another respect as well. Under the Republic electoral participation had rapidly expanded after a literacy requirement was substituted for income qualifications. But the bitterness of the contest for the state assembly helped raise the level of political participation even further. Between the parliamentary elections of August 1889 and the state constituent assembly contest of May 1891, the number of voters more than tripled, from 14,000 to 46,000. Many of the new voters were members of the middle class, fully able to meet the literacy requirements.[29] Yet there can be little doubt that since the election amounted to a struggle for survival on the part of the former Liberals and their allies, both sides illegally dipped into the illiterate gaúcho mass to increase their talleys. This political mobilization of the rural lower classes was to be followed two years later by military mobilization.

Before his resignation, Governor Costa had appointed a committee consisting of Assis Brasil, Barcelos, and Castilhos to draft a state charter. The document was entirely the work of Castilhos, however, as Assis testified a few months after he had first seen it.* In considering the proposed charter, the constituent assembly largely limited itself to debating measures that would have made the executive even more powerful than in the original draft. When the constitution emerged, almost unchanged from Castilhos' original version, its important provisions were: 1) a unicameral legislature whose authority was restricted to budgetary matters; 2) an executive with a five-year mandate empowered to pass laws by decree on all nonfinancial matters, unless a majority of the município councils rejected a given law; 3) the appointment of the lieutenant governor by the governor; 4) the indefinite reelection of the governor, provided he could obtain three-fourths of the votes cast; and 5) a strict and exaggerated separation of "spiritual" and "temporal" powers.

Provisions 2, 3, and 4 were clearly designed to strengthen one-man rule, Comte's republican "monocracy"; and provision 1, a legislature confined to budgetary affairs, was taken directly from the Frenchman's *Appel aux conservateurs*. Separation of powers covered the freedom of education and freedom of profession Castilhos had sought to have incorporated in the federal constitution. Here too he followed Comte in excluding state support of higher education and state licensing of professionals in his draft, though he, like the master, enthusiastically backed universal elementary education. The rubber-stamp assembly proclaimed the constitution on July 14, 1891, the centenary year of the first French constitution. On the same day the assembly unanimously elected Castilhos governor for the first five-year term, following the precedent of the federal constituent assembly in deferring popular elections until the second term.

Castilhos' alliance with Deodoro had paid off: he had achieved undiluted power in his native state at the age of thirty-one. Yet not all the Gaúchos were happy with the government in Rio (just as many

---

* The essential features of the draft had appeared almost a year earlier in a three-part article in *A Federação*, signed by Alfredo Varela but presumably authored by Castilhos (June 27–30, 1890).

opposed Castilhos), and even the PRR chief himself was obliged to criticize the federal government on several occasions. The establishment of the Republic had upset many traditional patterns of trade—both legal and illegal. In February 1890 Rui Barbosa, minister of the treasury in the provisional government, had attacked contraband, long a way of life in Rio Grande, by establishing a special customs jurisdiction in the state. Beyond that, the favorable tariffs Rio Grande had enjoyed under the Imperial regime, thanks to the efforts of Silveira Martins, were to be done away with: Rui had ordered the gap between Rio Grande's tariffs and those in effect elsewhere in Brazil closed in progressive steps. To prevent a concomitant increase in smuggling, a federal agent was sent to Rio Grande to stop goods from moving across the frontier from Uruguay. A diligent man, he set up special zones beyond which goods passing through the border municípios could not legally move, even if tariff receipts could be produced (since these were often notoriously forged). The agent did such an exemplary job that commerce in the frontier towns almost came to a standstill, to the benefit of the Litoral. By and large, the Republicans' views on the new regulations revealed a regional cleavage. Members of the state assembly (all PRR men) split on the question more or less along the lines of Litoral versus Campanha.[30] However, when a new treasury minister abolished the fiscal zones in October 1891, *A Federação* warmly applauded the measure, apparently seeking support from the merchants along the border, most of whom had backed Silveira Martins.

In export as well as import policies, the Republican regime brought changes in its wake, but this time the initiative lay with the state rather than the federal government. The major source of provincial revenue in the closing years of the Empire was a 4 per cent duty levied on all goods leaving the province. The first Republican legislature altered this policy by distinguishing between different types of goods. Now the highest rates were placed on the state's two traditional exports, charque and cowhides (6 per cent and 9 per cent, respectively), with the implication of a regional discrimination against the Campanha, since the Litoral and the Serra were turning increasingly to agriculture and beginning to produce manufactured goods. Again, however, the issue was one of relative emphasis, for many Republicans were also major cattle and charque producers.

A final issue on which the Republicans seemed to be more interested in defending the interests of the Litoral and the colonial region of the Serra was the commercial treaty of 1891 between Brazil and the United States. Essentially, this agreement was designed to secure a guaranteed market for Brazilian coffee in the United States (and consequently was defended by Fluminenses, Paulistas, and Mineiros) in exchange for Brazil's admission of American grains and manufactured goods at low duties. The Commercial Association of Pôrto Alegre and lard producers in particular from the German colonial area protested to the PRR delegation at the constituent assembly in Rio, and the Gaúchos denounced the agreement.*

Those who nursed economic and political grievances against the federal and state governments got their chance to strike at both in November 1891, when Deodoro reestablished his dictatorship in a coup d'état. Deodoro had run into repeated difficulties with his congress, and the state of financial affairs was deteriorating badly. Yielding to the urgings of the Barão de Lucena, minister of agriculture and *éminence grise* of the new government, Deodoro decided to ignore the constitution by dissolving congress and calling for new elections. On November 3 he struck, surrounding congress with troops.

Castilhos and his trusted associates in Rio de Janeiro had been forewarned and had tried to dissuade the President from his course of action.[31] When Deodoro sent word of the coup to Pôrto Alegre, Castilhos replied cryptically that public order would be "fully maintained" in Rio Grande do Sul. Despite a note of ambiguity in this laconic message, there could be no doubt that Castilhos decided to back the coup d'état: not only did *A Federação* run Deodoro's manifesto on page one, but even more significantly, the state legislature rejected a motion to protest the coup.[32]

Castilhos' acquiescence notwithstanding, other Gaúchos began a struggle to overthrow Deodoro that was soon to spread to the national capital itself. This movement was led by military officers and leaders of the former monarchist parties; the officers were chiefly concerned

---

* Castilhos let other Gaúcho congressmen take the lead in criticizing Deodoro's government. Another issue that had led the Riograndenses to make strictures on the regime was a concession to a relative of Deodoro for construction of the port of Tôrres, on the northern end of Rio Grande's coast. The same issue was chosen by Deodoro's first cabinet (for tactical reasons) as a basis for its resignation en masse on January 21, 1891.

with bringing down the national government, whereas the politicians aimed their wrath primarily at the state level. The first blow was directed at Castilhos. A revolt broke out in the Litoral município of Viamão, the site of recent Republican electoral fraud against the followers of Gaspar Silveira Martins. The unrest soon spread to nearby municípios, but more important, military units stationed in Bagé and the port of Rio Grande began to defy state and national authority, with the support of the Gasparistas. At the same time Livramento was invaded from Rivera and captured by an ex-Liberal caudillo. The rebel forces in Bagé were commanded by a resolutely anti-Castilhista general, João ("Joca") Nunes da Silva Tavares, the Barão de Itaqui and a brother of the former acting governor.

On November 11 *A Federação* registered a shift in Castilhos' position as his fear of deposition grew. The governor had opposed the coup d'état, the party organ asserted; he had agreed to maintain order only to avoid bloodshed. But Castilhos' change of heart came too late to prevent his ouster. The very next day a determined crowd led by Barros Cassal, Assis Brasil, and a rebel military commander forced Castilhos to resign. To whom did he wish to deliver the government, he was asked? Castilhos seems not to have previously considered the question. "To anarchy!" he raged.

A triumvirate composed of Assis Brasil, Barros Cassal, and Gen. Domingos Barreto Leite (an officer acceptable to the Gasparista faction) took over. The new authorities voided Castilhos' constitution, closed the port of Rio Grande, and, after consolidating power in the state, readied a force of some 6,000 men to march northward to overthrow Deodoro. The success of the Riograndense revolution greatly encouraged conspirators in other areas, and on November 23 Adm. Custódio de Melo, commander of the naval squadron lying off Rio de Janeiro in Guanabara Bay, raised the standard of revolt. After a shell lobbed into the city had damaged the Candelária, one of Rio's ancient churches, Deodoro yielded. Tired and sick, he relinquished authority to his constitutional successor, Vice President Floriano Peixoto. Without the success of the Gaúcho rebels, a revolt might eventually have occurred in the capital, but Floriano himself acknowledged the "uprising in Rio Grande do Sul" as the origin of Deodoro's fall.

Deodoro was finished, but was Castilhos? Rio Grande was governed by a junta based on a shaky coalition of ex-Liberals, ex-Conservatives, and dissident Republicans. In a series of bitter and mocking editorials in *A Federação*, to which he now devoted full time, Castilhos branded the triumvirate a *governicho*, a caricature of a government. The name stuck, even though the personnel changed, because of the junta's ineffectualness and the intransigence of a Republican Party bent on overthrowing it. From the beginning Castilhos made it clear that he did not consider any authority in the state legitimate except his own; on the day of his deposition he privately spoke of seeking a *revanche* and of "knocking down the dogs" who had replaced him.[33] In his newspaper a week later he appealed to friends in the army to overthrow the state government. But Castilhos was in no position to enforce his will. His party had been split by the coup in Rio: ill-concealed recriminations between the party chief and two of his most loyal lieutenants, Barcelos and Borges de Medeiros, illustrated the crisis in the PRR. Furthermore, Castilhos' brother-in-law Assis Brasil had definitively broken away and soon removed himself altogether from Gaúcho politics.* Castilhos began to rebuild slowly, using his newspaper to spark the flames of rebellion and temporarily turning away from the army as his mainstay to regional caudillos who could convert their electoral strength to military strength, and to the Military Brigade. That the governicho had failed to restructure the Brigade was prime evidence of the immobilism of the coalition controlling the state government.

Still, it would be quite incorrect to ascribe the tumult of the next few months entirely to Castilhos. With his fall, município governments were toppled as well, in most cases falling into the hands of former Liberals, who began to persecute their Republican predecessors. Private grievances were redressed through violence, and a number of Republicans were killed. At least one PRR border chieftain, João Francisco Pereira de Sousa, had to seek refuge in Uruguay. *A Federação* chronicled and exaggerated the plight of the Republicans in a stream of articles with inflammatory titles such as "Chaos," "Disorder," and "More Blood."

Tension mounted in February 1892 when Silveira Martins returned

---

* His role in the governicho in November 1891 lasted only five days. Thereafter he returned to the diplomatic corps (in which he had served under Deodoro) and did not actively participate in Riograndense politics again until 1907.

to Rio Grande from exile in Europe. His presence in the state caused the loose coalition called the Federal Republican Party to fall apart, for dissident Historical Republicans would not submit to the will of the Tribune. In March more confusion was added to the political nomenclature when a new organization, the Partido Federalista (Federalist Party), was born. Unlike the Federal Republican Party, the Federalist Party was no ephemeral grouping; it was to remain on the scene for three decades. The Campanha município of Bagé was chosen as the site of the new party's organizing convention, and it would continue to be the center of Federalist power. A wealthy município, yet one with a highly stratified and latifundium-based population, Bagé was not only the home of Silveira Martins, but also that of the powerful Tavares family; the former monarchist leaders and traditional political rivals had been definitively driven into each other's arms by Castilhos. By late March the Federalists were ready to present their program; it was virtually dictated by Silveira Martins.* Their principal goal was to introduce a parliamentary regime (in contrast to the established presidential system), with a chief of state selected by the parliament. The return of Silveira Martins imposed a new discipline on the anti-Castilhos forces, both in terms of ideology and in terms of leadership: if the new party lost some potential adherents who refused to accept Silveira Martins' preeminence, it most certainly gained cohesion and unity of purpose.

Meanwhile, Castilhos' forces were not sitting still. Even before the return of the Tribune, the Castilhistas had attempted to catapult their leader back into power. But the only results of an abortive uprising on February 4 had been several deaths across the state, most of the casualties being PRR members. Accordingly, the Republicans resolved to plan more carefully. Between Silveira Martins' reappearance on the scene and the founding convention of the Federalist Party, a meeting of great moment took place. Sixteen PRR leaders, among them Pinheiro Machado and Manuel Nascimento Vargas from the Missões District, Evaristo Amaral from the central Serra, and Hipólito Ribeiro and João Francisco from the Campanha, secretly gathered at Monte Caseros, Argentina, near the junction of the frontiers of Brazil, Uruguay, and Argentina. There at the spot where 40

---

* The term Federalist was a misnomer, for the former monarchists wanted to give the central government greater power to intervene in the states than did the PRR.

years earlier Brazilian and Argentine troops had sealed the fate of the
tyrant of Buenos Aires, Juan Manuel Rosas, the Riograndense Republican leaders decided to stake their political careers and perhaps
their lives on a conspiracy to restore Castilhos to power. At the same
time, in Pôrto Alegre Castilhos and Gen. Júlio Frota (now a senator)
were elaborating a related scheme to bring strategic elements of the
army into the plot.

Isolated acts of violence and even atrocities had been taking place
throughout the state under the governicho; one such incident, which
the Republicans laid at the door of the Federalists, concerned the
family of a Capt. Domingos Mancha, an elderly PRR member in
Palmeira das Missões. According to *A Federação*, "Federalist bandits"
entered the old man's house and bound him, forcing him to watch
as his five daughters were raped; Mancha then was castrated, and
after being stabbed and lanced, received a gaúcho-style coup de grace:
his throat was slit from ear to ear. (The last-named atrocity, called
the degola, would be repeated hundreds of times in the next three
years by both Federalists and Republicans.) The Palmeira outrage
was only one of 15 hideous crimes against Republicans that *A Federação* reported between Castilhos' fall in November 1891 and his
second accession to power seven months later.

Though the Federalists shared control of the state government
with dissident Republicans during the governicho, many Federalists
had a monopoly on power at the local level, and PRR militants
purposely failed to distinguish between the inaction of the state government and its active support of local tyranny. In May 1892 Republicans claimed to have uncovered a plot to assassinate all the leaders
of the PRR. To "depressurize" the political atmosphere, a private
meeting at the end of May was arranged between Castilhos and Silveira Martins by a mutual friend—to no avail; the two men were
irreconcilable. Following the appointment of a Federalist as chief
of the state police, a critical post for political domination, *A Federação* on June 14 shrilly proclaimed: "Gasparismo cannot perpetuate
itself in power, for the honor of the Republican Party! Against
[gasparismo], Republicans, aim your weapons!"

One of the reasons the Republican putsch in February had failed
was that the regular military units in Pôrto Alegre had remained
loyal to the governor, General Barreto Leite. This had led Castilhos

to conclude that if he were to recapture the governorship through a coup, he needed the support of key units of the federal army, which meant the support of Floriano, Deodoro's successor in Rio. Under the circumstances, Castilhos had got off to a bad start indeed, venting his choler against Floriano in *A Federação* after the collapse of Deodoro's dictatorship. In January 1892 the party newspaper accused Floriano of violating the constitution and sarcastically predicted that his sycophants would soon confer on him the title bestowed on Rosas, "Restorer of the Laws." Castilhos had even sent an emissary, Lt. Col. Antônio Adolfo Mena Barreto, to Rio to join the military circles plotting against the new head of state.[34]

Whether or not Floriano knew of Castilhos' complicity in the military plotting, he certainly had no illusions about the Gaúcho's initial hostility toward him. Moreover, as Castilhos and Mena Barreto soon learned, Floriano was not as inept in the exercise of power as his predecessor: the conspiracy was foiled, and officers implicated were retired or imprisoned. Floriano was in many ways the opposite of Deodoro: suspicious, inarticulate, and imperturbable, even cold, where Deododo was gullible, voluble, and irascible. Deodoro tended to speak of military honor and to indulge in blustering and quixotic gestures (as, for instance, when he challenged one of his ministers to a duel during a cabinet meeting); Floriano calculated and, if necessary, skillfully deceived. Nevertheless, the careers of the two marshals had been closely intertwined since November 15, 1889: Floriano, Ouro Preto's adjutant general, had refused to fire on Deodoro's rebellious troops on the day of the coup. His reward had been an appointment as minister of war; congress later elected him vice president of the Republic, a title he insisted on retaining after accepting the reigns of power from Deodoro on November 24, 1891.

Despite Castilhos' initial antagonism toward the new ruler of Brazil, the two men were slowly drawn to one another. Political instability in Rio Grande was paralleled by similar events across Brazil, and Floriano cast about for strong leaders to back his regime, which lived in the shadow of conspiracy and was plagued with economic and financial problems. He may also have been moved to consider the possibility of an alliance with Castilhos because of a troublesome border issue with Argentina. He felt that war with Argentina was a definite possibility,[35] a contingency that made it highly desirable to have a strong government in Rio Grande do Sul, the pivotal state in any military operations in the Plate.

The question Floriano had to answer was: who was best qualified to lead Rio Grande? One of the strong figures, Silveira Martins, was completely unacceptable, since his party was not only opposed to the existing constitution but suspect as a haven for monarchists; as for a military man, Rio Grande, unlike the other states, had seen a procession of military governors. Gen. Bernardo Vasques, the commander of the local Military Region, believed there was only one solution: by April 1892 he was urging Floriano to permit the PRR to resume power.[36] In May Floriano sent a special envoy to Rio Grande to determine whether Vasques was right. In the opinion of the agent he was. The government of General Barreto Leite was weak, the envoy reported, and the Gasparistas were sure to win in the partial congressional elections in June because the Republicans were going to abstain. He suggested a plan: let Castilhos take power in a coup and then resign, turning the state government over to a neutral figure to organize an election. As it turned out, the plan was executed somewhat differently, since the interim governor proved to be anything but neutral. Be that as it may, Floriano knew the essentials of the proposed coup and at least tacitly agreed to them in early June.[37]

On June 17 the Republicans launched their offensive. With the support of the Military Brigade in Pôrto Alegre, Castilhos marched on the governor's mansion to depose Pelotas, once again ruler of the state. General Vasques's troops stood idly by, refusing to defend the incumbent, who reacted by transferring the government to the commander of the garrison at Bagé, Gen. Joca Tavares. Since Castilhos asserted that his was the "restored legal government," Rio Grande now had two claimants to authority. PRR forces and federal troops from Uruguaiana and Quaraí began to converge on Bagé, and a major military clash appeared to be imminent. Silveira Martins, in Pôrto Alegre, wired Tavares, begging him not to permit a civil war. Whether in response to the Federalist leader or because he was militarily outclassed, Tavares surrendered to an army contingent under the command of Col. Artur Oscar de Andrade Guimarães. (Tavares and other Federalists soon emigrated to nearby Uruguay, fearing assassination by PRR militants.) The only other resistance to the coup was offered by the disaffected Republican Barros Cassal, who

boarded a naval vessel in the Guaíba estuary and convinced its commander to fire on Pôrto Alegre. Achieving nothing, the ship soon
steamed away into the Lagoa dos Patos.

The complex and frequently violent pattern of political instability
in Rio Grande during the first three years of the Republican regime
was partly a local aspect of national political and financial chaos, but
it also reflected internal dynamics in the state's economy and society.
At the national level, Brazil, like other countries with colonial economies, had been severely affected by the depression that began in
France in 1889 and spread to Britain a year later. The monetary
policies of the first Republican government in the years 1889–91,
contradictory but on the whole favoring easy credit, had produced
an orgy of speculation known as the Encilhamento ("Saddling up"),
followed by a crash in 1892. The exchange value of the milréis, the
Brazilian unit of currency, fell in every successive year between 1889
and 1892, from U.S. $0.54 to $0.24 (in current dollars).

Despite a remarkable increase in the number of banking firms in
Rio Grande in 1890–91 (from two to ten) there was less buoyancy
in the all-important but unstable export sector. The value of the
state's interprovincial and foreign exports had fallen from 20,000
contos (or thousands of milréis) in 1882 to 13,500 contos in 1888, and
managed to climb back to only 17,000 by 1890. Charque alone accounted for almost one-third of the export revenues in 1890, even
though sales outside the province had dropped over 50 per cent
since the slaughter of 1886–87.[38] The charque industry was hard-hit
by the abolition of slavery, which led not only to a labor shortage but
also to a temporary disorganization of the market; plantation owners
in other parts of Brazil had customarily fed their slaves Gaúcho
charque, but the demand decreased sharply as many freedmen left
the fazendas and headed for the city.

Undoubtedly the crisis would have been worse, had not financial
and economic crises of greater proportions hit Rio Grande's chief
competitors in the Brazilian charque market, Argentina and Uruguay. El Noventa, the political crisis of 1890 that brought down the
government of Juárez Celman in Argentina, was a political consequence of the European depression and the resultant financial collapse in the Plate. Uruguay, a stronger competitor than Argentina

in the Brazilian charque market, underwent a similar collapse, and though the government did not fall, Uruguay's foreign trade did not reach the levels of 1889 until a full decade later.[39] The political and economic problems in the Plate thus attenuated the Gaúcho charque crisis, since the export-oriented charqueadores of Argentina and Uruguay felt the repercussions of the European depression more than the Gaúchos. Cattle slaughters in Rio Grande continued to fluctuate, however, with a general upward trend between the low of 1889–90 and the high of 1893–94.[40]

A greater sensitivity to national and international economic trends was only one of the consequences of the commercialization of Gaúcho ranching, discussed in Chapter 1. Technological change, especially the introduction of railroads, wire fencing, and new breeds of cattle, created a new social phenomenon in ranching country, particularly in the Campanha: this was the increasing dislocation and marginalization of the gaúcho class as fewer and fewer unspecialized cowhands were needed on the big estâncias.[41] It was growth, therefore, not stagnation, that led to unemployment in the Campanha.

The 1890 census data on literacy in the state's municípios clearly show the gap between urban and "colono" Rio Grande on the one hand, and "estância" Rio Grande on the other: 58 per cent of the inhabitants of Pôrto Alegre (including ages 0–6) and 54.7 per cent of the inhabitants of São Leopoldo, the chief German colony, were illiterate, against almost 84 per cent in São Borja (in the Missões District) and only slightly less than that in Quaraí and São Francisco de Paula, in the Campanha and the central Serra, respectively. Furthermore, the census figures show that a shift in the relative demographic strength of the three regions was accompanying the economic transformation of Rio Grande: between 1872 and 1890 the Serra's population increased 159 per cent, whereas the Litoral's increased only 72 per cent and the Campanha's 93 per cent.[42] By 1890 only a fourth of the state's population lived in the Campanha, and two-fifths lived in the Serra. These social and economic shifts were occurring at the same time that sustained political instability and increasing political mobilization pitted two highly disciplined machines against each other in the three initial years of the Republic.

It was this setting of socioeconomic change, coupled with the political disarray of the opening years of the Republic, that had allowed

Júlio de Castilhos to seize power. In his climb to uncontested author-ity, he had had to overthrow an organization whose bastions had seemed impregnable only three years before; in achieving power he had become a despot and had alienated many of his fellow Republi-can propagandists. But by 1892 his political authority was complete: the Castilhista machine controlled the executive, the legislature, the município governments, and the state police organization. Still, the Gasparistas had only been dislodged, not destroyed, and neither side doubted that a bloody struggle was soon to come.

# CHAPTER THREE

# Terror and War

By 1892 the Partido Republicano Riograndense had become the regimented organization it would remain throughout the First Republic, and its leader moved swiftly after his coup d'état to secure his party in power indefinitely. Castilhos' first act was to reinstate his constitution of July 14; his second was to resign in favor of a party colleague, Vitorino Monteiro. As governor, Monteiro had two tasks: to prepare the Military Brigade and reserve forces for civil war and to arrange popular elections that would bring Castilhos back to power with renewed authority. Floriano Peixoto, who had met previous requests for help from governors of Rio Grande with notable indifference, sent warm congratulations and promises of support to Monteiro.

In the wake of the coup d'état, the Republicans systematically discharged Federalist officeholders. The consequences were predictable: an intensification of the internecine violence in Rio Grande do Sul. Almost all accounts of these events are biased—and exaggerated. Still, it does appear that there were more violent crimes in the second half of 1892 than in any comparable period since the rise of the Republic, though from the outset the regime had witnessed a high level of violence. And it seems clear that most of the terror, though by no means all of it, was the work of the Republicans.

The degola, the gaúcho's preferred form of execution (in the Plate as well as in Rio Grande), became a commonplace. Though the degola could be performed in a variety of ways, typically the gaúcho slaughtered his victim in much the same way he slaughtered a sheep. The victim was forced to kneel with his hands tied behind him and to place his head between the legs of his executioner, who ruptured the carotid arteries in a single swift stroke of his knife.[1] The degola was quick, silent, and cheap. In the last half of 1892, reports of degolas and other atrocities poured into the state capital from more than a dozen municípios across the state. Pôrto Alegre itself was the scene of three violent deaths of important figures. Facundo Tavares, septuagenarian brother of Joca and Francisco, resisted arrest in a midnight raid on his house by the Military Brigade, and in the process he was wounded and two of his sons were killed. Frederico Haensel, a German-Brazilian who had served as a Liberal in the provincial assembly, was shot "while trying to escape" in his own home. The story of an old man forced to witness the rape of his daughters was repeated, but this time the victims were Federalists. A Federalist historian lists the names of 134 persons across the state who were murdered in Republican reprisals between Castilhos' coup and his inauguration in January 1893.[2]

Whenever possible, the Federalists responded in kind. One of their most notorious atrocities was the murder in November 1892 of a high-ranking PRR member, Evaristo Amaral, one of the participants in the Monte Caseros meeting. A Federação carried the full details of this heinous crime, as related by José Gabriel da Silva Lima, a close friend of the victim and a fellow Republican militant. On the way from Cruz Alta to Itaqui, according to this account, Evaristo had been attacked, wounded, and overpowered by a gang of hoodlums hired by one Garcez, an ousted Serra delegado. After Evaristo's capture, José Gabriel reported, "The barbarians broke his shin and thigh bones, forearms and upper arms. The killer Filandro, according to his own testimony, cut open the abdomen of Colonel Evaristo, pulled out his intestines ... while he was still alive, and then gave him the degola, cutting the head from the trunk of the body." After laying out the rest of the details of this gory crime, the outraged José Gabriel concluded with a curse: "Eternal damnation on the Federalist Party, which wants to govern the state while preaching ... murder, robbery, and pillage!"[3]

As if there could be any doubt about the object lesson for loyal Republicans, the point was driven home the next day by Evaristo's son, who wrote in A Federação: "The assassination of my beloved father was not an isolated incident: it is linked, intimately linked, to the revolution which the Federalist Party [planned]. . . . My father was not killed as vengeance by Garcez [but] by the Federalist Party of Rio Grande do Sul, whose chief is the dissembling Dr. Gaspar Silveira Martins." As the word vengeance implies, Evaristo had not been gratuitously singled out for liquidation: some of his hirelings were accused of committing atrocities against Federalist families.[4] Whatever the truth of the matter, the Republicans could now make political capital of a martyr. "If I die," Evaristo is supposed to have said several weeks before the crime, "I will die for my Party."[5]

The murder of an important party member appeared to lend substance to the allegation made a few weeks earlier by Fernando Abbott (who had replaced Vitorino Monteiro as governor) that he had uncovered a plot to assassinate Republican leaders systematically. The Republicans now managed to create an atmosphere reminiscent of the Grand Peur of the French Revolution in Rio Grande, with repeated alarms about the Federalist menace. Many of the major Federalist leaders fled the state; those who did not were taken into custody. The effect of the constant (and almost certainly often exaggerated) reports of atrocities was to dispel any remaining reluctance on either side to retaliate with equal savagery.

Castilhos and his aides worked feverishly to consolidate PRR rule, concentrating especially on the state's military establishment. The outlay for the Military Brigade was already the largest single item in the 1892 budget. The total number of officers and men in this force, which amounted to a state army, had risen from 718 in the last year of the Empire to 1,265. The Republicans quickly took advantage of the provision in the restored constitution that allowed the governor to conscript able-bodied men into state forces. Furthermore, on September 22 they created município guard units to supplement the Brigade. In November and December a series of bond issues was floated for the "maintenance of public order." And at the end of the year "provisional corps" of the Military Brigade were set up, a step that allowed Republican estancieiros to militarize their gaúchos with official sanction.

Clearly, the Republicans were determined to avoid the fatal error of the governicho, which had failed to restructure the state's military and paramilitary organizations after Castilhos fell from power in

November 1891; the rulers of that period had been content to change only high-ranking personnel. Castilhos' lieutenant, Fernando Abbott, during his first stint as acting governor in 1891, had issued 222 executive orders reorganizing the Military Brigade and reserve units. In contrast, all the rulers in the governicho period together issued a total of only five such orders. The Castilhista concern was again evident under Monteiro and Abbott, who issued 20 orders concerning state military forces.[6]

The PRR could not rely solely on state troops and paramilitary units, however; that was one of the lessons of November 1891. In September 1892 Castilhos went to Rio to assure himself that Floriano Peixoto would make good an earlier promise to back the "true Republicans" in Rio Grande. Apparently any doubts of Floriano's position were laid to rest during this visit, and Castilhos returned to Rio Grande satisfied that he still had the Marshal's support. In November, in a contest supervised by Abbott, Castilhos was elected governor. Relative calm prevailed on election day, but only because the Federalists had chosen to boycott the polls.

On January 25, 1893, Júlio de Castilhos was inaugurated as the first popularly elected governor of Rio Grande do Sul; his was the eighteenth government in the state since the birth of the Republic in November 1889. According to a member of the state constituent assembly, Castilhos was Rio Grande's Danton, the leader who would rise "to point the way to the Terror" if necessary.[7] Castilhos himself did not put it quite so bluntly, but he did vow "energetic [action] when the security and tranquility of society demand the severe application of inexorable repressive measures."[8]

Meanwhile the harried Federalists had been streaming out of the state in increasingly large numbers, most of them moving across the borders into Uruguay or Argentina. Even if they escaped murder or imprisonment, their property was likely to be vandalized and their livestock slaughtered. (To cite just one example: after the war one of the Tavares brothers was indemnified for the loss of almost 19,000 head of cattle during 1893 and 1894.)[9] Under the circumstances, some 10,000 persons allegedly fled to Uruguay alone between June 1892 and February 1893. This general exodus to Uruguay, where many of the great estancieiros of Rio Grande owned estates, permitted what might otherwise have been an aggrieved but unorganized group to mass for an invasion under the protection of a friendly government.* Moreover, the rebels could count on the peons of their Uruguayan estates, along with a certain number of gaúchos from their Rio Grande estâncias, to participate in the invasion. A few regular army officers, most of them Riograndenses by birth and participants in Imperial politics, also joined the rebels.

What the Federalists wanted first was the dismantling of the constitution of July 14. At the same time, most of them realized that if this goal were to be achieved, Castilhos' protector Floriano would have to be ousted as well. With the memory of November 1891 fresh in their minds, many rebels expected quick and decisive aid from malcontent elements of the army and navy, who were continuing to conspire against Floriano in the national capital. A more long-range Federalist aspiration was to substitute a parliamentary regime for the presidential system established in the national constitution. But some of the rebels even went beyond this goal and unabashedly professed monarchism. Col. Manuel Macedo Fulião, for instance, always went into battle shouting "Long live H. M. the Emperor."[10] Silveira Martins, then in Montevideo, had considered the idea of restoration while in Europe, but now professed to reject the notion.† Finally, joining the parliamentarians and monarchists was a third faction: a group of dissident Republicans, led by Barros Cassal, who were willing to make common cause with the Federalists because of their abhorrence of the Castilhista machine. Recognizing the difficulty of holding such disparate elements together, the civilian leader and the military leader of the movement—Silveira Martins and Joca Tavares —decided to leave their ultimate objectives undefined.

In the end, however, the open question of monarchism, as well as certain personnel changes in key military positions, made the military situation radically different from the situation in 1891. Tavares still hoped that army personnel in Rio Grande (numbering between five

---

* In 1889 there were 7,191 Brazilian property owners in Uruguay, with combined holdings valued at 11,833:074$000, or $6.4 million (in current U.S. dollars). *A Reforma*, September 3, 1889. Silveira Martins had good connections with both the Blanco (Nationalist) Party, which was strong along the northern border, and the ruling Colorados.

† Silveira Martins was principally an advocate of parliamentarianism, and, says one biographer, he "never made a fetish of forms of government" in choosing between a monarchy and a republic. Osvaldo Orico, *Silveira Martins e sua época* (Pôrto Alegre, 1935), p. 329.

and six thousand men) would at least remain neutral in the struggle against Castilhos.[11] But General Vasques had been placing units in Rio Grande under the command of militant supporters of Floriano, and the real question was: would the army stand aside in a contest that also involved the fate of the government in Rio?

War finally broke out on February 2, 1893, when a Federalist band crossed the Uruguayan border into Bagé. A number of the Uruguayan gaúchos who accompanied their Brazilian landlords in the initial raids into Rio Grande were from a department of Uruguay that had been settled by Spaniards from Maragataría. Consequently, the Republicans soon began to apply the term Maragato to all Federalists, implying they were a group of foreign invaders. As often happens, the term of derision was accepted as a badge of honor, and Maragato rapidly became a synonym for Federalist in both camps.*

Not only did the Republicans brand the Federalists an alien force; they also charged them with separatism and monarchism, referred to more abusively as Sebastianism. It was the accusation of restorationist objectives that did the most damage. Tavares and his companions-in-arms made an unfortunate choice of words in their first manifesto, issued on February 5, ending their exhortation to the Riograndense people with the phrase "Viva a Nação Brasileira!" (Long live the Brazilian Nation!) rather than the by-this-time conventional "Viva a República!" The Castilhistas seized upon this implicit coolness to the republican system—genuine enough among some Federalists—to depict the Maragatos as unrepentant monarchists to the Brazilian public at large and the army in particular. There can be no doubt of the effectiveness of the charge, for Tavares soon issued a clarificacation, carefully ending with the words "Viva a República!"

From the beginning the Federalists were outclassed, both in numbers and in matériel. For manpower they relied chiefly on the gaúcho armies of the Campanha and Serra estancieiros. The Campanha force was particularly important, not only because of its numbers but also because of its strategic location along the frontier: the three major invasions of the state all originated in Uruguay. Most of the estan-

---

* In turn, the Federalists called the Republicans *picapaus* (woodpeckers), apparently because of the red field caps worn by the federal troops who fought alongside the Castilhistas. The nickname never gained the popularity of Maragato, however.

cieiro-politicians had been Liberals, and one researcher has shown that almost all of the commanders who signed the rebel manifesto of March 15, 1893, had held offices of one sort or another under Silveira Martins.* Many of those who lived along the frontier were engaged in commerce and smuggling as well; and a very few, such as Rafael Cabeda of Livramento, were primarily merchants rather than ranchers. In the Colonial Zone the rebels could count on sympathy among the Germans but little else. Silveira Martins had earned the support of the Germans for his championing of the right of non-Catholics to vote. Furthermore, the PRR had persecuted the most prestigious member of the German community, Karl von Koseritz, and it was a Castilhista official who had murdered Frederico Haensel. But sentiment notwithstanding, the German community was largely without arms and only too aware, from bitter experience, that it needed the goodwill of the state government. In addition, Castilhos gave some attention to rallying the Germans to his side, most notably by beginning the construction of schools in São Leopoldo for political effect. At the same time, he took the precaution of detaining suspect German-Brazilians. Among the Italian colonists, the Republican leader felt much stronger.[12] In the end, however, the sympathies of the colonos made little difference, for the war barely touched the Colonial Zone.

For the 5,000-man army of the first invasion, equipment was in perilously short supply; the Federalist army had only 700 modern weapons altogether[13] and was forced to rely primarily on lancer formations. When it became clear that the vast majority of the regular troops in the state would remain loyal to Floriano (and by extension to Castilhos),† the invaders understood they would have to use hit-and-run tactics, relying on surprise and mobility, and avoiding decisive combat whenever possible. Inevitably the Campanha, adjacent to Uruguay and the chief base of Federalist strength, became the major area of operations, though the Serra (except for the Colonial Zone) also saw extensive action; only the Litoral was virtually free

---

* Sérgio da Costa Franco, "O sentido histórico da revolução de 1893," in *Fundamentos da cultura riograndense: Quinta série* ([Pôrto Alegre], 1962), p. 199. The greatest number were former delegados, commanders of National Guard units, and members of município councils.

† Among the few officers who went over to the rebels, the two most important, apart from Tavares, were Isidoro Dias Lopes and Luís de Oliveira Salgado.

from attack—but the inability to dominate the administrative and commercial axis of the state had been precisely the reason the Farrapos had been forced on the defensive in 1836.

The leader of the first Maragato invasion and the man destined to be the outstanding rebel general during the war was Gumercindo Saraiva. Saraiva (spelled Saravia in Uruguay) was a product of the border culture that has played a leading role in the history of both Uruguay and Rio Grande do Sul. Whether he was born in Brazil or in Uruguay is still disputed;[14] his father, a Farrapo, had fled across the border and had taken up residence in Uruguay. Gumercindo's brother Aparício, who accompanied him in the Federalist campaign, later became the head of the Blanco Party in Uruguay. Aparício's son Nepomuceno continued to participate in military campaigns on both sides of the border 30 years after the Maragato invasion.

Gumercindo's formal education (limited to secondary school) was acquired in Montevideo, and his training in gaúcho-style military campaigns took place in Uruguay; his preferred language was Spanish. As he once jokingly remarked, "Hablo el castellano para no 'estropiar' nuestra lengua; prefiero 'estropiar' la de ellos" (I speak Spanish so as not to "massacree" our language [Portuguese]; I prefer to "massacree" theirs).[15]

Gumercindo's conception of the good life was ranching and politicking, with a good fight now and then in a quick raid across the cochilhas of Rio Grande and Uruguay. In 1873 he married a Brazilian girl from Jaguarão, a relative of João Francisco Diana, Liberal politician and last foreign minister of the Empire. Eight years later the couple took up residence in Santa Vitória do Palmar, the southernmost município of Rio Grande, across the border from the Saraiva estates in the Uruguayan department of Cerro Largo. With his wealth, connections, and military reputation, Gumercindo soon became the leading political figure of Santa Vitória, and in July 1889 he was appointed delegado; he also held the rank of lieutenant colonel in the National Guard. Though he summarily lost these posts when the Republicans replaced the Liberals as the rulers of Rio Grande, Castilhos sent Assis Brasil on a mission to the Saraiva estate to co-opt the Spanish-speaking caudillo into the PRR. Gumercindo refused, for in agreeing he would have had to share power in his município with former Conservative leaders who had entered the Republican Party in the last months of the Empire.

His refusal was not well received, and Gumercindo soon found himself in jail, charged with having arranged a murder in Santa Vitória. Managing to escape, he fled across the border to Aparício's estância, where he remained until Castilhos was overthrown in November 1891. He then returned to Rio Grande, faced trial, and won acquittal under a more friendly judge. But he had only a few months of peace. With Castilhos' return to power, Gumercindo's position was again precarious. Indeed, his cousin Terêncio Saraiva, an estancieiro in Bagé, had already been cut down by the degola, the victim of a marauding band of Castilhistas. Gumercindo withdrew across the frontier once more, but this time he had every intention of returning to dislodge the oppressor in Pôrto Alegre. In sum, this was no Cincinnatus reluctantly abandoning a bucolic existence, but a man who had long been involved in the stormy political affairs of both Uruguay and Rio Grande do Sul.*

Gumercindo invaded Rio Grande at the beginning of February and was soon joined by Joca Tavares (taking the field at age seventy-seven), Joaquim Pedro Salgado, and other Maragato leaders. In March Gumercindo attacked the town of Dom Pedrito, near Bagé, and easily overran it. He then permitted his soldiers to sack the town and to terrorize the inhabitants to such a degree that officers of the regular army were shocked; as a consequence the army's support of the state government hardened.[16] The first major battle of the war occurred when Gumercindo, Tavares, and Salgado joined forces at the Inhanduí River to engage the Division of the North, a Castilhista army jointly commanded by Gen. Francisco Rodrigues Lima, a retired army officer in the service of Castilhos, and the Republican militant Pinheiro Machado. There, on May 4, some 6,000 poorly armed Federalists faced 4,500 well-armed Republicans; the Castilhistas, dug in and disposing of artillery, repulsed a valiant Federalist cavalry charge, then took the offensive. The Federalists retreated, abandoning much of their meager equipment and weaponry; Tavares and Salgado withdrew across the frontier, leaving Gumercindo to continue the revolution on Brazilian soil with a force of 1,100 men.

The battle at the Inhanduí was crucial because of its effect on the

---

* According to his nephew, Gumercindo was prompted to enter the fray in order to establish a Federalist-controlled Rio Grande that would then help the Blancos to gain power in Uruguay. Though this may have well been a consideration, the fact is Gumercindo had reason enough without such aims. See Nepomuceno Saravia García, *Memorias de Aparicio Saravia* (Montevideo, 1956), p. 28.

morale of the Republicans—in Rio de Janeiro as well as in Rio
Grande. "Victory! Victory!" Castilhos exultantly wired Floriano.
If, as José Maria Bello states, Rio Grande was the testing ground for
the survival of the new Republican regime,[17] Castilhos and the Castilhista army had apparently demonstrated their indispensability.
There would now be no question of putting the state under the control of a military interventor, as one of Floriano's advisors had suggested shortly before the outbreak of hostilities. Floriano got permission from congress to declare a state of siege in Rio Grande, but
he did so only to sustain the incumbent machine. If any further indication of his support for Castilhos is needed, it can be found in his
appointment of two ardent Castilhistas, Abbott and Monteiro, to
serve as ministers to Argentina and Uruguay, respectively. In the
Plate they could keep a close eye on the rebels, now active in both
countries.

As federal troops and Castilhistas tracked Gumercindo's army in
the Campanha, Salgado regrouped his forces along the Uruguayan
frontier and invaded Rio Grande again in August with some 1,000
men. He managed to establish contact with Gumercindo, and together
the two commanders led their men northwest, hoping to link up with
a naval unit stationed at Itaqui. They planned to take advantage of
a naval revolt, led by Adm. Custódio de Melo, Floriano's former
minister of the navy, that had erupted in Guanabara Bay on September 6. Gumercindo believed or hoped that the entire navy would join
hands with the Maragatos. To his consternation, however, the naval
commander at Itaqui would promise nothing more than neutrality in
the struggle for control of Rio Grande do Sul. Pressed by a 2,500-man
force under Rodrigues Lima and Pinheiro Machado, Gumercindo
struck out eastward through the Serra to incorporate smaller rebel
forces into his army. Although the Maragatos had by no means been
able to dominate the Serra, they had made a series of hit-and-run
raids in the Central Plateau. They had also managed to convulse the
Missões District, thanks to the repeated attacks of a Federalist caudillo
from São Borja named Dinarte Dorneles, who had raided from Argentina.

The combined forces of Salgado and Gumercindo took Passo
Fundo in October, but they were unable to hold the town; from there
they continued to move north, crossing into Santa Catarina on No-

vember 7, 1893. In the meantime the naval rebellion had resulted in the capture of Desterro, the capital of Santa Catarina, and Salgado pushed eastward toward the coast to join forces with naval units. The impetuous Gumercindo, however, continued to drive north, determined this time to make Floriano his target rather than Floriano's deputy Castilhos.

Meanwhile the Maragatos had had a measure of success in the Campanha. General Tavares, again in the field, had taken the frontier town of Quaraí at the end of September, then had marched east. Two months later in the município of Bagé, he surprised and overwhelmed a group of Castilhistas and federal troops bivouacking on the banks of the Rio Negro. The enemy commander, Gen. Isidoro Fernandes, quickly surrendered—unwisely, as it turned out, for at Rio Negro the first mass atrocity of the war occurred. On the night of November 24, approximately 300 of the 1,000 prisoners were executed by the degola. Many of the victims were Uruguayans, since the Republicans like the Federalists had recruited mercenaries across the border. To determine which prisoners were foreigners, Tavares's men required each prisoner to pronounce the letter J. Those who failed to render the Portuguese pronunciation, "zhotah," correctly were presumed to be Castelhanos and were put to the knife. One man did all the killing—Adão Latorre, whose Spanish surname indicates he came from the same border culture as those he was arbitrarily executing.

Still, Brazilian throats also met cold steel on the night of November 24. Among those killed were army personnel, whose deaths undoubtedly strengthened the military's support of the Castilhistas. In at least one case there was a kind of rough justice in the execution: the victim was a Castilhista boss named Manuel Pedroso, who had sacked and murdered his way through the município of Bagé. When Pedroso learned that he was slated for the degola, he asked his mulatto executioner, "Adão, how much is the life of a good and brave man worth?"

"Brave, agreed. Good . . . I don't know! The life of a man is worth a great deal [but] yours is worthless because it's on the edge of my knife, and no money can buy it," Adão retorted.

Throwing back his head to make Latorre's task easier, Pedroso spat out, *"Then go ahead and cut, you black son of a whore!"*[18]

Most of the bodies at Rio Negro were tossed in a nearby lagoon, but Pedroso's corpse was left to rot in the sun for three days.

As might be expected, this episode led to new atrocities; the 300 victims were not to be forgotten. A Castilhista general, Firmino de Paula, retaliated with the slaughter of almost an equal number of Maragatos in April 1894, at Boi Prêto. Throughout the Serra and the Campanha, the rapes, castrations, and degolas that had marked the turbulent months before the invasion continued unchecked. The bishop of Rio Grande do Sul expressed the anguish of the Rio-grandense people to the Rio de Janeiro press in mid-1893, and confirmed that degolas were common and the destruction of property extensive.

Following the fateful events at Rio Negro, Tavares and his 3,000 men attacked the city of Bagé, the site of one of the most important military garrisons in the state. Col. Carlos Teles, the commander at Bagé, held fast with 1,000 loyal troops. After 30 days of siege, the troops were reduced to eating dogs, horses, and cats in order to survive, but the knowledge of what had happened to prisoners a few miles away at Rio Negro kept the defenders going. On January 8, 1894, after a month and a half of encirclement, a relief column arrived, forcing the Federalist army to lift the siege and retreat into Uruguay. The aged Tavares, his health failing, withdrew from the fight.

At this point we must briefly consider the naval revolt in Rio de Janeiro, for from late 1893 on, the Federalists attempted to coordinate their efforts with the navy rebels. The rebellion began when Adm. Custódio de Melo ordered the fleet in the bay facing Rio to bombard the city. Among other grievances, Custódio felt he had been "betrayed" by Floriano—just as Floriano had deceived Pelotas—on the question of support of Castilhos' coup of June 1892.[19] Custódio had resigned as minister of the navy in 1892, but he had not been able to translate his anger into action until September of the next year. He had participated in the naval rebellion against Deodoro in 1891, and it was his hope that Floriano too would resign when the first shots were fired. But he was to find that Floriano was made of sterner stuff than Deodoro; after a series of artillery duels and unsuccessful landings, Custódio and part of his fleet headed south, where navy insurgents already held the island city of Desterro.

As noted, when Salgado had wheeled eastward to establish contact with the "provisional federal government" at Desterro, Gumercindo had driven north. Crossing into Paraná, he had impressed local inhabitants into Federalist ranks as he went, and on January 20, 1894, he captured Curitiba, the state capital. From there he issued a demand that Floriano resign, threatening to march on São Paulo if he did not. Unimpressed, Floriano stolidly ignored the message, and troops in the federal capital, now no longer threatened by an attack from the naval forces in Guanabara Bay, made ready to move south. The state police of São Paulo, a unit similar to the Gaúcho Military Brigade numbering some 3,000 well-armed men, also stood between Gumercindo and Floriano. Although the Federalist troops had almost reached the Paraná–São Paulo border, Gumercindo realized that the silence from Rio de Janeiro meant his bluff had been called. Ordering his 4,000-man army to retreat and following his errant intuition now as always, he began a march back to Rio Grande do Sul. Meanwhile the rebels' situation was growing critical in Desterro. The rebel "capital" was being encircled by loyalist troops, and the despairing Custódio de Melo, in a last desperate gamble, sailed his fleet down the coast and in April attacked the port of Rio Grande with Federalist support. The city's defenders, however, were able to repulse a landing party until reinforcements were sent by rail from Bagé. Custódio gave up the effort, put to sea, and sailed to Buenos Aires, where he interned his ships and was given asylum. A week after the attack on the port, Desterro fell to loyalist troops. These defeats, together with a serious setback in the Campanha, where an army led by Hipólito Ribeiro had badly beaten the Federalists in February, made Gumercindo more than ever the chief hope of rebel success.

Once Gumercindo reentered Rio Grande do Sul, he joined forces with another Federalist leader, Antônio Prestes Guimarães, and their combined armies engaged the Division of the North near Passo Fundo at the end of June 1894. In a six-hour battle, the largest of the war, the Federalists suffered some 400 casualties and the Republicans 240; among the wounded were the Federalist Aparício Saraiva and the Castilhistas Rodrigues Lima and Firmino de Paula. For the Maragatos the battle was a defeat, if only because they could not replace their dead and wounded. They were soon to suffer an even worse loss. On a westward march to join forces with Dinarte Dorneles, Gumercindo and his men were involved in a skirmish at Carovi on August 10. Brashly exposing himself on the front lines, Gumercindo sustained a chest wound. Two hours later the most daring and inventive of the Maragato commanders was dead.

*A Federação*'s final judgment was harsh. Far from praising a valorous enemy, the paper printed a venomous curse: "May the earth which your hateful cadaver profanes lie on you as heavy as the Andes. On that revolting grave may there fall all the concentrated sorrows of the mothers you sacrificed, of the wives you offended, of the virgins you polluted—wild beast of the South, hangman of Rio Grande."\* To such white heat had passions been raised in Rio Grande do Sul! In point of fact, Gumercindo's conduct was no worse than that of most of the other field commanders—on both sides. Moreover, though he was guilty of permitting outrages like the sacking of Dom Pedrito, he never authorized a systematic slaughter on the order of those permitted by Tavares and Firmino de Paula.

The loss of Gumercindo was a crippling blow to the Federalists in the Serra, and they now split up. Aparício Saraiva, seeking to avoid combat, led most of the men formerly under his brother's command into Argentina in early September. In the next few months he reorganized his forces in northern Uruguay, and by early 1895 he was making disruptive but discreet sallies into the Campanha. Outside the Campanha Federalist resistance had been crushed by six divisions combining Castilhista and Federalist troops. Meanwhile Abbott in Argentina and Monteiro in Uruguay had finally obtained firm commitments from the neighboring governments to intern rebel forces, and this prospect now spurred some of the rebels to new action. But when the last attack came, it was not led by Aparício, who despite his daring had a healthy respect for military realities; the third and final invasion of Rio Grande, the most desperate and quixotic action in the whole uneven contest, was led by Adm. Luís Saldanha da Gama.

The aristocratic Saldanha, formerly the director of the Brazilian naval academy, was a latecomer to the revolt against Floriano; he was among the last, however, to abandon the campaign in Guanabara Bay. Unlike Custódio de Melo, he was a dedicated monarchist, a fact that added a final note of confusion to the rebels' goals, since Tavares

---

\* August 17, 1894. Gumercindo's grave was discovered by Firmino de Paula, who exhumed and mutilated the corpse.

and Gumercindo had repeatedly denied any interest in restoring the crown.* On April 22, 1895, Saldanha, who prided himself on his knowledge of military as well as naval strategy, crossed the Quaraí into Rio Grande with a contingent of navy rebels. One morning two months later an advance party of the Division of the West, led by the Castilhista João Francisco Pereira de Sousa, spotted Saldanha's camp. With the advantage of surprise, João Francisco's troops easily broke through the enemy lines and swept into the encampment, scattering the Admiral's forces. In vain Saldanha exhorted his men to turn and fight, until he himself fell when a Castilhista lance pierced his chest. The professor of military and naval science had scored somewhat less brilliantly than the unlettered caudillo, Gumercindo Saraiva.

The two original leaders of the revolt, Joca Tavares and Silveira Martins, at last recognized the futility of further combat. In Rio de Janeiro attitudes were also changing. Prudente de Morais, a civilian backed by the country's coffee-producing interests, had replaced Floriano Peixoto as chief executive in November 1894. In Prudente's view peace in Rio Grande was essential if civilian control of the Republic was to be secured at a time when "Jacobin" groups (so known for their demand for an authoritarian Republic purged of monarchists) were clamoring for military rule. In the first few months of the new administration, a border issue that had cast the shadow of war over Argentine-Brazilian relations was settled by the arbitration of the president of the United States, Grover Cleveland. Accordingly, the prospect of Brazil's involvement in a foreign war was greatly reduced, and Prudente could deal more freely with the Brazilian military. By settling the conflict in Rio Grande and thus eliminating the issue of la patrie en danger, Prudente could weaken the army as a potentially unified Jacobin organization.[20] In any case, Prudente seems to have sincerely desired peace for his fellow countrymen in Rio Grande do Sul.

In July 1895 Gen. Inocêncio Galvão de Queiroz, the commander of the Rio Grande military district, initiated peace talks with General Tavares. In a protocol signed by both men, Tavares stated he had not

---

* Saldanha, however, got Silveira Martins to agree to co-sponsor a proposal for a national plebiscite on the form of government Brazil should adopt, a move that implicitly repudiated the Republic and put Silveira Martins in the position of compromising with monarchism.

revolted against the federal government but only against that of Castilhos. And one of the conditions he insisted on was that a new constitution be drawn up for Rio Grande, written "in accordance with the federal constitution." Galvão agreed.

Predictably, Castilhos reacted sharply and insisted that the federal government repudiate Galvão's actions.* Castilhos' friend Bernardo Vasques was now minister of war and may have exerted additional pressure on Prudente. At any rate, there was a sound constitutional argument against the proposal, namely, that it was the duty of the congress, not the executive, to pass on the constitutionality of state charters. Prudente and Vasques wired Galvão to this effect, declaring that the administration could guarantee the ex-rebels their civil rights, but that only congress could deal with the constitutional issue.† Tavares and Galvão had to yield, and by August 23, 1895, Rio Grande do Sul was officially at peace. A full amnesty was declared two months later; furthermore, rebel soldiers from the regular army were allowed to return to active duty two years after their surrender.

I have dwelt at some length on the civil war of 1893–95 because of its far-reaching consequences for Gaúcho politics in the Old Republic. Abiding hatred was the inevitable result of the bloodiest civil war in Brazil's history, a war that lasted 31 months and produced ten to twelve thousand casualties in a state population of one million persons. The residue of hatred would play a role in Riograndense politics almost to the end of the Old Republic, and veterans of the war would rule the state for 33 years. The cruelties and atrocities of the struggle were notorious. One of the greatest tragedies was that, as in other

---

* No love was lost between Galvão and Castilhos. Castilhos privately fulminated against the "intrigues and perfidies" of Galvão in the peace talks, and in a public manifesto Galvão attacked Castilhos for his despotism and charged that the state constitution had been the "real" cause of the civil war. The lack of interest among congressmen in revising the Gaúcho constitution, Galvão asserted, stemmed from political deals between Vice President Manuel Vitorino and the majority leader in congress, Dep. Francisco Glicério Cerqueira Leite; both needed the support of the Riograndense delegation in the chamber and the senate. Castilhos to J. da Costa Fortinho, n.p., September 24, 1895, Archive of Borges de Medeiros; I. Galvão de Queiroz, *A pacificação do Rio Grande do Sul* (Rio, 1898), *passim*.

† In fact, the constitutionality of the July 14 charter had been challenged in the chamber of deputies in 1892: a bill offered by Justiniano de Serpa proposing that the congress intervene in Rio Grande and revise the state constitution failed by 16 votes out of 128 cast.

civil wars, families often became bitterly divided, with father set against son, or brother against brother. Angel Dourado, a physician who rode with the Federalists, tells of a case in which a Castilhista lancer ran through his own son before the shock of recognition.[21]

The brutalization of the rural lower class, especially the gaúcho element, was perhaps the greatest tragedy of all. Again to cite Dourado, "It was horrible to see those ever-exploited, anonymous masses slowly growing accustomed to criminal acts, becoming insensible to suffering, [and] losing all honor in the killing of the defenseless. They rose up as ignorant savages, no longer respecting anything and wanting to destroy everything."[22] For this savagery, much of the blame must be placed squarely on the shoulders of the leaders at the highest levels. At times Silveira Martins and Castilhos seemed utterly indifferent to the suffering their troops had inflicted on the enemy. Castilhos, for example, told one subaltern in the Campanha: "Don't spare the adversaries; punish them through their persons and their property, but respect families." Germano Hasslocher, a Gasparista, decided to abandon Silveira Martins after giving him an eyewitness account of the Rio Negro massacre, only to be brushed aside as a "neurotic."[23]

One of the most important results of the war was a further political polarization in Rio Grande. In contrast to the amorphous, governor- and notable-dominated system of most other states in the First Republic, Rio Grande's politics continued to center around two well-organized parties. Paradoxically, perhaps, both parties were at the same time more ideologically oriented (dictatorial presidentialism versus parliamentarianism) than parties elsewhere in Brazil. Family and station, which counted for so much in other parts of the country, meant relatively less in Rio Grande.[24]

Another political result of the war was the consolidation of the centralized political system. As powerful as Silveira Martins had been at his apogee, he had allowed Liberal *coronéis* (rural bosses) much more power in local affairs than Castilhos was willing to cede. Under the Republican ruler there were local and regional coronéis with personal power; but what separated Rio Grande from other states was the impossibility in the tightly disciplined PRR of a coronéis' revolt (as occurred in Bahia in 1919–20) or a coronéis' pact independent of the state executive (as occurred in Ceará in 1911).

The war had created military heroes who had reputations and followings of their own. The Division of the North alone had produced a clutch of them. The most outstanding was Pinheiro Machado, who was henceforth to spend most of his time in Rio de Janeiro as Rio Grande's congressional leader, though he still maintained extensive influence in the Missões District. Another was Firmino de Paula, author of the massacre at Boi Prêto. After the war Firmino became a subchief of police and was the political boss of the central Serra for decades. A third veteran of distinction was Manuel Nascimento Vargas, commander of an expeditionary force in the Division of the North; it was his advance column that killed Gumercindo Saraiva. Vargas came to exercise a sort of suzerainty over São Borja, formerly under the sway of the intrepid Dinarte Dorneles, to whom Vargas was related by marriage. Another veteran of the Division was Fernando Abbott, who had twice served as acting governor and who had managed to put in a brief term as a soldier before going to Argentina as Floriano's minister; Abbott became the boss of São Gabriel, in the central Campanha. Still another officer of the Division of the North was a relatively obscure lieutenant colonel, Antônio Borges de Medeiros, who was to be Castilhos' protégé and successor. In other Castilhista forces there were men of similar prowess and prestige. One of the most famous in the Division of the West was João Francisco, the son of an estancieiro-soldier with property on both sides of the Brazil-Uruguay border; João Francisco became Castilhos' frontier commander in the Military Brigade. But for all the power some of these former military lieutenants wielded in their own spheres of influence, none of them approached the autonomy of certain coronéis in other parts of Brazil. And once they decided to oppose the Republican machine—even after Castilhos' death—they found their power stripped away, as we shall see in the next chapter.

A third important political effect of the war was the forging of a solid link between the PRR and the national army, or at least a powerful segment of it. At the end of the conflict Tavares had complained to Prudente that the military personnel stationed in Rio Grande were too closely connected with Castilhos to offer firm guarantees to the returning exiles.[25] For many authoritarian members of the military, Castilhos seemed to be the legitimate heir of Floriano.

As to the social and economic effects of the war, these are difficult to estimate accurately in the absence of good data. Frontier estancieiros and their dependents were bound to be hurt most, and Litoral commerce (including the charque industry) least.[26] Broadly speaking, there was a shift in power from estancieiro elite to near-elite. Silveira Martins and the other leaders of the Liberal and Conservative parties had been the aristocracy of the province as owners of the largest and oldest estâncias; many of them bore Imperial titles. Castilhos and his associates were a little less wealthy and more tenuously connected with the provincial nobility.* At the local level Castilhos usually tried to install the rich and powerful (as his feeler to Gumercindo illustrates), but he placed unquestioning loyalty above preexisting prestige and authority. By and large, however, estancieiros would continue to rule Rio Grande do Sul under the Republic as they had ruled it under the Empire. At the same time, the new constellation of power was reflected in regional terms in the political elite. Where once most of the political leaders had come from the Campanha, more and more were now natives of the Serra. A related development was a new alliance between the Litoral and the Serra, replacing the close ties between the Campanha and the Litoral. But this change was to become apparent only gradually, as the Serra and the Litoral increased their lead on the Campanha in population and economic growth.

* Most Republican leaders were related to noble families but often only collaterally; such was the case with Castilhos, Borges de Medeiros, and Assis Brasil. Vitorino Monteiro and Firmino de Paula were sons of barons of the Empire. See Mário Teixeira de Carvalho, *Nobiliário sul-riograndense* (Pôrto Alegre, 1937), pp. 88, 92, 112, 229, 241.

# The New Order

THE EVENTS of the opening six years of the Republic cast Gaúcho politics in a distinctive mold. Unlike the Republican parties of most states, which allowed numerous "Republicans of November 15" to attain top posts, the PRR ruthlessly ousted the members of other parties from power. Júlio de Castilhos, furthermore, had made his party fully as authoritarian as the state government—to the point where even after he relinquished the governorship, he was able to rule Rio Grande through his control of the party, an almost unique situation in Brazil. The leadership of Castilhos, the discipline and sacrifice of the war years, and the political polarization of the postwar period—all had given shape to the relatively modern party that was now in firm control of Rio Grande do Sul. But there was another, less direct element that gave the party its peculiarly Riograndense character, and that was the secular tradition in the state. In most of Brazil priests occasionally figured as coronéis—but not in Rio Grande. Moreover, in all the years of the Old Republic no priest entered congress as a representative for Rio Grande do Sul or held a post in the state executive, and only two sat in the legislature. The party chief even implied he was not a Catholic. The lack of a strong religious tradition in Rio Grande has been noted by historians and can be supported statistically by comparing data from Rio Grande with figures from other states in Brazil.[1]

If the Gaúchos were not overly religious, still Castilhos had almost come to be regarded as a god by his followers. His insistence on one-man rule met no serious opposition after the defections of 1889–92. The practice of convoking party plenums frequently, as had been done during the years of agitation against the Empire, was abandoned in the chaotic period following the birth of the Republic, and after the war the party chief saw no reason to resume it. In fact, no PRR congresses took place between 1889 and 1923. As party leader, Castilhos reserved for himself all of the major political decisions, and most of the minor ones. Administrative duties he assigned to his loyal, efficient, and intelligent protégé, Borges de Medeiros.

Antônio Augusto Borges de Medeiros was not the charismatic figure Castilhos was. He had a jurist's mind, not altogether surprising in a man whose father had been a judge and who himself had sat on the state supreme court. Born in the Campanha in November 1863, he had graduated from law school in 1885, then had helped organize the Republican Party in Cachoeira, a município on the western edge of the Litoral where he thereafter made his home. During the civil war Borges had served as a lieutenant colonel in the Division of the North. Subsequently he had been appointed chief of the state police, then charged by Castilhos with the task of drafting the state's legal codes. His performance so impressed Castilhos that he made Borges his successor as governor, though Castilhos would retain real power as party chief. In an uncontested race, Borges was elected in November 1897. Like Castilhos, the new governor accepted the political tenets of positivism and federalism; and like Castilhos, he championed financial orthodoxy, and managed to achieve a budgetary surplus every year he was under the party chief's tutelage. Still, there was never any question that it was Castilhos who both proposed and disposed. Or as *A Federação* put it: Governor Borges was "entirely subordinated" to Castilhos' "supreme direction."[2]

The power of the Republican machine depended in large measure on its uninterrupted control of the state government. By the constitution of July 14 the governor had a legal authority tantamount to dictatorship. Even so, the backing of a disciplined party was important, and for this discipline the party chief relied on four things: the power of the governor to cancel município elections or to interfere by decree in local politics in other ways; the control of party affairs at the local level by coronéis loyal to him alone; the ability of the coronéis to mobilize the vote in their districts, employing violence and fraud when necessary; and the efficiency of a powerful state Military Brigade that could be deployed for political purposes.

Castilhos, and Borges after him, intervened repeatedly in local elections and administrative affairs.³ If local authorities defied an executive order, the governor had the constitutional power to declare void their resolutions or acts "when they infringe on federal or state law."⁴ Since state laws were made by the governor by decree (except those dealing with budgetary matters), this provision gave him a free hand in the municípios.

For muscle to back up these decrees, the governor relied primarily on the Military Brigade, a force that varied from 1,500 men (twice the size of the state force in 1889) to 3,200 over the course of the Old Republic. The Brigade was in fact a state army, as well equipped as its federal counterpart and commanded by a career officer on leave from the army. Nor was this the full extent of the Castilhista forces; two years after the 1895 demobilization, an enemy judged Governor Castilhos could count on seven to eight thousand troops, including provisional corps and município guards.⁵

As in prewar days, it was the incumbent machine that won the elections. In conformance with federal voting regulations and the practice in other states, ballots were cast publicly. Even where opposition forces almost certainly disposed of an absolute majority, as in Bagé, they were not permitted to register enough votes to win control of the local government, much less to challenge PRR hegemony at the state level. The opposition to the PRR was strongest in the frontier municípios, where the Federalists had found their greatest support during the war; it was weakest in the Serra communities populated by Italian and German colonos.

Nonetheless, despite all the forces at its command, the PRR could not maintain its monopoly on power without intimidation, violence, and fraud. Even with some accommodation of the opposition after the death of Castilhos, the party was forced to continue itself in power through these "regulatory" devices, though at a considerably reduced level. The type of fraud perpetrated was limited only by the imagination of the local party boss. The most common forms were the illegal registration of foreigners, minors, and residents of other municípios; the inflation or diminution of vote totals in a município's official count; the alteration of voting registers; the refusal to set up polls; the refusal by the local judge to register voters for the opposition; and the diversion of município funds into political campaigns. Coercion, too, took many forms, ranging from the deployment of units of the Military Brigade to the use of strongarm tactics by *capangas* (political hooligans); threats of dismissal were usually enough to keep civil servants in line. Since there was no secret ballot, intimidation was an especially effective form of political control.

The man who brought in the vote was not invariably an estancieiro, and in fact the exception was the rule in the Colonial Zone, where there were few latifundia. Typically, however, the coronéis of Rio Grande (like those in the other states of Brazil) were rural landowners, though not necessarily the largest property holders in their districts. What made the Gaúcho coronel unique was his role within the party structure. In other states the coronel usually obtained his position in the establishment party because of his economic power and social prestige within a certain area. Though these factors counted for something in Rio Grande, there was one indispensable qualification for a man to exercise local power: a willingness to accept decisions from above; hence the name *coronel burocrata*, or bureaucratic coronel. Intendants (*intendentes*, roughly county superintendents)* whether coronéis or subordinates, were not allowed to make important decisions. One intendant who tried to obtain a loan for a public project without telling Borges, then party boss, allegedly received a telegram reading, "Resign. Provisional intendant succeeds."[6] There could be no clearer example of party-government relations, with the PRR disciplining an errant member on the one hand, while on the other the governor (also Borges) used his constitutional authority to fill the vacancy until a new election could be arranged. So frequently were local authorities replaced that at any given time a considerable number of municípios had only provisional intendants. The lack of local autonomy was a source of friction within the PRR, and was probably the main grievance of those who went over to the opposition in the years after the civil war.[7] The *coronéis burocratas* were usually men of local stature, but occasionally not. Some of them came from the middle class. (One, Germano Petersen, was a tailor by trade; another, Dartagnan Tubino, was a grade school teacher.) An enemy of Castilhismo stated the opposition's problem as follows: "No person

* In urban areas they were more comparable to mayors, since no city could be incorporated inside a município, which always took the name of its seat (e.g., Pôrto Alegre).

of social prominence wants to join the opposition because he would risk finding himself [ground] under heel by persons of little consequence, perhaps even his own servants."[8]

Above the local coronéis were four subchiefs of police, one for each of the districts into which the state was divided for the purposes of law enforcement. These men customarily enjoyed a long tenure of office and functioned as "super" coronéis by Gaúcho standards. Though the subchiefs did not directly command units of the Military Brigade, they could requisition Brigade personnel. With larger areas of authority and some measure of autonomy, they were more like the powerful coronéis of the other states than the local bosses.[9] But they were still members of the official state bureaucracy and were appointed only when they met the same requirement as all other officeholders: unqualified loyalty to the party leaders.

Inevitably there were politicians who left the party for one reason or another. One of the first to do so was Congressman Pedro Moacyr, who had been editor of *A Federação* at the outbreak of the war. Something of a maverick in congress, he had refused to vote as directed in 1895. Though he was repudiated by the other Gaúcho congressmen, he would not give up his seat. However, the newspaper he had recently edited began a vigorous campaign against him, and he was not reelected in 1896. Moacyr subsequently went over to the Federalists, and years later entered the chamber of deputies as a Maragato.

Ousting a rebellious congressman was relatively simple; many deputies had no real constituencies, and the PRR chief sometimes shifted them from one district to another. It was much more difficult to dispose of some of the heroes of the civil war who retained local power bases. Yet this too was possible. When Hipólito Ribeiro, the man who had inflicted the largest number of casualties on the Federalists in a single battle, broke with Castilhos, he was effectively contained. João Francisco Pereira de Sousa, also of the Division of the West and later head of a frontier unit of the Military Brigade, rejected the authority of Borges after Castilhos died, and was rendered harmless to the PRR. The same occurred with Fernando Abbott, a power in São Gabriel and twice interim governor of Rio Grande.

An example of one local coronel's insubordination and punishment will illustrate the mechanisms at work. In December 1899 José Gabriel da Silva Lima, of Cruz Alta, refused to support a candidate for federal deputy who had been endorsed by Castilhos. At least in part the problem grew out of the war, for Castilhos' nominee, Germano Hasslocher, had started out an ardent Gasparista and had only left the Federalist Party after the Rio Negro massacre. José Gabriel, by contrast, had left the Conservative Party as early as 1889 and had become a fanatic Castilhista; it was allegedly he who directed a massacre in a section of Cruz Alta after the brutal murder of his friend Evaristo Amaral. When José Gabriel declined to support the PRR nominee in 1899, Castilhos decided to "smash the rebellion of the petulant and vain old man, but in a calm and cautious fashion"[10]— cautious because of José Gabriel's prestige in the party. Hasslocher won the contest handily of course, but Castilhos did not forget the incident. A year later a local election in Cruz Alta offered the party leader his opportunity for revenge. José Gabriel would have won easily had not the subchief of the Second Region, General Firmino de Paula, arrived with a contingent of the Military Brigade "to maintain order." José Gabriel was duly overwhelmed at the polls and eliminated as a local power.*

João Francisco was perhaps the most powerful man to oppose the machine. His military activities during and after the war were notorious. His men had killed Admiral Saldanha da Gama, and in the late 1890's he and his Military Brigade unit had continued to patrol the border, sometimes even crossing into Uruguay to terrorize politically active Federalists living there. The Maragatos considered him a ruthless killer, the very incarnation of all the evils of Castilhismo. A Federalist quatrain had it thus:[11]

| | |
|---|---|
| Nuvens negras no horizonte, | Black clouds on the horizon, |
| O céu cortado de um corisco | A sudden bolt of lightning, |
| O busto de Augusto Comte, | The bust of August Comte, |
| A faca de João Francisco. | The knife of João Francisco. |

Several years after the death of Castilhos, João Francisco quarreled with party chief Borges, who saw to it that João Francisco's command was dissolved. Loyal Republicans soon learned to agree with the Federalists on the enormity of João Francisco's crimes. A rising young Castilhista, José Antônio Flôres da Cunha (who was later to be governor), published an exposé of João Francisco's past, accusing

---

* After Castilhos died, a penitent José Gabriel made his peace with Borges and served one term in the state legislature.

him of several murders and—a major offense in gaúcho country—horse-rustling.[12] That such a powerful caudillo could be brought down was a warning for others not to offend the party hierarchy.

Borges began his first term as governor in January 1898; his record in office was so good in Castilhos' judgment that the party boss endorsed him for a second five-year term. In a manifesto issued in October 1902, Castilhos lauded his protégé and referred to the "continuity of views and action" between the two men. Again Borges was elected without an opponent, since the Federalists once more refused to participate in a rigged contest, and the PRR dissidents were weak and disorganized. Borges had just begun a five-year term when his protector's health began to decline rapidly.

Castilhos, a heavy cigarette smoker, had been complaining of a bad cough for some years. By 1903 he was in constant pain and was unable to sleep. The party boss began to consult specialists in September of that year, but it was already too late: he had an advanced case of throat cancer. His breathing became more and more difficult, and Protásio Alves, a PRR physician and politician, decided to attempt a tracheotomy. The operation, performed in Castilhos' home in Pôrto Alegre on October 24, was unsuccessful: Castilhos died on the operating table at the age of forty-three. Most Riograndenses were not even aware of his illness and were shocked by his death. His grieving followers staged the most elaborate obsequies the state had ever seen, and *A Federação* bordered its pages in black for months. In death Júlio de Castilhos assumed even more of a superhuman aspect, and henceforth was referred to as the Patriarch by his followers. A statue of him would eventually appear in the plaza opposite the governor's mansion, where it stands today.

Two days after Castilhos died, Borges wired Pinheiro Machado, leader of the Rio Grande congressional delegation, to come to Pôrto Alegre for consultations on party leadership. Pinheiro soon got the entire delegation to support Borges for party chief.[13] In a little over a year the transfer of power was complete—and total. On February 17, 1905, *A Federação* announced that candidates for the state legislature would no longer be selected by the PRR executive committee, but by the party chief.

The new PRR leader shared certain characteristics with his predecessor—sobriety, personal modesty, devotion to his family, unimpeachable honesty, and an unwavering faith in the principles of governance laid down by Comte. Like Castilhos, he came to power at an early age: he was thirty-nine when he became head of the PRR. Borges was also like Castilhos in his authoritarianism, a trait that was perhaps essential, given the "monolithic" structure of the party (to use Castilhos' word). An oft-repeated anecdote illustrates just how autocratic Borges could be. An intendant who had come to the capital to plead for public works in his município began his plea to the party chief with the words "I think. . . ." Cutting him short, Borges snapped: "You don't think; I am the one who thinks. You take inspiration from my instructions and act accordingly."[14]

Physically Borges resembled Castilhos in his small stature. He always stood erect, reinforcing a characteristic air of formality. He liked to receive petitioners standing, and in conformity with the positivist injunction to "live openly," he always spoke within the hearing of those still waiting to be admitted to his presence.[15] After a certain length of time he would extend his hand to his visitor, signifying that the interview was at an end. He granted such audiences to almost all comers, though they might have to wait for hours or even days for their chance.

The new PRR boss proved true to the continuity of views that had so impressed Castilhos. But his personality was quite different from the Patriarch's. He spoke without emotion and invariably appeared calm in time of crisis. He possessed neither Castilhos' passion nor his ability to inspire fanaticism in his followers. His accession to party leadership thus marked the institutionalization of the PRR system following the passing of its charismatic leader.

As PRR chief and governor, Borges faced no real test of his ability to lead a united party until 1907, when another gubernatorial contest took place. He chose not to succeed himself but instead selected a second-ranking member of the party to run the government while he devoted himself exclusively to his duties as party leader. The candidate he chose was Carlos Barbosa Gonçalves, one of the several physicians who had been active in forming the PRR. A Historical Republican from the southern frontier, Gonçalves had chaired the state constituent assembly, then had become president of the state legislature, a position he held until his nomination for governor.[16]

As always, the Republican machine ran smoothly; since those who opposed Barbosa Gonçalves realized they had no chance to prevent him from becoming the party nominee, they abstained from the primary, in which more than 61,000 voters accepted the "official" candidate. Yet the gubernatorial race of 1907, in contrast to those of 1892 and 1897, did not go uncontested. The leader of the PRR in São Gabriel, Fernando Abbott, left the party and entered the race as a Republican dissident. Abbott received the support of Assis Brasil, who had recently left the foreign service to return to Gaúcho politics. He was also supported by a number of Federalists, in spite of the persecutions that had taken place during his brief but critical term as governor in 1892.

The effort to get out the vote brought a new element into Gaúcho politics. The Generation of '07, a group of politically ambitious young men who were in their final years at Pôrto Alegre's new professional schools, joined the battle on behalf of the odds-on favorite, Barbosa Gonçalves. Calling themselves the Castilhista Student Bloc (Bloco Acadêmico Castilhista), they organized in April 1907 for the express purpose of campaigning for the PRR nominee. In a banquet given for the group, a party functionary raised his cup in a toast to the students, declaring that "from their ranks a new Júlio de Castilhos would surely step forth."[17] In fact, he was to prove a good prophet: one of the young men, Getúlio Vargas, a law student and son of a Castilhista general, Manuel N. Vargas, would direct the destinies of Brazil for almost 19 years as President and dictator. Maurício Cardoso and João Neves da Fontoura, also law students, would later hold key cabinet posts, and two cadets at the new Pôrto Alegre military academy, Pedro Góes Monteiro and Eurico Gaspar Dutra, would be ministers of war under Vargas; Dutra would be president as well.

Most of the leaders of the Bloc came from the law school, and Vargas, Neves, and several other young law students spent the second half of 1907 campaigning across the state for Barbosa Gonçalves. The Bloc also published a newspaper between June and December with the title O Debate (The Debate). Its editor was Firmino Paim Filho, who along with Vargas and Neves, showed great political promise at the time, and indeed lived up to that promise into the late 1920's. For senior law students like Vargas and Paim, the campaign represented a coming-of-age.

The students had made the right choice of candidates, for the

November 25 elections confirmed what was already evident—that Borges had firm enough control of the PRR to ensure his candidate's victory; the "official" nominee beat Abbott by a majority of nearly four to one. And Abbott's poor showing, thanks in part to the indifference of many Federalist voters, confirmed what was already clear to some—that there was no room for three parties.

Yet it was not easy to unify two distinct groups that had opposed each other so bitterly in the early 1890's. The chief thing the dissident Republicans and the Federalists had in common was their rejection of the Comtian charter as unconstitutional.

Most of the Federalists who had emigrated to Uruguay returned in the years following the war, and they formed the larger sector of the opposition. Despite the death of party caudillo Silveira Martins in 1901 and the inability of any single leader to take his place, the Federalists stood firm in their dedication to parliamentary organization at the federal level, calling for the election of the president by congress and the participation of cabinet ministers in congressional sessions. After the Tribune's demise, Joca Tavares called a party congress in Bagé, which again demanded the revision of both the federal and the state constitutions in order to strengthen the union, and to abrogate the positivist constitution of Rio Grande do Sul. Some Federalists still hoped to invade the state and overthrow the Castilhista machine from a Uruguayan sanctuary. After 1904, however, new international alliances and internal developments in Uruguay forced them to reassess the situation, and the new circumstances influenced some Federalists to back Abbott in 1907.

The other component of the opposition—those who had broken with the Republican Party leadership—was less cohesive; its members were generally chary of an alliance with the Federalists. Republican dissidents had formally organized a party in 1895, but it disappeared before Castilhos' death. New life was infused into the dissident movement, however, when Abbott defected and, more importantly, when Assis Brasil returned to Rio Grande. The dissidents even hoped to attract a Federalist following after Assis emerged as their leader in 1908, for he had been out of the state during the civil war, and though the brother-in-law of Castilhos, he had never been a real Castilhista, as Abbott had.

Assis, a member of the constituent assembly of 1890–91, had withdrawn from Gaúcho politics before the collapse of the governicho, in which he had participated. Returning to the diplomatic corps, he had been named minister to Portugal, then had served from 1899 to 1904 as minister to the United States. After another tour in Argentina (where he had been accredited in 1890), he reentered Riograndense politics in 1907, and the following year he founded the Partido Republicano Democrático (Democratic Republican Party) with Abbott's support.

To this new effort Assis brought more than broad experience; in addition to his other activities and accomplishments, he was a political theorist. By 1896 he had written two books on republican constitutional organization. He differed from the Federalists in insisting on a presidential form of government, but like them he wanted congress to choose the chief executive. Assis was eager to develop a truly representative political system with minority participation. One student of political history has called him the country's leading theorist of presidential government.[18] He was never a positivist.

The mature Assis Brasil was a highly principled, aristocratic, and somewhat stuffy exemplar of nineteenth-century liberalism. After the death of Castilhos' sister, he had remarried, this time choosing a Brazilian beauty who was living in Portugal during his tour of duty there. He had traveled widely in the Americas, Europe, and the Near East, and had his children tutored in English, French, and German by foreign governesses in his home at Pedras Altas, a fortress-like structure he had designed himself. A cultured man with a worldliness that was a rarity in the insular society of Rio Grande, he was also a man of many talents—one who would be called a *pensador* (lit., thinker) in Spanish America. Diplomat, lawyer, politician, and political theorist, he was a model rancher (he wrote a classic work on agriculture), a sharpshooter, and an amateur poet, historian, and architect as well.

At the founding convention of the Democratic Party, Assis Brasil called for revision of the state constitution, guarantees against voting fraud and corruption of the judiciary, and increased authority at the federal and municipal level, in addition to the constitutional change he had previously defended—congressional election of the president. He was the first to admit the essential conservatism of a program that was largely embodied in the slogan "Representation and Justice."[19]

But Assis was not interested simply in organizing a new party in Rio Grande do Sul; he made repeated attempts to build a national organization, an effort that finally bore fruit in 1927. As early as 1897, while still in the foreign service, he began looking for outside support to oust Castilhos. Writing to the "official" presidential candidate, Manuel Ferraz de Campos Sales, he painted his brother-in-law, whom he had known from childhood, as a cynical opportunist who respected only power. In reply, Campos Sales expressed interest in Assis's collaboration with the new administration; he declined, however, to interfere in Gaúcho politics,[20] and in fact he soon reached an understanding with Castilhos.

Faced with this Campos Sales–Castilhos entente, Assis attempted to found a national opposition party. He approached former President Prudente de Morais on the matter in 1901. Prudente, at odds with the administration, was more than interested. He was at the time trying to form a new party in his own state of São Paulo that might be linked to a national organization, and he urged Assis to return to Rio Grande and do the same.[21] Prudente died the next year, however, and the Paulista dissident movement all but died away. Assis's hopes for an opposition party at the national level would have to wait for an understanding with a new Paulista party toward the end of the Old Republic. Nor was he successful in the short run in attracting Federalists to the Democratic Party; memories of the war were still too vivid to bring the former enemies together on a lasting basis.

No member of the opposition held an official post in Rio Grande while Castilhos ruled; there were no anti-establishment politicians in congress, in the state legislature, or in positions of local power from 1893 until Castilhos died. Borges, however, was willing to make minimal concessions to the opposition to give a semblance of minority representation. In 1906, under the (federal) Rosa e Silva law, which provided for minority representation, three Federalists joined the 16-man Gaúcho congressional delegation. In the following year Borges introduced his own version of the federal statute, incorporating an understanding that up to one-fourth of the congressional seats would simply be given to the minority without contest. This 1907 law is noteworthy in two respects. First, the Riograndense regime refused to apply the 1906 federal voting regulations, and it later was sustained in this action by the federal supreme court, an indication of the strength of states' rights in Brazil. Second, this law made it clear that the only way to achieve minority representation in the Old Republic (in other states no less than in Rio Grande) was by the crude procedure of not contesting a stipulated number of seats; competition simply did not work.*

Relations between the establishment and the opposition at the national level, PRR leaders slowly discovered, were not much different. Castilhos had announced his policy toward the federal government at the end of the national constituent assembly: "Neither unconditional support nor systematic opposition." But during the tumult of the early 1890's his brave phrase remained an empty slogan because of his dependence on the two military presidents. After a civilian came to power in 1894, however, he strove to free Rio Grande from dependence on the federal executive and the PRR from enduring alliances in national politics. A doctrinaire who had condemned the lack of ideology in the parties of the late Empire, Castilhos recognized similar tendencies in the new Republican regime. Over time he came to look on Rio de Janeiro as a center of political corruption, a "putrefying Babylon."[22]

Nevertheless, the Gaúcho politicians had vital state interests to defend in the capital. There were of course economic interests, chief among them cattle products in general and charque in particular. And there was the related concern about the effects of tariffs, frontier regulations, and foreign trade. Political considerations also had to be taken into account, and even if Rio Grande seemed relatively secure against federal intervention, disorders in Uruguay from 1897 to 1904 had to be watched carefully. The possibility that the Federalists might profit from Platine upheavals kept the PRR leaders anxious about the federal executive's views on the border problem.

Another sustained theme in Castilhista policy toward the federation was the defense of Brazil's constitution against revisions that would weaken state authority, a stance that dovetailed with a rejection of any federal attempt to give the minority a measure of power in the state government of Rio Grande. Naturally enough, antirevisionism also appealed to other incumbent machines and became

---

* The congressional seats reserved for the minority in this period went to the Federalists rather than to Assis Brasil's Democrats.

a central feature in the meager ideological paraphernalia that bound the leading establishment parties together. Likewise, for the Gaúcho Federalists from the beginning, and for other critics of the federal regime later, revisionism was a cardinal objective.

Before the turn of the century advocates of revisionism were still few at the national level, and Castilhos concentrated on the more immediate problem of restricting presidential authority in Rio Grande. He put his policy of political independence into effect for the first time during the Prudente de Morais administration. In 1894 Prudente had been the unopposed nominee of a congressional coalition organized by fellow Paulista Francisco Glicério Cerqueira Leite, a coalition that was yet another Partido Republicano, this one with a second distinguishing adjective, "Federal," added. The PRF convention had unanimously chosen Prudente in September 1893, though machines from seven states, including those of Minas Gerais and Rio Grande do Sul, failed to participate in the formal nomination. Prudente was elected in March 1894 without the help of Rio Grande, Santa Catarina, and Paraná, all of which were still being wracked by the Federalist war.

As noted in Chapter 3, Brazil's first civilian president had been eager to achieve a lasting peace in Rio Grande. He believed the federal government could help attain such a peace by removing from the state all army officers who in the course of the conflict had become uncompromising Castilhistas and fierce enemies of the Federalists, and by pressuring the Gaúcho government to deactivate its extensive reserve forces. But relations between state and federal authorities deteriorated after peace was established in August 1895, for Castilhos distrusted both the President and the repatriated Federalists.* Nor was General Galvão (who negotiated the peace with Joca Tavares) the last commander of the Rio Grande Military Region to be publicly denounced by Castilhos.

Relations between the state and federal governments were complicated in 1896–97 by Prudente's bad health and by a military campaign against a Sebastianist millenarian movement in Bahia. Pru-

---

* So deep was this distrust that Castilhos consistently intercepted secret telegraphic communications between federal officials. When Prudente learned of this, he had the offending telegraph service employees removed and rebuked the governor of Rio Grande. (Morais to Castilhos, Rio, April 25, 1896, Archive of Prudente de Morais.) Castilhos, however, soon found new means of tapping telegraph lines.

dente had been taken ill in November 1896 and went to a mountain retreat, leaving Vice President Manuel Vitorino Pereira in charge. Manuel Vitorino, who carried on in Prudente's absence for some three months, became the cynosure of the Florianistas (or Jacobins), who felt he was more aware than Prudente of monarchist threats to the Republic. A movement rapidly perceived as monarchist did in fact arise, though in an unexpected quarter, the *sertão* (backlands) of Bahia. In the hamlet of Canudos a mystic named Antônio Maciel, better known as Antônio Conselheiro (the counselor), had defied the Republic as a godless political monstrosity, and was predicting the second coming of King Sebastian of Portugal at the turn of the century. When the millenarian movement fell afoul of the Bahiano government, Gov. Luís Viana sent in state forces. But the Sebastianists routed their adversaries almost without effort, and Viana requested federal troops, the first expedition of which fared no better. When the news of their defeat reached Rio, the Florianistas chose to blame Prudente de Morais, accusing him of having truckled to monarchists in his eagerness to pacify Rio Grande do Sul. Manuel Vitorino now ordered one of the heroes in the struggle against the Federalists, Col. Antônio Moreira César, to lead a thousand men against Antônio Conselheiro's *sertanejos*. This expedition was even more disastrous: not only was the federal force defeated, but its leader, Moreira César, was killed in February 1897. The rout was primarily the result of the Sebastianists' expert use of hit-and-run tactics against troops unfamiliar both with that kind of warfare and with the hostile terrain of the Bahiano sertão.

On March 7 Rio de Janeiro learned of Moreira César's death. Only four short days before, Prudente had quietly returned to the presidential residence, Catete Palace, and reassumed his duties. Now he saw news of the debacle touch off a rampage through the streets of Rio. Suspected monarchists were attacked and the presses of three monarchist newspapers destroyed. The rioting continued a second day; this time a mob killed a leading monarchist publisher, Gentil de Castro. The situation was precarious, and if Prudente had not already been in Rio, there is some question whether he would have been allowed to take charge again. (As it was, he chose to enter Catete Palace when the Vice President was absent.) And among those who had unsuccessfully conspired to keep him from returning to power was Júlio de Castilhos.[23]

In May Jacobin elements took over the military academy in Rio, and a number of cadets rebelled against the government. But loyal troops easily put down the mutiny and moved quickly to disarm self-styled patriotic battalions of militia patrolling the streets. The "defusing" of Rio had an important political consequence. Bahia congressman J. J. Seabra offered a resolution in the chamber of deputies, proposing that a comittee be sent to congratulate the President for safeguarding the civilian Republic. The PRF leader, Francisco Glicério, had not been consulted, and aware that the President was seeking to replace the PRF as an undependable instrument in time of crisis, managed to defeat the proposal. His success was short-lived, however. Soon after the tables were turned in a vote for the presidency of the chamber. Prudente's candidate found the necessary support in the delegations from Minas Gerais, São Paulo, Pernambuco, and Bahia; Glicério had the backing of the delegations of Rio Grande do Sul, the Federal District, Amazonas, and Ceará, and of a few other deputies who had not yet sensed which way the political winds were now blowing. There is some irony in the fact that the Gaúchos, who had initially been cool to the PRF, threw their weight behind it just in time to participate in its decline.

Meanwhile another veteran of the war against the Federalists had been sent to defeat the millenarians at Canudos. This was Gen. Artur Oscar, who was no more successful than Moreira César in defeating the enemy but a good deal more adept at staying alive and keeping Jacobin sentiment aflame in Rio. Ultimately, a new minister of war, Carlos Machado Bittencourt, succeeded where all others had failed. Taking personal charge, he organized the critical transport services needed for a successful assault on the sertanejo redoubt, and with some 6,000 troops, finally overwhelmed Canudos in October 1897, as the last of the rebels died in their trenches. The story of the religious exaltation and the grim resistance of the sertanejos, of the forbidding backlands, and of the incompetence of the Republic's army was later immortalized by Euclides da Cunha in Os sertões.[24]

While the inhabitants of Canudos were being exterminated, a related event took place on the fringes of Rio Grande do Sul. In this case, however, what was involved was a massacre, not a long-drawn-out struggle. In the município of Lajes, just across the border from Rio Grande in Santa Catarina, a millenarian community was thriving. In August 1897 a Lajes newspaper, picking up the Sebastianist-restorationist dimension, suggested that the 300-member hamlet (called Entre Rios) had links not only with Antônio Conselheiro but also with the Gaúcho Federalists. This "evidence" was sufficient for Castilhos. He immediately made plans with the governor of Santa Catarina for a joint attack by the two state police forces on the village, but only Gaúchos seem to have participated. The subchief of the First District directed the operation. Launching a surprise attack on Entre Rios, his troops killed all the men in the community and burned their huts, leaving the women and children alive but homeless. On receiving a report on the operation at the end of August, a satisfied Castilhos remarked that the subchief "conducted himself as I hoped he would" and deserved "only praise and applause."[25]

Canudos was taken five weeks later, but the victory did not calm Carioca spirits as the government hoped. Glicério's PRF, now a minority faction in congress, remained hostile to the President in a loose alliance with Jacobin elements. Suddenly, however, Prudente's authority received a major boost. The President and the minister of war had gone to an arsenal in Rio to greet a detachment of soldiers returning from the Canudos campaign. Inside the compound a Jacobin soldier aimed a pistol at the President. Fortunately for Prudente, the gun misfired. In the ensuing scuffle the assassin drew a dagger and killed Marshal Bittencourt, while his original target, Prudente, was led away unharmed.

The bungled assassination attempt and the murder of the minister of war swung popular opinion swiftly toward Prudente. He obtained a declaration of a state of emergency from congress and closed the Military Club, a center of Jacobin agitation. A mob, this time progovernment, wrecked the offices of the newspaper *O Jacobino*. Francisco Glicério went into hiding, and Senator Pinheiro Machado of Rio Grande do Sul was arrested and confined to a warship for more than a month.*

Prudente's new authority allowed him to increase the pressure on the Riograndense establishment. Two anti-Castilhos generals were assigned to frontier garrisons, where they conspired against the PRR.

---

* Pinheiro had been under surveillance by the administration. The immediate cause of his arrest was a mistaken interpretation of an intercepted telegram from his ranch foreman. The confusion concerned the movement of *tropa*, which means both troops and a herd of cattle.

The President had already turned over the main federally owned railroad in the state to a private Belgian concern, despite the vehement protests of Castilhos. In February 1898 the President closed the Pôrto Alegre customs house, which had been operating for 50 years. This was presumably a move to increase disaffection among the commercial interests in the Litoral, once it became clear that Castilhos could not defend them against federal reprisals. Prudente also tried to bring together Republican dissidents and Federalists in Rio Grande, but this effort came too soon after the close of the war and miscarried.[26] Though PRR leaders feared there would be an attempt to overthrow the Castilhista machine before Prudente's term was out (and said so publicly),[27] the attempt was never made. Castilhos could count not only on most of the military commanders in the state (many of whom had fought the Federalists), but also on the Military Brigade and several provisional corps attached to the Brigade.

Not only the PRR, but the Brazilian army as well, bore the weight of presidential discipline. It saw its leverage in national politics sharply reduced by the events of 1896–98. The army, which had dominated politics until 1894, reached a nadir in political influence at the end of the Morais administration. Canudos had humiliated the officer corps, and Prudente had deftly used Marshal Bittencourt's assassination to shore up presidential power. The Military Club remained closed until 1901, and an unsuccessful military putsch in 1904 involving generals as well as cadets further weakened and divided the army. Accordingly, an alliance between the PRR and the military against a president backed by Minas, São Paulo, and Bahia was unthinkable.

In the 1898 presidential election, the military counted for little. In July 1897 Governor Campos Sales of São Paulo, with the support of the incumbent President, was formally nominated by the same group of states that split the PRF: Minas Gerais, São Paulo, Pernambuco, and Bahia. Glicério's faction and the Jacobins decided to name their own slate, rejecting the single-candidate precedent of 1894. Since Floriano had died in 1895, his admirers were forced to cast about for a new Iron Marshal. The leading contenders were Lauro Sodré, the positivist officer who as governor of Pará had defied Deodoro's coup in 1891, and Júlio de Castilhos, esteemed for his determination and ruthlessness during the "monarchist" onslaught of

1893–95. Both men had been honorary presidents of the Military Club. But Glicério considered Castilhos too radical and opposed his nomination at the PRF convention in October 1897. Though Pinheiro Machado fought hard for his chief's nomination, Sodré was triumphant in a run-off against Castilhos. In any case, the nomination took place before Prudente's "coup" of November; thereafter a victory for Campos Sales was a certainty. Sodré could count only on the votes of the three southern states and Pará. Shortly before the election in March 1898, the PRF disintegrated, and *A Federação* advised Gaúcho voters to abstain. Only some 3,000 votes were cast in Rio Grande, almost all of them by anti-Castilhistas. Yet however independent of federal power Castilhos wished to be, his bouts with Prudente made him eager to establish better relations with the new President, Campos Sales. Witness the ambivalence of *A Federação,* which even as it urged PRR voters to abstain because Campos Sales was the "candidate of Catete," asserted that except for this he would have been worthy of support.

Manuel Ferraz de Campos Sales, like Prudente, was a Historical Republican and a former governor of São Paulo. He owed his election not only to Prudente, but to the Republican organizations of São Paulo and Minas and to the coffee-growing interests of these states. Between his election and his inauguration, he had made a trip to Europe to renegotiate Brazil's burdensome external loans; he returned from London convinced of the necessity of achieving financial stability in Brazil after almost a decade of speculation and excessive currency issues, exacerbated by disorders and civil war. In order to reestablish Brazil's foreign credit, he was willing to set aside all other considerations, and he clearly saw that a rebellious and secure political leader like Castilhos would not reassure foreign investors about Brazil's stability. Despite some initial doubts about the possibility of an accommodation with Castilhos,[28] the new President was soon willing to forget past slights and to begin afresh with Castilhos and with Borges de Medeiros, who became governor the same year Campos Sales became president.

In an economy move during his first month in office, Campos Sales drastically reduced the funds for patrolling the frontier against contraband. The state government, Borges informed the President, would be more than happy to step into the breach. In August 1899, a month after the state had assumed the responsibility for patrolling the border, the president of the Pôrto Alegre Commercial Association (Praça do Comércio) lauded the efficiency of the new system. Another measure that benefited the commerce of the Litoral (and indirectly that of the Serra) was the restoration of the customs house in Pôrto Alegre, which Campos Sales agreed to put back into operation in 1899. Finally, at Castilhos' insistence, the President removed the unfriendly generals billeted in Rio Grande by Prudente, even though one reassignment caused him some embarrassment.* In exchange, the Gaúcho congressional delegation under Senator Pinheiro Machado cooperated with Campos Sales in his austerity programs.

The Campos Sales–Castilhos entente worked smoothly enough until early 1900, when Campos Sales introduced what was quickly labeled the *política dos governadores* (politics of the governors). This arrangement institutionalized the existing tendency of establishment parties at different levels and in various branches of government to maintain each other in office indefinitely. The name derived from an understanding between the governors (usually the leaders of the state parties) and the president for mutual support. The term also meant the "politics (and policies) of those who govern"—in short, the Establishment. In particular, the política was a means of ensuring that the president would always have a majority in the chamber of deputies. After consulting the governors of São Paulo, Minas, and Bahia, Campos Sales pushed two important procedural changes through the chamber. One made the presiding officer of the last session the president pro tem in the new session, setting aside the established precedent of allowing the oldest member of the chamber to preside initially. This was a crucial innovation, for the president pro tem appointed the credentials committee. Thus, assuming the president of the chamber supported the president of Brazil (which he always did), the executive was in a position to control the recognition of congressional mandates. The second change reinforced this control. It required that a majority of the município councils of each congressional district certify the winners' vote. Because the establishment

---

* The general in question was out of Rio Grande when reassigned, and stubbornly insisted on returning briefly to his post before his transfer to Paraná. Characteristically, Campos Sales feared the general's behavior would produce rumors of militarism abroad and cause the exchange rate to fall! [Manoel Ferraz de] Campos Salles, *Da propaganda à presidencia* (São Paulo, 1908), pp. 283–85.

party at the state level supported local politicians and vice versa, this was another safeguard against the entry of rebellious deputies into congress.[29] The 1900 elections showed how effective the rules changes were. Uncooperative congressmen-elect from two states, Paraíba and Mato Grosso, were refused recognition in large numbers. This cancellation of mandates by the credentials committee was sarcastically known as the degola.*

Campos Sales introduced the *política dos governadores* to make certain he had congressional support for his fiscal and monetary policies.[30] His most pressing problem was meeting the obligations of the Rothschild funding loan contract of 1898, which consolidated Brazil's external debts and introduced a payments moratorium to restore the nation's credit rating. The contract called for such unpopular measures as increasing taxes, decreasing the currency in circulation and government expenditures, and placing a lien on the Rio customs revenues for the House of Rothschild. In effect, then, the *política dos governadores* was simply a response to the reality of Brazil's colonial economy.

One machine that tried to resist the imposition of the *política* was the Partido Republicano Riograndense. Though Castilhos sanctioned fraud in his own state, he was not willing to countenance it on the national level. He correctly viewed the President's rule changes as measures to reduce the authority of congress.[31] The Gaúchos were at least consistent: they had resisted (albeit unsuccessfully) Prudente's efforts to obtain a pliant majority in congress in 1897. But the issue of the *política dos governadores* was a difficult one for them; though Castilhos staunchly opposed it on principle, Pinheiro Machado made clear it would certainly be implemented.[32] To oppose the *política* meant a new break with the federal government, and the Gaúchos had already had a taste of the consequences of such action under Prudente. In the end, fearing a reversal of PRR fortunes in Uruguay, Castilhos chose not to risk a rupture with the President over the issue.

Campos Sales soon asked the Gaúchos to swallow an even bitterer pill: to accept Francisco Rodrigues Alves, the governor of São Paulo,

---

* The term was not such a misnomer after all, for the congressional degolas of 1900 had gruesome enough results: they signaled a revolution in Mato Grosso, where the faction of Joaquim Murtinho (the minister of treasury in the Campos Sales administration) massacred a group of rivals. Francisco de Assis Barbosa, "A presidência Campos Sales," *Luso-Brazilian Review,* V, 1 (Summer 1968), 12.

as the next president. Castilhos and his advisors were repelled by the proposal, not only because an incumbent in Catete was again naming his successor but even more importantly, because Rodrigues Alves had not been a Historical Republican—a weighty consideration for the doctrinaire Castilhos. On the contrary, the governor of São Paulo had been a successful Conservative politician and a Counselor of the Empire.

Campos Sales had chosen a third Paulista for president not so much because of regional cliquishness but because of his high regard for the financial and administrative acumen of Rodrigues Alves. The all-important task of restoring Brazil's finances had to be carried on, and the President had satisfied himself that his candidate would follow his lead.[33] Campos Sales approached Rodrigues Alves about the nomination only after the governors of Minas Gerais and Bahia had been consulted and had assented. The Mineiros knew of the President's preference in November 1900; the Gaúchos (through Pinheiro) only learned about it the following January, after the matter had been decided.[34] Catete, São Paulo, and Minas, with the backing of Bahia, had again settled the succession.

When Castilhos was told of the choice of candidates, he professed to believe that Rodrigues Alves's accession would be the first step toward a restoration of the monarchy.[35] Pinheiro wanted Castilhos to enter the lists, but the PRR boss refused. As the months wore on, Pinheiro tried to get Campos Sales to consider several Historical Republicans, without success; Sales was adamant, even on the point of designating the vice president (Gov. Silviano Brandão of Minas). The President "is convinced a subjugated nation will accept all impositions," Pinheiro wired Borges.[36] With a president backed by São Paulo, Minas, and Bahia, the Gaúchos knew their cause was lost. Yet Pinheiro continued to hope that some contretemps would allow a new name to surface, a game of patience he was to play with profit in later contests.

Castilhos decided to avoid unconditional surrender by publicly abstaining, as in 1898. After relaying this decision to the President, Pinheiro reported back to Castilhos that such a course of action would be interpreted as an out-and-out rejection of Rodrigues Alves, and emphasized that Republican unity would be destroyed to no purpose.[37] At length, sheer necessity forced a reversal of the Gaúcho position. In mid-1901 a new Federalist invasion seemed imminent, and Castilhos asked Pinheiro to obtain arms from the federal government for the defense of the state. The realistic Pinheiro was quick to reply: if the Gaúchos refused to accept Rodrigues Alves, did Castilhos really believe the administration would give them military support?[38] Pinheiro privately purchased some 5,000 weapons for the Gaúcho government in July, but the PRR leaders still wanted assurances of federal support.

The end of the civil war in Rio Grande had by no means brought peace to the border area. In 1896, Aparício Saraiva, then head of the Blanco Party in Uruguay, had taken control of the region around Rivera; he had launched a full-scale revolt against the ruling Colorados a year later and then succeeded in establishing Blanco hegemony along most of the length of the Uruguay–Brazil frontier. The Colorados and the Blancos seemed more evenly matched in the stormy years between 1897 and 1904 than they had been for decades, and Aparício was playing for high stakes—control of the Uruguayan Republic. For the Riograndenses, the question was not so much who sat in the presidential palace in Montevideo, but who ruled along the border. As early as 1896 Aparício and João Francisco had begun negotiations for a PRR-Blanco alliance, a plan that was subsequently approved by Castilhos in order to forestall a Blanco alignment with Silveira Martins. In 1898 Castilhos authorized secret shipments of arms to the Blancos,[39] in deliberate contravention of agreements between the Brazilian and Uruguayan governments.* In the meantime Silveira Martins and his lieutenant Rafael Cabeda had formed strong ties with the Colorados (of the two Uruguayan parties, the one the Tribune had been closest to during the Empire). The PRR leaders received enough reports from spies in Uruguay and Rio de Janeiro in 1901 to fear that a Federalist invasion of Rio Grande, with Colorado support, might come at any time. Even after the death of Silveira Martins in July, their apprehension did not diminish. Under these circumstances and at Pinheiro Machado's urging, Castilhos decided to capitulate on Rodrigues Alves's candidacy, thus assuring his machine of federal military backing. Pinheiro's practical politics had

---

* One of the main reasons the Gaúchos had been so eager to assume responsibility for patrolling the frontier against contraband was precisely their desire to conduct their own foreign policy.

carried the day. In this instance (as in many later instances) he was nevertheless concerned about the appearance of power when the substance was absent. Rio Grande participated in the convention that nominated Alves—a concession so distasteful to Castilhos that Pinheiro had to threaten to resign to get his way.[40]

To the Jacobins and other purists who did not like the patently undemocratic transactions of presidential politics, Castilhos had appeared something of a potential savior of the Republic. They were now shocked and dismayed by the PRR's behavior. Edmundo Bittencourt, editor of Rio's leading opposition newspaper, *Correio da Manhã*, had considered the Gaúcho party chief the only man worthy of the presidency. Learning in mid-August that the PRR would back Rodrigues Alves, Bittencourt concluded that either Castilhos was betraying the Republic or he was himself being betrayed by Pinheiro Machado, his spokesman in Rio.

In broader perspective, however, the Gaúchos had no chance of stopping the presidential juggernaut backed by the ascendant coffee interests in Minas and São Paulo. The Riograndenses received little enough for their surrender to Campos Sales. Pinheiro got Rodrigues Alves to oppose constitutional revision in his platform,[41] a position hotly defended by the PRR but one that also appealed to other establishment parties across the country. In addition, Campos Sales gave the Gaúchos war materiel and assurances of federal military support. He also kept unfriendly army commanders out of the state.

The invasion the PRR officials so firmly believed was certain to come did not take place, primarily because of federal military backing for the Gaúcho establishment and PRR aid to Aparício Saraiva, still in control of most of the border. But clandestine arms shipments continued to flow across the frontier in the next few years, for Castilhos had become convinced that his party's interests were best served by keeping Uruguay divided.[42] And divided it was: in 1904 civil war erupted when Aparício finally made his bid for national power against the new Colorado president, José Batlle y Ordoñez. The war was an uneven contest in which the old-style Blanco caudillo moved through Uruguay with an army on horseback, while Batlle's government troops made effective use of the nation's new rail network. In September Aparício was gravely wounded, as Gumercindo had been ten years before, while risking his life on the front lines. The Blanco chief crossed safely into Brazil, under the protection of the Castilhistas, only to die of his wounds soon after. The war ended in a complete Colorado triumph, but the consequences were not what the Maragatos hoped for. Batlle did not attempt to make the Gaúchos pay for João Francisco's meddling in Uruguay, but instead devoted his energies to reconstructing his country and introducing economic and social reforms.[43] Caudillo rule—or at least the horseback variety —had ended in the Uruguayan Republic.

Rio Grande's troubles with its southern neighbor were not limited to the political sphere. Throughout the nineteenth century the Gaúchos had faced stiff economic competition from the ranchers of Argentina and Uruguay, and were both outproduced and undersold except when political upheaval disrupted production in the Plate. The relative inefficiency of the Gaúcho pastoral economy persisted well into the twentieth century, and was a permanent fact of life throughout the period under study. Gaúcho ranchers and statesmen studied the problem, focusing their attention in the main on the Uruguayan economy, since Uruguay was the foremost producer of charque. (By the early years of the twentieth century Argentina was turning out higher-quality beef products). One problem for the Riograndenses was the distance from the estâncias to the major charqueadas; with a less developed railway system than Uruguay, Rio Grande still had to move most of its animals to slaughter in the late 1890's by means of cattle drives of 10 to 25 days.[44] (There was some improvement after 1901, when cattle cars began to be used by the railroads in increasing numbers.) Transportation between the charqueadas and the markets was also a problem. The Uruguayan charqueadas were located near good harbors or on the Uruguay River, where they could take advantage of cheap transportation to Brazil's coastal cities. Still other problems were the higher quality of livestock in Uruguay and the fact that the Uruguayan charqueadas had access to cheaper salt.[45]

At the beginning of the century about half of the Gaúcho charque was still produced in Pelotas, despite the opening of new plants elsewhere in the state; Bagé accounted for another quarter of the total output. In 1902 Rio Grande slaughtered a few more cattle for charque than Argentina (455,000 head compared to 432,000), but Uruguay slaughtered almost twice as many (725,000). Although Rio

Grande was Brazil's main charque supplier, it could not meet the total domestic demand at the customary prices. For reasons discussed in the next chapter, neither could the Gaúchos eliminate foreign competition. Large quantities of Platine charque were imported to supply the Brazilian market. The Gaúcho ranchers resented the fact that Uruguay sold far more to Brazil than it bought in return: in 1901, for example, the value of Uruguay's charque exports alone to Brazil was almost two-and-a-half times the value of its total imports from Brazil. Another irritant for Gaúcho estancieiros was the fact that charqueadas in Rio Grande were not averse to smuggling cattle from the other side of the line, especially when this meant higher quality (and often cheaper) meat. Corrupt Riograndense officials even illegally "nationalized" foreign cattle by supplying false receipts to prove the animals were from Riograndense estâncias.[46] At the same time, state and federal governments were eager to see regulated numbers of Uruguayan cattle enter Rio Grande to improve the breeding stock—but this was another source of abuse because of the potential for smuggling.

Impressed by the upsurge of exports in Argentina and Uruguay following the investment of British capital in those countries, Borges de Medeiros was eager to have foreign investors open frigoríficos in Rio Grande. Negotiations were begun with the London-based Brazilian Cold Storage and Development Company, but plans never got off the drawing board; Rio Grande would have to wait for the First World War to make frigorífico investment attractive to foreign capital. The major foreign investment in the state's beef processing industry during the early years of the century was made by a Uruguayan firm, which established a charqueada in the border town of Livramento—another invitation to cattle smuggling.

Gaúcho politicians were anxious to control contraband, and one way to do it was to reduce the costs of shipping Serra and Litoral beef to Rio de Janeiro and points north. This could be done by opening a new Atlantic port north of Pôrto Alegre and building good rail feeder lines, thus freeing ranchers in the northern half of the state from the high costs of transporting their products via the Plate or the bar of Rio Grande. The construction of a major port at Tôrres, which had been a political issue during the provisional government, was raised again in 1904,[47] but with no concrete results; in the end, the state government settled for major improvements of the existing facilities and further dredging at the port of Rio Grande, which had been initiated by the Rodrigues Alves government.

In fiscal matters the PRR regime instituted some progressive measures in the years following the civil war. One of Castilhos' cherished projects was a rural property tax that would gradually replace the incentive-killing export tax on which Rio Grande (like the other states) depended most heavily for its revenue. Introduced in 1904, the property tax was the leading source of revenue from 1915 through 1918.[48] On the outlay side public education headed the list, usually accounting for about a quarter of the state expenditures; education took second place only during wartime or a period of mobilization, when the Military Brigade came first. Rio Grande devoted a larger share of its revenues to education than São Paulo or Minas Gerais, neither of which was able to enforce a significant rural property tax. Indeed, the state government's ability to enforce a meaningful property tax and its emphasis on public education gave Riograndense fiscal policies a decidedly progressive cast compared with those of other members of the federation.

As powerful as the state government was, before World War I it restricted its participation in economic life to conventional areas like railroad ownership. In urban affairs Castilhos minimized the role of both the state and the município governments. Not only was the state capital a small town at the turn of the century (with a population of 74,000 in 1900); it afforded little in the way of public works, which remained primitive despite the promising start made at the end of the Empire. In the opening years of the new century, electric lighting, which was supplied by a private company, was available only in the center of the city, and then only until 10:00 P.M.; most of the city still depended on gaslight. Nor was there a public water supply. Worst of all, Pôrto Alegre had no sewer system, a fact that was more than obvious to anyone walking the garbage-littered streets. Social life was limited in the Riograndense capital: there were a few downtown cafés and a few private clubs (the most prestigious of which was the Commerce Club, an outgrowth of the Commercial Association and the preserve of wealthy merchants and ranchers). Except for the enticements of bars and bordellos, and occasional performances by traveling opera companies and theater troupes, night life was non-existent.

With three bookstores and two theaters, the city had attained at least the same cultural level as most of the other state capitals. But Pôrto Alegre's cultural life in no way matched the brilliance of the national capital, with its flourishing literary bohemia. The closest thing to bohemia in Pôrto Alegre was student society; and the most striking development in the intellectual progress of the city was the founding of several *faculdades* (professional schools) at the end of the nineteenth century.

Beginning in 1896 four of these schools sprang up in less than a decade where none had existed before; no longer did Gaúcho students have to journey to São Paulo, Rio, or Recife to complete their education. Since the Castilhista constitution prevented state interference in higher education, three of the four schools (law, engineering, and medicine-pharmacy) were privately organized; the fourth, the Escola de Guerra, was federally controlled. The Escola was transferred to Pôrto Alegre after the cadet mutiny against Rodrigues Alves in 1904; though the federal government moved this military school back to Rio in 1910, another federally supported military academy, the Colégio Militar, was established in Pôrto Alegre.*

Positivism continued to be a strong current in the intellectual life of the capital. Positivists had extensive influence in the new faculdades, especially in the military and engineering schools; the engineering school was in fact founded by three positivists. In 1897 a positivist study group was founded in Pôrto Alegre, and a few years later a chapel was erected by the orthodox, or religious, positivists. The followers of the Apostolate in Rio were not permitted to hold political office, but they had close connections with high political circles. One such believer was Protásio Vargas, son of Manuel and brother of Getúlio, both of whom also gave money to the Positivist Church.†

Among the heterodox positivists—those who chose Castilhos over Miguel Lemos, the head of the church in Rio—were three future congressmen: Domingos Mascarenhas, João Simplício Alves, and Ves-

---

* In fact, government-run military schools of lesser importance had existed in Rio Grande since 1877.

† Religião da Humanidade, *Edifício da sede pozitivista em Porto Alegre* (Pôrto Alegre, 1913), pp. 4, 8. In Pôrto Alegre, as in Rio, members of the professions, and most notably engineers, dominated the positivist chapel. Of the 117 donors to the chapel whose occupations are listed in the pamphlet cited here, 69 held professional degrees, and 45 of these were engineers. One of the leading orthodox positivists was Antônio Pereira Prestes, a military engineer, whose son, Luís Carlos Prestes, became the leader of the Brazilian Communist Party.

púcio de Abreu. Castilhos and Borges continued to insist on the validity of the philosophic, if not the religious tenets of Comte. After Borges succeeded Castilhos, official tributes to positivism became increasingly evident in Pôrto Alegre. A portrait of Comte was on display—along with portraits of Borges and Castilhos—in the governor's salon of the state library. Busts of Comte's lay saints— the French anatomist Marie François Bichat, Aristotle, Descartes, Frederick II, Shakespeare, Gutenberg, Dante, Charlemagne, Saint Paul, and Julius Caesar—were encased in the facade of this building, which was erected during the Barbosa Gonçalves administration (1908–13). Yet for most members of the PRR, positivism remained ideological window-dressing with little real meaning. Even Teixeira Mendes, Lemos's successor as leader of the Apostolate, acknowledged it was Castilhos' personality rather than his creed that brought him so many devoted followers.[49]

From the vantage-point of non-positivists, who constituted an overwhelming majority of Brazilian intellectuals by the middle of the Old Republic, the Comtian dictatorship and its trappings were less to be admired than criticized and even ridiculed. José Veríssimo and Sílvio Romero, founding members of the Brazilian Academy of Letters and professors at the famous Colégio Pedro II in Rio, were among the social critics who found little to admire in Rio Grande do Sul. Veríssimo deemed the pastoral industry "extremely retarded, not bearing comparison to Argentina's or even Uruguay's." It was Rio Grande's constitution that prompted Veríssimo to call the state "a foreign body in the Brazilian federation." In his opinion, time would abolish the "monstrous creation" of Júlio de Castilhos.[50]

Sílvio Romero, the leading folklorist and literary historian of his day, considered São Paulo the only state in the union with progressive leadership. He was even harder on Rio Grande than Veríssimo. Romero agreed that the constitution of July 14 violated the federal charter and condemned what he called "positivoid Castilhismo." Rio Grande do Sul had the worst government in Brazil, he declared. The Gaúcho state was controlled by a "dictatorial, positivist absolutism, instituted by Júlio de Castilhos and ridiculously adulterated by the smiling and Jesuitical simplicity of his mummified successor." In his fulminations against Pinheiro Machado, Romero contributed to the myth that the state was one where only a Spanish-American-style caudillo could arise—in a milieu of "semi-barbarian" nomads.[51]

A few years later another out-of-state critic focused on the bizarre elements in positivism—the elaborate use of the characteristic color green, the devotion to Comte's female companion, Clothilde de Vaux, and the secular but Catholic-derived liturgy. Simão de Mantua found the Rio Grande of Borges de Medeiros a fantastic Comtelândia. He spoke for most of the new generation in describing his reaction to a positivist pamphlet: after reading one paragraph, he fell into a deep sleep.[52]

This was Rio Grande do Sul in the opening years of the new century. Underdeveloped by European standards and undemocratically governed, it shared these qualities with other members of the Brazilian Federation. Castilhos had built a political machine durable enough to survive a civil war, and with a peculiar dictatorial organization that paralleled the organization of the state government. The Riograndense Republicans were well-connected with military personnel, but an alliance between the PRR and the officer corps was of little value when the army was demoralized and the machines of Minas and São Paulo acted in concert. For this and other reasons, Castilhos kept his party aloof from the politicking for the presidency, the key to federal power. An indication of the isolation of the Gaúcho Republicans was the fact that they supplied no cabinet members to the five administrations between 1894 and 1910. But after Castilhos' death, Borges de Medeiros was to permit Pinheiro Machado to assert a claim for Rio Grande in the presidential succession of 1906; and by 1910 the Gaúchos, allied with a reinvigorated army, would be leading competitors for national power.

# PART TWO

# State and Nation

# CHAPTER FIVE

# Rio Grande and the Federation

To ACCOUNT for the rise of Rio Grande in the last half of the First Republic requires a comparative analysis of the state political machines, as well as an examination of relevant national institutions. Accordingly, in this chapter we shall interrupt the chronological narrative to lay a theoretical basis for the second and larger part of this study—Rio Grande do Sul in national politics. From the preceding pages it should be clear that Brazil had fragile national political structures; enduring parties existed only at the state level, and then only in some states. Only three states, however, had effective autonomy in the second half of the Old Republic. In a sense these states are political regions in themselves, though the term region can also be applied to the groupings of "satellite" states that attempted to act in concert. Regionalism for the period in question can be defined as political behavior that accepts the existence of a larger nation-state but that seeks economic favoritism and political patronage from the larger political unit, even at the risk of jeopardizing the political system itself.

Since the basic unit of political organization was the state party, this investigation focuses on the political machines of the leading states rather than on the less cohesive regional groupings of parties. Cleavages among the states and their parties will be treated primarily in terms of differences in political, economic, and military organization and strength.[1] The three autonomous states were Minas Gerais, São Paulo, and Rio Grande do Sul, and the political parties of the first two usually acted together to the exclusion of the third. We are concerned with political competition from the perspective of Rio Grande, which, allied with the army, formed an alternate base for attaining national political power. Specifically, the detailed examination of national politics begins with the presidential campaign of 1909–10 and ends with the revolution of 1930, which terminated the Old Republic.

Though some attention is given to economic interests, my primary concern here is with politics, and specifically with the question of presidential succession, since the presidency was the key to economic legislation and patronage. My study of economic factors is limited to two aspects: economic structure as a major variable in political behavior, and economic legislation as a form of compensation for political defeat of the parties of any of the three autonomous states.

Political mobilization remained low throughout the period under study, and Republican politics continued to be dominated by an elite. The ability of political leaders of the states to choose a consensus candidate in a "normal" presidential election, together with elite control of the final tabulation in a contested race, usually made popular elections little more than a formality. It is generally more useful to examine the presidential races from the viewpoint of the pre-electoral bargaining among the state elites than to study the voting figures themselves. In the following pages we shall see how three powerful states dominated Brazil (with the active or passive participation of the army) and how the political system functioned. We shall also examine internal developments in Rio Grande over the period 1910–30, in order to understand what prompted the Gaúchos to enter national politics.

Together Rio Grande, Minas, and São Paulo accounted for only 13.3 per cent of the area of Brazil, but they maintained a much larger and almost constant proportion of the national population between 1910 and 1930—about 41 per cent. Minas, the largest of the three (at 169,164 sq. miles, about midway in size between Texas and California), was twice as large as either of the other two states. Minas also led the federation in population, and there were twice as many Mineiros as Gaúchos between 1910 and 1930; São Paulo was second, Bahia third, and Rio Grande fourth.

One could expect economic and political leadership from the most populous states of the federation. But in fact the economic and polit-

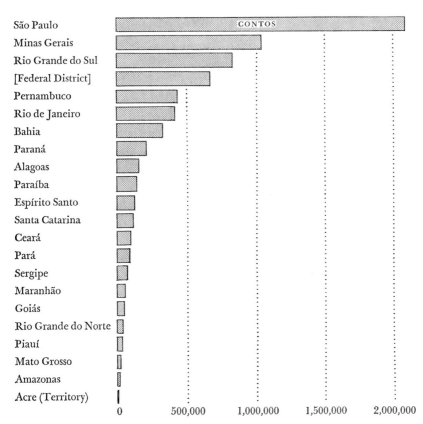

Fig. 1. Gross agricultural and industrial production of the states, 1920. Adapted from João Lyra, *Cifras e notas (Economia e finanças do Brasil)* (Rio, 1925), pp. 44–45.

ical influence of Minas, São Paulo, and Rio Grande was greater than their demographic weight, whereas Bahia ranked much lower in economic and political affairs than it did in population. In 1920, the middle of the period under consideration, Rio Grande, Minas, and São Paulo accounted for more than half the agricultural and industrial production of the nation (by value), excluding the non-autonomous Federal District.* Figure 1 shows the disparity among the states in economic output.

* The Federal District (containing the city of Rio de Janeiro) was important in industry, but it did not possess a powerful and cohesive party comparable to the more important state parties. The prefect of the district was appointed by the president.

São Paulo was first among the states in per capita industrial and agricultural output in 1920 with 587 milréis (about U.S. $123); Rio Grande was second with 376 milréis and Minas ninth, with 178.[2] The output per man in Minas, therefore, was well under half that of the other two states. São Paulo also led in industrial production; one-third of all the Brazilian capital invested in industry was invested in São Paulo. It was followed in decreasing importance by Rio Grande do Sul, with 12 per cent, Rio de Janeiro State, with 7 per cent, and Minas, with 5 per cent. But even in São Paulo, the industrial labor force numbered only 229,000 men in 1920, or about 15 per cent of the economically active population in the state.[3]

In 1920 São Paulo was first among the 20 states in the value of rural properties, Rio Grande second, and Minas third. São Paulo understandably took first place in the value of state revenues; Minas and Rio Grande were second and third, respectively. The three together took in more than half the revenue collected by the 20 states.[4] The same three states also predominated in the transportation field. By 1930 almost half the total mileage of all roads in Brazil was in these states, and better than half of the first-class roads. Minas had the most extensive rail system in 1930, São Paulo the second most extensive system, and Rio Grande the third. Together the three states possessed more than 55 per cent of the nation's total rail network.

The concern of the leaders of these states with achieving national power is understandable. Apart from the opportunities for patronage and the power to influence events beyond their frontiers, the three states had a direct interest in gaining control of the federal administrative apparatus to support their economies. Taking control of the executive was also important in securing the desired economic and financial legislation because of the president's great influence in congress.

Agriculture was the mainstay for every state during the Old Republic, and in São Paulo and Minas agriculture meant coffee. Coffee dominated Brazil's export economy: in the decade 1911–20 coffee accounted for 53 per cent of the total value of Brazilian exports; in the next ten years the figure rose to almost 70 per cent. If the coffee tree is taken as the basic unit of capital stock, São Paulo and Minas had more than two-thirds of the nation's productive capacity in this uniquely important export activity at the end of the Old Republic.[5]

Rio Grande, which was much less export-oriented than the two great coffee producers, was primarily interested in protecting its internal markets for pastoral products.

Large-scale agriculture required transportation facilities to supply domestic and foreign markets, and political leaders in the big three states sought control of the federal executive in part to develop roads, railroads, and, except for land-locked Minas, port facilities. From 1906 on, the major coffee-producing states (São Paulo, Minas, and Rio de Janeiro) attempted to influence the international market for their product by controlling supply. For this purpose they became increasingly dependent on the federal government for loans to buy and store surplus coffee stocks.

Since the coffee interests were paid in foreign currencies and converted their funds into milréis (in which their costs of production were calculated), they profited from the devaluation of Brazilian currency abroad, and therefore sought control of Brazil's financial policy.* The Riograndenses, by contrast, were not so interested in international market operations as they were in keeping foreign beef products out of the Brazilian market. They also favored stable domestic prices, an objective not always compatible with currency devaluation.

São Paulo, the leading coffee-producing state, had built the strongest Republican party in the last years of the Empire. The various export economies, and especially the economies of the coffee-producing states, were well served by the triumph of the federal idea in 1889–91. For many Brazilians the constitution of 1891 fulfilled the promise of decentralization stressed in the Republican motto of 1870. The Brazilian constitution provided for a wider dispersion of authority than did those of Argentina (1853, revised in 1860) and Mexico (1857 and 1917), the other large federal republics in Latin America. Both of these countries placed greater restrictions on their states (or provinces) than did Brazil, notably in not allowing their member states to levy export taxes on goods shipped across state lines; in Brazil, taxes on products shipped out of state (including exports) were the chief source of revenue for the members of the federation.[6] The Bra-

---

* Coffee planters and coffee exporters were, of course, two distinct though overlapping groups. Further research is needed on the complex relations (including conflicts) between the two.

zilian states could also tax imports. Although the revenue from such taxes reverted to the federal treasury, theoretically the Brazilian states could build tariff walls around their particular industries.* This constitutional provision led to interstate conflicts. One of the most notable was a six-year squabble between Rio Grande and Pernambuco, which began when the Gaúchos placed a tax on rum "imports," a leading product of Pernambuco; the Pernambucano government retaliated by slapping a duty on Riograndense charque.

Unlike the Brazilian constitution, the constitutions of Argentina and Mexico specifically prohibited the states of those countries from raising troops except in time of emergency. In Argentina the provinces were given no authority to set up civil, commercial, penal, or mining codes, and in Mexico the constitution of 1917 reserved all mineral rights for the nation. In Brazil, by contrast, the states could write their own procedural codes and were given authority over the mineral deposits within their boundaries. The Brazilian states were also allowed to negotiate foreign loans and to sell bonds abroad, a power that the constitution of 1917 denied the states of Mexico.

By Latin American standards, then, the Brazilian constitution of 1891 permitted a high degree of decentralization. It failed, however, to make adequate provision for the poorer states. Just as the chief source of income for the states during the Old Republic was the export tax, so the major source of income for the federal government was import duties. At the constituent assembly, deputies from the depressed northeastern states had argued for a share of import revenues, asserting that neither export levies nor property taxes would provide sufficient funds to run their governments. Time was to prove this concern justified.

Another way in which the constitution tended to favor the strong states was in the relationship between the three branches of the federal government. From the earliest years it was clear that the executive branch dominated the other two, and the *política dos governadores* went a long way in spelling out the subordination of congress. Consequently, as the Republic developed it became increasingly clear that the selection of a president was of critical importance in controlling the political system. And it was clear, too, that the ad-

---

* In practice, some states unconstitutionally taxed imports under a variety of legal guises simply for revenue purposes.

vantage lay with the stronger states, since the president was chosen by a direct popular vote of literate males, and the economically powerful states tended to be those with the largest populations and the best educational systems.

The economic preeminence of São Paulo, Minas, and Rio Grande had a clear parallel in political life in the period 1910–30. In absolute numbers, Minas, São Paulo, and Rio Grande led the other states in registered voters (in that order). In 1910, 47 per cent of Brazil's electorate resided in the three most powerful states, and in that year's presidential election the three states provided 51 per cent of the votes cast; by 1930 the respective figures had climbed to 52 and 54 per cent.[7] In the 1930 contest, São Paulo and Minas each supplied a little more than 19 per cent of the total vote, and Rio Grande a little less than 16 per cent.

National political affairs during the Old Republic were controlled by coalitions of the establishment state parties, usually with the explicit or implicit backing of the army. These coalitions were organized for the express purpose of supporting a presidential candidate and seldom survived the elections. Rarely did the formation of "national" political parties result in a real contest. In the popular elections for the presidency during the Old Republic, the winner's share of the vote fell below 70 per cent on only three occasions, attesting to the noncompetitive nature of the system, which in turn reflected the low level of political mobilization.*

From a national perspective the state parties might be seen as caucuses in a loose national party.† Like caucuses, they had a restrictive membership and were not controlled by the national "party." In Maurice Duverger's terms, they were cadre groupings, characteristic of the caucus system.[8] Unlike mass parties, they had no formal enrollment procedure and no precise criteria for membership.

One important reason the parties of the powerful states sought to

---

* The correspondence between competition and mobilization is evident in the results of the elections of 1945 and after. As more and more voters entered the political system, candidates won by increasingly narrow margins.

† Eul-soo Pang has recently shown that parties in Bahia were short-lived, and argues this was true elsewhere in the northern half of Brazil. ("The Politics of *Coronelismo* in Brazil: The Case of Bahia, 1889–1930" [University of California, Berkeley, unpublished Ph.D. dissertation, 1969], pp. 37–38 and *passim*.) For most northern states during most of the Old Republic, the "party" might best be defined as the men in power in the state capital and the coronel substratum.

TABLE 1

Size of Police Forces (Active) of Leading States, 1909, 1917, 1928

| State | 1909 | 1917 | 1928 |
|-------|------|------|------|
| São Paulo | 3,508 | 8,618 | 7,622 |
| Minas Gerais | 2,502 | 2,976 | 4,111 |
| Rio Grande do Sul | 1,552 | 2,528 | 3,212 |
| Bahia | 2,126 | 2,200 | 3,153 |

SOURCE: Directoria do Serviço de Estatistica, *Força policial militar: 1908–1912* (Rio, 1914), pp. 4–5; Directoria Geral de Estatistica, *Relatorio* (Rio, 1921), pp. 39–40, and *Relatorios* (Rio, 1930), p. 199.

NOTE: Figures for 1917 include Guarda Civil for 1916. The size of the state forces varied annually, and Rio Grande's contingent was sometimes slightly smaller than Bahia's and Pernambuco's in the decade 1921–30.

elect a president from their own ranks was that the presidency was a key to controlling the governments and congressional delegations of the smaller states. The president not only could distribute federal patronage, but also could deploy the army to depose governors who opposed his policies in any state except São Paulo, Minas, and Rio Grande. To be sure, the governors of these three states were deposed in 1891, along with 16 other governors who supported the abortive coup of Deodoro da Fonseca; but after the consolidation of the Republic and the election of the first civilian president in 1894, the Federal government did not attempt to unseat incumbents in the powerful states, though it did not refrain from intervening in most of the others.

This lack of federal intervention in Minas, São Paulo, and Rio Grande was not all a matter of self-restraint. The existence of formidable state police forces was an effective deterrent. Table 1 shows the size of the police forces of the top four states at three intervals.

Although Bahia's state police force was larger than Rio Grande's in 1909, it was qualitatively inferior, for Rio Grande's Military Brigade had more rifles than any other state force.[9] Moreover, the Bahiano police were spread across an area twice the size of Rio Grande do Sul, and so had less strategic mobility. Finally, politicians in Bahia were frequently at odds with one another, and the state police suffered from rifts among powerful leaders. When state forces came up against powerful coronéis, they were defeated.[10] The relative solidarity of the political machines of Rio Grande, Minas, and São Paulo, and the loyalty of their police forces to the state governments, had no counterpart in Bahia or Rio de Janeiro, or in the weaker states. And the ruling party in Rio Grande was perhaps in a stronger position than that of Minas or São Paulo: it could mobilize provisional corps on short notice by calling on local political bosses, who remained prepared for military action after the civil war of 1893-95. If the Gaúcho government had not been able to field some 12,000 men in the statewide civil war of 1923, a hostile president would probably have intervened against the PRR.

Where intervention occurred, it was carried out by the army. The total number of federal military personnel for the same years represented in Table 1 was roughly equal to the total strength of the state police forces. It was only in the 1930's that the army finally (and definitively) outnumbered the combined strength of the state police forces and began to employ equipment the states could not afford. As we have seen, the army's role in politics tended to vary according to its strength relative to other contenders. The military's propensity for close connections with the PRR developed into something like an alliance as the Gaúchos began to bid for national power. The Republic continued the Imperial practice of stationing a quarter to a third of the army in Rio Grande do Sul, and the command of the Rio Grande military district (the Third Region after 1919) was one of the most important army assignments; eight commanders of this region became ministers of war in the Old Republic. In addition, the only professional military academy in Brazil outside of the capital was in Rio Grande do Sul. In 1907 there were more cadets in Pôrto Alegre than in Rio de Janeiro (712 as compared to 639).

The myth about the Gaúcho's military vocation had a basis in fact in the Republican era, just as it had in the Imperial era. Rio Grande continued to contribute more than its share of military leaders. In this respect the contrast with Minas and São Paulo is particularly striking: in 1895 eight of the 30 generals of division and brigade had been born in Rio Grande; none were from Minas, and only one was from São Paulo. At the end of the Old Republic eight of 30 were again Gaúchos, and none were Paulistas or Mineiros. Of the 25 presidents of the Military Club in the Old Republic, five came from Rio Grande, one from São Paulo, and none from Minas. And of 20 war ministers between 1889 and 1930, seven were from Rio Grande, none from São Paulo, and one—the only civilian to hold the post—from Minas.[11] This trend continued into the 1930's.

There were several good reasons for the close ties between the PRR and the federal army. Ideological convictions (positivism), bonds established during the struggle of 1893–95, and regional loyalty have been mentioned. Another factor was the PRR's unflagging defense of military appropriations in congress, where Riograndenses sat on key committees. Finally, the PRR was the army's only potential ally in a contest for power: the officer corps alone could not overthrow the Mineiro-Paulista alliance, nor could it rely on the other state machines to stand up against the most powerful organizations. When the Gaúchos did not contend for national power, the army remained loyal to the president.

The political system of the Old Republic was characterized by a low degree of institutionalization at the national level, and by a low degree of mobilization as well. The first resulted in part from the history and states' rights ideology of the various Republican parties, and in part from the nonintegrated economies they defended. The rate of political mobilization, defined in terms of the electorate as a percentage of population, began to accelerate only toward the end of the Old Republic. The percentage of the population voting in presidential elections from 1910 to 1930 was only 0.3 per cent more than the 1894–1906 average of 2.4 per cent, and one-fifth the rate in the presidential election of 1945, the first after the period under study (see Table 2). The Old Republic's maximum rate of voter participation, 5.7 per cent, which was achieved in 1930, was only about one-sixth the rate for the United States in the 1928 presidential election. Thus Brazil failed to extend suffrage to the masses even in a formal sense during the 41 years of her First Republic: there was no Brazilian equivalent to Argentina's Saenz Peña Law of 1912 or the Mexican constitution of 1917, both of which made voter registration mandatory for all citizens.

Low political mobilization was related to coronel control in rural areas, where about 90 per cent of the Brazilian people still lived as late as 1920.[12] Coronel control was by no means unique to Rio Grande; on the contrary, rule by rural bosses, usually (but not always) the owners of latifundia, characterized the political system of the nation as a whole. The coronel was the local leader of the establishment party in his state; it was his duty to bring in the assigned number of votes—and to keep the opposition from voting. The coro-

TABLE 2

*Presidential Elections in Brazil, 1894–1945*

| President elected and date of election | Number of voters (millions) | Per cent of population voting | Per cent of total vote for winner |
|---|---|---|---|
| Prudente de Morais (3/1/94) | .3 | 2.2% | 84.3% |
| Manuel Campos Sales (3/1/98) | .5 | 2.7 | 90.9 |
| F. Rodrigues Alves (3/1/02) | .6 | 3.4 | 91.7 |
| Afonso Pena (3/1/06) | .3 | 1.4 | 97.9 |
| Hermes da Fonseca (3/1/10) | .6 | 2.8 | 64.4 |
| Venceslau Brás (3/1/14) | .6 | 2.4 | 91.6 |
| F. Rodrigues Alves (3/1/18) | .4 | 1.5 | 99.1 |
| Epitácio Pessoa (6/13/19) | .4 | 1.5 | 71.0 |
| Artur Bernardes (3/1/22) | .8 | 2.9 | 56.0 |
| Washington Luís Pereira de Sousa (3/1/26) | .7 | 2.3 | 98.0 |
| Júlio Prestes (3/1/30) | 1.9 | 5.7 | 57.7 |
| Eurico Gaspar Dutra (12/2/45) | 6.2 | 13.4 | 52.4 |

SOURCE: Guerreiro Ramos, *A crise do poder no Brasil* (*Problemas da revolução nacional brasileira*) (Rio, 1961), p. 32. I have corrected Ramos's electoral data for 1910. See *Diario do Congresso Nacional*, XXII, 82 (July 27, 1910), 559–60.

NOTE: Percentages of population voting were calculated on retrospective rather than contemporary population estimates.

nel often courted voters in his bailiwick with personal favors, finding jobs for them, or arranging loans, or simplifying bureaucratic procedures. Where enticement failed, he resorted to violence and fraud to meet his vote quotas, calling on a force of armed men who were personally loyal to him. In exchange for delivering the votes of his município (or group of municípios), the coronel was granted control of local patronage, which extended to such "civil service" positions as schoolteaching. If the leaders of the state party became dissatisfied with a coronel, they could often oust him through their control of the state police, the judiciary, and patronage.[13]

At the next level of political authority, the party in power was characteristically led by the governor, who gave his political support to the president in exchange for participation in the distribution of federal patronage in the state, federal support against rival parties or factions, and economic legislation and public works for the state. Just as the coronéis typically depended on the state party (at least in southern Brazil), so the governors and their parties were, in general, dependent on the goodwill of the president. The parallel is not valid, however, for the three most powerful state machines.

The mutual dependencies and obligations of the four-tiered system (with the voters at the bottom) have led some commentators to

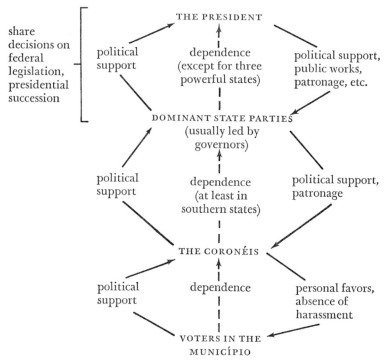

Fig. 2. Scheme of the political hierarchy in the Old Republic.

liken the Old Republic to a feudal state, with its hierarchy of lords and vassals (see Figure 2).[14] The Brazilian system did in fact resemble a feudal political structure in the lack of a centrally controlled bureaucracy at the local level (resulting in a civil service that was subject to political pressure) and in the granting of quasi-military power to the coronel and his private army. Without pushing the analogy too far, the fact remains that the absence of a genuine bureaucracy in the countryside and the lack of national parties, together with the patrimonial way in which "government" was understood, made the political system of the Old Republic only slightly more democratic than the Imperial regime before it.[15] Each level of government tended to support the others. Since the entire system was based on the manipulation of the rural vote, it had a low potential for adaptation in a country beginning to industrialize.

Nevertheless, for several decades the system seemed stable enough.

The politics of the Old Republic is often seen as an alliance between Minas and São Paulo that was based on common economic interests and that permitted the two states not only to alternate in the presidency, but also to take the lion's share of lesser positions of power. Those who hold this view have dubbed the arrangement the politics of "coffee and cream" (lit., *café com leite*), in recognition of the fact that Minas was also a dairy state. In fact, Mineiro-Paulista alternation was only a tendency, not the rule. In only three of the 11 direct presidential elections in the Old Republic did a Paulista succeed a Mineiro, or vice versa. This period saw three full-term presidents from São Paulo, one Paulista who died shortly after taking office, and another who was unseated shortly before his term expired. A sixth Paulista was elected but was prevented from taking office by the revolution of 1930. In the same period three of the presidents came from Minas and a fourth from the little state of Paraíba. Whether or not Rio Grande do Sul is to be seen as contributing a president depends on whether one classifies Marshal Hermes da Fonseca as a Riograndense or as a military officer without state ties. (The ambiguity of his relationship with the PRR will be treated in the succeeding chapters.) Rio Grande's Getúlio Vargas, who was defeated in the presidential election of 1930, came to power through the revolution that terminated the Old Republic. There is no doubt that in a general sense the presidency did "belong" to Minas and São Paulo; but in the second half of the Old Republic, the Mineiros held the presidency for eight years and the Paulistas only four.

Cabinet posts are another indicator of the strength of the state parties within the executive. In the years 1910–30 the cabinet consisted of the heads of seven ministries: transportation, justice, agriculture, foreign relations, war, the treasury, and the navy. In all but one administration, the war and navy ministers were appointed from the ranks of professional officers. The most important posts for the state political parties were the treasury, transportation, and justice ministries. The first two were important because of their large budgets: between 1910 and 1930 the treasury got the largest share of federal revenue of all the ministries, averaging more than 34 per cent of the total budget; transportation was second, with an average of 29 per cent.[16] The treasury controlled financial policy and thus had enormous influence with respect to exchange rates and coffee policy. The transportation ministry, charged with building roads, railways, and telegraph lines, had the power to help or hinder a state's economic growth. The minister of justice held a sensitive and important position because he presided over federal elections and could influence the outcome of congressional and presidential contests. The machines of the three most powerful states accounted for almost half (48 per cent) of the total number of years that members of state machines held ministerial portfolios between 1910 and 1930; and members of the parties of the three big states headed the principal civilian ministries (transportation, the treasury, and justice) 63 per cent of the time. In the second half of the Old Republic, Rio Grande and Minas predominated in the cabinet; São Paulo placed a distant third in both the total number of years in ministerial positions and in the three major posts. As Table 3 shows, there was a marked and significant change in the distribution of ministerial posts in the second half of the Old Republic, when nine of the 20 states of the federation were not represented at all in cabinet posts. In the earlier period cabinet posts were distributed more evenly among the states, with only six unrepresented. Moreover, in that period Rio Grande do Sul ranked twelfth both in the total number of ministry years and in the three most important positions.

From the data in Table 3 it is clear that the hegemony of the Paulista-Mineiro alliance is too simple an explanation of Brazil's national politics. The *politica dos governadores,* which was maintained by São Paulo and Minas, had two dysfunctional elements. The first was the potential crisis that accompanied every transfer of power at the national level. For the transition to be smooth, the Mineiro and Paulista parties had to agree on a candidate, and the other states had to go along with the decision. Gubernatorial succession also often produced a crisis within a state, since control could be wrested from the establishment party only through violence and federal intervention. A second and longer-range problem was the inability of the coronel-based system to absorb new urban bourgeois and working-class groups, which began demanding a voice in politics toward the end of the era, and increasingly turned to revolutionary alternatives.

Crises resulting from the inability of the Mineiro and Paulista elites to agree on a presidential candidate—sometimes compounded by an incumbent's desire to name his successor—tended to bring into play the other two autonomous elements in the political process, the

TABLE 3

*Number of Years Cabinet Posts Were Occupied by*
*Representatives of State Parties*

| States (ranked by total years) | Years in all ministries | Years in treasury, transportation, and justice |
|---|---|---|
| A. November 15, 1910–October 23, 1930 | | |
| 1. Rio Grande do Sul | 18.13 | 15.14 |
| 2. Minas Gerais | 16.09 | 15.45 |
| 3. São Paulo | 12.37 | 6.71 |
| 4. Santa Catarina | 9.14 | 3.92 |
| 5. Bahia | 9.12 | 1.20 |
| 6. Rio de Janeiro | 6.91 | 2.92 |
| 7. Pernambuco | 6.82 | 3.46 |
| 8. Rio Grande do Norte | 6.29 | 6.29 |
| 9. Ceará | 4.00 | 4.00 |
| 9. Piauí | 4.00 | 0.0 |
| 11. Pará | 3.92 | 0.0 |
| B. November 15, 1889–November 14, 1910 | | |
| 1. Minas Gerais | 12.64 | 7.69 |
| 2. Bahia | 9.73 | 9.35 |
| 3. São Paulo | 9.02 | 7.29 |
| 4. Pernambuco | 5.51 | 4.74 |
| 5. Goiás | 5.41 | 5.41 |
| 6. Mato Grosso | 4.66 | 4.66 |
| 7. Rio Grande do Norte | 4.41 | 4.41 |
| 8. Rio de Janeiro | 4.25 | 3.07 |
| 9. Santa Catarina | 4.00 | 4.00 |
| 10. Ceará | 3.12 | 2.36 |
| 11. Paraíba | 2.73 | 2.73 |
| 12. Rio Grande do Sul | 2.56 | 1.51 |
| 13. Pará | 2.27 | 1.08 |
| 14. Sergipe | 1.30 | 1.30 |

SOURCE: Compiled from Dunshee de Abranches, *Governos e congressos da Republica dos Estados Unidos do Brazil* (São Paulo, 1918); *Almanach de Gotha*, 1923–31 (Gotha, 1922–30); Augusto de Bulhões, *Ministros de fazenda do Brasil 1808–1954* (Rio, 1955); Max Fleiuss, *Historia administrativa do Brasil* (São Paulo, 1922).

NOTE: Four more or less arbitrary decisions were made in compiling this table: 1) professional military officers were excluded, except those making a career in a state machine (e.g., Lauro Müller); 2) ministers who held office less than three months were considered interim appointees and were excluded on the assumption that they did not have sufficient time to manipulate patronage and power for the benefit of their state; 3) Francisco Sá, though he began his career in Minas, was classified as a Cearense on the ground that he belonged to the ruling machine in Ceará at the time of his ministerial service; 4) cabinet members from the Federal District were excluded (the principal officeholder from the District, the Barão do Rio Branco, was not machine-connected).

PRR and the army. But the *politica dos governadores,* predicated on mutual support of incumbents at all levels, was in danger the moment a contested presidential election took place. Indeed, the very existence of autonomous units of power (or crudely put, the alternate formula of Rio Grande and the army) was a source of instability. For that matter, the participation of the Gaúchos in the decision-making process (even if the army was absent, as in 1919) signaled that the *política dos governadores* was in crisis. When the PRR and the military lost, the regime reeled before abortive revolts (though the Gaúchos were often appeased with economic legislation). To win, however, the Riograndenses needed the support of at least a faction of one of the other major machines.

There was yet another factor that ultimately contributed to the demise of the *política dos governadores*, viz., the relationship between the states and the central government. In the early part of the era, decentralization and modernization went hand in hand, at least for the southern members of the federation. The states became the foci of new responsibilities and services, taking on obligations the national government was not ready to assume. The most notable example is the valorization of coffee, an instance of intervention in an international market to stabilize export prices. The responsibility for valorization tended to seesaw in the Old Republic between the state and federal governments. São Paulo pioneered the first price support program in 1906; 11 years later a second program was established, again by São Paulo but this time with federal financial backing. In 1921, at the coffee growers' insistence, the federal government shouldered the entire burden of valorization and it continued to do so until 1924, when an economy-minded president turned coffee protection operations back to São Paulo. In the late 1920's an interstate agreement (initiated by São Paulo) brought the coffee-producing states into concert, and in 1930–31 coffee "defense" reverted to the federal government.

Other fields where the states took the initiative were utilities, public transportation, and banking. In Rio Grande do Sul, for instance, state economic and social responsibilities grew faster in the years 1910 to 1930 than those of the federal government. In 1912 the operation of the port of Pôrto Alegre became a state responsibility, and in the late 1920's, the federal government ceded the ports of Pelotas and Tôrres to Rio Grande. A privately owned railway running east-west from the state capital to Uruguaiana was bought out by the Gaúcho government in 1919. In financial affairs the state chartered a development bank in 1928 and began to intervene in domestic commodity markets, as the Paulistas had in the international sphere. As early as 1917 the Riograndense government intervened in the economy temporarily to halt the shipment of foodstuffs out of state, and the governor forced employers in Pôrto Alegre to raise wages.

It must be noted, at the same time, that the Gaúcho ranchers were not willing to rely exclusively on the state for financial assistance; they also wanted federal support in certain areas, as did the Paulista planters. In general, as coffee growing spread from state to state and as both investments and markets began to assume national dimensions, demands for federal controls increased. Coffee interests needed the federal government to establish conversion funds to keep the value of the milréis from rising; they also wanted treasury issues for the expansion of credit (as did other agricultural interests and industrialists). The charque producers and other Gaúcho manufacturers naturally wanted to control import policies that affected their products.

The rise of the external debt of both the states and the union in the mid-1920's, together with the resumption of amortization payments on the federal debt, was a matter of such concern for the incumbent president, Artur Bernardes, that he had the constitution amended in 1926 to give the federal government greater latitude to intervene in the states in the case of financial mismanagement. Bernardes introduced this measure, according to future chief of state Getúlio Vargas, because he feared American intervention in the state of Amazonas, the most notoriously insolvent and debt-ridden member of the federation.[17]

Though it is difficult to detect a clear direction in the union's share of total governmental revenues in the last 20 years of the Old Republic,[18] it seems plain that economic and social crises led to new demands for federal controls. This was true in the wake of World War I, when congress enacted a workmen's compensation law (1919) and a national coffee valorization program (1921). Similarly, in the wake of the Great Depression of the 1930's came a revolution that gave the national government sweeping new powers. And another trend is plain as well, namely, an increase in governmental intervention in economic affairs in the 1920's, not only on the part of the federal government but also on the part of the important members of the federation: the states as well as the government in Rio were abandoning laissez-faire liberalism.

Given the pivotal role we have assigned the Gaúchos in the decline of the Old Republic, it is important to turn now to a discussion of the economy and activities of Rio Grande in that period. The Riograndense economy continued to be oriented primarily toward the Brazilian market. Unlike São Paulo, which depended on overseas demand, Rio Grande sold two-thirds to three-fourths of the goods it shipped across its boundaries in the 1910–30 period in other parts of the nation.[19] Foodstuffs accounted for about two-thirds of the total value of goods sent out of state from 1920 to 1930; or put another way, ranching and its ancillary industries accounted for roughly one-third, fluctuating between 30 and 40 per cent. In a word, the Riograndenses had a rural-based economy.

Comparative figures on state economic production are sketchy at best, but Rio Grande's relative position clearly improved during the Old Republic. From sixth place in the value of agricultural output in 1886, it rose to third in 1920, the same rank it held in the overall value of production. Rio Grande was second only to São Paulo in the value of rural properties in 1920, and first in the federation in the number of cattle. Herds increased from 6.7 million head in 1910 to 10.7 million in 1930. The greatest concentration of cattle was along the frontiers with Argentina and Uruguay. Of the eight municípios with the greatest number of cattle in 1920, all were either on the border or separated from it by only one município.[20] The frontier location of many Campanha cattle ranches, together with the relatively high-cost operations of the Riograndense railroads and port facilities, allowed Montevideo to remain a leading entrepôt for Gaúcho beef destined for the northern cities of Brazil into the late 1920's.

The production of charque continued to be the principal derivative activity of cattle ranching in Rio Grande throughout the Old Republic; and at the end of the period the state accounted for about 80 per cent of the nation's output. Rio Grande's best customers for charque were the lower and lower-middle classes of the cities of Rio de Janeiro, Salvador, and Recife. At the beginning of the Republic charque had amounted to a quarter to a third of the value of goods shipped out of state, and by the end of the era this share had declined only slightly, to one-fifth, despite attempts to introduce large-scale frigorífico operations and the rise of other industries.[21]

The problems that had plagued the cattle growers and charque producers throughout the nineteenth century continued to do so through 1930. The Argentine and Uruguayan meat industries had far outdistanced Riograndense operations. As early as 1906 the bulk of Argentine beef destined for export was frozen or canned. Argentina got its first frigorífico in 1883, a year in which charque was still competing with cowhides as the most important export in Rio Grande do Sul. No significant frigorífico operations were undertaken in the Brazilian state until 1917, when American companies began production there. Not until 1940 were there more cattle slaughtered for frozen and canned beef than for charque in Rio Grande, and in many of the years thereafter charque regained the lead.[22] Ironically, Uruguay, with its more modern cattle industry, could still sell charque in Brazil at a lower cost than Rio Grande. One of the few advantages the Gaúchos had was that Uruguayan charque production was decreasing relative to Gaúcho output in the late 1920's. In general, the Riograndense estancieiros could make the same complaints in the 1920's as they had made at the beginning of the century: Uruguayan cattle were being illegally shipped into the Riograndense charqueadas, and Uruguayan charque was being sold more cheaply in Brazilian port cities, either because of lower production and shipping costs or because of the smuggling that continued to breach the tariff wall.

Nor were Rio Grande's ranchers and charque producers in a position to shut foreign producers out of the Brazilian market, for the Gaúchos could not meet the total national demand at the going prices. To be sure, duties on foreign charque might have been raised to the point where the supply of the Riograndense product would be equilibrated at a much higher price with effective demand, but this was only theoretically possible. There were three practical considerations that worked against maintaining artificially high prices: charque had long been a staple of the diet of the urban lower classes and the administration that permanently priced these classes out of the market was certain to face serious political problems; a dramatic price rise would inevitably induce charque producers in São Paulo and Mato Grosso to enter the market in greater force, partially offsetting any gains the Rio Grande producers would make; and, finally, smuggling, already a major problem with moderate duties, could be expected to increase sharply if steep tariff walls were erected.

That Gaúcho ranchers repeatedly found themselves in an unfavorable position with respect to their Platine competitors is not to suggest that the Gaúchos had less entrepreneurial ability; they did in fact open a domestically financed frigorífico in Pelotas, but large-scale operations could not be undertaken without major foreign investments, of the kind made in the Plate. Despite a good start in Rio Grande at the end of World War I, the American firms of Armour and Swift sharply cut back production in the middle 1920's. Concerned primarily with providing frozen and chilled beef for North Atlantic consumption in the postwar era, the foreign packers produced where operations were most efficient. Because of poorer pastures and less efficient transport (mostly owing to the accidents of geography), Rio Grande could not compete on equal terms with Uruguay and Argentina.

The most important agricultural enterprise in the state was the cultivation of rice. This crop, which had appeared in Rio Grande only in the first decade of the century, became the state's leading commercial grain by 1920. Here was a field in which the Gaúchos showed considerable efficiency: their rice yields were the highest in the nation. After beef and its byproducts, rice was the most important commodity shipped out of state in the last decade of the Old Republic.[23] Rice cultivation in Rio Grande employed irrigation, unlike the poorly capitalized rice production in other states. In this activity as in the cattle industry, only wealthy landowners could compete.[24] Rice growing continued to expand rapidly in the 1920's, to the point where overproduction led to falling prices; thereafter an effort was made to control supply.

In manufacturing, Rio Grande was outdistanced in 1920 only by São Paulo and the Federal District; even so, only some 11 per cent of the state's work force was employed in industry. The census for that year shows a higher percentage of individually owned industrial firms in Rio Grande belonging to Brazilians than in any other state.[25] Rio Grande also had more Brazilian-controlled banks than the other leading states. In this connection, the contrast with São Paulo is particularly striking. Foreign-chartered banks played a leading role there, whereas in Rio Grande deposits in foreign banks accounted for only one-eleventh of the total deposits in 1920.* The sources of

* Though the available data do not permit a precise comparison of the two states, of the banks with headquarters in the capital of São Paulo, foreign banks held

foreign investment in Rio Grande were also considerably different from those in São Paulo and Minas. Whereas British capital was predominant in Minas and São Paulo, American investment led in the southernmost state at the end of the Old Republic. American firms had invested heavily in both utilities and transportation in Rio Grande, as well as in frigoríficos. The United States consul in Pôrto Alegre estimated in 1930 that Americans had at least $25 million in direct investments, and that the value of American-held bonds of the city of Pôrto Alegre and the state of Rio Grande exceeded $50 million.[26]

Toward the end of the era, the state's economy was clearly expanding. Although São Paulo and Minas led the Brazilian federation in production, there are indications that Rio Grande was pulling abreast of Minas in the 1920's. There are no statistics for annual gross product by state, but other figures point to a more rapid rate of economic growth in Rio Grande than in Minas. In 1920 Minas and Rio Grande were second and third, respectively, to São Paulo in state revenue; in 1930 Rio Grande moved up to second. Even in 1920 the federal government was collecting more revenue in Rio Grande than in Minas. The federal sales tax brought in a larger sum in Rio Grande than in Minas for the first time in 1929 and continued to do so in the ensuing decade.[27] Although Rio Grande do Sul lagged behind Argentina and Uruguay in the development of the beef industry, the state had a dynamic economy that was of increasingly greater importance at the national level.

Rio Grande's economic growth was reflected in significant social changes, the most notable of which was the Serra's widening demographic margin over the other two regions.[28] Table 4 shows the extent of this change, which was in large part due to the development of small-scale industries and a high birth rate in the Italian and German areas in the region. In the main, small farms continued to be the rule in the Serra (and in a few enclaves in the Litoral), making Rio Grande first in the nation in the number of owner-operated

---

about two-thirds of the total deposits at the end of 1920. In the state as a whole, however, the foreign share was only one-fourth in 1936. See Rio Grande do Sul: Repartição de Estatistica, *Relatorio: 1920* (Pôrto Alegre, 1921), p. 287; São Paulo: Repartição de Estatistica e Archivo do Estado, *Annuario estatistico de São Paulo (Brasil): 1920* (São Paulo, 1922), II, 90–91 (Table 2); and Instituto Nacional de Estatística, *Sinopse estatística do Estado*, no. 2 (São Paulo, 1938), p. 130.

TABLE 4

*Population Growth in Rio Grande do Sul, 1890–1920*
(*by region*)

| Area | 1890 | | 1920 | | Per cent of growth 1890–1920 |
|---|---|---|---|---|---|
| | Population | Per cent | Population | Per cent | |
| Serra | 375,039 | 41.8% | 1,088,410 | 49.9% | 190.2% |
| Campanha | 224,195 | 25.0 | 436,594 | 20.0 | 94.7 |
| Litoral | 298,221 | 33.2 | 657,709 | 30.1 | 120.5 |
| State | 897,455 | 100.0% | 2,182,713 | 100.0% | 143.2% |

SOURCE: Directoria Geral de Estatistica, *Sexo, raça e estado civil, nacionalidade, filiação culto e analphabetismo da população recenseada em 31 de dezembro de 1890* (Rio, 1898), pp. 426–29, and *Recenseamento do Brazil realizado em 1 de setembro de 1920*, Vol. IV (Part 1): *População* (Rio, 1926), pp. 228–54.

farms. In the state as a whole, however, the latifundium still dominated. In 1920 less than 3 per cent of the rural properties in the state represented more than 45 per cent of the value of all rural real estate; and just over 10 per cent of the holdings accounted for almost two-thirds of the total value. Predictably, the concentration of land was greatest in the Campanha. In 1909 the five municípios with the largest average holdings in the state were all in the Campanha.[29]

Rio Grande had the highest rate of literacy of all the states by 1890 (25.3 per cent), and it held the lead in the following decades. The rate of literacy (including ages 0 to 14) rose to 38.8 in 1920, 9 per cent higher than that of the second-ranking state, São Paulo, and over 14 per cent higher than the national average of 24.5 per cent.[30] The German and Italian colonos helped put Rio Grande in the top position; São Leopoldo, the leading German-populated município, had almost 62 per cent literacy (for all ages) in 1920, and the Italian-dominated Caxias do Sul, 46 per cent.

The German-Brazilians were especially prominent in the industrial activities that were unrelated to pastoral pursuits. Of the total value of output in 1915, industrial firms with German surnames accounted for almost as much as those with Portuguese names; the Italians were about a quarter as important as the other two.[31] Charque and yerba mate continued to be dominated by Luso-Brazilians, and wine and butter by the Italians; in all other fields the Germans were preeminent. The colono groups were also pushing their way into large-scale trade. In 1924 three of the six officers and 40 per cent of the members

of the Commercial Association of Pôrto Alegre were German-Brazilians. There were also 17 Italians among the 327 members. In 1930–
31 the association had 464 members, of which 198 had German surnames and 43 Italian.[32]

Despite the increasingly active role of the colono population in
the state's economic affairs, the colonos played a minor role in politics. The traditional estancieiro's economy had its analogue in political life. The vast majority of the establishment and opposition
leaders of Rio Grande were members of the landowning class. Estancieiros also predominated among the political leaders at lower levels.
When the first statewide congress of cattle ranchers took place in
1927, 13 of the 16 Gaúcho congressmen either attended the event or,
as ranchers, sent statements of support; and almost a third of the 74
local committees of the state party were represented by one or more
members.[33]

At the município level the PRR, which continued to hold a near-
monopoly on political offices, was usually led by a rancher. Coronelismo thrived in a rural milieu dominated by the large estate, and the
population of Rio Grande do Sul was overwhelmingly rural. In 1920
Pôrto Alegre was the only município in Rio Grande with a population over 100,000; only five other municípios had populations over
50,000. At that time 77 per cent of the inhabitants of the state lived
in municípios with populations under 50,000.

The fraud and violence that formed part of the coronel system in
Brazil continued to be a feature of the local political scene in Rio
Grande in the second half of the Old Republic. In the years 1913 to
1927, when the leader of the Republican Party also held the governorship, he received 69 reports of electoral fraud and politically motivated violence.[34] Though by no means an exhaustive list of instances
of fraud and violence, these incidents can be considered representative of the type and relative magnitude of political irregularities.
About three-quarters of the incidents involved violence or physical
intimidation. More than half the reports referred to the use of
capangas. Almost 80 per cent of the cases involved fraud in elections
or in voter registration. Sixty of the 69 incidents were attributed to
the PRR, the remainder to the opposition. Two students of coronelismo assert that most fraud and violence in rural Brazil arose from

the competition of rival coronéis for the support of the dominant state party.[35] This judgment is more valid for other states than it is for Rio Grande do Sul, where a well-organized opposition party faced the establishment in most municípios. Nonetheless, 39 per cent of the 69 cases could be identified as resulting from intra-party struggles among rival Republican coronéis.

There is no clear pattern of the distribution of fraud and violence by município population. Yet it is interesting to note that Pôrto Alegre, with a population of 179,000 in 1920, was the site of a single (reported) incident, and Pelotas, the second most populous município, with 82,000 inhabitants, had none. Given 71 municípios and 69 reported cases, Pôrto Alegre had an average incidence. On a per capita basis, however, the capital had an extremely low rate of fraud and violence. This fact tends to substantiate the correlation between coronelismo and a low rate of urbanization. Still, it is also possible to interpret a low level of fraud and violence in rural municípios where the PRR's totals were unusually high simply as an indication of tight political control by the party in power.

The municípios bordering Argentina and Uruguay had a much higher rate of violence and fraud than the others, better than twice the rate for non-border municípios. The very presence of the frontier contributed to this frequency, offering a reservoir of non-Brazilians for fraudulent voter registration and providing a sanctuary from which the opposition could launch invasions. An impending Federalist invasion was rumored almost every year and finally materialized in the mid-1920's.

Fraud and political violence, as Figure 3 shows, increased dramatically in the early 1920's; the sharply rising incidence was probably a contributing factor to the opposition's decision to launch a statewide civil war in 1923. Though the number of reported instances fell off during the period 1924–26, each year was marked by a minor revolt. Something approaching an era of good feeling began in the late 1920's, culminating in a political alliance of the governing and opposition parties in the presidential election of 1930.

If coronelismo generally implied the existence of latifundia, we might then expect a greater degree of electoral autonomy in the colono areas. But this was not the case. The colonos were mostly immigrants and descendants of immigrants who had received modest

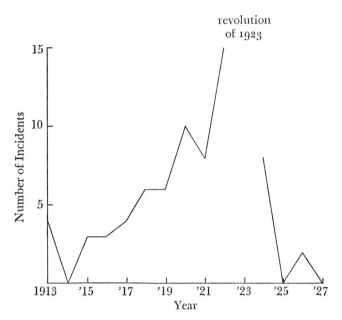

Fig. 3. Incidents of electoral fraud and political violence reported to the governor of Rio Grande do Sul, 1913–27. Compiled from the Archive of A. A. Borges de Medeiros.

plots of public lands from the government. One foreign observer judged Rio Grande do Sul the most successful of all the states in creating numerous and prosperous colonial settlements.[36] Politics was something else. In the 11 colono municípios, the number of incidents of fraud and violence between 1913 and 1927 was slightly lower than average; at the same time the colono population was even more faithful to the governing party than most non-colono Gaúchos.* In the political districting of 1897, the German-Brazilians had 24.7 per cent of the registered voters, but they were so effectively gerrymandered as to be powerless. By 1914 the Germans constituted one-sixth of the

---

* Classification of colono and non-colono units presents a problem of defining a sufficient percentage of colonists in the total population. The colono municípios I accept include those so classified by Borges de Medeiros in his political correspondence: Alfredo Chaves, Antônio Prado, Bento Gonçalves, Caxias, Encantado, Garibaldi, Guaporé, Santa Cruz, São José do Norte, and São Sebastião do Caí. (Borges, circular letter to local PRR leaders, Pôrto Alegre, August 17, 1917, Archive of Borges de Medeiros.) In addition, I add São Leopoldo, the município with the largest German population, which was no longer an area for state-sponsored colonization in the twentieth century.

state's population, but they remained firmly affixed to the ruling party.[37] Electoral statistics confirm the PRR's firm control of the predominantly colono municípios. In the voter registration for 1905, for instance, more than a quarter of the total electorate registered as Federalist; in the principal German município, São Leopoldo, by contrast, only two Federalist voters were registered against 2,788 Republicans. In three of the predominantly Italian communities (Garibaldi, Alfredo Chaves, and Bento Gonçalves), the Federalists did not register a single voter; in another, Caxias do Sul, the Republican-to-Federalist ratio was almost ten to one. Of the total number of registered voters in the 11 colono municípios in 1918, only 1.2 per cent were listed in the opposition party; the corresponding figure for all other municípios was 13 times greater.[38]

Coronel-inspired violence certainly had something to do with keeping the colonos under PRR control, and capangas made raids from neighboring municípios. But coronelismo seems to have been slightly muted in the colono-inhabited areas. The reason for the tight control over the 11 colono municípios appears to lie in the relationship of the settlers to the state government and in their lack of integration into Brazilian culture. An imperfect command of Portuguese alone hampered political mobilization outside the "official" party. In addition, the government could raise the colonos' taxes, suspend land grant policies, and use other forms of harassment. The leading student of the German-Brazilians in Rio Grande concludes that this group did not assert its political independence until after World War II.[39]

The Castilhista machine controlled the colono and non-colono municípios alike in Rio Grande, and the PRR's continuity of personnel and discipline helped its leaders project themselves onto the national scene by 1910. The Gaúchos' participation in national politics in the Old Republic can be divided into four phases: 1) dependence on the military presidents, Deodoro and Floriano, 1889–94; 2) autonomy and relative isolation under Castilhos in the years following the civil war, 1895–1903; 3) gradual emergence as a major political force under Pinheiro Machado and Borges de Medeiros, 1904–08; and 4) full-scale participation in national politics, 1909–30. The PRR's chief economic interests were to protect ranching and ranching-related industries. The party's conservative financial policies, partly ideological in inspiration, tended to coincide with objectives of the treasury, specifically when the federal executive's interests conflicted with those of the coffee growers over external depreciation. And despite the Gaúchos' reputation for "non-Brazilianness," Rio Grande's leaders were economically oriented toward Brazil more than their competitors in Minas and São Paulo.

The Riograndenses were to enter politics on a sustained basis in the presidential contest of 1910. The presidency was not only the key to control of the executive branch of government, but a powerful tool for controlling congress and most of the states as well. In the Old Republic, as in other periods of Brazilian history, succession of the chief of state occasionally produced a crisis in the political order; and in 1930, as in other periods of Brazilian history (1889, 1937, 1945, 1961, 1969), the crisis ended in the breakdown of the constitutional system.

The remainder of this study focuses on the presidential elections in the years 1910–30, or more precisely, on the contests where the political system was strained and finally destroyed by Rio Grande's efforts, with military support, to provide an alternative for the Minas–São Paulo alliance. These were the successions of 1910, 1919, 1922, and 1930. Throughout the 41 years of the Old Republic, only three regular presidential elections were seriously contested (1910, 1922, and 1930), and in each Rio Grande figured prominently. Though ruled by a conservative elite whose values were not dissimilar to those of the elites of other states, Rio Grande do Sul was a source of instability in the second half of the Old Republic. Its disruptive role in the political system dominated by Minas Gerais and São Paulo is the central theme of the following chapters.

# CHAPTER SIX

# Pinheiro and His Party

THE TREND Castilhos had condemned during the Campos Sales years—the decline of ideologically based politics and the mutual support of incumbents—became even more pronounced as the new century developed. With the consolidation of the Republic on the basis of the *política dos governadores*, politics became a game of patronage and economic privilege, and state parties became little more than oligarchies. Politically ambitious young men could achieve high positions only by joining a ruling clique, and even then they had to have powerful protectors. The simplest way to move up was to marry the boss's daughter. This path permitted a certain amount of social mobility for men of obscure origin, but only if they had the indispensable university degree. In a political culture still responsive to a great oratorical tradition, the *bacharel* (law school graduate) who could declaim with skill and who knew how to lard his speeches with classical allusions was a familiar figure. However humble his origins, the bacharel with the right connections—and above all the right marriage—could go to the top in most of the state oligarchies, though he might always be known as the "son-in-law." *Bacharelismo* was both a career pattern and a state of mind.*

---

* The bacharel type was brilliantly satirized by the novelist Affonso Henrique de Lima Barreto in *Numa e a nympha: Romance da vida contemporanea* (Rio, 1915). The greatest achievements of the protagonist, Numa de Castro, are earning a law degree and marrying the daughter of Neves Cogominho, the boss of the (mythical) state of Sepotuba. Numa enters the chamber under Cogominho's protection and is universally referred to as the "son-in-law of Cogominho." Among other things, the novel is a *roman à clef*, set during the presidential campaign of 1909–10. The novelist's General Bentes is Hermes da Fonseca; Dr. Bastos is Pinheiro Machado, Xisto is Davi Campista, and *o Velho* (the Old Man) is Afonso Pena.

Oratory was at a premium not only in the state legislatures and congress, but also at the frequent formal banquets where politicians honored each other and where political platforms were solemnly revealed. The banquet was the characteristic social event of turn-of-the-century Brazil, as it was in France and other countries in the *belle époque*. Typically, sumptuous feasts were accompanied by orchestral music and pompous oratory.

The political elite was as confident as it was ostentatious in the years between 1898 and 1910 as one administration succeeded another in an orderly fashion. Yet the nature of politics was subtly changing, and one of the differences apparent by 1910 was the rise of Rio Grande do Sul in national politics. Under Castilhos the Gaúchos had made no attempt to assert leadership in presidential politics, but after his death and the attenuation of the Federalist menace, PRR leaders began to take a greater interest in national affairs. The state's economic ties with the rest of Brazil were also expanding, and in 1910 a rail line finally connected São Paulo (and Rio) with Rio Grande do Sul. Five years later, the dredging work was completed that allowed ocean-going vessels to reach Pelotas, thus facilitating the shipment of Riograndense beef to ports in central and northern Brazil. Other factors that accounted for Rio Grande's new presence in national politics included Gaúcho links with a revitalized military organization and the influence and power of the state's chief representative in Rio de Janeiro, Senator Pinheiro Machado.

The machines of other states had to make room as the PRR demanded its place in the sun, and the principal losers were the Bahianos; the Gaúchos effectively replaced the Bahianos as the third most powerful group in national politics. In the all-important presidential elections, Bahia's vote fell from 103,000 ballots in 1898 to 61,000 in 1910, at a time when the national total rose from 462,000 to 628,000. Rio Grande's vote rose from only 3,000 in 1898 (when Castilhos directed PRR members to abstain) to 42,000 in 1906, the year in which Rio Grande passed Bahia for the first time, and to 67,000 in 1910. By 1930 Rio Grande do Sul contributed almost twice the number of votes as Bahia in presidential elections. Since literacy was a requirement for suffrage, in part the shift was due to a faster-growing number of literates in Rio Grande than in Bahia, though in absolute numbers Bahia still had more literate persons aged fifteen

and over in 1900. The other major reason for the decline of the Bahianos was that congress decided to cut the vote in Bahia down to
size, since the totals there were more inflated than in most states by
illegally registered voters. Congress simply declared Bahiano ballots
void in large numbers. Politicians from Bahia apparently got the
point, for the state's total registration in 1910—some 100,000 voters—
was 3,000 fewer than the votes cast and validated in 1898, despite a
population increase of half a million persons. Rio Grande's registration in 1910 was 117,000.[1]

A large share of the credit for Rio Grande's displacement of Bahia
must be given to José Gomes Pinheiro Machado, the most powerful
man in the senate in the years 1905–15. Pinheiro had been a senator
ever since the constituent assembly, and by 1910 he had more seniority
than his colleagues from the two most powerful states in Brazil,
Minas and São Paulo. In 1902 Pinheiro was elected vice president
of the senate, the highest honor his peers could bestow upon him.
(The position of president of the senate was held by the vice president of the Republic, and so was not open to a senator.) He held this
position until 1905, and then again from 1912 to 1915. Unlike most
of his fellows, he commanded the loyalty of the other two senators
from his state as well as that of the delegation in the chamber, except
for a few Federalists.

Pinheiro Machado was an imposing figure. Like Borges de Medeiros, he was slight of stature and carried himself erect. But there
the resemblance ceased; Pinheiro was as flamboyant in style as Borges
was conservative. With his curly locks flowing down the back of his
collar, a flashy pearl stickpin in his silk cravat, a walking stick deco-
rated with ivory (from a unicorn, he insisted), and high-heeled boots,
he reminded some contemporaries of the romantic poets.[2] Occasionally he even decked himself out in a specially styled gaúcho outfit.
But however unorthodox his dress, it did not keep him from dominating other senators and congressmen. In 1905–6 he assumed the
leadership of the majority faction in the senate (simply called the
Bloco, or the Bloc), easing out Francisco Glicério of São Paulo. Pinheiro was a major supporter of the policies of President Rodrigues
Alves, a Paulista, and his personal links with São Paulo were extensive. His father had come to Rio Grande from Sorocaba, and Pinheiro continued to hold properties in São Paulo state. Moreover,

he had gone to law school in São Paulo and had married a Paulista. He generally supported Paulista claims on the national treasury for coffee support programs, but he was considerably more independent in this respect than the client of São Paulo who succeeded him in 1915 as vice president of the senate—Antônio Azeredo of Mato Grosso.[3] Pinheiro also maintained good relations with high-ranking military leaders. He was a veteran of two wars (Paraguay and the civil war of 1893–1895) and held the rank of general, which he had been granted by Floriano in 1894. His chief source of power, however, was an increasing control over the credentials committees in congress that enabled him gradually to make satellites of the political groups of northeastern Brazil.

Pinheiro figured prominently in the succession maneuvers of 1905, when the PRR became a major participant in presidential politics for the first time. The pre-electoral bargaining in that year represented a transition from the quiet consultations between the president and the governors of São Paulo, Minas, and Bahia in 1901 to a full-fledged race at the polls in 1910. The selection of Rodrigues Alves's successor required a change in strategy: Rio Grande was pushing aside Bahia, and the Mineiros seemed indisposed to accept a fourth consecutive Paulista. The succession of 1906, as it turned out, was the first in which the issue had to be settled by labyrinthine negotiations to arrive at a single "unity" candidate.

The first name to surface was that of Vice President Afonso Pena of Minas, who in 1904 seemed to be favored by Rodrigues Alves. But the following year the Partido Republicano Paulista (PRP) put forth Bernardino de Campos, who had served as minister of the treasury and more recently as governor of São Paulo. Rodrigues Alves now leaned toward Bernardino as an administrator who would continue the financial policies initiated in 1898. Pinheiro Machado, meanwhile, was trying to split the Paulistas by raising the hopes of former President Campos Sales. In June Pinheiro helped persuade the Partido Republicano Mineiro (PRM) to reject Bernardino de Campos, despite the protests of Rodrigues Alves.[4] Bahia opted for its renowned senator, Rui Barbosa, in mid-1905. The Mineiros at this time had not yet made a decision, though they preferred one of their own PRM members; some Mineiro leaders backed Afonso Pena, who also enjoyed the support of the boss of Pernambuco, Sen. Francisco

Rosa e Silva. Pinheiro by now had managed to gather seven states, led by Rio Grande, behind Campos Sales.

Ultimately an understanding between the Mineiros, the Gaúchos, and the Bahianos determined the outcome. Pinheiro and the Bahianos agreed in July to back a Mineiro if the PRM would close its ranks.[5] By the end of the month PRM leaders had agreed to unite behind Pena, though he was by no means the most powerful politician in Minas. In fact, it has been suggested that Pinheiro Machado was especially eager to support Pena precisely because of his weakness in Minas Gerais; the president would need Pinheiro's support to govern.[6]

Pinheiro's acceptance of Pena represented a distinct departure from the Gaúcho stand in the previous succession: like Rodrigues Alves, Pena had been a Counselor of the Empire and a Republican of November 15, but Pinheiro did not raise the cry of "restoration" in 1905 as Castilhos had in 1901. After meeting with Pinheiro at the resort of Caxambu, in Minas, Campos Sales decided to abandon his candidacy in favor of a unity candidate. By August 11 enough states had fallen in line behind Pena to ensure his victory,[7] though Campos Sales, Bernardino de Campos, and Rui had not yet publicly withdrawn.

The PRP continued to hold out for Bernardino de Campos, even though he had already lost many backers in his home state because of an interview published in June.[8] A former minister of the treasury, Bernardino had announced his support for a stable exchange rate and a more modern tax structure. He called for a federal income tax and also for a sales tax to replace state export taxes, the major source of revenue for the states, including São Paulo. The leaders of the richer states were unwilling to risk the loss of financial autonomy. Moreover, Bernardino's program implied revision of the constitution, the thought of which was anathema to most establishment politicians.

All the same, Bernardino's interview contained a positive feature for Brazil's coffee planters. He supported the principle of governmental intervention to help the states protect coffee sales abroad. This had become a critical issue by 1905.[9] In the early years of the Republic international prices for coffee had been high and exchange depreciation rapid, leading to an overplanting of coffee trees. By the time of the succession maneuvers of 1905, coffee growers and merchants realized that the 1906–7 harvest was likely to yield more than 20 million bags (the largest harvest ever) at a time when there was already a surplus of 9.5 million unsold bags. In addition, coffee prices abroad had fallen to about half what they had been in the early 1890's; and the coffee growers had also begun to realize that the overseas retail prices of coffee fluctuated much less than the prices they received because New York and European buyers warehoused stocks as a buffer against heavy buying when output was low (e.g., in drought years) and wholesale prices were high.

Ultimately, however, it did not matter whether Bernardino de Campos's position was "correct" on the issue of federal price supports for coffee or not. With his radical proposal to abolish export taxes, which would have deprived the Paulista government of two-thirds of its revenues[10] and denied it any initiative in coffee marketing, his political support faded away. On August 16 he abandoned the struggle, throwing his weight behind Pena, the unity candidate who had obtained the support needed to win the nomination before outlining his policies.

Before Pena's election in March 1906, the governors of São Paulo, Minas, and Rio met at Taubaté, São Paulo, where they agreed to institute a coffee valorization program. The Convention of Taubaté called for an agency to withdraw surplus coffee from the market by purchasing it from the growers. These surpluses would be stored and released in periods of low output; in this fashion the price of coffee could be stabilized at an acceptable figure. The project was to be funded by obtaining a foreign loan, which would be amortized by taxing each bag of coffee shipped abroad. The scheme presupposed a near-monopoly on the world supply of coffee, a realistic enough assumption at the time. Although this project was a state initiative, the three states expected to receive support from the federal treasury.

It soon became clear, however, that the new Pena administration would not underwrite the plan, whereupon Rio State and Minas withdrew. But São Paulo remained committed to the program and undertook to maintain the price of coffee on its own—using the vital state power to tax (coffee) exports. Nevertheless, the coffee interests obtained a major concession from the Pena government. Thanks to Brazil's sustained favorable balance of trade, the value of the milréis had steadily increased, adversely affecting the coffee exporters, who were paid in foreign currencies. In 1906 the federal government created a Conversion Fund (Caixa de Conversão), undertaking to stabilize the milréis at a lower value than its real worth and thereby prevent financial loss to the coffee producers. In thus yielding to the coffee interests, the Pena government in effect abandoned the conservative monetary policies of its two immediate predecessors.

In certain areas, however, Afonso Pena exerted more presidential power than Rodrigues Alves had. Pena attempted to curb the influence of Pinheiro Machado by vesting authority in a new generation of congressmen, so young they were quickly tagged the Jardim da Infância, or Kindergarten. Carlos Peixoto, the Mineiro leader of the Jardim, became president of the chamber of deputies at age twenty-four. Another member of the group was the Gaúcho James Darcy, who was elected majority leader in the lower house when Pena took office. In 1908, however, Pinheiro Machado punished the young man for his lack of loyalty to the PRR by forcing him to resign his seat in congress. Cassiano do Nascimento, an older and more reliable Gaúcho, replaced Darcy as majority leader.

During the presidency of Afonso Pena, the political process grew more complex with the appearance of a reinvigorated army. Elsewhere in South America governments were restructuring and professionalizing their armies at this time, and the establishment of a modern reserve force had been a plank in Pena's platform. He lived up to this campaign promise, continuing the reorganization of the army (which had been begun by Rodrigues Alves) and raising its morale to new heights. The man chiefly responsible for the transformation was Pena's minister of war, Hermes Rodrigues da Fonseca. Hermes, the son of an army officer and a nephew of Deodoro da Fonseca, was born in 1855 on the Riograndense frontier, where his father was stationed. Hermes took up a military career as well, advancing rapidly through the ranks in the early years of the Republic. He gained national fame for putting down a cadet revolt in Rio in 1904. Rodrigues Alves subsequently made him the commander of the military region that protected the national capital. In this capacity he supervised Brazil's first field maneuvers in 1904 and helped restructure military education in 1905. He rose to the rank of marshal as Afonso Pena's minister of war, a post in which he continued to demonstrate his talent as an administrator by creating a reserve force, reorganizing Brazil's military commands, and theoretically instituting conscription (which was not, however, enforced until 1917). He not only sent officers to Europe for advanced training but also went himself to Imperial Germany, where he was awed by the Kaiser's modern army. To be sure, the success of the Marshal's programs rested on congressional approval of military appropriations; and for success in that area he could largely thank Pinheiro Machado, an old friend.*

When the next struggle for succession took place, it was only natural that the Marshal figured prominently among the contenders. But the front-runner at the beginning of 1909 was the candidate of Catete, Treasury Minister Davi Campista from Minas Gerais. Pena had originally favored Gov. João Pinheiro da Silva of Minas as his successor, but João Pinheiro died in October 1908, not only depriving President Pena of his favorite, but also opening a breach between the older Mineiro leaders and the Jardim da Infância.[11] Campista, Pena's next choice, began to run into trouble toward the end of January 1909, when a powerful leader of the PRM, Crispim Bias Fortes, publicly opposed him. The President's inability to control the machine of his home state, a situation that Pinheiro Machado must surely have hoped for, left the succession question open in the early months of 1909. The names of Hermes, Rui, Sen. Quintino Bocaiuva (a Historical Republican from Rio State), and Foreign Minister Rio Branco were suggested by Pinheiro and others in talks with the President; not until mid-May did Pinheiro firmly support Hermes. Pena in the meantime stood by Campista, and members of the Bloc (principally representing Minas, Pernambuco, Rio Grande, and part of the Bahiano machine) decided to resolve the matter without presidential help. Led by Sen. Francisco Sales of Minas and Pinheiro Machado, the Bloc decided, on May 17, to support Hermes, who already had the backing of a once-again politicized army; he accepted the following day and soon resigned as minister of war. The new governor of Minas, Venceslau Brás Pereira Gomes, was chosen for the vice presidential post to assure the adherence of the PRM. On

---

* Just how close the two were is indicated by the fact that Hermes was Pinheiro's second in a duel with Edmundo Bittencourt, the editor of Rio's *Correio da Manhã*, in May 1906. The quarrel arose from the newspaper's acerbic personal attacks on Pinheiro, dating back to 1901. Bittencourt received a minor wound and the matter was closed.

May 19 Pinheiro reported that all the state machines except those of São Paulo and Bahia had accepted the ticket.

The same day Rui Barbosa rejected Hermes, and he was rapidly seconded by Gov. Manuel Albuquerque Lins of São Paulo. Congressmen from Bahia and São Paulo, with scattered support from other delegations, soon met to select a slate to oppose Hermes and Venceslau. Yet Pinheiro was not particularly worried by this move; he believed Lins had acted without the consent of the Paulista party. Furthermore, Bahia was divided, with Sen. J. J. Seabra and several Bahiano deputies backing Hermes. A convention of state congressional delegations nominated Hermes and Venceslau in late May, and by June Pinheiro Machado could boast that a large majority of the deputies and all but nine of the 63 senators had pledged themselves to Hermes.[12]

Events were shaping up well for the Hermistas: Davi Campista's candidacy had fallen by the wayside with the Bloc's May 17 decision to support the Marshal, and almost simultaneously came the resignation of the precocious president of the chamber of deputies, Carlos Peixoto. The leader of the Jardim da Infância resigned because of the rift between the PRM and Afonso Pena, who had sponsored Peixoto's presidency of the lower house. With the Jardim in disarray, Pinheiro Machado was able to reassert his influence in the chamber.

For all of this, the opposition candidate backed by São Paulo and Bahia might have won if he had enjoyed the resolute backing of the incumbent president. Here the Hermistas had a great stroke of luck: President Pena died on June 15, and the presidency devolved upon Nilo Peçanha, who wished to return to power in Rio State and believed that Pinheiro and Hermes could best help him to achieve this goal. Accordingly, the full weight of presidential authority was thrown behind Hermes. Support from the army was also an important factor in the Marshal's favor, since the commanders of the garrisons in the satellite states were not above bringing pressure to bear on his behalf.

In Rio Grande do Sul the PRR leaders were elated that a Gaúcho, even one in uniform, would be the next president. Flôres da Cunha, then a member of the state assembly of Rio Grande, proposed that the legislature express its wholehearted backing of Hermes and Venceslau. His motion was quickly seconded by young Getúlio Vargas and was adopted unanimously by the Castilhista-populated house.[13]

Although it was clear that Hermes would be elected, the Paulistas and Bahianos held an opposition convention in August, nominating Rui Barbosa for president and Albuquerque Lins as his running mate. Judging by Rui's ineffectiveness in upsetting the establishment candidate in later elections, it is evident that the ability to wage a major battle in 1910 lay principally with the Paulista Republican machine. After losing out in the nomination in 1905, the PRP leaders had adhered to the unity candidate. Now, largely ignored by the Bloc in its deliberations, they judged the political system was mature enough—after four uncontested popular elections—to sustain a race. They also believed, as Campos Sales had argued earlier, that "militarism" would hurt Brazil's foreign credit. Rui picked up this theme in his attacks on Hermes, even labeling his crusade the Civilian Campaign (Campanha Civilista).*

For many Brazilians, Rui represented the highest hopes for liberal democracy. A masterly orator and jurist, he had begun a brilliant career in the Imperial chamber of deputies. Though he had not been a Republican propagandist in the 1880's, he participated in the conspiracy that toppled the old regime, and had briefly dominated Deodoro's provisional government as minister of the treasury. He had actively opposed the dictatorship of Floriano Peixoto and spent two years in exile. Rui had represented his native state, Bahia, in the senate since 1895, earning there a reputation for eloquence, integrity, and ambition. In 1907 he led Brazil's delegation to the Second Hague Peace Conference, where he demonstrated his knowledge of international law and several European languages. In Brazilian eyes Rui put his country on the map at the Hague, even if the leader of the German delegation privately considered him the "most boring" member of the conference.[14]

The platforms of the two candidates were alike in many ways, though there were differences in approaches to economic problems and to federal-state relationships. Rui backed São Paulo's proposal for federal assistance in supporting the price of coffee. He also offered a series of constitutional amendments to strengthen the federal government, among them proposals to unify Brazil's judicial system and to establish sanctions against state governments that violated the federal constitution. He wanted to give congress the right to inter-

* To this the Hermistas retorted that theirs was a national candidate, for the army was above state and regional interests.

vene in economic conflicts between states and to regulate the states'
authority to contract foreign debts. In addition, he called for a secret
ballot. Rui's program presumably appealed to members of minority
parties and urban voters in general, groups that saw in increased
federal power and the secret vote a means of weakening the coronel-
based state oligarchies. Several months after his nomination, Hermes
produced a platform of a decidedly more conservative nature, calling
for a balanced budget and the stabilization of the milréis, and rejecting any revision of the constitution.

Although Rui was the better qualified of the two candidates, his
impassioned speeches had little effect on the outcome of the contest.
The leaders of the state machines had decided in advance who would
win. Minas, Rio Grande, and the lesser states were not persuaded by
Rui's oratory, which focused on the somewhat irrelevant issue of
civilian versus military authority in Brazil. On March 8, 1910, a week
after the election, Pinheiro Machado exultantly wired Borges that
Hermes had won in all the state capitals except São Paulo, and that
the Marshal would have a two-to-one victory. In some of the capitals
of Pinheiro's satellite states, the early returns showed the election
to be a runaway: in Fortaleza, Ceará, figures showed 1,230 votes for
Hermes and two for Rui; in Recife, Pernambuco, it was 3,226 to
seven. Even in Rui's home state, Hermes took the capital, Salvador,
by a three-to-one margin. A "stupendous victory," proclaimed the
Gaúcho Senator.[15] Though the election was not as much a rout as
these first returns suggest, the final tally gave Hermes almost a two-
to-one edge—404,000 against 223,000 for Rui. Rio Grande do Sul,
which had the third-largest voter turnout (after Minas and São
Paulo), handed Hermes a handsome victory; he triumphed in his
home state by a margin of better than three to one. São Paulo was
the only state where a majority went to Rui, and there as elsewhere
the vote was controlled by the state machine. Despite the evidence
to the contrary, Rui never admitted that he lost the election; Pinheiro, he charged, had manipulated the congressional committee
that counted the votes.[16]

Hermes, who went to Rio Grande toward the end of the campaign
and spent election day in Pôrto Alegre, was impressed by the way
Borges de Medeiros ran the state and by the division of authority
that allowed Gov. Carlos Barbosa Gonçalves to devote himself ex-

clusively to administrative questions; the Marshal was soon to try to apply the same division of labor at the national level. The man on whom he would rely for political leadership was Senator Pinheiro Machado; indeed, after leaving office, Hermes acknowledged to Borges that he had governed Brazil with Pinheiro's aid.[17]

Pinheiro Machado's dominance stemmed not only from his unique influence with the Marshal, but also from his authority within the ruling elite. His power in congress derived in the first instance from his control of the credentials committee of the senate, and usually of its counterpart in the chamber as well.[18] Through this control, Pinheiro could deny a seat in congress to an opponent by getting the appropriate committee to declare enough votes fraudulent to make the opposition candidate the winner. An anecdote has it that the Senator once said to a young congressman-elect of doubtful loyalty: "Son, you won't be recognized [in congress] for three reasons. The third is you weren't elected."[19] The first two were Pinheiro's power in the credentials committee and his desire to punish insubordination. This sort of treatment was reserved, however, for the politicians of the 17 weaker states, not for those of Minas, São Paulo, and Rio Grande. Moreover, Pinheiro's control of recognition allowed him to participate in the selection of congressional candidates from his northern satellites. One striking instance of his use of this power was arranging the election of Flôres da Cunha, a Gaúcho, as a deputy from Ceará; Flôres had never even visited that state! This was by no means an isolated incident; there were many other cases where Pinheiro chose the candidates to represent the satellite states.[20]

Pinheiro was both an elitist and an opportunist. His election in Rio Grande do Sul was automatic, and as he once proudly proclaimed, he had "never cultivated popularity."[21] But on the whole, his approach to politics won little favor outside his home state, not only because of his obvious disdain for public opinion but also because of his crude Gaúcho ways. (Rui Barbosa, for instance, once corrected his grammar on the senate floor.) Pinheiro's vulgarity and lack of tact irritated many bacharéis, especially those who went to his home on Rio's Morro da Graça to seek favors and were kept waiting until he chose to interrupt a billiard game or throw in a poker hand; some spent whole evenings there without ever receiving the nod to speak.[22] As could be expected, Pinheiro had close connections with many leading capitalists, including Percival Farquhar, the American magnate who controlled the Brazil Railway.[23] It was not unheard of for powerful businessmen or important politicians to lose heavily to him at the card table in order to curry favor. To put it bluntly, Pinheiro simply made more money than he should have in politics; there was an unmistakable air of corruption about him.

The gaudy banquets of the period seemed to fit the free-spending style of Pinheiro, a master of the art of conspicuous consumption. One such instance was a feast given in his honor in 1905 at the Hotel dos Estrangeiros. The banquet hall was festooned with lilies, camellias, roses, chrysanthemums, and orchids, with a central bouquet inscribed with the words "Hail Pinheiro Machado," spelled out in white camellias and tiny electric lights. Among the 170 guests were Hermes da Fonseca, three ministers, two governors, the prefect of the Federal District, and numerous senators and deputies, including Rui Barbosa, Venceslau Brás, and Davi Campista. The guests could choose from the following menu:

> *Potages*—consommé riche à la Cavour, bisque d'écrevisses
> *Relevé*—favorites
> *Poisson*—badejo, sauce mousseline et sauce genevoise
> *Entrées*—filet de boeuf Richelieu, noisettes d'agneau fédora
> *Milieu*—sorbet aux liqueurs des Iles, suprême de volaille en belle vue
> *Légume*—asperges à la polonaise
> *Rôti*—dindonneau en surprise
> *Entremets*—timbales magicienne
> *Glace*—corbeilles de fruits glacés
> *Dessert*—petit fours, bonbons, fils d'or, marrons glacés,
> fruits européens, primeurs de long-champs, violets de Parmos,
> corbeilles fleurs Petropolis
> *Vins*—Madère, Hauts Sauternes, Pontet Canet, Rhum Jamaica,
> Vieux Bourgogne, Veuve Cliquot
> *Café et liqueurs*

During the meal a 30-piece orchestra played selections from Wagner's *Tannhäuser* and Carlos Gomes's *Il Guarany*. Then came the inevitable speeches, one by Pinheiro and another by Sen. Francisco Ferreira Chaves of Piauí.[24]

At a 500-plate banquet in his honor on September 1, 1910, Pinheiro announced his plan to create a national party in support of the government.* There could be little doubt about the significance of such an organization after Hermes announced, in October, that "the chief executive does not deal in politics but in administration, relying on . . . the political forces that represent the majority." The division of politics and administration in Rio Grande do Sul was his "ideal," he declared.[25] Clearly, Hermes had a concept of the presidency that bore little relation to reality, for the office was an eminently political one and a post that had been held by some of the country's most astute politicians.

In fact, the President-elect was a man of weak character and undistinguished intelligence ("a complete mental zero," as the usually temperate Melo Franco puts it);[26] and as Hermes became more and more dependent on Pinheiro it became increasingly clear that his initial definition of his duties was no mere piece of rhetoric.

Pinheiro formed his Partido Republicano Conservador (Conservative Republican Party) in the first week of November 1910; it brought together a majority of the state machines, though the dominant faction in São Paulo was conspicuously absent. Sen. Quintino Bocaiuva was elected president of the new party, but only because Pinheiro did not want the job. From the beginning, the Gaúcho Senator was the real boss of the PRC, as Bocaiuva was quick to acknowledge;[27] and when Bocaiuva died in 1912, Pinheiro agreed to become the party president.

The PRC bore a great resemblance to an earlier national political conglomerate—Francisco Glicério's Partido Republicano Federal.

* One critic saw Pinheiro as a would-be dictator, or very close to it. Simão de Mantua, in his essay on Pinheiro, imagined these thoughts running through the Senator's mind: "To lead a party, to govern a nation! What's so superhuman about that? Can't I run an estância . . . ? I'll take command—and be more of a chief, more of a lord, more of a boss than Glicério. The Gaúcho, after all, is a man among men. Above all, I and only I must give the orders, just like on the estância. I'll have aides, confidants; you can't know everything. I have assistants on the estância, one for every specialty. And when you come right down to it, the nation is nothing but a huge estância: the people are the livestock . . . ; the deputies, senators, ministers, [and] high functionaries are the foremen and peons; I'll be the owner, the estancieiro." Mantua [pseud. for Antônio Gomes Carmo], *Figurões vistos por dentro (Estudo de psicologia social brasileira)* (São Paulo, 1921), I, 165. However exaggerated Mantua's picture, it does express the widespread opinion that Pinheiro had little interest in developing a viable democracy in Brazil; and it shows as well how Pinheiro was viewed by the cultivated but powerless bacharéis who made Rui Barbosa their idol.

For one thing, many of the same men were leaders in both parties. Bocaiuva, for instance, had been on the PRF executive committee. Other PRC officials who had previously been PRF leaders included Pinheiro himself; Augusto Tavares de Lyra from Rio Grande do Norte; Tomás Delfino and Alcindo Guanabara from the Federal District; Antônio Azeredo from Mato Grosso; Urbano Santos from Maranhão; Firmino Pires Ferreira from Piauí; Severino Vieira and J. J. Seabra from Bahia; Leopoldo Bulhões from Goiás; Tomás Acioli, Pedro Augusto Borges, and Francisco Sá from Ceará; and Rodolfo Miranda of the PRP minority in São Paulo.

There were also structural similarities between the two caucus parties. In both, each state (and the Federal District) was represented by a two-man delegation at the national conventions, and in both, these assemblies were to elect seven-man executive committees. Even the names of the two parties were similar; in fact, in 1893 Nilo Peçanha had suggested the name Partido Republicano Conservador for Glicério's party.[28]

Like the PRF, the PRC was anti-revisionist and stood for states' rights and fiscal responsibility. Freedom of education, the peculiar positivist measure denying the government any control of higher education, and protection of the pastoral industry were included in the PRC program to satisfy the Gaúchos; to accommodate the army, the new party championed the development of Brazil's military power.[29] With considerably less fanfare, the PRC leaders agreed to continue conversion fund operations for coffee interests.

State branches of the PRC were duly set up across the country; most of the units in the satellite states of the north were extremely heterogeneous, often including both the ruling and the opposition factions. Conventions were held in the state capitals, at which the local parties adopted the national program verbatim, along with pledges of loyalty to the national PRC leadership, President Hermes, and the bosses of the various state machines.[30] The PRC was a convenient tool for Pinheiro, a means of institutionalizing his authority and legitimating his *de facto* control of the political oligarchies of satellite states under the rubric of party discipline. With Minas Gerais and Rio Grande do Sul it was an entirely different matter, however. The machines of these two states did not give up their sovereignty to join the PRC; they did no more than join *with* it in a national coalition. Before the new party was organized, Borges de Medeiros stipulated that any organization receiving PRR support must be controlled by Pinheiro himself. Moreover, he hand-picked the leaders of the Rio Grande branch of the PRC from PRR ranks and emphasized to Pinheiro that the local unit would concern itself exclusively with federal affairs.[31]

Pinheiro dominated the senate with his new party, and he moved swiftly to strengthen his position in the chamber. In the lower house Minas Gerais often won the presidency, partly because Minas had the largest delegation. Rio Grande frequently won the post of majority leader, and two Gaúchos had held the post during the Pena administration. João Severiano da Fonseca Hermes, a brother of the President, entered the chamber for Rio Grande in 1911 and immediately became the majority leader.*

Like other important state parties, the PRR tried to influence public opinion in the national capital by giving financial support to various Carioca newspapers, notably *A Tribuna, Correio da Noite, A Imprensa, Gazeta de Noticias,* and the prestigious *Jornal do Commercio.*[32] Outside the federal capital the role of public opinion was minimal, owing to the low degrees of urbanization and literacy, and to the consequence of coronel control. In Rio de Janeiro there was much less evidence of machine domination, and a relatively high literacy rate (well over 50 per cent by 1910) made newspapers an important political instrument. Although popular opinion in Rio was a minor factor in a presidential election, the public reaction to deliberately circulated political rumors at least affected political tactics. Even so, Pinheiro Machado made little effort to conceal his contempt for the Carioca populace; his power was in no way dependent on the voters in Rio and his reelection in Rio Grande was a certainty. Popular appeals and charismatic leadership were not part of Pinheiro's political style; his dominance depended solely on his authority in the ruling elite.

The consistent backing of a "permanent" government in Rio Grande do Sul; the control of the credentials committees in congress, as well as the control of two crucial congressional posts, those of vice president of the senate and majority leader of the chamber; the tool

---

* Fonseca Hermes inverted his name to distinguish himself from the Marshal.

of party discipline exercised through the PRC; the free use of subventions to influential newspapers; and a personal ascendancy over the President: these were the keys to Pinheiro Machado's power. But his "system" was one of personal relationships and was therefore subject to the shifting allegiances of the political elite.*

Pinheiro's preeminence in national politics was predicated on the authority granted him by Borges de Medeiros. In Rio Grande Pinheiro was consulted on politics in most border municípios. Since his home was in São Luís (in the Missões District), he could reach Rio de Janeiro most quickly via Montevideo, a route that took him through areas Borges never visited; along the Argentine and Uruguayan frontiers he had the authority to settle local disputes. Borges permitted Pinheiro to help in the selection of congressional candidates, for the Senator needed a state delegation personally loyal to him.[33] The party chief, however, reserved for himself the exclusive right to distribute federal and state patronage within the state.

Borges relinquished the governor's office to Carlos Barbosa Gonçalves between 1908 and 1913, but he retained control of party politics and had the final word on all significant political and administrative decisions.[34] President Nilo Peçanha asked him to come to Rio as minister of agriculture in 1909, a request that had Pinheiro's blessing. Borges declined, perhaps reluctant to lose contact with the minutiae of município politics and administration. In 1912 he was returned to office without an opponent, and he remained governor until 1928. In congress, as in the state executive, the PRR continued to enjoy a virtual monopoly of office in the Hermes era. (One to three seats in the chamber of deputies were still reserved for the opposition,

---

* The system of control Pinheiro Machado had developed by 1910 was not unlike that of his contemporary Giovanni Giolitti, who dominated Italian politics in the era 1903–14. Like Giolitti, Pinheiro manipulated a political hierarchy whose strength lay in rural areas where suffrage had preceded social and economic development, and where as a consequence new voters were still bound by the old patriarchal political structures. Both Pinheiro and Giolitti managed client groups from the most underdeveloped regions of their countries (the northeast in Pinheiro's case, the Mezzogiorno and the islands in Giolitti's), and neither had any compunctions about letting his underlings use fraud and violence to meet assigned vote quotas. Just as the leaders of *fin-de-siècle* Italy cast aside their democratic aspirations in their hour of triumph, so did the Brazilian Republicans. In Italy it was said that "liberalism is dead because we're all liberals now"; the same was true, *mutatis mutandis*, for republicanism in Brazil. See A. William Salomone, *Italy in the Giolittian Era: Italian Democracy in the Making, 1900–1914* (2d ed., Philadelphia, 1960).

whose representatives continued to seek constitutional reform and to deny the legitimacy of PRR rule.)

In economic affairs Rio Grande's participation in national politics continued to revolve around cattle and charque production. The middle- and lower-income groups of Brazil's major coastal cities remained the chief customers for Gaúcho charque. Inflation, the Gaúchos argued, tended to cause the substitution of (cheaper) *bacalhau*—dried fish—for charque in these markets.* Throughout the Old Republic, the PRR insisted on a policy of stable prices and fiscal conservatism. Although this position found support in the writings of Comte, it also fitted in neatly with the Gaúchos' interpretation of their interests in the pricing of charque. Shortly before Hermes took office, Borges wrote Pinheiro that recent deviations from the strict financial conservatism of the Campos Sales government had been an egregious error.[35]

The organization of the Hermes cabinet was a matter of concern to the Riograndenses, for Borges had his own interpretation of the Marshal's program. Pinheiro and Hermes wanted Borges to enter the government as minister of the treasury, where he would be in a powerful position to carry out conservative financial policies. But Borges would not be lured away from Rio Grande.[36] Pinheiro regretted the decision, arguing Rio Grande's "organic program" could be put into effect only if Borges and a second Riograndense entered the government. For his part, Borges was certain that whatever the makeup of the cabinet, Hermes would govern jointly with Pinheiro; and with Gaúcho congressman Rivadávia Correia as minister of justice, Borges contended, federal control of higher education could be terminated.[37] This positivist-inspired aim, along with financial conservatism and defense of states' rights, was the heart of the "organic program," of which the remainder was public works and patronage for Rio Grande do Sul.

A serious problem on the composition of the cabinet developed three weeks before Hermes took office in mid-November 1910, and its resolution sheds light on the personalities of Hermes and Pinheiro. Hermes had invited a brother-in-law, Amarílio de Vasconcelos, to

---

* *A Federação*, October 15, 1910. This argument implies that prices rose faster than wages—probably a realistic assumption in a country where wage labor was poorly organized.

head the ministry of transportation, an act that Pinheiro and Borges roundly condemned. The proposed minister had a reputation as an unrepentant monarchist, and the issue of consolidating the Republic had some lingering meaning for the two Gaúcho politicians.* After a conference with the Marshal, Pinheiro, who found Hermes "well-meaning but indecisive," wryly confided to Borges that Hermes once again proved to be "open to suggestions in the public interest." The transportation ministry went to Senator Seabra of Bahia and later to José Barbosa Gonçalves of Rio Grande do Sul. In explaining to the press why he had dropped the appointment of his monarchist relative, Hermes stated that he had yielded to "public opinion and republican sentiment."[38]

The new government soon began to meet its promises to the Gaúcho party in the areas of positivist ideals and economic affairs. After only a few months in office, Minister of Justice Correia satisfied Borges on the issue of freedom of education, the point the Gaúchos had so vigorously fought for at the constituent assembly of 1890–91. In a decree dated April 6, 1911, Correia abolished the special recognition and privileges granted to federally sponsored faculdades and made them autonomous in their internal administration.

In economic affairs Hermes emulated his recent predecessors by professing a belief in, but only indifferently practicing, a conservative fiscal policy. Despite lip-service to such a program, the Republic's record before 1910 had been spotty because of contradictory pressures in economic and financial matters. On the one hand the coffee growers pushed for devaluation, while on the other treasury officials resisted it in order to avoid increasing the federal government's financial burden, fixed in "hard" currencies. Depreciation of the milréis also contributed to higher domestice prices, and inflation in turn generated new pressures to devalue. Pushed one way and pulled the other, the presidents and ministers of the treasury in successive governments tried to check the pressure to devalue the milréis and to meet the coffee interests halfway by trying to obtain stable exchange rates and stable prices. The coffee producers, however, were satisfied with stable exchange rates only when the milréis was rising in value;

---

* As late as 1913 Pinheiro Machado was still talking of a restoration plot in the federal capital. Pinheiro to Borges, Rio, March 2, 1913, Archive of Borges de Medeiros.

when it was not they generally obtained devaluation. Campos Sales and Rodrigues Alves alone among the early presidents repeatedly balanced the budget, thereby removing a major source of inflation. As for Hermes, his "sound finances" program turned out to be something much less than that; each year of his term ended with a deficit.[39] To be sure, he had some successes. His administration kept the value of the milréis stable until the outbreak of the First World War. Yet however distasteful the coffee growers found the stable exchange rate, they generally applauded government policies, particularly when the treasury ministry reestablished the Conversion Fund soon after Hermes took office.

In the union's relations with Rio Grande, Borges took advantage of the President's dependence on Pinheiro to extend the authority of the state government. One notable instance was a dispute in 1913 between the state and the federal government over control of the port of Pôrto Alegre. The principal ports of the other coastal states were under federal jurisdiction, and the administration contended that the same practice should apply in Pôrto Alegre, a port of call for foreign ships. Borges dismissed this argument, insisting that the port fell under state jurisdiction because it was situated on an internal waterway (the Guaíba estuary). In March 1913 Borges appealed to Pinheiro to intercede with Hermes; two weeks later Pinheiro reported that the President had "seen the validity" of the party chief's argument.[40] In railway construction in Rio Grande, Borges also extended the state's authority. More importantly, the Gaúcho-headed transportation ministry ordered the federally controlled railroads running between Rio Grande and São Paulo to acquire refrigerated meat cars and to install frigorífico depots, to the obvious benefit of the Gaúcho ranching industry.

Borges reassumed the governorship of Rio Grande in 1913. In one sense he was no different from any governor, anywhere: he was interested in federal patronage. But he was more successful than most. He managed to secure more important posts for Riograndenses under Hermes than had been obtained in any previous administration. Rivadávia Correia began as minister of justice and later headed the treasury; José Barbosa Gonçalves, a brother of the former governor, directed the transportation ministry for three years; Borges himself had been offered the treasury post in 1910. From a political point of view, the appointment of a Gaúcho to head the federal telegraph service was useful to Borges, as was the appointment of a PRR member to the supreme court; both men regularly reported political gossip to the Governor. Moreover, the director of the telegraph service was in an excellent position to gather information, since urgent messages were usually transmitted by wire. Federal jobs in Rio Grande were meted out by Borges, who simply sent his nominations to the various offices and ministries in Rio.[41]

The PRR was not the only group expecting to benefit from the Marshal's victory in 1910. Another was the army, which quickly began to challenge Pinheiro for control of the satellite states. When Hermes won the presidency, a number of high-ranking officers decided the time was ripe to enter politics; their aim, they let it be known, was to "redeem" their native states from the entrenched political oligarchies, an avowal that soon earned them the name *salvacionistas* ("salvationists"). Within two years after Hermes took office, army officers had won the governorships in four northeastern states, in contests where the threat of military interference was a new element. The officers' rush for power in the states, initially so successful, threatened Pinheiro's position, and even the machines of the major states. One indication of the seriousness of the threat was an incident in May 1912, when a gun battle broke out between army personnel and the civil guard in Belo Horizonte, the capital of Minas Gerais. The affair might have been made the excuse for an attempt at military intervention in Minas, if Hermes had not interceded to support the state government.[42]

The danger to Rio Grande's ruling party was greater yet. Gen. Antônio Adolfo Mena Barreto, a Gaúcho by birth, became minister of war in September 1911; seeking to follow in the footsteps of other salvacionistas, Mena planned to run for governor in Rio Grande do Sul. He had been a friend of Castilhos and a PRR deputy in the state assembly in the 1890's, and had fought the Federalists in the civil war. He later broke with Castilhos and conspired against the Gaúcho establishment in the last years of the nineteenth century. In 1911 the Maragatos encouraged Mena to run against the PRR candidate. In January 1912, however, Hermes learned of his minister's plans and informed him that the government could not support a candidate against the PRR. Yes, said the President, he could remain "neutral" in the forthcoming elections in Ceará and Alagoas, but not in Rio Grande, where the opposition had campaigned for Rui Barbosa. A month later Mena had another disagreement with Hermes and resigned his post; shortly thereafter he retired from active duty. To what extent Pinheiro played a role in vetoing the candidacy of the Minister of War is uncertain, but Mena lamented a year later that the country was falling under the power of the "caudillo" Pinheiro Machado.[43]

Federal intervention was a sure way to effect a change of government in the satellite states—the only way, in fact, short of civil war. Article 6 of the constitution established a set of conditions necessary for intervention. The two most easily met were the need to reestablish order and tranquility at the request of the state government in question and the need to preserve "federal republican" institutions and guarantees. The tactic most frequently used for intervention under the first condition was the division of the state legislature into two rump bodies, both of which then claimed legitimacy and validated only the credentials of their own adherents. If the group hostile to the governor could demonstrate a numerical majority to the satisfaction of the federal government, they could obtain federal intervention. A legislative division of this sort had occurred in the rubber-exporting state of Amazonas (followed by the violent overthrow of the governor) during Nilo Peçanha's administration, with the connivance of Pinheiro Machado.[44] In that case, however, Pinheiro had been unsuccessful; Nilo had used federal authority to reinstate the deposed incumbent. During the Hermes administration rump assemblies were formed in Rio State, Bahia, Ceará, and Amazonas, with varying results. The second method of obtaining intervention—pleading the need to guarantee republican institutions—was used to oust the governors of Bahia (1912) and Ceará (1914).

The four governorships the military captured in 1911–12 were those of Ceará, Alagoas, Pernambuco, and Sergipe. In the first three cases the incumbent governor was forced out of office after a series of angry demonstrations and disorders in his state capital. Gen. Emídio Dantas Barreto, Hermes's first minister of war, began his salvacionista career as Pinheiro's ally against the long-time political boss of Pernambuco, Senator Rosa e Silva, whom Pinheiro wished to eliminate as a rival for control of the northeast. Dantas initiated the "salvations" by resigning his ministerial post in 1911 and entering the gubernatorial race. After a tempestuous election, Gov. Estácio Coimbra was forced out of power, and the state assembly recognized Dantas as governor in December 1911. Another irregular change of government occurred in Ceará, where Col. Marcos Franco Rabelo took office without the confirmation of a clear majority in the state legislature. Military interference was also the key to Gen. Clodoaldo da Fonseca's triumph in Alagoas.

In January 1912 Bahia suffered the same humiliation Amazonas had experienced in 1909—the bombardment of its capital by a military commander. Salvador, however, was no frontier boomtown but the cradle of national traditions and the capital of Brazil for most of the colonial period. Factional infighting had begun the chain of events that led to the disaster. Three rivals vied for control of the state, and in a climate of disorder the incumbent governor resigned. His successor, Aurélio Viana, moved the government away from the capital, but the opposition refused to acknowledge his authority and won a court order granting them control of the state legislature. When Viana refused to obey the court, Gen. Sotero de Menezes, the commander of the military region, ordered the local garrison to bombard the city. In the confusion that followed, Senator Seabra was able to gain control of the Bahiano government.

Even as the salvacionistas were moving into the northeast in late 1911, Pinheiro Machado was pondering a still greater feat: taking over São Paulo. He hoped to capitalize on a rift in the Paulista party between Governor Albuquerque Lins and a faction led by the minister of agriculture and a federal senator. Pinheiro soon had to abandon the idea of intervention, however, for Lins held his party together and obtained a pledge of loyalty from the state police force. With a federal army little more than triple the size of São Paulo's well-equipped state police and spread across the continent, there was clearly no question of intervening in Paulista politics.[45]

Except for Pinheiro's ineffective maneuvers in Paulista affairs, intervention in state politics during the first two years Hermes was in office was the work of the army, or of the army in league with local politicians. Pinheiro did not initiate the moves in Pernambuco, Alagoas, Ceará, Sergipe, and Bahia, though he made every attempt to improve the position of the PRC when a fluid situation arose. It was in 1913–14, the last two years of the Hermes administration, that interventionist schemes originated with the Senator, who grew more powerful as the salvacionistas' power waned. With the most politically oriented officers abandoning important posts in Rio to "conquer" state governments, salvacionista forces were spread thin and weakened. Moreover, to a certain extent the military was divided against itself, for the Bahiano crisis provoked the resignation of the war and navy ministers. Another factor was a deterioration in relations between Hermes and his son Mário, the salvacionista leader in the chamber, an estrangement that began when the Marshal remarried shortly after his first wife's death. Extensive and sometimes unethical entanglements in state politics also diminished the prestige of the salvacionistas, and probably lowered morale in the army as well. Nor did the military manage to increase its share of the federal budget during the Marshal's government.

Although Pinheiro Machado had helped put at least one military officer in a governor's mansion (Dantas Barreto), the salvacionistas began to rebel against him once they took office, since they considered the PRC part of the oligarchic system. By 1913 Dantas in Pernambuco and Clodoaldo da Fonseca in Alagoas were openly defying the PRC's authority. The rupture came when Pinheiro attempted to name Hermes's successor. Early in the year Dantas and Clodoaldo, supported by other salvacionistas, launched a revolt against the PRC that had the effect of reactivating the Minas–São Paulo alliance. Pinheiro retaliated quickly. Candidates elected to the chamber from Alagoas, Amazonas, Ceará, Pernambuco, Rio, and Paraná—the states rebelling against the national party—failed to gain recognition. The Senator had assumed the offensive. In June Governor Clodoaldo reported that his followers in Alagoas were being persecuted—at Pinheiro's instigation. Loyal federal bureaucrats were being fired, and Pinheiro's agents were routinely intercepting mail and telegrams, Clodoaldo complained. It was essential, he said, for Brazil to liberate itself "from the man who had transformed the country into a slave-compound."[46]

Pinheiro singled out Ceará to demonstrate the price of rebellion, and the crisis there illustrates the political ills that troubled the Old Republic. In that state, political maneuvering, religious exaltation, and ill-defined social protest led to a minor civil war. The political upheaval grew out of the usual local power struggle. The points at issue were the relationship of local groups to the PRC and the legality of Governor Franco Rabelo's election; the opposition revived the second question after Rabelo had already served two years. Relations between the traditional political oligarchy, led by the Acióli family, and the new urban-oriented organization of the salvacionista governor ultimately degenerated into violence. In late 1912, Rabelo's partisans attacked the homes of their enemies in Fortaleza, the state capital.

The tension subsided, and violence might not have erupted again if Governor Rabelo had not joined Dantas Barreto and Clodoaldo da Fonseca in opposing Pinheiro's bid to name the presidential candidate. The Governor had good cause to regret this decision, for Pinheiro now decided to collaborate with the Acióli faction in Ceará against him. In the interior of the state, the Acióli family had a coronel client named Floro Bartolomeu da Costa; this erstwhile Bahiano physician had become the secular leader of a movement headed by a priest suspended from orders, Cícero Romão Batista.[47] Padre Cícero was virtually worshiped by thousands of illiterate devotees throughout the northeast hinterland, and Floro had successfully harnessed the religious enthusiasms of these backlanders for political objectives. In August 1913 Floro made a visit to Rio de Janeiro and there conferred with Pinheiro and Dep. José Acióli. Several months later, on December 9, a revolt against Rabelo broke out in the city of Juàzeiro, Padre Cícero's New Jerusalem. Acióli's followers in the state legislature summarily retired to that town, where they convened a rump assembly and proclaimed Floro the new governor. In mid-January Floro's sertanejos took the offensive, sacking towns as they approached the coast; they soon invested Fortaleza. The embattled Rabelo wired the President on February 23 that the uprising was the handiwork of Pinheiro, who was punishing Ceará because the state "would not let [itself] be politically enslaved." He also asserted that the army, except for the local garrison, was abetting the revolt against the legitimate government. Further, he claimed that his supporters in the federal bureaucracy, like Clodoaldo's, were being dismissed.[48]

The foes of the PRC still held a trump card, however: the stand taken by the officers of the Fortaleza garrison. Learning that Hermes

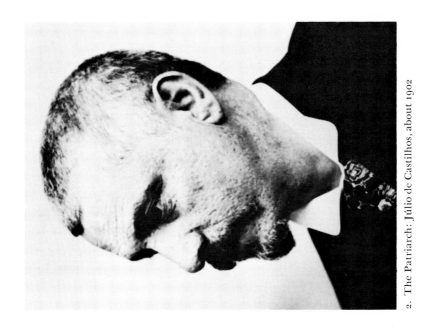

2. The Patriarch: Júlio de Castilhos, about 1902

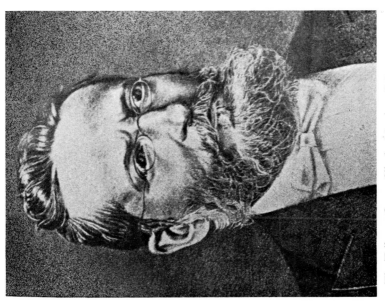

1. The Tribune: Gaspar Silveira Martins, 1878

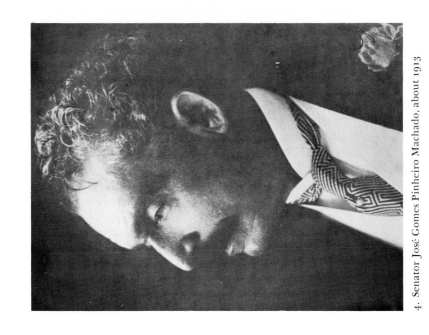

4. Senator José Gomes Pinheiro Machado, about 1913

3. Antônio Augusto Borges de Medeiros in his first year as leader of the Riograndense Republican Party (1904)

6. Getúlio Vargas as a deputy in the state assembly, 1910

5. Pinheiro Machado in dandified gaúcho attire

8. Borges in his last year as governor (1927)

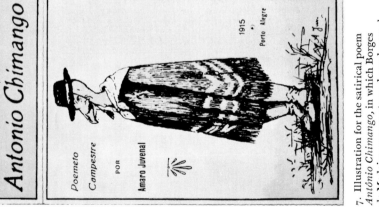

7. Illustration for the satirical poem
*Antônio Chimango*, in which Borges
de Medeiros was portrayed as a buzzard

9. Politics as a soccer match: Senator Pinheiro Machado of Rio Grande do Sul impresses the cartoonist as leading the PRC (Conservative Republican Party) to victory in the 1913 presidential succession maneuvers. Pinheiro's goal gives the nomination to Minas Gerais. Other figures are Nilo Peçanha (holding his bruised foot in foreground), Venceslau Brás (in PRC sweater behind Pinheiro's raised leg), and Hermes da Fonseca (standing in center of the reviewing stand). From *O Malho*, July 26, 1913

10. Governor Vargas and Osvaldo Aranha, 1928

12. Getúlio Vargas as presidential candidate (1929)

11. Joaquim Francisco Assis Brasil, about 1930

13. Victorious Gaúcho revolutionaries hitch their horses to the obelisk on Rio's Avenida Rio Branco, November 1, 1930

was about to intervene against Rabelo, the Governor's brother officers in Fortaleza protested to the Military Club in Rio that such action would be "incompatible with military dignity." The Military Club, the center of political activity in the army, had a strong anti-Pinheiro faction led by General Mena Barreto, the disappointed office-seeker. A violent dispute developed in the club over the Ceará question, and Mena and his group were subsequently expelled. This was not enough for Pinheiro. He argued that the conspiratorial plotting of Mena and his associates made it necessary to declare a state of siege in the Federal District—and Hermes complied.[49] The crisis was overcome, albeit somewhat messily.

Nor had Pinheiro finished with Ceará. He now contended that Franco Rabelo was incapable of preserving federal republican institutions; the President's envoy to Ceará, Col. Setembrino de Carvalho, concurred.[50] On March 14 Hermes issued an intervention decree, and Setembrino took charge. In the next election a candidate backed by the Aciólis and by another member of the PRC faithful, Tomás Cavalcanti, won with the support of Setembrino. Pinheiro had reasserted PRC hegemony in Ceará, a fact that augured ill for the other party rebels.

Dantas Barreto, who had once been an enthusiastic admirer of the Castilhista machine, saw Pernambuco as the next victim of Pinheiro's vengeance, for it had been Dantas who had initiated the resistance to Pinheiro's dictating a presidential candidate in 1913. Pernambuco and Ceará had a common frontier, and a series of border incidents following Rabelo's fall prompted Dantas to strengthen his state police organization—a wise move, as it turned out, for the federal government promised Setembrino several thousand troops to apply pressure to Dantas. Simultaneously, the Gaúcho treasury minister, Rivadávia Correia, acted to prevent ammunition from reaching Recife, Pernambuco's capital. Meanwhile, Pinheiro reversed his position on the political leadership in Pernambuco and allied himself with Rosa e Silva against Dantas. Pinheiro was not able to turn Governor Dantas out of office by force, but in 1915 he arranged for Rosa e Silva to be seated in the senate over the candidate of Dantas. According to the local count the Dantista had outpolled Rosa seven to one; the powerful Pinheiro simply had these votes disqualified as fraudulent.[51]

The last state to bear the consequences of thwarting Pinheiro was Rio de Janeiro, which had also joined the coalition against a PRC-dictated nomination. Political irregularities were no novelty in Rio State. Just one day before Gov. Alfredo Backer's term expired in 1910, he had been deposed by the faction of former president Nilo Peçanha. Earlier that year Nilo had reestablished his control of Rio politics, with Pinheiro's support, by provoking a division of the state legislature; on December 31, 1910, a *Nilista* named Francisco Oliveira Botelho had replaced the ousted governor. After Nilo's machine participated in the revolt against the PRC, Pinheiro took steps to ensure that the next governor of Rio State would be one of his own protégés. In this enterprise he secured the aid of Governor Botelho, who broke with his mentor, Nilo. Feliciano Sodré ran as the PRC candidate against Nilo himself in 1914. The state assembly split into two bodies, with what was probably the majority faction recognizing Sodré. Nilo nonetheless requested and received a judgment from the federal supreme court recognizing him as governor.

Pinheiro reacted sharply to the court's intervention. He held that the tribunal had interfered with the constitutional system by stepping into "a matter beyond its jurisdiction," ignoring the fact that the court had taken similar action before. The larger of the Rio assemblies, probably at Pinheiro's prompting, lodged a protest against the supreme court's ruling. Pinheiro put the question on the congressional agenda; he was certain that with the support of President Venceslau Brás, who had replaced Hermes in November 1914, he could install Sodré.[52] At the end of December both Sodré and Nilo were inaugurated by their respective rump legislatures. Though Pinheiro got a senate committee to deny the supreme court's jurisdiction in the Rio case, the congress as a whole never overruled the court, and Nilo ultimately consolidated his authority.

There was little Pinheiro could do to punish the parties of Minas Gerais and São Paulo for their "insubordination" to the PRC. For their part, the leaders of Minas and São Paulo were willing to tolerate Pinheiro's strong-arm tactics until the end of the Hermes administration, perhaps fearing, as Dantas suggests in his memoirs, that Pinheiro would try to maneuver Hermes into declaring an out-and-out dictatorship if his power were suddenly challenged. The outbreak of war in Europe in August 1914 might have provided an excuse. In fact, the state of siege instituted during the Military Club incident was extended until two weeks before Venceslau's inauguration. Governor Clodoaldo had remarked considerably earlier that the Marshal seemed "hypnotized" by Pinheiro;[53] the leaders of the two coffee-producing states must have had similar misgivings in the last anxious months of the Hermes administration.

Whether or not the "redemptions" of the salvacionistas brought new social and economic groups into the political process is far from clear. The commonly accepted view is that the victories of the salvacionistas simply ended in the replacement of one oligarchy by another. Still, in Ceará at least, the salvacionista experiment seems to have mobilized new urban and commercial elements to challenge the political domination of traditional landowning clans.[54] The introduction of the army into politics was again only a temporary phenomenon; but the myth of military "redemption" from a corrupt political system, which was already present in the 1880's, lived on into the 1920's, when junior officers rebelled against President Artur Bernardes and the political system he represented. To Pinheiro Machado the question of control of the northeast by old or new elites was a matter of indifference, as long as the group in power served the interests of the PRC. Dantas, Rabelo, and Clodoaldo accused Pinheiro of standing behind the traditional oligarchies; yet in Pernambuco the Gaúcho first supported Dantas Barreto against Rosa e Silva, and then turned back to Rosa. Clearly, Pinheiro's chief concern was maintaining control of a national machine, and through it, control of congress and the executive.

The years 1910–14 were a period of disillusionment for Brazilian intellectuals, and some of the best criticism and satire of the Old Republic was written in, or just after, the Hermes era.[55] One of the problems critics noted was Brazil's debility in the world market. Not only did the superior methods of East Indian rubber plantations drastically affect rubber production in the Amazon, but the outbreak of World War I produced severe (though temporary) contractions in coffee sales and foreign investments. On the domestic front, hatred of the excesses of the Hermes government—both by the bacharéis and by urban elements in general—focused on Pinheiro Machado, even though he was often not in control of the situation. After all,

Pinheiro's violations of state autonomy had the backing of Borges de Medeiros, who accepted the Senator's interpretation of federal-state issues as long as Rio Grande was not affected. The salvacionistas, too, shared responsibility with Pinheiro for the violence of the Hermes years, as did the President himself, through his willingness to be manipulated. On the other hand, Pinheiro's haughty disregard of electoral majorities in the congress made him a symbol of the distortions of republican government in Brazil.

Like other political manipulators, Pinheiro took advantage of unstable coalitions within a state machine, groupings that proved extremely fragile when gubernatorial succession produced a local crisis. But Pinheiro alone was able to shape the struggles for state control into a system of domination at the national level. Political combinations were constantly shifting in the states and therefore in congress. The governors, once in power, often turned against their benefactors, as Dantas and Clodoaldo did against Hermes and Pinheiro, and as Botelho did against Nilo. Confusion and flux were part of Pinheiro's political style, for he more than any other knew how to wait for the right opportunity; still, his own combinations were no more stable than those he exploited. Political irregularities continued after 1914, but the power of an assertive chief executive, backed by Minas and São Paulo, was to bring the political process under presidential control again. The split between Mineiros and Paulistas, the political activation of the army, the death of a hostile president in office, and the pliability of the feckless Marshal were temporary circumstances that Pinheiro turned to his advantage. Nevertheless, the PRC would remain a threat to President Venceslau as long as Pinheiro was able to control entry into congress.

# CHAPTER SEVEN

# Resurgence of the Coffee Alliance

THAT Pinheiro Machado's influence in national politics was on the wane became evident soon after Venceslau Brás succeeded Hermes as president. But the Senator, anxious to retain the appearance of power if not the substance, wanted at all costs to avoid an open break with the new president in order to avert a repetition of the Prudente–PRF conflict of 1897. This would be no easy task, for the PRC was badly split: the salvacionistas had risen against it, and the Paulistas had remained aloof from the beginning. The key to the PRC's survival as the dominant political aggregation was the attitude of the Mineiro leaders.

Pinheiro's first major defeat was his inability to control the process of presidential nomination. The political elite had begun discussing the question of succession more than a year in advance of the election. On February 28, 1913, Pinheiro had asked Governor Dantas Barreto if the PRC could count on Pernambuco's support in selecting the next president, and it had been his reply (insisting on a "national convention" rather than a PRC choice) that set off the rebellion against Pinheiro Machado and his party. Gov. Clodoaldo da Fonseca of Alagoas soon followed suit, asserting in early March that domination by Pinheiro's organization must end. The PRC, he complained, offered candidates not victory at the polls but recognition in congress. Another member of the salvacionista group, Marshal Mena Barreto, would soon attempt to put together a coalition of northern states to oppose the PRC.[1] In the view of the salvacionistas, reform at the national level could be achieved only by overthrowing Pinheiro's caucus party. Yet the military rebels were too weak to impose a president without support from other political forces; inevitably the northern coalition had to work within Pinheiro's party or else adhere to the choice of Minas and São Paulo.

Would Pinheiro himself run? In Rio Grande do Sul Borges de Medeiros was attempting to drum up support for the Senator's candidacy. Pinheiro was the obvious choice of the PRC establishment, and Hermes favored him.[2] But the PRC was in trouble: even if it could contain or neutralize the salvacionista rebellion, it would have to expect independent action on the part of the PRM and the PRP. As early as January, Hermes had sent a messenger to the governor of Minas, Júlio Bueno Brandão, inquiring whether the Mineiro party would support a slate of Pinheiro for president and Brandão for vice president. The PRM would not. Brandão stated his preference for Campos Sales as the standard-bearer and within a few months initiated a movement to stop Pinheiro. Aware of the likelihood of an attempt to intervene in his state if Pinheiro were chosen, Brandão told his friends he would prefer to "fall *with* Minas rather than *in* Minas."[3]

In mid-April 1913 Brandão met with a spokesman for Rodrigues Alves, once again governor of São Paulo. It was agreed that the Mineiros and the Paulistas would consult each other before committing themselves on the succession. With the force of this agreement to back him up, Brandão convoked the PRM executive committee on May 4, which unanimously vetoed the candidacy of Pinheiro, just as Pinheiro had earlier vetoed the candidacy of Sen. Francisco Sales of Minas. Pinheiro did not take this as a serious setback, however; he was more interested in keeping the PRC the dominant force in national politics than in becoming president. Given the support of Marshal Hermes, Pinheiro did not doubt that he could win the presidency; but he was willing to forgo the office "to avoid tremendous unrest in the country."[4]

Pinheiro chose instead to suggest candidates that would divide his opponents. He first threw his weight behind his friend Campos Sales just as the former president was running into trouble in the PRM. The Campos Sales ploy was an attempt to attract São Paulo and upset the Coligação (Coalition), as the opponents of the PRC were now known. By May this group included Minas, São Paulo, Pernambuco,

Rio State, Bahia, Alagoas, and Ceará. In Minas the Campos Sales candidacy foundered on the question of a choice for vice president that would demonstrate the Coligação's independence of the PRC. The salvacionistas fought the nomination because they considered Campos Sales too closely connected with Pinheiro. He finally withdrew on July 18, and died two weeks later. Meanwhile, Rodrigues Alves surfaced as a possible compromise candidate; but the boomlet for him also failed, as did a Bahiano effort on behalf of Rui. By July the Mineiros were backing the incumbent vice president, Venceslau Brás, a PRM leader from southern Minas, for the presidency.

Pinheiro had earlier considered, and rejected, Venceslau. By July 7 the Gaúcho had resolved to find a "frankly partisan" candidate for the PRC. When the PRM leaders proposed Venceslau to him two days later, he countered with the name of Borges de Medeiros. The Mineiros vaguely professed interest. However, Pinheiro soon had to report that Borges refused to be considered; furthermore, said Pinheiro, the PRC would accept Venceslau as its candidate.[5] Clearly, by this time the Senator felt that playing this game would give him his only chance to have a major voice in president-making. On July 12 Governor Rodrigues Alves committed the Paulista party to Venceslau, but as the candidate of Minas not of the PRC. That settled the matter. After the salvacionistas had defied Pinheiro and split the PRC, it was almost inevitable that presidential succession would again depend on a *café-com-leite* entente.

Although the PRC had only adhered to a candidate, not selected one, as Rui later pointed out,[6] Pinheiro attempted to salvage what he could and to give the impression that he and his party had chosen Venceslau. He managed to get Venceslau to agree to have Sen. Urbano Santos of Maranhão, one of Pinheiro's minions in the PRC, as a running mate. Pinheiro was also allowed to preside over the convention that nominated Venceslau, a face-saving device that Pinheiro reported to Borges as a personal victory. Emphasizing in the same report that the new vice president was a loyal PRC member, Pinheiro then lauded Venceslau, a man he had previously termed unacceptable. The Venceslau-Santos ticket, he concluded, had broken up the Coligação.[7] Borges accepted Pinheiro's interpretation of Venceslau's triumph, and in July 1913 *A Federação* endorsed the Mineiro as a conciliation nominee.

The political concessions Pinheiro extracted from Venceslau for the coming administration mostly had to do with Gaúcho participation in the government. A Riograndense would get the ministry of justice, and Rivadávia Correia, the treasury minister in the Hermes cabinet, would become prefect of the Federal District. The future president was officially connected with the PRC, and his nomination held the organization together. He was no creature of the PRC, however. He insisted on writing a platform without Pinheiro's assistance; and between his election in March 1914 and his inauguration in November, he remained at his fazenda in the interior of Minas, thus isolating himself from contact with Pinheiro and deemphasizing his relationship with the PRC.

The Mineiro party gave the new president the backing he needed to free himself from Pinheiro's influence. Fonseca Hermes of Rio Grande, the Marshal's brother, lost his post as majority leader in the chamber of deputies to a Mineiro, Antônio Carlos de Andrada; Minas also retained the presidency of the chamber. Pinheiro acquiesced in the Gaúcho defeat in the lower house, appreciating that a test of strength on the majority leader issue could lead to a rupture between Venceslau and the PRC. The Senator preferred to maintain the semblance of harmony and probably still had hopes of bringing Antônio Carlos under his sway. He also accepted revisions of the "positivist" educational reforms that Rivadávia Correia had instituted under Hermes.

The question of succession in Rio State, discussed in Chapter 6, was a burning issue in Venceslau's early months in office, and he handled the matter with consummate skill. Borges and Pinheiro had denounced the supreme court ruling recognizing Nilo Peçanha over Feliciano Sodré. When both claimants were simultaneously inaugurated in December 1914, Venceslau sent troops to Niterói, the capital, to back Nilo. At the same time he deplored the supreme court's "interference" in state politics. Venceslau thus at once publicly declared himself opposed to the court's action and acknowledged his obligation as chief executive to uphold the judiciary's ruling. Pinheiro brought the issue before congress, and at the beginning of January 1915 was satisfied—or pretended to be satisfied—with Venceslau's stance. But only one week later he was reporting to Borges that he had narrowly averted a split between the President and the PRC.

Still, he was optimistic: despite Venceslau's "contradictory deliberations," Pinheiro believed the President would eventually accept the
PRC position on the Rio question.[8] Pinheiro next pushed a bill
through the senate that effectively turned Rio State over to Sodré,
but it was blocked in the Mineiro-controlled chamber. Meanwhile,
Nilo was running the state with the support of the federal executive.
Although the question dragged on as a legal issue during the ensuing
months, Nilo's *de facto* authority ended in a *de jure* victory. In October 1915 he acquired a majority in the state assembly, and the rival
body was dissolved. In the State of Rio de Janeiro, the revolt against
the PRC had been successful—thanks to Catete and the Mineiros in
congress.

Pinheiro's empire was crumbling, but in January 1915 he was still
powerful enough to pick a PRC politician for a seat in the senate
from the State of Espírito Santo. He was also able to punish the Dantas faction in Pernambuco, as described earlier, by seating Rosa e
Silva in the senate against the rival claimant, José Bezerra. This was
a hollow victory, as it turned out, for in July Venceslau made Bezerra
his minister of agriculture.[9]

While the PRC suffered setback after setback, the PRR remained
firmly in power in Rio Grande. And though there were threats to
Borges's authority in the Venceslau years, they were minor compared
with the challenges to Pinheiro's authority in the arena of national
politics. In fact, the PRR boss's rule was brought into question on
only two occasions. The first was in May 1915, when the Governor
was stricken by an illness that compelled him to retire to a fazenda
near the state capital; he did not return to Pôrto Alegre until the
following year. In his absence, party affairs were handled by a trusted
aide, Protásio Alves.[10] Meanwhile, however, Lt. Gov. Salvador Pinheiro Machado directed the state government, and his brother, the
Senator, had full control of the Riograndense delegation in congress.[11] Pinheiro invited the ailing Borges to come to Rio for a rest,
but the invitation was declined; as on previous occasions, the PRR
leader refused to leave the state. It is possible that Pinheiro was
thinking of ousting Borges, or at least of taking over the Riograndense party if the PRR chief should die. In fact, a PRR coronel
later alleged that the Senator's brother had wanted to overthrow
Borges during his protracted illness, and that the plot had failed

only because the Military Brigade remained loyal to the party chief.[12] In any case, Borges never gave another congressman the authority in the Riograndense delegation that Pinheiro had enjoyed. The only other challenge to Borges in the Venceslau years was a near-successful attempt on his life in 1917. Except for the congressional seats allotted to the Federalists, the PRR continued its monopoly on political posts; and Borges was returned as governor in 1917 in a one-man race.

The only election that aroused much interest within the state between the presidential elections of 1910 and 1922 was a contest for a senatorial post in August 1915. Pinheiro recommended Hermes to Borges for a vacant slot in June, and Borges agreed. But the incompetence of the former President had not been forgotten, even in his native state. In July 1915, shortly after Pinheiro's brother had taken over the state government, anti-Hermistas staged a rally in Pôrto Alegre. Shouting "Death to Hermes," demonstrators inflamed the crowd; the assembly rapidly became a mob, and state police fired on the group. Seven persons were killed and two dozen were wounded. A few days later Ramiro Barcelos, a former senator from Rio Grande and a member of the federal constituent assembly of 1890–91, decided to oppose Hermes in the August election. Barcelos broke with Borges to run against Hermes, "the man who dragged the country into bankruptcy and political ruin."[13] As a follower of Castilhos, Barcelos criticized the heterogeneous PRC, charging that it was no more than a vehicle for Pinheiro Machado's ambition. Meanwhile Pinheiro made use of his connections with Percival Farquhar, the American master of a far-flung economic empire in Brazil, to uncover evidence that Barcelos had engaged in unethical financial dealings as a public official,[14] and the news was widely publicized in *A Federação*. In any event, the victory of the former president was a foregone conclusion, for the Party coronéis stood by Borges. In one município the results were 1,300 to 0 for Hermes. The statewide returns showed 61,329 for Hermes da Fonseca and 3,519 for Ramiro Barcelos.

The significance of the contest lies in the subsequent action of the losing candidate. At the end of 1915, Barcelos wrote a satirical epic poem, *Antônio Chimango*, directed at Borges and his machine. The work was loosely modeled on José Hernández's *Martín Fierro*, and like the Argentine epic, it purported to be a story of life on the range told in cowboy dialect. Its protagonist is a ranch foreman whose sole concern is dominating his peons. The chimango, a scrawny scavenger bird of southern Brazil, represents the slight and long-necked Borges de Medeiros—"gaunt as a werewolf and nasty as the devil"[15]— the ranch and its peons, Rio Grande do Sul and its citizens. The state police tried to suppress the work, but nonetheless it gained wide circulation clandestinely. "Chimango" and "chimangada" (his stooges) rapidly entered the political vocabulary, and the epithets became war cries when the opposition revolted in 1923.

If Borges successfully weathered the Venceslau years, Pinheiro did not. The President had not only Mineiro and Paulista support in his maneuvers against the PRC, but also the enthusiastic approval of the populace in the federal capital. The general hostility toward Pinheiro has already been noted: urban groups hated him, and some sectors of the political elite viewed him as a barbarian from a state only tenuously Brazilian. One of his greatest sins, as a contemporary pointed out, was his trampling on Brazil's "bacharelesque" traditions.[16] Always careful to accord respect to real power, Pinheiro nevertheless had a tendency to treat many of his colleagues with a familiarity usually reserved for persons of inferior station. Whether his peers were more dedicated than he to democratic practices is doubtful, but at least they observed the niceties of oligarchic democracy with greater consistency.

Yellow journalism fanned the flames of hatred against him, with the tacit approval of many members of the political elite. During the gubernatorial crisis in Rio State, the Carioca daily *A Rua* proclaimed: "The Vice President of the senate knows he has given the people more than enough reason to hate him, and that the people . . . could be pushed to the point of demanding that he be brought to account for his conduct."[17] In a bitter jest, Deputy José Gonçalves Maia of Pernambuco told another Rio newspaper, *A Noite*, that he was going to present a bill in congress reading: "Article 1, Pinheiro Machado is to be eliminated; Article 2, All provisions to the contrary are revoked."[18] Disorders frequently accompanied Pinheiro's arrivals and departures at the senate. Agitation against him increased in July after the anti-Hermista riot and massacre in Pôrto Alegre. Pinheiro knew he was a likely candidate for assassination, and had even prepared a political testament.

On the afternoon of September 8, 1915, he left the senate to meet Albuquerque Lins, the former governor of São Paulo, at the fashionable Hotel dos Estrangeiros, scene of the 1905 banquet. Two Paulista deputies met Pinheiro in the lobby, and the three men exchanged pleasantries while waiting for Lins to appear. Suddenly a man with a dagger approached Pinheiro from behind and thrust the blade into the Senator's back. Pinheiro turned, shouting *"Canalha!"* (you filthy dog!), and took several steps toward the fleeing assailant. The blood drained from his face; he stopped; and before his stunned companions could get him to a couch, he died. According to one account, there was widespread jubilation in Rio when the news broke. Leading politicians "mentally embraced" the murderer, and merry crowds swarmed into the Avenida Rio Branco "as at Carnival time."[19]

Pinheiro's assassin, captured a few blocks from the hotel, was identified as Manso de Paiva Coimbra, an unemployed and semiliterate baker from Rio Grande do Sul. In captivity he showed no remorse. "Tyrants have to be done away with," he said, "[and] I got the real boss." When asked whether he had intended to assassinate other political leaders as well, the prisoner answered "no," volunteering: "I wouldn't kill Marshal Hermes just as I wouldn't kill any other zero."[20] Few political leaders believed that Paiva had acted alone. He had carried a note that was meant to justify his action in the event he was killed; the language of the note, which emphasized the suffering of the Brazilian people under Pinheiro, seemed to be that of a better educated man than Paiva. Responsibility for the crime was laid at the door of a number of men; the Senator had had many enemies. Borges, the Riograndense congressmen, and Hermes had no doubts, at least at first, that Paiva was carrying out orders.

When the assassin was brought to trial, Gaúcho deputy Flôres da Cunha led the prosecution. Although the trial revealed inconsistencies in the defendant's account of the events of September 8, he stuck to his story that he had acted alone. Borges and his congressmen believed that political considerations were preventing a thorough investigation of the murder, despite Venceslau's assurances that every effort would be made to discover additional conspirators. Deputy Ildefonso Pinto thought Venceslau was moving slowly because he feared disorders and a consequent attempt at a military coup.[21] Still, the Gaúchos did not remain wholly committed to the conspiratorial theory of the assassination. *A Federação* charged the press in the capital with partial responsibility for the crime because of the incendiary attacks on Pinheiro in *A Rua* and other papers. The PRR organ also censured the President for allowing irresponsible journalism to flourish in Rio. Thus, to the extent that the Gaúchos blamed the popular press, they implicitly denied a conspiracy. In his long years in prison, Manso de Paiva never implicated other parties.

In October Pinheiro Machado's widow disclosed his political testament, written in March 1914. In it he declared that his political ideal "was and is the establishment of the Federal Republic in our fatherland." In the realm of doctrine, he wrote, "I made no concessions to the ambitions that surrounded me. I remained faithful to the convictions that seemed to me necessary to ensure the purity of the form of government we adopted." His last instructions were clear: preserve that purity; the system must not undergo changes that would pervert it.[22] Behind the rhetoric lies Pinheiro's view of his role in Brazilian history—that of a guardian of the Republic. In principle and in a literal sense, he had fought parliamentarians and monarchists to preserve the purity of the republican system as he saw it: a presidential form of government with broad powers for the states. But he had no quarrel with a system that allowed meaningful autonomy for only three states, and that gave him the opportunity to establish an extraofficial hegemony over the weaker members of the federation. His system depended on an executive branch too weak to control the three major states; otherwise, the phenomenon of Pinheiro Machado could not have occurred, nor could the machine of Borges de Medeiros. For this reason Pinheiro was always suspicious of the revisionism of Rui Barbosa and his followers.

Foremost in the ranks of the defenders of the Republic, Pinheiro Machado violated both the letter and the spirit of its institutions. More to the point, he was less delicate about it than his colleagues from Minas and São Paulo, who could generally count on the executive for heavy-handed discipline. Pinheiro had both great personal authority and political acumen, a combination of qualities that allowed him to exploit a weakness in congressional procedure; and once he could control the process of recognition, he was partially successful in molding a political apparatus he could manipulate in the selection of presidential and gubernatorial candidates. When outmaneuvered, he knew how to retreat with the appearance of triumph. He had had good connections with the army, at least until the wave of salvacionista revolts. His reputation as a fearless soldier in the Paraguayan War and in the campaign against the Federalists contributed to his prestige. His personal power was immense, if widely resented. Yet his political style excluded appeals for popular support; his milieu was the governing oligarchy in a politically unmobilized society.

The PRC continued to exist for a time after Pinheiro's assassination, but the locus of power unmistakably gravitated toward Catete. In October 1915 Sen. Vitorino Monteiro of Rio Grande warned Borges that President Venceslau was seeking to turn the party to his own ends; at the time the organization still had more than two-thirds of the votes in the senate. Vice President Urbano Santos, a Pinheiro protégé, put it more bluntly: "There is no longer a [national] party. The party is the President of the Republic."[23]

Perceptive politicians in the satellite states quickly took advantage of the shift in the national power structure. In Amazonas the PRC suffered a reverse in Venceslau's first year in office. One of two rump legislatures there had been suppressed since 1912, when the incumbent governor was unseated by Jonatás Pedrosa, one of the state's representatives in the national PRC. In a gubernatorial election held shortly after Pinheiro's death, the opposition assembly reappeared and recognized its own claimant. Rival governments continued into the 1920's, by which time Amazonas was in a state of administrative and financial chaos. Better than any other, this case illustrates the failure of federalism in the Old Republic. In 1915, however, the duality of governors and assemblies redounded to the benefit of the President, since it ended the PRC's monopoly of power in the northwest.

In 1916 Venceslau demonstrated his strength in Piauí, located in the northeastern hump. In January Borges received a plea from a Piauiense congressman for backing against federal interference in the forthcoming gubernatorial election. Since the incumbent governor, Miguel Rosa, had been a faithful follower of Pinheiro, Borges ordered the Riograndense congressional delegation to oppose presidential interference in Piauí. Rosa's faction elected a new governor in April; but in what was by this time classic fashion, a majority in the assembly recognized another candidate and organized a second legislature. In June Rosa appealed to Borges for support, alleging that the federal government was supporting the opposition, led by Félix Pacheco and Marshal Pires Ferreira. Moreover, he said, an upheaval was imminent, since his adversaries were using federal funds to arm 600 capangas for a march on the state capital.[24] The civil war in Ceará two years earlier seemed about to be repeated in Piauí. Fortunately, it was not; the supreme court's resolution of the same problem in Rio State without violence led both claimants in Piauí to file briefs requesting recognition. The court upheld the appeal of the Pires-Pacheco candidate, Eurípides Aguiar. The federal government's military support of Aguiar before and after the court's ruling further undermined the independence of the PRC. Moreover, although both Pires Ferreira and Pacheco had previously represented Piauí in the PRC executive, they had seized the opportunity to realign with Catete against Governor Rosa. The Riograndenses could do little more than protest. Even the method of settlement was a defeat for Borges, the same kind of defeat the Gaúchos had experienced when they had tried to stop the court's "interference" in Rio State a year earlier.

Rio Grande's reaction to the reassertion of the presidential prerogative and to the destruction of the PRC was primarily one of withdrawal from political commitments. Nine days after Pinheiro's assassination, Borges fell back on Castilhos' dictum of isolation and independence. In issuing instructions to the PRC congressmen, Borges declared: "It is not proper for us either to give unconditional support or to offer systematic opposition [to the President]." As for the PRC, the Gaúchos would remain faithful to the party as long as its policies were "consistent with the autonomy of the Riograndense party."[25] This had a familiar ring: in 1910 Borges had told Pinheiro that the PRR would participate in the PRC only if the programs of the two parties were consistent and Pinheiro led the national party. With Pinheiro no longer at the helm to guarantee the autonomy of the state party in the national organization, Borges virtually abandoned the PRC, and this fact undoubtedly strengthened presidential authority.

Rio Grande's disengagement from national politics was reflected in the PRR's diminishing interest in improving its image in the federal capital. One Gaúcho senator complained in 1917 that his state got no favorable press coverage in Rio de Janeiro, whereas São Paulo controlled *Correio da Manhã*, Minas *O Paiz*, Rio State and Pernambuco *A Razão*, and the ministry of the treasury[!] the *Jornal do Commercio*.[26]

The collapse of the PRC presented an opportunity for the redefinition of political allegiances. One of the first politicians to make a move was Sen. Antônio Azeredo of Mato Grosso, who contacted Borges about a new alliance 11 days after Pinheiro's assassination in September 1915. Azeredo, Pinheiro's replacement as vice president of the senate and a client of the Paulistas, sought to interest the Riograndense chief in an association with the PRP. A Gaúcho congressman made the same suggestion. In the following months Azeredo renewed his appeals on São Paulo's behalf, and Governor Rodrigues Alves expressed interest in a Riograndense-Paulista alliance in March 1916.[27]

But nothing came of the efforts to draw the PRR out of its self-imposed seclusion. Like Castilhos, Borges considered isolation the best guarantee of state autonomy in periods when the Gaúcho party had little influence over the president. Even so, Rio Grande was a power in the federation and could not altogether avoid entanglements in the politics of the dependent states. In the last two years of Venceslau's administration (1916–1918), Borges was asked to give his support to the recognition of congressmen or governors in Espírito Santo, Mato Grosso, Piauí, Alagoas, and Rio State. In each case, whether by action or by inaction, Rio Grande necessarily had an impact on the politics of these states. Moreover, Rio Grande's previous stand in the cases of Rio State and Piauí showed that the Borges interpretation of autonomy included occasional opposition to the president, though in neither case did the Gaúcho-backed candidate win.[28]

Secure as it was, the PRR had a few problems of its own. One was an embarrassing move by Hermes da Fonseca. Following Pinheiro's death, rumors were aired in the Carioca press that Borges considered Senator-elect Hermes useless without Pinheiro and was insisting on his resignation. A Riograndense deputy reported to the party chief that Hermes believed the stories and was contemplating resigning before taking office. When Borges learned of the Marshal's intentions, he labeled them "impolitic, unjustifiable, and self-defeating," but he could not deter Hermes. The old soldier told Borges in his letter of resignation that he had run for the presidency only because Pinheiro had wished him to, and had subsequently entered the senatorial race at Pinheiro's insistence. "With his death," wrote Hermes, "my political career also comes to an end."[29] To the consternation of Borges, the former president withdrew from public life and remained aloof from politics until 1922.

The PRR's retreat in national politics did not mean the Gaúchos would cease to expect economic favors from the federal government. Europe was at war, and Rio Grande like other states stood to profit by the huge import requirements of the Allies. Brazil began to export frozen and chilled beef during World War I, though it was not Rio Grande, as one might expect, but São Paulo and Rio State that first entered the market, in part because of Rio Grande's poorer port facilities. The government of Rio Grande do Sul sought to aid in the modernization of beef processing, relying on federal help primarily to protect the long-established charque industry.

In 1915 Borges offered a series of tax advantages to foreign frigorífico companies. The main attraction was a 30-year exemption from state taxes for the firms, an exemption that applied as well to animals slaughtered and to canned and refrigerated meat sent out of state. These concessions produced no immediate results, however, and in 1916 further tax exemptions were decreed.[30] This time government action was successful. Both Armour and Swift set up plants at the end of the war, and they continued to operate after frigoríficos in other parts of Brazil succumbed to competition from the Plate.

With the assistance of Venceslau, the Riograndense delegation in congress was able to defeat a proposal to restore an old ad valorem tariff of 8 per cent on equipment and machinery imported by frigoríficos for their operations. In addition, Borges successfully pressured the Farquhar-controlled Compagnie du Port de Rio Grande to provide facilities to Swift and Armour for their projected frigorífico depots at the port. Simultaneously the Governor promoted a Gaúcho-owned frigorífico, sponsored by the state cattlebreeders' association. He called on his congressional delegation to secure a suitable tract of land from the federal government at the bar of Rio Grande, and Venceslau granted the concession at the end of 1916. In raising capital for the domestically owned frigorífico, Borges appealed to local PRR leaders to solicit funds from the ranchers in their municípios.[31] The Companhia Frigorífica de Pelotas was chartered in 1917 and began production two years later.

On behalf of the charque industry, Senator Monteiro obtained a federal tax exemption for the salt used in charqueadas. Venceslau got the Gaúcho congressional delegation to vote for his sales tax bill in 1916 on the proviso that charque would specifically be exempted from the levy. Furthermore, the ministry of agriculture agreed to subsidize livestock shipments on federally controlled railroads and coastal freighters.[32] Rio Grande's close cooperation with the Mineiro president on issues affecting cattle seems to have been a factor in Borges's lack of interest in an alliance with São Paulo.

The Paulistas opposed the administration's bills on sales and income taxes, which Gov. Altino Arantes believed would unduly burden his state.[33] Nevertheless, the sales tax was enacted in 1916, and this was followed two years later by an income tax. The blow to the Paulistas was somewhat softened, however, by a federal loan in 1917 of 110,000 contos (then equal to U.S. $27.5 million) to the State of São Paulo for coffee valorization. Borges and his party accepted the sales tax, not only because charque was exempted but also because the Gaúchos feared rapid inflation (and a decrease in charque consumption) if the government were forced to issue unduly large amounts of paper currency. But Borges preferred the income tax to the sales tax,[34] presumably because Rio Grande (unlike São Paulo and Minas) was primarily dependent on its sales in Brazil.

Congress had to deal with social as well as economic issues. Brazil became involved in the affairs of Europe with a declaration of war on the Central Powers in October 1917. By the end of the war Brazilian political leaders were worried that the native proletariat might try to follow the example of revolutionary workers' organizations in Europe. In November 1918 the Paulista delegation put a bill before congress regulating labor, but the Riograndenses, with the support of other delegations and the fledgling national Federation of Labor Unions (Federação dos Sindicatos), forced the Paulistas to withdraw the measure.[35] It was Borges who dictated the Gaúcho position. In July 1918 he had sent a long set of instructions to his delegation, outlining his objections to the labor bill before congress. The influence of Auguste Comte, whose works the party chief had carefully restudied during his illness in 1915–16, was unmistakable. Borges saw a national labor code as an infringement on states' rights, though with true Comtian paternalism he favored the enactment of workers' compensation measures. Citations from the works of Comte and his Brazilian disciples, Miguel Lemos and Teixeira Mendes, were sprinkled through the message.[36]

In December the Gaúchos again opposed the Paulistas, and again successfully. The issue was workers' compensation, with the Gaúchos demanding that employers pay compensation for all accidents, and the Paulistas attempting to have employers absolved of all financial responsibility in mishaps caused by the workmen.[37] In the bill signed into law on January 15, 1919, the Gaúcho-backed position prevailed: Brazil's first workers' compensation law—timid enough—required employers to pay three years' wages for total disablement, whatever the cause of the accident.

Borges had demonstrated his own approach to the labor problem in August 1917. In July the state Workers' Association (Federação Operária) had declared a general strike in Pôrto Alegre to obtain higher wages. Believing the workers' demands justified and seeking to avoid violence, Borges responded with an increase in wages for state employees (including railway and port workers) ranging from 5 to 25 per cent, and temporarily prohibited the shipment of foodstuffs out of state in order to meet local shortages. He also instructed the state police and the intendant of the capital to "intercede with" local employers, many of whom thereupon raised wages. Though such interference in the private sector of the economy was born in a wartime atmosphere, it was unprecedented in Brazilian history.*

On the whole, war brought little economic disruption to Rio Grande. There were a few flare-ups, notably when Brazil broke diplomatic relations with Germany over the sinking of the freighter

---

* Ivan Lins argues that positivist labor paternalism was a recognized precedent for the legislation that Getúlio Vargas, the protégé of Borges, extended to the whole nation after 1930. When it comes to specifics, though, the argument is far from convincing. The central feature of Vargas's post-1930 labor system was governmental arbitration to prevent strikes and lockouts. Yet in 1918 Borges (citing Teixeira Mendes) explicitly rejected the notion that a labor court was a better means of settling disputes than direct negotiations between workers and management. See Lins, *História do positivismo no Brasil* (São Paulo, 1964), pp. 190, 201; and Borges to Abreu, July 24, 1918, Archive of Borges de Medeiros.

*Paraná* in April 1917. Riots broke out in Pôrto Alegre; and mobs sacked and burned German-Brazilian firms and the Sociedade Germânia without any real effort on the part of police and state troops to contain the violence. However, there were few subsequent incidents, and Borges was reluctant to adopt the kind of nationalistic measures in force elsewhere in Brazil—e.g. requiring that all schools teach in Portuguese—presumably because he did not want to offend the German-speaking population.*

Brazil was at war when the 1918 presidential succession was settled, and the question brought fewer problems than in 1910 or 1914. Francisco Rodrigues Alves of São Paulo became the first second-term president. His unanimous nomination, which was tantamount to election, was the result of the smooth functioning of the Mineiro-Paulista entente. But the question of who would rule Brazil for the next four years was not to be settled so easily, for the health of the new president and that of his vice president were soon to collapse, producing a crisis in the Republic. The election of two dying men was symptomatic of the failure of the Historical Republicans to transfer power to a younger generation, and the Riograndense party shared responsibility for the political crisis by acquiescing in the Alves nomination.

The selection of one of the last elder statesmen of São Paulo was as quiet as any succession in the Old Republic. As early as August 1916, Borges learned from a cabinet member that São Paulo and Minas were setting up a slate of Rodrigues Alves and Delfim Moreira, the governors of the two states. The Riograndense congressional delegation and Carlos Maximiliano Pereira dos Santos, the Gaúcho minister of justice, reported other possible combinations in the ensuing months; the drift of these speculations was that Minas might drop Rodrigues Alves and try to put Moreira or another Mineiro in the presidency. However, differences between President Venceslau and Francisco Sales, leader of the strongest faction in the PRM, kept Minas divided. Three weaker states—Pernambuco, Bahia, and Rio de Janeiro—unsuccessfully attempted to block all Paulista candidates. In March 1917 Senator Soares dos Santos of Rio

* In November 1917 President Venceslau expressed his displeasure at the fact that Borges was the only governor who had failed to respond to the President's messages on the war, and who did not require that all classes be conducted in Portuguese in his state. (Pereira dos Santos to Borges, November 16, 1917, Archive of Borges de Medeiros.)

Grande believed that Venceslau would back any nominee selected by the Paulista party and approved by the governor of Minas. Another Gaúcho senator, Vitorino Monteiro, reported at the same time that Francisco Sales had arranged a Rodrigues Alves–Delfim Moreira ticket. Unfortunately, wrote Monteiro, Moreira was stupid and "totally incompetent." Moreover, the Mineiros knew Alves's health was poor, and believed Minas could dominate his second administration. The Alves-Moreira slate did not "correspond to the gravity of the moment," Monteiro warned Borges.[38] In mid-April 1917 the candidates were "officially consecrated," as one Gaúcho deputy put it.[39] Rio Grande was one of the last states to define its position when Borges finally instructed Santos to relay Gaúcho endorsement of the "official" slate. As late as May Rui Barbosa was still running hard, but without any real chance; and by the time of the election, in March 1918, Rodrigues Alves and Moreira were unopposed.

In forming his cabinet, Alves asked Borges to let a member of the Riograndense government, Ildefonso Pinto, serve as minister of agriculture; but the PRR chief refused. Borges had previously sought one of the three major posts (justice, transportation, or the treasury). After this effort failed, he showed no interest in securing a cabinet post for Rio Grande. He informed Rodrigues Alves that the PRR did not require a ministerial slot to support the new government.[40]

In any case the President-elect was dying. In October 1918 Carlos Maximiliano, who had earlier advised Borges of Rodrigues Alves's poor health, reported that Minas and São Paulo were preparing for the succession of both Alves and Moreira, who was apparently suffering from tertiary syphilis. On the day of his inauguration, Rodrigues Alves was already planning to resign. The ailing President promptly turned over his duties to Moreira, who demonstrated little ability to govern. At the end of 1918 one of the Gaúcho senators lamented that the nation had no leader; each minister did as he pleased, and social unrest was rising in the capital.[41] Unemployment, the outbreak of Spanish influenza, and the appearance of radical workers' organizations—all caused alarm in the ranks of the Brazilian political elite.

After the murder of Pinheiro Machado in 1915, Mineiro-Paulista control of the presidency was to continue uninterrupted until the end of the Old Republic, except for the *sui generis* succession of 1919.

No one would duplicate Pinheiro's feat of holding together a national establishment party that did not revolve around the president. In point of fact, however, the PRC was already in decline before his assassination; Venceslau Brás hastened its end, seeking to eliminate all threats to presidential power during his remaining years in office. The destruction was complete by 1918: the PRC played no role in the nomination of Rodrigues Alves or in subsequent contests.

After Pinheiro's death, Borges de Medeiros immediately disengaged his state from attempts to wrest control of the presidency from the two more powerful state parties. He did not follow up hints that São Paulo was interested in a new bi-state alliance, probably in the hope of securing economic benefits for Rio Grande from Venceslau's government. In 1918 the Mineiro-Paulista system seemed to function even more smoothly than it had four years earlier. Yet by entrusting the leadership of the nation to two sick men, the parties of São Paulo and Minas Gerais jeopardized their control of presidential succession.

# CHAPTER EIGHT

# Two Elections: Concert and Discord

THE YEAR 1919 opened with a political crisis. President
Rodrigues Alves was dying, and Vice President Moreira was inca-
pacitated. The two, a Paulista and a Mineiro, had been chosen by
the political leaders of their own states—men who could not possibly
have been unaware of their candidates' ill health. Alves died on
January 16. Faced with the necessity of arranging a special election
(as required by the constitution when an incumbent died during his
first two years of office) and recalling how the campaign of 1910 had
strained relations within the political elite and between the elite and
the army, the establishment parties were united on one point: they
wanted to obtain a successor without a contested election.[1] The parties of Minas and São Paulo might still have imposed a candidate,
had they been able to agree on a nominee. But each wished to name
its own governor to the remaining three-and-a-half years of the 1918–
22 term. It thus fell to the state parties, acting through their agents
in congress, to settle the issue. The candidate that emerged from
their consultations would then be proclaimed the choice of the nation at a national convention (mainly composed of congressmen).

The first candidacy to arise was that of Altino Arantes, governor
of São Paulo. PRP leaders began to circulate his name in mid-January, but they soon ran into stiff opposition from Minas. The Paulistas
wanted their full four-year term, whereas the Mineiros reasoned that
São Paulo had had its "turn" with Rodrigues Alves. When Borges
de Medeiros learned that Minas and São Paulo were promoting their
own candidates, he saw a rare opportunity to make his influence felt.

His position was further strengthened by his refusal to place his own name in the hat at the invitation of São Paulo, Bahia, and several lesser states. On January 21 he instructed the Riograndense delegation to endorse a nominee favored by Minas and São Paulo—provided the candidate came from neither state.[2]

With the Mineiros and Paulistas deadlocked and Borges refusing to run, contenders came forward from Bahia, Santa Catarina, Paraíba, and Pernambuco, though the three most important delegations remained uncommitted. Of the would-be nominees in early February, Rui Barbosa of Bahia seemed to be the front-runner. Borges let it be known he would support Rui if the Senator would forswear his old program for constitutional revision. To Rui's disadvantage, however, his long-time rival J. J. Seabra controlled the Bahiano delegation in congress, and Seabra doggedly opposed the candidacy, probably fearing the loss of control of Bahia if Rui became president. The Mineiros were on the point of accepting Rui Barbosa, but the Paulistas hesitated, then balked when Seabra revived their hopes for an Arantes candidacy. Negotiations began anew, and São Paulo and Minas Gerais again turned to the possibility of a bilateral accord. On February 17 they agreed to run Arantes if Rio Grande (that is, Borges de Medeiros) assented; he did not. Instead he cautiously committed his state—for the first time—to Sen. Epitácio da Silva Pessôa of Paraíba; the PRR was the first machine of any importance to back Epitácio. On February 20 delegates of the three major states, together with representatives of Pernambuco and Bahia, quietly met in a politician's home in Rio, where they decided on Epitácio as the "national candidate." The selection of a consensus candidate who was not from the southern states was unprecedented. The anomaly was doubled in that the mantle went, not to a Bahiano or a Pernambucano, but to a senator whose state party was a political cipher. In a polemical memoir, Epitácio acknowledged the critical role of Rio Grande do Sul in the negotiations leading to his nomination; Gov. Camilo Holanda of Paraíba also gave the Riograndenses credit for Epitácio's victory.[3]

Although Borges admired Epitácio Pessôa for his integrity and political ability, he had made his decision only after the range of candidates had been narrowed to exclude representatives of the three powerful states and Rui. Borges seized the opportunity to stop Minas and São Paulo, whose prestige had fallen to a low point because of the disastrous Rodrigues Alves–Delfim Moreira ticket. Moreover, by backing a candidate from a third-ranking machine he created a political debt—a claim he could not have made on a candidate named by Minas and São Paulo. At least two of the "big three" were needed for victory, however, and Mineiro and Paulista backing swiftly followed that of Rio Grande. This of course also put Epitácio in the debt of the PRM and PRP leaders.

The candidate had a long career of public service. As a member of the first federal congress, he had vociferously opposed Floriano Peixoto's dictatorship in 1892, thereby ensuring his defeat in the next election. He then became a professor of law. Epitácio reentered politics to serve in the cabinet of Campos Sales and was subsequently appointed to the supreme court. In 1912 he left the bench to become a federal senator from his home state of Paraíba; by 1915 he was boss of the state machine. Epitácio had attracted the attention of Rodrigues Alves in the succession maneuvers of 1917, and the President-elect had chosen him to lead the Brazilian delegation to the Versailles Peace Conference. Just as Rui's performance at the Hague had impressed his compatriots, so did Epitácio's at Versailles, where with American support he was successful in arranging for German reparations payments to Brazil. Epitácio was still in France when he was tapped for the presidency. In March 1919 a national convention formally proclaimed his candidacy.

Rui Barbosa, who had come close to victory in the political dealings of February, now decided to give Epitácio a race even without the backing of the important establishment machines. In his campaign he concentrated on two issues—greater authority for the federal government and increased welfare legislation for industrial workers—making more of an effort to attract urban groups than he had in 1910. The surprise of the April election was not that Epitácio won a majority, but that the plucky Rui got almost 30 per cent of the vote, winning a majority in Pará, the State of Rio, and the Federal District. In São Paulo, Minas, and Bahia, he got one-third of the votes cast.[4] Perhaps the most significant aspect of the election was that urban voters were beginning to play an independent role in Brazilian politics.

Epitácio took office on July 28. Whether or not he owed his election more to Rio Grande than to the two coffee giants was not directly relevant to his choice of ministers and his program. Since he had to govern without a powerful party of his own to assist him in congress, he wanted the support of all three autonomous state machines. This backing was all the more important to him because he had plans for an ambitious public works program to combat the drought cycle in his native northeast, the most poverty-stricken area of the country. To secure the support of the powers in the federation, he took a logical but unprecedented step: of his seven ministerial appointments, six came from the "big three" states. This meant naming civilians to head the war and navy ministries, the first such appointments since the birth of the Republic. Both these positions went to Mineiros; the treasury and agriculture posts went to the Gaúchos, and transportation and foreign affairs to the Paulistas. The ministry of justice was given to a Pernambucano.

The Paulistas soon let Epitácio know how much he was beholden to them. In the international depression of 1920, coffee sales declined sharply; at the same time the 1920–21 crop promised to be almost twice the size of the frost-damaged harvest of the preceding season. Carlos de Campos, the majority leader in the chamber and a Paulista, threatened to resign his post in 1920 if the President did not meet São Paulo's demand for a large issue of paper currency to ease credit and devalue the milréis.[5] The intransigence of the PRP allowed the Mineiros to intercede as mediators, though their state, like São Paulo, stood to gain by the devaluation scheme. Epitácio yielded, and Campos stayed on.

The coffee-producing states scored an even greater victory the next year, when the federal government assumed the burden of protecting coffee prices in the international market. São Paulo had pioneered in the defense of coffee sales, purchasing stocks when foreign prices fell below a specified level and storing them against the day the prices rose again. In order to pay the planters and store the coffee, the state government had resorted to foreign loans. In general planters considered the Paulista program a resounding success, despite the lack of direct support from a somewhat skeptical federal government concerned with foreign debts and exchange problems.

By 1921, however, the number of coffee-growing states was increasing, and the Paulistas demanded federal support for the industry that earned the greater part of Brazil's foreign exchange. Overproduction was again a problem. Between 1919 and 1921 the price of coffee on the New York market fell from $0.25 to $0.10 per pound. In October 1921, congress created the Coffee Defense Institute (within the treasury ministry) to superintend a price-support program. A sum of 124,-000 contos (approximately U.S. $16.1 million in 1921) was provided for stock purchases, and two foreign loans totaling £9 million were obtained for the institute's operations. Under the plan, the Pessôa government bought 4.5 million bags of coffee from Brazilian producers.[6]

Like Minas and São Paulo, Rio Grande won favors for its principal industry in Epitácio's term, though not until his last year in office. From the outset, however, all three states profited by the President's public works program. Most of the federal railway expansion between 1919 and 1922 took place within their boundaries. With these and other concessions to the three leading states, the President won the votes he needed in congress for his prized public works program in the drought-stricken northeast. Replying a few years later to the charge that this program had been a waste of money, Epitácio pointed out that though the regional development scheme had cost the government 304,000 contos (about U.S. $41 million), it had aided eight states; moreover, the government had spent almost the same amount on railroads alone in Rio Grande, Minas, and São Paulo.[7]

Part of Epitácio's package for Rio Grande was the acquisition of the Farquhar-dominated Compagnie Auxiliaire, the state's principal railway, which was purchased by the federal government and then transferred to the state in 1921. Epitácio also agreed to help the state government obtain the Compagnie du Port de Rio Grande do Sul, another Farquhar interest. Borges de Medeiros's objective was to increase the efficiency of Riograndense transport, and especially to make frigorífico exports more profitable by improving facilities and subsidizing freight. (The Armour company, which had begun operations in Rio Grande in 1917, had located at Livramento and shipped through Montevideo; the Swift plant was situated at the Port of Rio Grande, and started packing in 1919.) More direct forms of federal aid for the ranching industry were extended in 1922.

The maneuvering among the "big three" for economic privilege was accompanied by political maneuvering for control of the presidency in the next term of office, a process that began two years in advance of the election. From the opening months of Epitácio's term, the Mineiros made it clear that the PRM was the central pillar of the Pessôa administration. Where the Paulistas forced the President's hand and reduced their political options in order to achieve economic legislation, the Mineiros played the role of mediators, making Epitácio dependent on their good offices to work with São Paulo. In late 1919 Minas clashed with Rio Grande over an election to name the president of the chamber, and a Mineiro emerged victorious.

The first skirmish in the president-making battle came in 1920, when a disputed gubernatorial contest in Espírito Santo led to a divided assembly and federal intervention. Subsequent congressional deliberations on the legality of the new governor's claim to office were viewed as a test of power for the 1922 election. The PRM supported the governor, the PRP the opposition faction in Espírito Santo.[8] As for the PRR, Borges instructed his delegation to vote on the legal merits of the case in defense of state autonomy, and the Gaúchos voted for the Mineiro-sponsored victor. This earned Borges the thanks of the governor of Minas Gerais, Artur Bernardes; but in terms of national politics the Mineiros had earned much more: they had made a satellite of Espírito Santo for the presidential election of 1922.

Only a month after the Espírito Santo case had been settled, the death of Vice President Delfim Moreira, in July 1920, brought about another series of maneuvers based on plans for 1922. The constitution required an election to fill the vacant post, and Epitácio insisted that Moreira, a Mineiro, be succeeded by a member of one of the three autonomous parties. Unlike the presidency of the chamber, the half-term vice presidency was not regarded as a prize by the state machines interested in presidential succession. Despite the fact that vice presidents had twice been elected to the presidency (Afonso Pena and Venceslau Brás), the post was largely honorific, and political leaders in São Paulo and Minas regarded it as a hindrance to winning the presidency two years later. Epitácio seems to have preferred a Paulista for the office, but when he failed to obtain the PRP's approval he sought a Mineiro or a Riograndense. Governors Borges and Bernardes tried to get each other to take the post, or at least to name a subaltern to accept the honor. Finally, at the end of July, the Mineiros agreed to put up one of their own senators, Bueno de Paiva. Bernardes asserted that Minas accepted the vice presidency only because the Mineiros and the Paulistas believed Rio Grande wanted a Mineiro. Having resolved the issue, Borges and Bernardes congratulated each other on their political solidarity. With a touch of irony, Bernardes wrote the Gaúcho that "your feeling that the candidate should be chosen by Minas brought us [Mineiros] real moral and political satisfaction."[9] Paiva was duly proclaimed the vice presidential candidate by senate leaders and was elected on September 5, 1920.

It became increasingly clear that the next "official" presidential candidate would be from São Paulo or Minas; as early as 1919 the governors of the two states, Washington Luís Pereira de Sousa and Artur Bernardes, impressed one Gaúcho congressman as the leading contenders. In 1920 the two state parties drew closer together in their congressional strategy, agreeing to elect a Paulista the next majority leader in the chamber. By April of the next year the Paulista and Mineiro leaders had reached an accord on a common front for the 1922 election.[10] Bernardes was to be the *café-com-leite* candidate.

The Governor of Minas was to become one of the most controversial figures in Brazilian political history. The Mineiro historian and biographer A. A. Melo Franco, a friend of the conservative Bernardes, saw him as possessed by "an almost religious faith in the . . . mission reserved for him by God or destiny." Congressman Getúlio Vargas described him in similar terms in 1925. "More than a reactionary [*retrógrado*]," wrote Vargas, Bernardes was "almost a fanatic about religion and the presidential mission which he believes to be his lot."[11] Born in 1875, Bernardes was too young to be a Historical Republican; by the time he graduated from law school the Republic was 11 years old. The young lawyer advanced rapidly in the PRM, thanks in part to his marriage to the daughter of Carlos Vaz de Melo, boss of the patriarchal *zona da mata* in the early 1900's. He became a federal deputy in 1909, then served as state secretary of finance under Gov. Bueno Brandão from 1910 to 1914. He himself became governor in 1918, and with the aid of Sen. Raul Soares quickly consolidated his power in the Mineiro party, this at the expense of Francisco Sales, who was forced to resign from the PRM executive committee the following year.

After the party leaders of São Paulo and Minas decided on the Bernardes candidacy, they informed their counterparts in other states and began making arrangements for a nominating convention in June 1921. By April 27 all the state parties had accepted the nominee—all, that is, except one. The PRR would not agree. Borges wrote the PRM's congressional leaders that the Riograndense party would not go along with the plan to "sanction" Bernardes in a rigged convention; and a Gaúcho deputy declared in the chamber that Brazil could not "accept what comes from Minas [just] because it comes from Minas."[12]

Borges de Medeiros's chief objection was that the Paulistas and Mineiros had imposed a man whose program, though unannounced, seemed likely to favor the easy-money and coffee-support schemes championed by São Paulo. The veteran PRR chief believed Brazil had to have a "sound finances" program of the sort initiated by President Campos Sales. By 1921 prices had risen about 75 per cent above the 1912 level, and Borges was particularly interested in currency stabilization.[13] One of his concerns was presumably keeping charque prices competitive with those of bacalhau. Borges also wanted a concerted effort made to develop a national transportation network, a program that would inevitably have decreased the proportion of federal highways and railroads built in Minas and São Paulo. In the political sphere, the Gaúchos feared Bernardes might try to revise the constitution to strengthen the federal government, and thus endanger PRR autonomy. At the nominating convention in June, Bernardes was in fact vague to the point of equivocation on the revision question.[14] The PRR leader's boldness in rejecting the Mineiro-Paulista candidate may have stemmed in part from his success in 1919 in throwing the nomination to Epitácio Pessôa. Epitácio still owed a political debt to Borges, and unlike most of his predecessors he tried to stay out of the politics of succession.[15]

In the end, a struggle over the second slot on the Bernardes ticket was to transform Rio Grande's dissent into a full-scale opposition campaign. Epitácio had indicated to Mineiro and Paulista leaders that he would like to see the vice presidency go to a northern state, and the establishment parties of Bahia and Pernambuco entered the competition. In early June 1921, however, the President and the Bernardista leaders opted for Urbano Santos of Maranhão, the vice president in the Venceslau Brás administration.[16] The decision from the top to jettison both Pernambuco and Bahia in favor of Maranhão led the parties of those two states to withdraw their support from Bernardes.

The defeated rivals for the vice presidency soon joined Rio Grande to back an opposition slate. Borges had suggested former President Nilo Peçanha of Rio State as a candidate even before Bahia and Pernambuco broke away from Bernardes, perhaps as a bid for Rio's support.[17] On June 12 representatives of Rio Grande, Rio State, Pernambuco, and Bahia, joined by Francisco Sales's dissidents from Minas, agreed on a ticket. Nilo was to be the opposition's standard bearer. J. J. Seabra, who had become governor of Bahia in 1920, was chosen as his running mate.

Though Rio Grande's rejection of Bernardes had touched off the four-state revolt, there had been earlier indications of restiveness over the Minas–São Paulo hegemony. Three of the four dissenting machines (Rio, Bahia, and Pernambuco) had unsuccessfully attempted to thwart a Paulista candidacy for the 1918 succession, and Bahia had joined several northeastern machines in suggesting an alliance with Rio Grande against the two dominant parties in the 1919 crisis.[18]

Nilo Peçanha was still a prominent figure in national politics. Since the days of his alliances and feuds with Pinheiro Machado, the wily ex-President had usually managed to control the State of Rio, and he had served as foreign minister during World War I. In the view of his supporters, he had a real chance to win. If the PRR was the third most important party in national politics, the ruling groups in Bahia, Pernambuco, and Rio ranked (in some order) fourth, fifth, and sixth. Nilo could count on heavy support in the Federal District, where he was popular, and hoped that Sales was still powerful enough to deliver a significant share of the Mineiro vote. Nilo also expected to draw more support from the army than Bernardes.

At Nilo's suggestion, Borges wrote the manifesto of the "rebel" candidates, whose campaign was christened the Reação Republicana (Republican Resistance). The Gaúcho chief called for a monetary and fiscal program that would end inflation and restore the milréis to gold convertibility. He also championed a balanced budget, citing Riograndense practice as a model of financial comportment. During the campaign Nilo praised Rio Grande's budgetary austerity, and quoted Borges and even Comte on the paramountcy of the budgetary issue, though no one had previously accused him of being a positivist. (In private conversations he went so far as to refer to the PRR leader as "our chief."[19]) Nilo also suggested that the fiscal policies of Campos Sales, long favored by Borges, be reinstituted.

Despite the emphasis on a return to lost virtue, the aging Historical Republicans who led the opposition also had something new to say. In his manifesto Borges had blamed the satisfaction of "regional interests," meaning those of Minas and São Paulo, for Brazil's financial troubles. This charge was developed fully during the campaign. Nilo protested against the economic and political "imperialism" of the two most powerful states, and demanded that rubber, cacao, sugar, and other Brazilian products be protected in the international market, just as coffee was.* The Reação leaders did not oppose valorization—Nilo's own state was an important producer of coffee—but they objected to special treatment for coffee alone. Riograndense propagandists took the same tack, arguing that the alternation of Mineiros and Paulistas in the presidency had led to the progress of two members of the federation and the neglect of the 18 others; a PRR publication cited the defense of coffee and the extensive construction of railroads in Minas and São Paulo as examples of selfish regionalism.[20] The 1921–22 campaign was unique in the Old Republic in pitting lesser powers against the combined strength of Minas Gerais and São Paulo. Almost as rare was the development of a large and disciplined congressional minority, led by Otávio Rocha of Rio Grande do Sul.

Since the Reação leaders were the underdogs, they took the logical step of approaching the army, which had played an important role in Brazil's last real race, in 1910. After the fiasco of the Hermes administration, the military had again withdrawn from politics; the salvacionista movement had died with the PRC, albeit more quietly. But in contrast to 1910, when the army took an active hand in the

---

* Nilo Peçanha, *Politica, economia e finanças: Campanha presidencial (1921–1922)* (Rio, 1922), pp. 7, 14, 93. Goods for which Brazil did not have a near-monopoly on world supply were not subject to valorization, though the producers could be subsidized. Nilo had almost nothing to say in his campaign about protection for industry in the domestic market, despite the fact that manufacturers had obtained relatively few privileges from the federal government as compared with the coffee growers.

selection process, the 1921 contest did not see the army involved in politicking until after the leaders of the four state parties had already named a candidate to oppose Bernardes.[21] The first person to approach the military was apparently Rui Barbosa, who in mid-June was willing to forget his anti-military sentiments of 1910 and to seek a "conciliation" solution revolving around himself or his former rival Hermes da Fonseca![22] But the leaders of the Reação remained united, and by August prominent generals were declaring their support for Nilo. In a further bid for army backing, Nilo even offered to step down in favor of Marshal Hermes, if Bernardes would do likewise. Nilo knew his adversary well enough, however, to appreciate that this bow to the military entailed little risk.

The PRR of course tried to revive its previous alliance with the army on behalf of Nilo. The state party had several retired officers in leadership positions, among them Deputy Rocha. Furthermore, Borges was a close friend of Gen. Cipriano da Costa Ferreira, who had led the Riograndense Military Brigade for six years. Ferreira was now commander of the Third Military Region—coextensive with Rio Grande do Sul—where more than a quarter of the army was garrisoned. Finally, Borges and his party still had ideological affinities with several of the positivist officers who had come out of the academies in the 1880's and 1890's. Among these were Generals Ximeno de Villeroy and Cândido Rondon, explorer of the Amazon and founder of the Indian Protection Service. Ferreira, Villeroy, and Rondon actively supported the Reação Republicana. Nevertheless, the Bernardistas were able to exert more pressure on President Epitácio than the Reação, with the result that military leaders who were outspokenly pro-Nilo were reprimanded.[23] This prompted the Reação leaders to defend the officers involved, thereby thrusting the military deeper into the campaign. An additional irritant to the army was the fact that disciplinary action was administered by the civilian war minister, João Pandiá Calógeras, a member of the PRM.

Military passions erupted with new intensity in October 1921 over two sensational documents that were openly derisive of the army. Edmundo Bittencourt's *Correio da Manhã*, which had stirred up hornets' nests before, revealed a pair of letters on the ninth and tenth that insulted Nilo Peçanha and, more importantly, Brazilian army officers. These missives, allegedly from the pen of Artur Bernardes, derisively called attention to Nilo's mulatto ancestry, termed Hermes "that overblown sergeant" [*êsse sargentão*], and cast aspersions on the generals who backed the Reação Republicana. With the publication of these letters, the Military Club, whose members included the army's highest-ranking officers, stepped into the fray. Hermes, who was president of the club, had by now quite forgotten his disenchantment with politics in 1915. The sometime social group quickly became a quasi-political organization, just as it had on many occasions in the past. A special committee was organized in the club to determine whether the letters published by the *Correio* were genuine, for Bernardes had immediately denounced them as forgeries. Relying on the reports of handwriting analysts, the committee proclaimed the documents authentic. On December 28 a plenary session of the Military Club resolved "to commit the case to the judgment of the nation" because the club had no judicial authority.[24] This resolution, implying that the letters were genuine, brought the army solidly into Nilo's camp. After the election a forger confessed that he had written the letters, but the damage had been done.

The candidates of the Reação Republicana meanwhile made serious efforts to garner support in the satellite states. With Nilo covering the north while Seabra took the south, the Reação candidates made appearances from Amazonas to Rio Grande do Sul in the most extensive political campaign Brazil had ever seen. The strategy was to bring in a heavy opposition vote in the states the Reação did not control. The election took place on March 1, 1922. Nilo Peçanha and his supporters across Brazil immediately claimed victory; so did Bernardes. Neither claim had any real meaning, however: both candidates knew that the election depended on the final count made by congress, not on the tallies of local and state authorities.

In a relatively close contest congress could declare enough votes fraudulent to make either man the winner. This gave Bernardes a decisive advantage; a congressional majority under Mineiro-Paulista discipline was sure to pronounce in his favor. Nilo, realizing his plight, quickly came up with a novel plan that he asserted would ensure a fair count. He proposed a "court of honor," composed of congressmen, supreme court justices, and military officers, to replace congress as the verifying body. Borges agreed to the plan in April, and the two Reação leaders rapidly obtained military backing for the idea. The Military Club and several prominent officers, among them General Ferreira, publicly endorsed the scheme.

Epitácio was in a difficult position. His government had come to depend on the goodwill of Minas and São Paulo, but the army's hatred for Bernardes was reaching a point of open revolt against the incumbent. The President was casting about for a conciliatory solution that would require both candidates to withdraw, Gaúcho congressmen reported to their leader. Borges was willing to discuss that alternative.[25] But were Minas and São Paulo? On May 1 the President held a meeting with Mineiro and Paulista politicians in Catete Palace to sound out the other side. A revolution was imminent, Epitácio declared, and 90 per cent of the army officers were pro-Nilo; or rather, as his war minister more accurately put it, they were 90 per cent anti-Bernardes. The President asserted that the Mineiro would not last 24 hours in Catete. Though Epitácio later denied it, a participant in the meeting reported to Bernardes that the President had wanted both candidates to retire from the field.[26] But the Mineiros would not be intimidated; and their Paulista ally, Governor Washington Luís, stood by them. The two state parties refused to consider a court of honor or a Bernardes withdrawal.

Under the circumstances Epitácio decided he had no choice but to see Bernardes through. He felt relatively secure in doing so, for he believed that Borges and the Riograndense Party would not join a revolt against constituted authority. On May 16 Epitácio notified Borges of his rejection of the court of honor, with the irrefutable—and convenient—argument that the constitution explicitly empowered congress to count the votes in a presidential election.[27] Borges attempted a last-ditch ploy, trying to get an equal number of majority and minority members of the senate and chamber on the joint credentials committee, but this too failed. Efforts at conciliation ended after the pro-Bernardes committee went to work on May 18. Borges broke with Epitácio, and instructed Luís Simões Lopes, the Gaúcho minister of agriculture, to resign. In an attempt to discredit the credentials committee, the congressional minority refused to participate in the vote tabulations. The counting proceeded as predicted, and on June 7 Bernardes was declared president. According to congress, Nilo had won in the four states whose machines had supported his candidacy, as well as in Amazonas and the Federal

District. As expected, Rio Grande do Sul gave him his largest state count (some 89,000 votes). The Reação leaders had apparently overestimated the remaining strength of Sales in Minas, where (according to the final count) Nilo drew less than 10 per cent of the votes.[28] Two days after the "official" certification, however, Nilo and Seabra were still claiming victory, based on the tallies of local election boards.*

The military, meanwhile, had been increasingly restless since the election. By April the leaders of the garrison in the federal capital were considering rebellion to obtain a second election, and Nilo was toying with the idea of military intervention.[29] The rejection of the plan for a court of honor led to insubordination and flare-ups in the garrisons of Santa Catarina and Maranhão. The situation deteriorated in early June, when rumors of federal intervention in the states of Rio de Janeiro and Pernambuco intensified the animus against Epitácio and Bernardes. Following the proclamation of Bernardes's victory, a Gaúcho congressman with military connections wired Borges that the conspirators awaited only Riograndense adherence to launch their revolt. The garrisons of São Paulo and the federal capital, said the deputy, "confide in the support of their comrades in the south."[30]

Epitácio Pessôa, however, had not erred in his assessment of Borges. The PRR chief was not willing to risk civil war to stop Bernardes from taking power. General Villeroy, representing a group of high-ranking military plotters, visited Borges in April to discuss an uprising, but the Governor would agree only to consider a plan of passive resistance. His scheme was to get political and military leaders to pledge noncompliance with Bernardes's directives. A manifesto to that effect would be published on inauguration day, November 15. Even so, Borges tried to cloak the proposed sit-down strike in a constitutional cover, citing a provision of the 1891 charter that by implication denied the duty of obedience to an illegitimate power. Borges de Medeiros, the former judge and member of the constituent assembly, was morally and psychologically indisposed to a patently extra-legal attempt to stop Bernardes. "My overriding preoc-

---

* Urbano Santos died in May, and Seabra had petitioned the federal courts to recognize him as vice president. In a seven-to-five decision at the beginning of June, the supreme court denied his claim.

cupation [is] to prevent any violent solution," he wrote a Gaúcho deputy.[31] Borges probably reasoned that any decision to intervene in the pro-Reação states would not be extended to Rio Grande, where the establishment party could count on both a formidable state police force and several easily mobilized provisional corps in a confrontation with the army. Moreover, most military commanders would be loath to oust Borges to gratify Artur Bernardes.

In addition, the "pacifying" mechanism of economic compensation for political defeat continued to operate for Rio Grande, even after Borges had broken "political" relations with the President. On June 19, 1922, a law was enacted extending government aid to producers of rubber, cotton, cereals, and pastoral goods, in addition to coffee planters. The statute reduced railroad tariffs for livestock and derivative products, subsidized frigorífico production, set up special credits for foreign governments willing to buy Brazilian agricultural and pastoral products, and temporarily suspended the importation of charque from the Plate. (This sweeping law also set up an Institute for the Permanent Defense of Coffee.) Thus congress under Epitácio Pessôa realized one of the measures proposed by the Reação Republicana.* Another concession to the pastoral industry of Rio Grande was the establishment of a rural credit division of the Bank of Brazil. Gaúcho congressmen had sponsored the credit scheme,[32] which was projected in the June 19 law and enacted in Epitácio's last months in office. The program was to be underwritten with a bond issue of 400,000 contos (U.S. $52 million in 1922).

Despite the federal government's effort to seek accommodations with the Riograndenses, the legitimacy of the political system was already decaying. São Paulo and Minas Gerais were imposing their choice on the other states, and a campaign had been openly waged against domination by the coffee giants. The refusal of the Reação minority in congress to participate in the verification of election tabulations had damaged the prestige of that body. Nilo Peçanha concluded that no candidate could win against the "autocracy" of São Paulo and Minas, and that the president and the two parties would impose a successor or face a revolution every four years.[33] The fact was, as he was finally forced to see after the campaign, that the PRM–

---

* Most of the provisions of the act, however, had yet to be put into force at the time Bernardes came to power, and he let the program die.

PRP alliance could always get its man elected, even against determined opposition. Rio Grande had been successful in 1919 only because Minas and São Paulo were divided, and the prestige of the *café-com-leite* alliance was at an unprecedented low. Once reunited in 1922, the Paulista and Mineiro leaders were able to pull the strings that made Bernardes the victor. In neither election was any attempt made to hide the fact that a tiny political oligarchy had selected the winning presidential candidate. Early in the 1921–22 campaign, a congressional debate between the Riograndense deputy Gumercindo Ribas and his Mineiro and Paulista opponents led to the admission that Bernardes had been chosen by a canvassing of state governors (an exaggeration in itself). Ribas protested that this practice was undemocratic, to which the Paulista majority leader Carlos de Campos retorted, "At any rate, it's the traditional policy in Brazil."[34] Although the charge of elite control applied equally well to the Reação Republicana machines, the victors inevitably bore the opprobrium.

Yet discontent with the system could be transformed into action (necessarily extra-legal) only when the army entered the fray on behalf of the losers. Each contested presidential election during the Old Republic (1910, 1922, and 1930) occasioned allegations of fraud, and a succession crisis drew the military into active political participation. As long as the civilian political elite remained united, the army was neutralized. In 1910, when the elite was divided, the military-backed candidate won; therefore, Rui and the other civilian leaders who charged fraud had no opportunity to form an alliance with the military. In 1922, the situation was radically different. The election had damaged the prestige of the political system; it had divided the national elite, and had produced the mutual alienation of civilian and military authority. In mid-1922 the nation wondered, along with Epitácio Pessôa, whether Bernardes would survive his first day in Catete.

# CHAPTER NINE

# Political Discipline and Military Revolt

AT THE end of June 1922 it seemed likely that Epitácio as well as Bernardes would fall victim to the wrath of the military. The incumbent President became embroiled in a bitter quarrel with Hermes da Fonseca that many officers took as yet another affront to military honor on behalf of the Bernardistas. The quarrel arose when Gov. José Bezerra of Pernambuco, one of the Reação Republicana leaders, died in office, and the state elite divided over the succession. Elections at the end of May 1922 were marked by violence in Recife, and Epitácio prepared to intervene with troops from the local garrison. At this point, Hermes, who was still president of the Military Club, urged the garrison commander to resist the President's instructions to interfere in local politics, an action the Marshal considered unworthy of the army's mission. Epitácio learned of Hermes's intercession in late June, when the appeal to the garrison commander was published in Recife newspapers. The President quickly reprimanded the old soldier, who replied defiantly on July 2, referring to himself as the "chief of the national army." Epitácio's reaction was immediate: he arrested the Marshal for a day and closed the Military Club. In the chamber Otávio Rocha, the Gaúcho leader of the Reação, excoriated Epitácio for his actions.[1]

On July 5 a revolt broke out in the national capital. For Brazilians of a later generation, that date marked the beginning of contemporary history, for the uprising of the fifth touched off a series of revolts that finally destroyed the Old Republic. The plot involved military men of many ranks and ages, but the most heroic scenes were enacted by junior officers from the fort on Copacabana beach. Because of their role, the insurrection was later considered the first of the *tenentes'* (lieutenants) rebellions. The revolt was hastily organized to respond to the President's handling of Hermes and the Military Club; moreover, it had no unified program other than keeping Bernardes from taking office in November.[2] Since Nilo Peçanha and Deputy Rocha were not informed until the last minute, they had no opportunity to marshal the support of the Reação machines. Epitácio declared a state of siege, and local commanders arrested military and civilian suspects. The army quickly isolated the rebellion at Copacabana, and on July 6 loyal troops took the fort. Several rebel tenentes died on the beach at Copacabana in a hopeless attempt to offer resistance.

Meanwhile, in the state of Mato Grosso, Gen. Clodoaldo da Fonseca was preparing to lead his troops in a march on Rio de Janeiro. As the salvacionista governor of Alagoas, Clodoaldo had defied Pinheiro Machado in 1913. Now he needed assistance from the PRR if his revolt were to succeed. Congressman Rocha's stance on the Hermes arrest gave Clodoaldo hope, but Borges had already made his decision.

On July 7 an editorial appeared in *A Federação* entitled "In Defense of Order" (Pela Ordem), which supported constitutional authority and condemned the insurrections. Though the editorial criticized Epitácio's treatment of Hermes, it proclaimed that Rio Grande would never sanction civil strife. In part because of Clodoaldo's dismay at the PRR chief's attitude, the Mato Grosso movement immediately collapsed.[3] Other plans for military revolts were aborted in São Paulo and Bahia, and in Rio Grande itself. For the time being the military situation seemed under control. Lacking coordination and cut off from the civilian opponents of Bernardes, the army conspirators failed to block federal intervention in Pernambuco, and a pro-Bernardes faction came to power there, breaching the Reação Republicana. In August a Bernardista from Pernambuco, Estácio Coimbra, was elected to fill the vice presidential slot left vacant by the death of Urbano Santos.

The Reação was in full retreat, and more interventions seemed likely, since Bernardes could count on an opposition party or faction to make trouble in Bahia, Rio State, and Rio Grande do Sul. Committed to the rejection of a coup d'état to keep Bernardes out of power, Borges now saw the possibility of a sit-down strike disappear in the confusion among the military after the failure of the July 5 uprisings. He was eager to appease Bernardes, and in any "every-man-for-himself" maneuver, he scuttled the Reação Republicana. On July 18 *A Federação* declared that Rio Grande's role in the opposition movement had ended. The Riograndenses hurriedly beat a retreat to a position of political isolation in the federation. The PRR withdrew from the Reação in congress, though Gaúcho voters were urged to abstain in the vice presidential contest.

Gubernatorial elections were due to be held in Rio Grande in November 1922, and even before congress had solemnized Bernardes's victory over Nilo, Borges had decided to "protect" his state by seeking his fifth five-year term.[4] No other governor in Brazil had served as long as Borges de Medeiros, and the opposition had hopes of forcing him from office. Since Borges's political enemies in Rio Grande had supported Bernardes against Nilo Peçanha, they counted on their good relations with the President-elect for federal support and, if necessary, intervention. Moreover, the opposition included not only the Federalists, who had continued their legal and extra-legal struggle against the Republicans since the war of 1893–95 and still represented some of the great estancieiro families, but also Assis Brasil's Democrats, who had been inactive since the defeat of Rui Barbosa in 1910.

Memories of the Gaúcho civil war and ideological differences had previously made it impossible for the opposition parties to unite. Now, however, the war was almost 30 years behind them, and they managed to table the ideological issue by keeping the demand for constitutional reform as vague as possible. Though the two groups did not yet form a unified party, they merged into an Aliança Libertadora (Alliance of Liberation) for the purpose of ending Borges's rule. They styled themselves Liberators (Libertadores) and chose Assis Brasil to run against Borges in November.

The chances of defeating or overthrowing the PRR had never been greater in its 30 years in power. The gubernatorial election found the opposition united, if only loosely, behind a popular candidate.

Federal intervention had already taken its toll in one of the Reação Republicana states, and Nilo's power in Rio and Seabra's in Bahia were gravely threatened. Bernardes, who was to take office ten days before the election in Rio Grande, was unlikely to forget the troubles arising from Borges's initial rejection of his candidacy. For the first time since 1906, no member of the PRR was invited to join the cabinet.[5] A final advantage for the Liberators was that Borges's mandate had to be overwhelming, since the state constitution provided that a governor seeking to succeed himself had to garner 75 per cent of the vote. This requirement meant that extensive fraud was likely, grounds enough for a revolt to provoke federal intervention. The most common means of triggering federal action—the division of the state legislature—was not possible. With only three members of the 32-man assembly, the Aliança could in no way claim a majority in a rump body to deny the Governor's authority.

The election of 1922 was the first contested gubernatorial race in Rio Grande since 1907, and charges of fraud were to come from both the Liberator and the Republican camps. Rumors of a revolution against Borges had preceded the election, and violence resulting in two deaths broke out in one western town while the polls were open. Whether or not Borges got the required majority was to be resolved in a procedure analogous to that used in presidential elections. According to the state charter, the legislature was to make the final count and could cast out any ballots it judged fraudulent. This meant that on the state level as on the national level the party controlling the legislature would get its man "elected." And just as Nilo had tried to circumvent the established procedure, so did Assis Brasil. He proposed arbitration to ensure a fair count. Borges initially agreed to consider appointing a judge to make an unofficial check on the state assembly's tally, but the two candidates could not find a mutually acceptable man. Bernardes and former President Venceslau both declined.

A three-man committee of the legislature began counting the votes in December, but the Liberators were not represented on it. Thirty-nine-year-old Getúlio Vargas headed the group. On January 17 the committee reported that Borges de Medeiros had won the election by a vote of some 106,000 to 32,000, and the assembly quickly pronounced him reelected.* Predictably, Assis did best in the state capital, where fraud was more difficult, and in the Campanha, where the Federalists and Assis had always been strongest. However, in only one município, São Sepé, was he officially accorded a majority.[6]

The conviction that fraud was used against them and the hope for federal intervention led Assis and his followers to rebel against the state government.† Their movement was to be significant for national politics for two reasons: first, because it provided a link between civilian and military malcontents, and second, because it temporarily diminished the PRR's autonomy in national affairs, making the Gaúchos less of a threat to café-com-leite domination. The rebellion should not have come as a surprise to the PRR leaders; in December Gaúcho opposition spokesmen had warned that revolutionary disturbances were inevitable if the legislature recognized Borges. On January 25, 1923, the day of the Governor's fifth inauguration, a series of regional uprisings began as bands of rebels wearing scarlet neckerchiefs spread across the countryside. Most of the rebel leaders had been Federalist caudillos, some of them veterans of the war that broke out following Castilhos' inauguration 30 years before. The rebel rallying cry was "Down with the Chimango!"; Ramiro Barcelos's 1915 satirization of Borges had not been forgotten. The rebels not only wanted to unseat Borges but hoped to turn the Republicans out of office and to abrogate the "positivist" constitution. Crucial to the fulfillment of these plans was the assistance of the federal government and the support of the leaders of Minas and São Paulo.

---

* According to a widely circulated anecdote, the committee initially concluded that Borges had lost the race by failing to obtain three-fourths of the vote. But when the committeemen went to the governor's mansion to break the bad news to the party chief, he had rushed forward, exclaiming that he knew they had come to congratulate him on the victory. Lacking the courage to contradict their boss, the assemblymen returned to the legislative chambers to perform the necessary "electoral alchemy." See José Antônio Flôres da Cunha, A campanha de 1923 (Rio, n.d.), pp. 7–8. (This work, a bitter but incisive memoir, is especially useful for its comments on the personalities involved.)

† The year 1922 was a depression year for the ranchers of the Campanha, and this factor may have also figured in the Liberators' decision to rebel. Political considerations were foremost, however, for Borges's continuation in power was announced beforehand as the casus belli. On economic conditions, see Alcibiades de Oliveira, Um drama bancario: O esplendor e a queda do Banco Pelotense (Pôrto Alegre, 1936), p. 61.

Assis Brasil went to Rio de Janeiro to sound out Bernardes. He simultaneously approached the Paulista and Mineiro parties—but with little success. Though the governor of Minas, Raul Soares, gave some indication of sympathy, Washington Luís of São Paulo declined to interfere in the internal politics of another state.[7] The attempt to secure federal support was no more successful. Aware of the problems of intervening in Rio Grande, President Bernardes was elusive when it came to the question of concrete aid. The PRR strategy was similarly to seek support from out-of-state powers, and the first step in that direction had been the abandonment of the Reação Republicana.

Although Bernardes was not one to ignore past affronts, his power to repay Borges for his defection in the 1922 campaign was limited. The President could not use the pretext of a divided assembly, as he did in the State of Rio; nor did he have any assurance the military would act against Borges at his bidding. The upper echelons of the army were divided on the civil war in Rio Grande, with the minister of war and the commander of the Third Region (Rio Grande do Sul) leaning in opposite directions. Gen. Eurico Andrade Neves, who had replaced Cipriano Ferreira in the Third Region, was, like his predecessor, a friend of Borges. In any event, the army would have had to face the state police in an intervention against the incumbent government—always a deterrent to a military adventure in the three autonomous states. Furthermore, the majority of Brazilian officers were still hostile to Bernardes, and many could not be trusted to intervene against the only Reação machine capable of standing up against the President.[8] Yet the threat of intervention was credible enough to make Borges compromise on some issues with his local enemies.

With the army officially on the sidelines, the confrontation between the rebels and the state government was bound to be an unequal match. Borges was able to mobilize some 12,000 men, supplementing his 3,500-man Military Brigade with about 8,500 provisional corpsmen. The Liberators could muster only half that number, and their equipment was vastly inferior. In some cases the Liberators emulated their Federalist fathers in 1893–95 by organizing lancer formations, which had to face the machine guns of the loyalist forces.[9] Essentially, the rebels' strategy was to keep the war alive by moving rapidly and avoiding combat, in the hope the federal government would eventually intervene. Their struggle earned them the respect and sympathy of many regular army officers stationed in Rio Grande, who occasionally provided the Liberators with arms and other materiel. In March one army general joined the rebellion, but when his troops refused to follow him, he returned to his billet—"ready to follow orders."[10]

In April Borges injected an international issue into the war by hiring the mercenaries of Nepomuceno Saraiva, a border caudillo of the same stripe as his father Aparício and his uncle Gumercindo, and a Blanco Party chieftain. In return for his participation in the war, the younger Saraiva expected to receive political and military backing from the PRR in Uruguay.* As in the Castilhos era, the Riograndense government was conducting its own foreign policy in Uruguay. Yet in a sense that policy backfired, for the state's use of foreign mercenaries increased support outside Rio Grande for the Liberators; it also led to tension between Rio de Janeiro and Montevideo, where the Colorado Party ruled.

Most of the fighting on the loyalist side fell to the provisional corps, whose members wore green bandanas to distinguish themselves from the scarlet-bedecked Liberators. Since these corpsmen were led by political caudillos, the conflict inevitably created a name for a new generation of Riograndense politicians, notably Firmino Paim Filho, Osvaldo Aranha, and Getúlio Vargas. The Liberators too had their share of heroes, among them Batista Luzardo. But the most outstanding figure of the war was José Antônio Flôres da Cunha, who commanded the Brigade of the West for Borges and trounced the rebels in every combat he could provoke. On May 15 Flôres and Nepomuceno inflicted a major defeat on the Liberators in the município of Dom Pedrito. There, at the battle of Santa Maria Chico, loyalist machine-gun fire raked the ill-equipped Liberator ranks, producing more than 100 casualties and destroying the supplies for an army of 2,500. It seemed to be a reenactment of Inhanduí in 1893.

Still, if the Aliança Libertadora could keep the revolution going

---

* Saraiva wanted to establish a regular alliance between his party and the PRR, but other Blanco Party leaders rejected the arrangement. Saraiva claimed that another reason he entered the war was to repay the PRR for the aid his father received from Castilhos in 1904. Nepomuceno Saravia García, *Memorias de Aparicio Saravia* (Montevideo, 1956), p. 624.

long enough, it might sustain several military disasters and still obtain federal intervention. This fact was not lost on the other side. The Republicans decided to demonstrate their solidarity with the embattled state government in order to publicize the PRR's strength and unity; for the first time since 1889 they held a party congress. Meeting in October 1923, the delegates unanimously pledged loyalty to Borges in the struggle against the "parliamentarians." Here too, the second generation of Gaúcho Republicans made its mark. The outstanding figures at the convention were João Neves da Fontoura, Maurício Cardoso, and Lindolfo Collor, who delivered addresses to the plenum and drew up several fiery manifestos. In the meantime the PRR had renewed its subsidies to newspapers in Rio and São Paulo to ensure that stories favorable to the Borges regime would find their way into print.[11]

During much of this period Bernardes had been preoccupied with events in Rio State, where he had intervened to end Nilo Peçanha's power. In January 1923 he overthrew the Nilista governor, Raul Fernandes, even though Fernandes had obtained a supreme court writ recognizing him over a rival backed by Bernardes and a rump legislature.[12] By mid-1923, assured of congressional approval of his intervention in Rio State, the President was ready to direct his full attention toward Rio Grande. He would sustain Borges's authority, but he exacted the price of Gaúcho support in congress against leaders of the Reação in other states.[13] Bernardes had sent an official envoy to Pôrto Alegre to discuss an armistice in April, to no avail. In June he began to exert pressure on Borges to make concessions to the Liberators, again without immediate results. Finally, in November, he sent his minister of war, Gen. Setembrino de Carvalho, to Rio Grande to act as mediator.

Setembrino had a curious relationship with the Riograndense party. A native Gaúcho and a member of Castilhos' hand-picked state constituent assembly, he had served the ends of Pinheiro Machado in 1914 as interventor in Ceará. The Minister was no friend of Borges de Medeiros, however; on the contrary, he had opposed the Governor's reelection in 1922.[14] Setembrino arrived in Rio Grande with the knowledge that Borges was finally willing to entertain negotiations with Assis Brasil.

In the early stages of bargaining, the issues were not clearly defined. Many of the rebels demanded the resignation of the "Chimango."

The remaining questions concerned the various provisions of the state constitution that concentrated power in the hands of the governor. Assis directed negotiations for the Liberators from his ranch at Pedras Altas, near the Uruguayan frontier. Setembrino, also in Pedras Altas, transmitted communications to Borges in Pôrto Alegre and pressed both parties to end the war. Independent of these efforts, Borges again obtained assurances from the federal government that no attempt would be made to overthrow him. Hostilities provisionally ended with the opening of negotiations in early November.

The Liberators did not succeed in unseating Borges. They did, however, succeed in limiting his authority. Reluctantly yielding to the mounting pressure from Bernardes, he accepted a change in the constitution that prohibited a governor from serving consecutive terms; he also agreed to sacrifice the "positivist" constitutional provision that allowed the governor to appoint the lieutenant governor. With the negotiation of guarantees for minority representation at state and national levels (six seats in the assembly and five in congress), the issues were resolved, and the Pact of Pedras Altas was signed in mid-December. The agreement ended the 11-month war, but it did not satisfy all the Liberators; some remained disaffected and reiterated their intention to unseat Borges.

Like their predecessors in 1893, the rebels of 1923 were outnumbered and outclassed in materiel; their only significant military triumph was a brief seizure of the state's second-largest city, Pelotas. On the whole the Liberator movement only superficially disrupted the economic life of the state, and the conflict witnessed few of the barbarities of the war of 1893–95. Once peace was established, it was, if not a peace among equals, hardly the victor-vanquished relationship of 1895. Although Borges was still in power, the Liberators had managed to alter the constitution to prevent still another term for him. The peace settlement also provided for federal observation of the next congressional elections. When the ballots were cast a few months later, local counts gave the Aliança Libertadora only five seats in the chamber; nevertheless, the pro-Bernardes credentials committee recognized seven of the minority candidates, ousting two veteran Republicans to do so.

The real victor of 1923 was Artur Bernardes. To be sure, he had not been able to overthrow the establishment party in Rio Grande (as he was to do in the other three states of the Reação Republicana).

But he had weakened Borges in his own redoubt. Moreover, he had humiliated the PRR by forcing the Gaúchos to support the administration in congress. To obtain Bernardes's backing in Rio Grande, the PRR congressmen voted for federal intervention in Rio State. They also voted for some of his constitutional amendments in 1925, despite a long tradition of anti-revisionism. These amendments (effective in 1926) gave the president broader powers of intervention in the states, particularly in the event of mismanagement of a state's public debt. (Still, the Gaúchos defeated several other amendments designed to strengthen the federal government, principally through agreements with the Paulista delegation concerning the 1926 succession.[15])

The revolution of 1923 had been directed exclusively at the PRR. Other revolts in Rio Grande were soon to threaten the national establishment. Borges stood by Bernardes in these uprisings—not, it should be noted, out of love for the President; the need for mutual support was clear, since some of the movements were avowedly directed against the system of political control at the state and national levels alike. Three revolts specifically involved the governments of both Rio Grande do Sul and the Republic.

Bernardes's unpopularity stemmed from several sources. For one thing, his relations with the military had been bad since the "false letters" episode. For another, his handling of political opponents was anything but conciliatory. Epitácio had punished the Pernambuco machine in June 1922; the next year Bernardes humbled Borges and broke Nilo's control of Rio State. During the final weeks of Seabra's term as governor, the axe of intervention fell in Bahia; the official reason was to assure Seabra's successor (and political rival) of a peaceful inauguration.

A third source of dissatisfaction with Bernardes arose from his economic and financial policies. In a drive toward budgetary austerity, he abruptly terminated Epitácio Pessôa's cherished northeast development program. Furthermore, he did not implement the major provisions of the comprehensive 1922 law, which provided for the "permanent defense" of coffee and other agricultural and pastoral products. Bernardes was aware that amortization payments on the external debt (dating back to the 1898 funding loan) would fall due in 1927, and the interests of the treasury clashed with the expensive protectionist schemes of agricultural lobbies. During the first half of his administration Bernardes built federal warehouses for stockpiling coffee, but when coffee prices began to rise, he seized the opportunity to reverse Epitácio's valorization program. At the end of 1924 the responsibility for coffee defense once again devolved upon the State of São Paulo. In January 1925 Bernardes dismissed his Paulista treasury minister, who had favored large currency issues and devaluation, and replaced him with an advocate of balanced budgets and exchange stability.

Whatever his financial policies, to Brazil's growing urban groups Bernardes personified the evils of coronel-based politics; many of them felt he was almost totally unresponsive to the needs of the cities. Brazilian industry, inadequately protected against foreign imports, faced increasing competition as Europe and the United States recovered from the First World War, and industrial production in Brazil fell off in the years 1924–26. Doctrines of economic nationalism appealed not only to industrialists but also to another bourgeois group —the junior military officers.

On July 5, 1924, the second anniversary of the tenentes' revolt, military insurrections erupted in São Paulo, Sergipe, and Amazonas. The movements in the latter two states were quickly put down, but the rebels in São Paulo captured the state capital and held it for three weeks. The tenente insurgents were led by Isidoro Dias Lopes, a retired general and Federalist veteran of the war against Castilhos and Floriano. Isidoro had come to Rio Grande in 1923 to confer with the Liberators,[16] a fact that must have planted some doubt in Borges's mind about the General's true objective, ostensibly the ousting of Bernardes. Furthermore, Borges suspected the rebels of 1923 might join any revolt that could be turned against the Gaúcho regime. He therefore sent a 1,200-man contingent of the Military Brigade to São Paulo to help crush the rebellion. The Mineiro government also sent state troops. In addition, Bernardes dispatched federal troops, the overwhelming majority of which remained loyal to the government. The combined strength of the army and the state police forces of Minas, Rio Grande, and São Paulo soon amounted to more than 15,000 men; Isidoro commanded only 3,500. At the end of July the insurgents abandoned the Paulista capital and headed west.

A related problem soon developed in Rio Grande, which also had its share of army revolutionaries. Borges had learned of revolts brewing in the garrisons of the Missões District as early as December 1923;[17] when in fact an uprising did occur some ten months later, the PRR and the commander of the Military Region were ready for it. A young captain named Luís Carlos Prestes issued a manifesto on behalf of the rebels, linking their revolt to Isidoro's. Their purpose, Prestes declared, was to overthrow Bernardes and to prevent Britain from taking over Brazilian customs for the amortization of foreign debts in 1927.[18] Prestes, the Rio Grande–born son of a positivist military officer, had pursued an engineering course in military school and had graduated at the top of his class in 1918. He was later to be the head of the Brazilian Communist Party. Three of his fellow rebels—Juarez Távora, Osvaldo Cordeiro de Farias, and João Alberto Lins de Barros—were to follow an entirely different course; all participated in post-1930 governments as ministers or interventors.

Once again the insurgents in Rio Grande were outnumbered and outclassed, despite the fact that several Liberator caudillos had allied themselves with the young officers before the Prestes pronunciamento. The officers' revolt immediately became the occasion for a Liberator uprising against Borges. Some of the tenentes (who were avowedly moving against Bernardes) attached themselves to a Liberator band led by an old campaigner of 1893, Honório Lemes. For two months several insurgent groups managed to maintain a foothold in northwestern Rio Grande, but ultimately they were forced to take refuge in Argentina. Many of them then marched to Iguassu Falls (where Brazil meets Argentina and Paraguay), and there merged with Isidoro's troops. Earlier, another veteran of 1893, João Francisco, had revolted against the state machine he had served so well under Castilhos; he too had made his way to Iguassu. However, the rebels soon split again into two groups. For Prestes this was the beginning of a two-and-a-half-year march through the backlands of central and northeast Brazil to generate peasant opposition to Bernardes and the political and social system he represented. Though ultimately unsuccessful, the "Prestes Column" became a symbol of defiance of the regime, with an even greater mystique than the Copacabana revolt of 1922. The column included a few civilian Gaúchos, but most of the Liberators accompanied Isidoro back to Argentina, to continue their conspiratorial activities in exile.

The disparity of the aims and of the participants in the 1924 rebellions was underscored by the fact that prior to the arrival of Prestes at Iguassu, Isidoro's troops had proclaimed Assis Brasil the civilian chief of the insurgency, even though he had not been consulted about the July conspiracy. Assis accepted the title, without, however, any attempt to disguise the fact that his primary concern was ousting Borges, "the usurper" who had failed to assure free elections in Rio Grande do Sul.[19]

Borges, receiving continual warnings of new uprisings, kept his state forces at peak strength. His combined military forces remained at 12,000 men. With Catete's approval, he sent an expedition after Prestes (then at Iguassu) under politician-soldier Firmino Paim Filho. To gather information about rebel activities in frontier areas, Borges obtained consular appointments to Argentine and Uruguayan bordertowns for PRR members. He also arranged to have a Riograndense deputy, Nabuco Gouveia, named ambassador to Uruguay. Gouveia had led the Gaúcho delegation in congress; Borges now replaced him with freshman deputy Getúlio Vargas, chairman of the state assembly's vote-counting committee in 1922.

In October 1925 a third revolt hit Rio Grande do Sul, this one an invasion led by the stubborn Honório Lemes, still bent on unseating Borges; the movement was hostile to Bernardes only because Lemes thought the President had betrayed the rebels of 1923 by keeping Borges in power.[20] Again the revolt was quickly suppressed; Flôres da Cunha and Osvaldo Aranha, Republican heroes of 1923, joined battle with the old caudillo and captured him. Yet three defeats did not prevent still another revolt in the state, the fourth in four years. On the eve of the inauguration of Bernardes's successor in November 1926, Lt. Alcides Etchegoyen (later to be a prominent general and president of the Military Club) led a quixotic insurrection against the federal government from his garrison in southwestern Rio Grande. This was Liberator territory, and the battle-scarred opponents of Borges joined Etchegoyen's movement, just as they had joined Prestes in 1924. Like their predecessors, the tenentes and Liberators were soon chased across the border.

Suppressing the various revolts did not alter the revolutionary climate, and the literature of discontent mounted rapidly in the mid-1920's as tenentes and civilian radicals began to publish their indictments of the Bernardes regime and the system of political control it represented.[21] The early stages of industrialization and urbanization were creating new political forces that could not be absorbed into the coronel-dominated politics of the state machines. By 1920 the total value of industrial output in Brazil had already risen to two-thirds that of agricultural production.[22] For groups connected with industrial society, and especially the new middle sectors, the tenente revolts seemed to portend a change in the structure of Brazilian politics that would destroy the power of rural-based cliques.[23] Although many of the urban-oriented critics were also vaguely committed to an anti-imperialist position, their censure significantly focused on the failure of the political system to close the chasm between the ideals of popular sovereignty and the reality of elite control and coronelismo.

Since the dialogue among the critics was often limited to alternatives in political organization, Assis Brasil still exercised a broad influence in their ranks. From 1924 to 1927 Assis remained in voluntary exile in Uruguay. In this period he gave much thought to the political ills of the Brazilian nation, and by 1925 he concluded that the federal republican system was a failure. Still championing "representation and justice" as in 1908, the longtime antagonist of the PRR called for electoral reforms that would grant a place to minority parties at all levels of government and end coronel control of the Brazilian município, where political influence in the judiciary made a mockery of justice and elections. His specific remedies were compulsory and secret male suffrage, and federal appointment of judges on the basis of professional qualifications.[24] With considerable regret, Assis termed himself a revolutionary; revolution, he decided, was necessary to obtain political reform in Brazil.[25] Assis Brasil's arguments appealed to minority factions in São Paulo and the federal capital, groups that would soon join the Liberators to form a national opposition party.

Among the ruling circles of the major state parties, a desire to end the political unrest and military plotting was emerging by 1925. Bernardes had kept various parts of the nation under a state of siege during most of his term of office, and the political elites realized that if peace were to be achieved, the rebels would have to be repatriated. In March 1925 a Gaúcho congressman took an early initiative by unofficially approaching (with the tacit approval of Bernardes and

Borges) General Isidoro and other rebel chieftains, in Libres, Argentina, on Rio Grande's western frontier. Ultimately the talks bogged down over the rebels' refusal to surrender their arms in exchange for a promise of amnesty,[26] and the discussions broke off. The repatriation issue, however, was to persist into the presidential campaign of 1930.

Despite the upheavals of the Bernardes years, the Mineiro-Paulista alliance functioned smoothly in choosing the next president. It was São Paulo's "turn" to occupy Catete in 1926, since the last full-term Paulista administration was that of Rodrigues Alves in 1902–6. The *café-com-leite* candidates, Washington Luís of São Paulo for president and Fernando Melo Viana of Minas for vice president, were named by the leaders of the Republican parties of the two states and Artur Bernardes; the other state parties were simply told to fall into line. At the "suggestion" of Bernardes, each state held a convention of município leaders; these were followed in September 1925 by a national convention at which the candidacies were formally proclaimed. On March 1, 1926, the unopposed slate received 98 per cent of the vote in one of the quietest elections in Brazilian history.

Borges passively accepted the Paulista-Mineiro formula and the rigged convention system he had rejected in 1922. A major consideration was undoubtedly a recently acquired respect for the consequences of opposing the two-state alliance, since the troubles of the Bernardes years were in some measure traceable to the campaign of 1922. Moreover, Rio Grande do Sul owed a political debt to São Paulo. In exchange for Paulista intercession to minimize the effect of Bernardes's constitutional revisions in 1925, Vargas had promised Gaúcho backing for São Paulo's presidential ambitions.[27]

Borges de Medeiros also had financial and economic reasons to support Washington Luís. Although Bernardes had given the Gaúcho charque industry temporary advantages in the domestic market, the Riograndenses were on the whole dissatisfied with his policies. Gaúcho cattlemen, charque producers, and rice growers were coping with an economic crisis in 1926, and Deputy Vargas believed Bernardes was quick to assist the Paulista economy while ignoring Riograndense needs.[28] In addition, the Mineiro's austerity measures had been something less than a complete success, partly because of the military establishment needed to keep his government in power.[29]

Washington Luís intended to make exchange and price stabilization the first priority of his administration. Borges had repeatedly expressed his concern for domestic price stability, and the Paulista's platform meshed well with the Gaúcho's interpretation of Rio Grande's needs.[30] In his platform Washington Luís had announced his decision to return the milréis to gold convertibility and to introduce other financial reforms. Though he did not promise specific concessions to Rio Grande before his inauguration, he chose Getúlio Vargas as his minister of the treasury, a position in which Vargas would have ample opportunity to assist his home state. Despite Vargas's private disclaimers of his qualifications as a financial expert and his generally low opinion of the character and ability of the new president, Borges insisted he accept the post.[31]

With the aim of reconciling Rio Grande to the Minas–São Paulo alliance, Washington Luís made another gesture of goodwill before taking office. He went to Pôrto Alegre in June 1926 to reaffirm his solidarity with the PRR, becoming the first president or president-elect to visit the state in 20 years.* As further proof of his rapprochement with Rio Grande, he later reappointed the Governor's friend Andrade Neves commander of the Third Military Region.

Washington Luís's overtures were welcome to the Gaúchos after Bernardes had shown "what a [strong] government is."[32] However unpopular he was, there is no doubt Bernardes was decisive and knew how to manipulate the political elite. As president, he brought Riograndense power to its lowest level since the period of the Paulista "dynasty" (1894–1906). The civil war of 1923 gave him the opportunity to discipline Borges; recognizing and working within the limits of presidential power in handling an "autonomous" state, Bernardes still ably settled his score. The Governor of Rio Grande bowed to the will of the President and the leaders of São Paulo and Minas Gerais. Borges abandoned his allies of the Reação Republicana, accepted major changes in the state charter, and reversed the Gaúcho position on revision of the federal constitution. He saw congress throw out the mandates of two of his deputies to permit the seating

* Afonso Pena was the last to do so; he visited the state in August 1906. Hermes da Fonseca was in Rio Grande at the time of his election, though his victory was not recognized by congress until several months later.

of his Liberator opponents. Finally, he quietly submitted to a Paul-ista-Mineiro decision on the succession of 1926. Unlike the party lead-ers of Bahia, Rio State, and Pernambuco, however, he still managed to maintain the PRR in power by means of a political and military mobilization unequalled since the war of 1893–95.

The revolts of 1923–26 brought fame to a new generation. The tenentes, like their Riograndense contemporaries, gained national reputations. Still, in joining forces with an older generation of Lib-erator caudillos, the young officers inevitably contributed to a con-fusion about their objectives. This lack of definition applies as well to the uprisings in the federal capital and Mato Grosso in 1922, and to the one in São Paulo two years later.*

Although the motives for rebellion were diverse, even among the military rebels, what clearly emerges from the Bernardes era is a fur-ther deterioration of the legitimacy of the political system, a process that had begun in 1910 with the "salvations." To the excluded rural-oriented minority parties, urbanization and industrialization were adding articulate but unrepresented groups in the cities. By the mid-1920's even Assis Brasil had recognized that the problem of develop-ing democracy went beyond capturing state governments from en-trenched oligarchies, and that extra-legal measures were required to obtain fundamental political change.

Yet as Washington Luís entered office, the *política dos governa-dores* and its coronel substratum seemed to have weathered the storm. The state machines of the Reação Republicana had been punished, and the Reação's only autonomous party, the PRR, was suitably con-trite. With the military purged of its insubordinate elements by the revolts of the mid-1920's, the only threat to a tranquil administration seemed to be the possibility of a failure of the President's financial and economic policies or a division among the elites of the autono-mous states on the succession of 1930. At the end of his term, the Paulista would have to face both problems.

* Clodoaldo da Fonseca and Isidoro Dias Lopes represented a generation of officers out of touch with tenente currents. Both chose Bernardes as their target rather than the colonial agricultural economy to which the *política dos governadores* cor-responded. Meanwhile the tenentes were groping for an economic explanation of Brazil's problems.

# CHAPTER TEN

# The Last Crisis

In his final message to the state legislature, in September 1927, Governor Borges de Medeiros emphasized that the PRR remained "fundamentally conservative" and could be counted on as a "defender of order and authority." Prohibited by the Pact of Pedras Altas as well as by a federal constitutional amendment from succeeding himself as governor, Borges nevertheless kept his post as party chief, and so was able to choose a replacement he considered capable of continuing his conservative policies. In July Borges had informed Treasury Minister Getúlio Vargas that he was to head the next administration. In October a PRR convention nominated Vargas by acclamation; in November he won an election in which the Liberators refused to field a candidate; and on January 25, 1928, he took office at the age of forty-four.

Vargas's assumption of executive authority in the state symbolized the rise to power of a second generation of Riograndense politicians, most of them sons of Historical Republicans. The new group were to make their mark on national history; four became cabinet ministers, one became an interventor and governor, and Vargas himself alternately dictator and president of Brazil for a total of almost 19 years. The other members of the group were José Antônio Flôres da Cunha, Osvaldo Aranha, Lindolfo Collor, João Neves da Fontoura, (Joaquim) Maurício Cardoso, and Firmino Paim Filho. Fourteen years separated the oldest, Flôres (born in 1880) from the youngest, Aranha; all had been active in the Republican Party since their student days, and all except Collor were lawyers. Four had graduated from the law school in Pôrto Alegre in 1907 or 1908 (Vargas, Neves, Paim, and Cardoso) and had made their political debut in 1907 as members of the Castilhista Student Bloc during the gubernatorial campaign of Carlos Barbosa Gonçalves; I have chosen to apply the name Generation of '07 to the whole group.

Six of the Generation of '07 were sons or close relatives of coronéis, and five came from estancieiro families. All seven could claim varied and extensive political experience by the late 1920's. Five had been intendants of their home municípios, and all had been state assemblymen. Four had made their names in the field during the Liberator revolt of 1923, the other three by defending the Borges government at the special PRR convention. By 1928 all but one had been federal deputies, and in that year four were serving in the state executive. As their careers make clear, these men were successful members of the establishment party, enjoying rapid and regular promotion into posts of greater and greater responsibility.

Getúlio Dorneles Vargas, the foremost member of the Generation of '07, came from a politically prominent family on the Argentine border. His father, Gen. Manuel Nascimento Vargas, had been a PRR leader in São Borja since the days of the Federalist rebellion. The violence associated with coronelismo was not lacking in the Vargas fief. Local political opponents accused one of Getúlio's brothers, Viriato, of two assassinations, and 76 citizens of São Borja wrote Borges in 1919, complaining about the Vargas clan's violence. Getúlio himself tended to avoid the cruder aspects of coronelismo, however, though he once reported that he had participated in a voter registration campaign in which 214 Republicans and no Federalists were added to the rolls.[1]

After a false start in a military career, the young Vargas had displayed his considerable ability in student politics. When President-elect Pena visited Pôrto Alegre in 1906, Vargas was chosen by his fellow students to deliver an address at the reception; he spent most of his senior year campaigning for Carlos Barbosa Gonçalves. From the beginning Borges's interest in young Getúlio was clear. Immediately after graduation Getúlio served as public prosecutor in the state capital, and he soon entered the state legislature from his home district. In 1916 Borges offered him the job of state police chief, but he turned it down. This was evidence enough of his special relationship with the Governor: far from holding the refusal against the young man, Borges tapped him for majority leader of the Rio Grande legislature the following year. (Later Vargas got the delicate job of counting the votes in the gubernatorial race between Borges and Assis Brasil.) Getúlio went to congress in 1923 but came home to fight the Liberators. In 1924 he became leader of the Gaúcho delegation in the chamber of deputies. Two years later President Washington Luís named him minister of the treasury.

Vargas's extreme caution and skill at turning the course of events to his advantage would be evident in the following years. Short and stocky, affable and efficient, Vargas inspired confidence in the mellowing Borges de Medeiros, who saw in the younger man an effective administrator and able politician, not an ideologue. Those who view Vargas in the post-1930 era as a Júlio de Castilhos writ large exaggerate his "positivist dictator" heritage.[2] As a rising and ambitious politician in a party that took the works of Comte and Castilhos as dogma, Vargas knew how to offer the appropriate libations, and at one time even contributed money to the Positivist Church. He had eulogized Castilhos at a PRR commemoration service in 1903, and in 1908 in another speech, notable for its effusion if not its taste, he compared the Patriarch to Hercules, Buddha, Napoleon, and Garibaldi.[3] In point of fact, however, Vargas had little interest in the rigid doctrines of Castilhos; witness, for example, his assertion that Castilhismo broke through "theoretical and purely doctrinal requirements to adapt itself to the practical necessities . . . of [Rio Grande do Sul]."[4] As a student Getúlio was more interested in Spencer and Darwin than Comte. In any case he preferred fiction to philosophy; Emile Zola was his favorite writer. Both his philosophical and his literary tastes were eclectic. In his address honoring President-elect Pena in 1906, he declared that even "if the constancy of truth is a natural law, the thinking process can never be contained in a single frame of reference."[5]

Unlike Castilhos, Vargas liked to rule by conciliation rather than domination. Possibly his political style was influenced by the tragedy of 1893, which saw his relatives in the Dorneles family fighting on the Federalist side. In any event, it was said of the post-1930 Vargas that he never made enemies who could not later be made into friends. Shortly before taking office as governor in 1928, he hinted that the ideological battle in Rio Grande should be abandoned in the inter-est of peace with the Liberators.[6] After 1930 Vargas paid no homage to Castilhos or positivism, in contrast to some of the other Riogran-denses of his generation. As a political personality, he could hardly have been less like Castilhos. In his ability to recognize and make use of winning political combinations (regardless of doctrinal in-consistencies), as well as in his complete self-possession, Vargas was quite the opposite of the near-fanatical Castilhos. "More like a Mi-neiro than a Gaúcho" was one contemporary's judgment of him.[*]

Flôres da Cunha, also from a frontier family, was interventor and governor of Rio Grande from 1930 to 1937; during his last three years in office he became Vargas's most powerful opponent at the national level. If Vargas failed to measure up to the stereotype of the voluble, proud, and daring Gaúcho, Flôres preeminently fit that stereotype. Where Vargas relied on calculation and was careful to mask his true sentiments, Flôres had a reputation for bluntness and bravado. He was the man on horseback, the military hero of 1923, in many ways the successor of Pinheiro Machado. But even Pinheiro, who had engineered Flôres's first congressional post as a deputy from Ceará, once called him a hothead (doidivanas).[7] In recognition of his military campaigns against the rebels of the 1920's, Flôres had been made an honorary general in the army; in 1929 he went to congress as a senator.

Among the members of the Generation of '07, Osvaldo Aranha was to be second only to Vargas in his place in national history. Aranha was the principal architect of the revolution of 1930; he subsequently became the minister of justice, was twice appointed minister of the treasury, served as ambassador to the United States, and held the post of foreign minister during the Second World War. His father, like Vargas's, was a coronel in a Missões município facing Argentina. Aranha worked closely with Flôres to bring in the vote in western Rio Grande; on one occasion they were even jointly accused of fraud.[8] But Aranha had a more cosmopolitan background than his colleagues, having studied in Rio and Europe; he also had ties with São Paulo, where he had relatives in the political elite. Aranha's "ductile intelligence," as Vargas put it, won him a reputation for

---

[*] Virgilio de Mello Franco, Outubro, 1930 (n.p., 1931), p. 300. Since Mello Franco was a Mineiro, the remark was presumably intended as a compliment.

resolving dangerous disputes. He once settled a quarrel verging on violence between Flôres and an army commander, and became something of a trouble-shooter along the western border. But despite his role as peacemaker, he was willing to risk his life for the party, and was twice wounded in the revolts of the 1920's. He was an assemblyman less than a year before being elected a federal deputy. In 1928 the handsome and youthful Aranha (age thirty-four) became secretary of the interior of Rio Grande, overseeing the Military Brigade.

Lindolfo Collor, the nation's first minister of labor, made his mark in Brazilian history by organizing the urban proletariat into government-manipulated unions. His career up to 1928 was the least typical of the new Gaúcho leadership. He was born in the German-Brazilian community of São Leopoldo, was a Protestant, and had studied pharmacy before taking a degree in social sciences in Rio. Perhaps the most intellectual member of the rising generation, Collor came to the attention of Borges through his flair for combative journalism, which earned him the editorship of *A Federação*. In his partisan attacks in *A Federação* and later in the chamber of deputies, Collor was—at least rhetorically—as violent as Flôres.

João Neves, who replaced Collor as leader of the Gaúcho delegation in the chamber, was one of the initiators of Vargas's bid for the presidency in 1930, and later served twice as foreign minister. He came from Cachoeira, Borges's home, where his father, Isidoro Neves, was the coronel. João Neves was a brilliant speechmaker and debater, who extemporized glibly in the florid tradition of Rui Barbosa. After serving in the chamber, he was elected lieutenant governor in 1928. Because the post had no administrative duties, Borges allowed Neves to return to congress, where he served as head of the Riograndense delegation while retaining his office in the state government.

Both of the other two members of the new Gaúcho team, Maurício Cardoso and Firmino Paim Filho, came from the Serra, and both had been PRR activists since the days of the Student Bloc. Cardoso was to be a cabinet minister twice in the 1930's; Paim, however, reached his zenith in the late 1920's. Paim had served as chief of the state police after Getúlio turned down the job in 1916. He had led a "legalist" expedition in pursuit of Luís Carlos Prestes at Iguassu Falls and, like Flôres, had been made an honorary general. The most con-

servative member of the group and a Republican who took the Castilhista tradition more seriously than his fellows, Paim became a federal
senator in 1930, and unwittingly played a vital role in smoothing
the path for a revolution he thought he was averting. Cardoso, the
last member of the Generation of '07, vied with Collor as the leading
intellectual of the seven. The son of a judge, he had carried off the
prizes in his law school class of 1908, and his legal talents prompted
Vargas to appoint him minister of justice in 1931. He later became
Getúlio's minister of agriculture.

The head of the new team, Getúlio, ruled Rio Grande only two
years, but his achievements as governor were impressive. In that brief
period he obtained important economic concessions from the federal government and made peace of a sort with the PRR's rivals
within the state. He was aided in his demand for federal economic
assistance by the increasingly strong voice of Rio Grande's ranchers
and farmers, who were organizing rapidly to meet new problems.
Some of those problems were simply the result of an expanding
economy. Rising output, for instance, was precisely the problem the
rice growers were facing. The cultivation of flooded rice, introduced
in the Litoral at the beginning of the century, had accelerated after
World War I. The 1926–27 harvest was almost double the harvest of
1919–20, and the consequence was falling prices. In 1926 Vargas, then
a federal deputy, found President Bernardes indifferent to the "overproduction" crisis in rice. Accordingly, the Gaúchos took action
themselves. As Brazil's most efficient producers of high quality rice
and the nation's leading suppliers,* the Riograndense fazendeiros
were in a position to follow the example of the coffee planters to
"valorize" their commodity. To this end, they organized a rice syndicate to control supply and maintain prices at a high and fairly constant level. (Organization was not difficult, since the cultivation of
rice required high outlays and was consequently limited to wealthy
growers.) In 1927, the year after the syndicate was organized, out-of-
state shipments were reduced by 20 per cent; in the same year the
overall value of sales rose 25 per cent.[9]

---

* Rio Grande do Sul exported flooded rice to other members of the federation,
many of which grew only "Indian" rice, an inferior variety that did not require
irrigation. São Paulo's total rice output was greater than Rio Grande's, but the
Paulista rice was of generally lower quality, and a larger percentage of the crop
was consumed within the state.

Cattle ranchers and charque producers were also facing a crisis in 1926–27. There had been violent fluctuations in price and output in both the charqueadas and the frigoríficos since the First World War. Frigorífico production had been stimulated by the huge Allied food requirements during the war and in the immediate post-war period, but by the early 1920's the Armour and Swift plants in Rio Grande could not always compete with packing houses in the Plate, largely because of transportation costs. In 1922 frigorífico output in Rio Grande fell to one-tenth the 1921 figure. Production rose again in the next few years, only to fall off precipitously in 1926. The virtual frigorífico shutdown in that year, though temporary, was a major stimulus to the reconstitution of the defunct Rural Federation (FARSUL), in 1927.* Another fillip was the rapidly declining price of charque in the same year.

The interests of the charqueada owners did not always coincide with those of the ranchers; the smuggling situation is a case in point. Yet both groups were interested in keeping sales at a high level, and many estancieiros had investments in charque plants. Impressed by the effectiveness of the rice growers' organization, the charque producers organized a syndicate of their own in 1928. Since they furnished the bulk of the charque consumed in Brazil's coastal cities, they too were in a position to manipulate prices in the domestic market.

The charque producers and the ranchers, organized better than they had ever been before, asked the state government for help in cutting off the supply of smuggled charque from Uruguay. Vargas in turn asked for, and obtained, federal legislation to put an end to the contraband trade. The problem was that charque from the western state of Mato Grosso could be most profitably shipped to Brazil's coastal cities via the Plate tributaries to Montevideo, thence dispatched by freighter to Brazilian ports. The amount of charque shipped via this route would have been insignificant but for the traffic in false receipts, which allowed Uruguayan charque, disguised as the Matogrossense product, to enter Brazil under the tariff barriers. Not only could Uruguayan producers still offer charque at lower rates than the Gaúchos, but freight costs from Montevideo to Brazilian ports continued to be lower than those from Rio Grande.

* The Federação das Associações Ruraes do Estado do Rio Grande do Sul, an organization of local rural associations, was originally established in 1910.

In 1927 freight charges from Montevideo to Recife, for instance, were almost 30 per cent below those from the port of Rio Grande to Recife.[10] The contraband trade rose in the mid-1920's, seriously threatening the new Gaúcho charque syndicate, the success of which depended on a near-monopoly position in the market. In November 1928 Neves and Vargas got a bill through congress banning the transshipment of Brazilian charque via foreign ports, a measure that almost exclusively benefited Rio Grande do Sul. To lower freight charges, Vargas got the federal administration to match state funds on a three-to-one basis for the expansion of the state-owned railway system, and to turn over the ports of Tôrres and Pelotas to the state for development.[11]

In his own sphere of competence the Governor set up the Bank of Rio Grande do Sul, using state funds for two-thirds of the initial capital. This institution, established in 1928, was expressly created to extend low-cost credit to pastoral and agricultural interests and their derivative industries; in its first year of operation, the bank granted more than half its loans to charque producers.[12] Vargas also subsidized the infant export trade in charque and rice by lowering railway rates on shipments of the two products destined for foreign ports. The improved transport system, the credit facilities, and the freight subsidies mollified the group of charque producers that had previously shipped through Montevideo.

The organizational drives of the ranchers, charqueada owners, and rice growers were symptomatic of a general rise of "associativity" in Rio Grande in the late 1920's. Vineyard owners and lard producers also formed syndicates, and merchants formed a state Federation of Commercial Associations. Of the 70-odd commercial, agricultural, and pastoral associations extant in Rio Grande in 1930, almost half were formed between 1926 and 1929.[13] Vargas applauded this trend; indeed, his government encouraged it by sponsoring new interest-group associations.

One of the men most responsible for the innovations in Rio Grande do Sul was the intendant of Pôrto Alegre, Alberto Bins, whose career illustrates the increasing importance of the German-Brazilians in the state's economic life. The son of an immigrant tailor who became a merchant in Rio Grande, Bins was born in Pôrto Alegre in 1869 but received part of his education in Germany. As a young man he joined a metal works firm in the capital; he became the manager of the firm in 1904 and expanded its range of products. He later went into rice farming, and as the president of the Pôrto Alegre Commercial Association, organized the rice growers' syndicate with several other German-Brazilians in 1927, becoming the syndicate's first director. In the same year he became the president of yet another enterprise, and again German-Brazilians and Germans took the initiative. This was the Viação Aérea Riograndense (VARIG), today the largest airline in Latin America and one of the most highly capitalized corporations in Brazil. VARIG was the nation's first domestic-chartered commercial airline; its original fleet consisted entirely of seaplanes to make the short hops between the state's major ports, Pôrto Alegre, Pelotas, and Rio Grande.*

Alberto Bins's success as an organizer was in part based on his administrative experience and connections as a PRR official. A member of the Pôrto Alegre município council from 1908 to 1913, he subsequently entered the state legislature and served as an assemblyman until 1928, when he became intendant of the capital. He remained intendant (a title that was later changed to prefect) for almost ten years, during which time he presided over the modernization of the city. He provided Pôrto Alegre with potable water, expanded water mains and the sewer system, widened and paved the streets, and tripled the city's electrical power capacity.†

Bins's talents as a syndicate organizer and Vargas's strong backing

---

* VARIG initially had financial ties with the Berlin-based Condor Syndikat, which began commercial aviation in Brazil. This organization should not be confused with the Rio-chartered (and Lufthansa-sponsored) Syndicato Condor, Ltda., also founded in 1927. See [VARIG], Início da aviação comercial no Brasil (documentário) (n.p., n.d.), pp. [1, 3].

† As an industrialist, Bins was more a paternalist than a progressive in his labor-management relations. He supported the government-controlled labor system that Vargas and Collor introduced in 1930, and applauded the quasi-fascist Estado Nôvo coup of 1937. Antônio Jacob Renner, another Brazilian of German extraction, had a similar career, though, unlike Bins, he was a member of the Protestant community of Rio Grande. Renner began as a lard producer, but soon went into the textile field, where he pioneered in the production and sale of waterproof ponchos for gaúchos. An admirer of the industrialized society of the United States, Renner introduced a three-shift schedule at his textile plant in Pôrto Alegre. With the support of Bins, he organized the Textile Industry Center in 1931 to promote the interests of mill owners. Renner too favored paternalism as a solution for the "social question" and, like Bins, welcomed the 1937 coup. For details on the careers of these two men, see Erich Fausel, Alberto Bins, merlense brasileiro (São Leopoldo, n.d.); and Ernesto Pellanda, A. J. Renner: Um capitão da indústria (Pôrto Alegre, 1944).

of the pastoral interests helped improve the PRR's relations with the opposition party. But Vargas did not rely on economic measures alone to come to terms with the Liberators; he also made direct political concessions to them. In certain municípios where the opposition was numerically strong, he took steps to ensure honest elections. Borges had allowed the Liberators six uncontested seats in the 32-man legislature after 1923; Vargas let them win a seventh in March 1929. Moreover, he invited Liberators to visit him at the governor's mansion, a gesture never considered by Borges de Medeiros. To be sure, Getúlio could afford to be more flexible than Borges; he was not a usurper in the Liberators' eyes. More important, the PRR was less ideologically oriented after Pedras Altas removed the *raison d'être* of the party's anti-revisionist posture.

Meanwhile the prestige of the Liberators had risen in national politics, for Assis Brasil had at last realized his 30-year-old dream of forming a national opposition party. In September 1927 the Aliança Libertadora joined the fledgling Partido Democrático of São Paulo to form the Partido Democrático Nacional (National Democratic Party); the new party also included a small group from the Federal District. Assis Brasil was elected president of the loose-knit structure.*

The Paulista Democratic Party had been organized in 1926 by men who repudiated the corruption of the entrenched PRP; its mildly reformist program centered on new electoral legislation. The PD represented urban groups as well as coffee growers in São Paulo, though it was more closely tied to banking and the professions than to industry.[14] The Paulistas did not go along with Assis's strategy of reform by revolution; they were, however, united with their Riograndense colleagues in their opposition to the fraud used against the minority parties by the Republican machines of their respective states.

Of the three most important state organizations in national politics, only the PRM did not face a formal opposition party after 1926, and Antônio Carlos Ribeiro de Andrada, the governor of Minas, expected to swing his state's massive vote behind a Mineiro candidate for president in 1930—presumably himself. It was "Minas's round" in the presidency, and Antônio Carlos hoped for the placet of President Washington Luís. However, chances seemed slight, for the two

---

* In 1928 the Aliança Libertadora was reorganized as the Partido Libertador (PL).

had not seen eye to eye on matters of mutual interest in economics and administration. Temperamentally, too, the refined and subtle Mineiro (scion of one of Brazil's founding fathers) had little in common with the plain-spoken, less aristocratic President. By late 1928 Antônio Carlos suspected that Washington Luís might try to put another Paulista in Catete, breaking the pattern of Mineiro-Paulista alternation.

João Neves, the head of the Gaúcho delegation in congress, learned in November that Antônio Carlos and his party would veto a Paulista candidate, a development that in his opinion made Vargas an excellent prospect for a compromise nominee. But Vargas was reluctant to join in the speculation about the matter, even when Flôres da Cunha reported that Washington Luís would consider a Gaúcho candidacy if Minas blocked the President's favorite, Gov. Júlio Prestes of São Paulo. Both Vargas and Borges (who was informed immediately) remained skeptical and discreet;[15] they saw no reason to alter their position as succession rumors continued to circulate in the first half of 1929.

By June Antônio Carlos had concluded that the President would definitely back Prestes, and Neves was able to report to Vargas that the Mineiros would stand by their word to stop São Paulo. Neves and Francisco Campos, a representative of the PRM, met in Rio on June 17 to sign a pact, subject to the ratification of Borges. According to the terms of the agreement, if the President accepted a Mineiro as his successor, the PRR would support the candidate; if he did not, Minas would back Getúlio Vargas or Borges de Medeiros.[16] It was a foregone conclusion that Washington Luís would reject any Mineiro candidate; but if for some reason he had decided to support Minas, Rio Grande's attitude would have been a negligible factor in the succession. The pact thus was extremely advantageous to the Gaúchos, since the Mineiros did all the giving.

Yet both Borges and Vargas were wary. The old party chief saw the debacle of 1922 as proof that no candidate could win against the opposition of the president. In any case he would not run, he told Vargas. For his part, Vargas had already decided on his own that no one could beat the favorite of an incumbent president, and he had written Neves shortly before the pact was signed that the Governor of Rio Grande could not make any deal with Minas without consulting Catete. The truth is, Vargas distrusted the silky Antônio Carlos and feared that the Mineiro might be using him as a pawn to obtain a Mineiro candidacy at a later date.[17]

Nonetheless, the Minas offer was tempting. Except for Marshal Hermes, a Riograndense had never occupied the presidential palace. And the strategy of Neves and the Mineiros seemed sound enough: to work for a near-unanimous vote for Vargas in Minas and Rio Grande. These two states alone could approach an absolute electoral majority, if they suffered no internal division. Neves reckoned on some 500,000 votes from Minas and about 200,000 from Rio Grande.* (The Rio Grande figure was based on the assumption that the Liberators would support Vargas.)

After some hesitation Borges and Vargas agreed to the terms of the pact, though Vargas still seemed to hope that he might receive the President's endorsement in a compromise with Minas. In July 1929 Vargas wrote Washington Luís of the Mineiros' offer; but, he asserted, he would not stand in the way of another mutually acceptable candidate. The President's reply was that 17 governors—all except those of Minas, Rio Grande, and little Paraíba—had expressed their support for Júlio Prestes of São Paulo. At this show of strength, Vargas realized that his chances of winning were extremely slim. Accordingly, on July 29 he wrote Washington Luís again, declaring that he would retire from the race provided the PRM gave its approval.[18]

The Mineiros did not, as Vargas had probably foreseen. Early the next month, João Neves opened the presidential campaign in congress. Washington Luís, nettled by the continued resistance of the Gaúchos and Mineiros, then published his correspondence with Getúlio and Antônio Carlos concerning the succession. In Vargas's opinion, this breach of confidence dealt a fatal blow to negotiations to avoid a contested election.[19]

Washington Luís did not doubt his candidate would win without Minas and Rio Grande. Presumably he and the leaders of the PRP reasoned that they deserved an extended residence in the presidential

---

* Neves to Vargas, Rio, June 15, 1929 (copy), Archive of Borges de Medeiros. In 1928 Minas had only some 320,000 voters, the record to that date; in 1930, however, registration more than doubled, to 646,000. See Directoria Geral de Estatistica, *Relatorios* [1928, 1929] (Rio, 1930), p. 195; *Diario do Congresso Nacional*, XLI, 16 (May 21, 1930), 545.

palace, since São Paulo had headed only one administration since 1906 (excluding the short-lived victory of 1918). Furthermore, São Paulo had led the federation in population growth and by 1929 was the most under-represented state in the chamber, for no reapportion-ment had been made since the first legislature in 1891–93.* São Paulo's under-representation in congress could be compensated by a longer tenure in the presidency. Still another consideration was that Júlio Prestes had guided the President's monetary reform bill through congress before becoming governor of São Paulo; Washington Luís seems to have had faith in him as a conservative administrator, much as Campos Sales had had in Rodrigues Alves in 1901. Finally, there was a psychological element as well. Washington Luís was not a man who was disposed to compromise solutions. Having committed him-self to Prestes, he would not yield to pressure with the malleability of a pragmatic politician like Vargas. The President maintained he was "too old to run" from a fight, Neves reported.[20]

In September representatives from the establishment parties of Minas, Paraíba, and Rio Grande, along with opposition leaders from other states, met in the capital of Minas to officially launch Vargas's campaign. Lindolfo Collor wrote a manifesto for the coalition, hence-forth known as the Aliança Liberal (Liberal Alliance). The conven-tion unanimously nominated Vargas for president, and as previ-ously arranged, chose Paraíba's governor, João Pessôa (nephew of former President Epitácio Pessôa), as Vargas's running mate. In the same month a Paulista-led convention of delegates from the estab-lishment parties of the other states nominated Prestes for president and Gov. Vital Soares of Bahia for vice president. Like the campaign of 1910, the contest of 1930 pitted Minas and Rio Grande against São Paulo and Bahia.

Although Vargas had had second thoughts about his candidacy in July and August, he had not lost time in securing his position. Lib-erator representation in congress had been cut from seven to three seats in 1927, and Vargas now promised the opposition two more un-contested seats, bringing the Liberator total to five of 16 places. Hold-

---

* In 1930 São Paulo had one deputy for every 291,000 inhabitants, Rio Grande one for every 185,000, and Minas one for every 201,000 (based on contemporary popu-lation estimates).

ing out the bait of electoral reform if he should win, Vargas told the Liberators flatly that he would not run without their full support.[21] These were rear-guard actions to make sure that in the event Prestes won, he and his patron, Washington Luís, would not be able to use the Liberators to punish the Republicans as Bernardes had done in 1924. Assis Brasil agreed to Vargas's proposals in July, and for the first time in the history of the Republic, Gaúcho politicians united behind the same candidate. Assurances about electoral reform and guarantees for minority representation in Vargas's program brought the whole PDN into his camp at the beginning of September. At a party meeting that month, dissident politicians from an earlier age, among them Pedro Moacyr, Dantas Barreto, and Clodoaldo da Fonseca, cast their lot with Vargas. While negotiating with the Liberators in July, Vargas had insisted that the Mineiros take the lead in proposing his candidacy,[22] thereby making Minas a more likely target for presidential wrath than Rio Grande; and it was also at Vargas's insistence that the Aliança Liberal convention was held in Belo Horizonte.

Despite these adroit maneuvers, Vargas remained singularly unenthusiastic about the campaign. Bearing the responsibility for the state government, he was apprehensive about the consequences of opposing the President. In mid-1929 he had been eager to maintain good relations with the administration to get a loan for the charque industry; by August, even before he was formally a candidate, the federal government was exerting pressure on the states supporting Vargas. In Rio Grande, Vargas sadly noted, the government was suspending the construction of new telegraph lines. He also worried about what he saw as a federal military buildup to isolate Rio Grande and crush Minas.[23]

In July 1929 Vargas had sought a compromise on the succession that would have sacrificed his own candidacy. When the possibility of averting a race seemed to vanish in August, he had proposed to his allies that the opposition slate be made up of candidates from Pernambuco and Ceará; this scheme would bring five establishment parties into the anti-Paulista coalition, guaranteeing an absolute majority. When Ceará and Pernambuco rebuffed the offer, Vargas had turned again to the idea of a compromise candidate, despite his recent conviction that Washington Luís had burned the bridges by publishing their confidential correspondence.[24] But the President and the PRP had remained firmly behind Prestes.

Vargas could not withdraw without the concurrence of the PRM and his own party. After the Aliança convention, both organizations would have been badly divided if Vargas suddenly backed down. Yet if he lost the race, the federal government might retaliate against the Aliança states. Vargas's way of meeting the dilemma was to encourage both the militants of the Aliança Liberal and those who sought conciliation with the administration, until the day he would have to choose between the two groups. He let Neves, Collor, Aranha, and the Mineiros pursue a belligerent course. At the same time he privately agreed with Paim that the conflict could still be resolved amicably and urged him to maintain the vital link with Rio de Janeiro. Paim probably saw a personal political advantage in this role, since Vargas would require his good offices with Júlio Prestes after 1930; in any event, he accepted the task.

Winning with only three state machines and the minority vote elsewhere postulated virtual unanimity at the polls in Minas, Rio Grande, and Paraíba. In an epoch when the influence of the press was still limited to a few urban areas, large vote totals depended on the unity and enthusiasm of the state parties. Minas was the key state because of its huge electorate, and Antônio Carlos had assured Vargas that the Mineiro party would stand united. However, at a meeting of the PRM executive committee in October 1929, Vice President Melo Viana broke with other PRM leaders over succession in the state government and withdrew his support from the Aliança Liberal. Vargas consequently felt he had been betrayed by the Mineiros, since he calculated Melo Viana's dissidents would divert 20 per cent of the Minas vote to Prestes. The hope of victory, dim at best, now faded, and Getúlio sought another compromise: not a third candidate, but simply face-saving concessions in Prestes's platform.[25] The offer was spurned.

With the last avenue to compromise closed, Vargas decided to save his own party from reprisals at all costs, whatever might happen to the Mineiros and Paraibanos, and to the Liberators of Rio Grande. He called on Paim to negotiate a secret pact with Washington Luís and Júlio Prestes. Getúlio agreed not to leave the state during the campaign and, if beaten, to accept Prestes's victory as legitimate. For their part, Washington Luís and Prestes agreed to support the seating of all Gaúcho deputies elected in March, not to aid the Liberators against the Republicans, and to reestablish normal relations between the government of Rio Grande and the federal government after the election.[26]

At the end of December Vargas violated the new pact by flying to Rio de Janeiro, where he revealed his platform on January 2. This document differed little from the Aliança Liberal manifesto of September; for the most part it was a warmed-over version of Assis Brasil's long-standing demands for minority representation and judicial and electoral reform, including the introduction of a secret ballot. In addition, Vargas promised a new effort to develop the northeast, and more effective protection in the international market for coffee and other Brazilian products. He pledged to repeal the extraordinary laws of censorship and siege in force since the Bernardes administration, and to extend amnesty to the rebels of the 1920's.

What was new in his platform was a nod to the idea of agrarian reform, which he probably had no intention of implementing, and a promise to enact social security legislation and draw up a labor code for Brazil's urban workers. Vargas's initial draft of a program said nothing about the labor question; this idea apparently came from Collor, who was both ahead of his contemporaries in recognizing the need to modernize Brazilian society and aware of the vogue of corporativism in Europe.[27] The provisions concerning labor, agrarian reform, and the state of siege were largely directed at Brazil's new urban classes, still excluded from meaningful participation in politics. These groups naturally shared an interest in honest elections with the traditional opposition parties and factions. A final innovation in Vargas's platform was the manner in which it was presented. Instead of reading his program at a banquet of the political elite as Júlio Prestes and all previous candidates had done, Vargas addressed his words to a milling throng in the national capital.

The climax of the campaign came in February, when disorders in Minas prompted Washington Luís to intervene in certain sections of the state; he also prevented an official statewide vote tabulation in Belo Horizonte, an action that aided Prestes. Rio Grande escaped this humiliation, though it appeared for a time that a Communist-scare involving the Military Brigade might become a pretext for intervention. In any case the public at large viewed Júlio Prestes's victory as a certainty; witness the lyrics to one of the most popular sambas for the 1930 carnival (written by the celebrated Sinhô):[28]

| | |
|---|---|
| Eu ouço falar | I hear it said |
| Que para o nosso bem | That for our own good |
| Jesús já designou | Jesus has already decreed |
| Que Seu Julinho é que vem. | That Julinho is the one. |

The Riograndenses apparently did not agree. In the election of March 1, Rio Grande do Sul delivered what it had promised, and more. As usual, the voting rate was proportionately higher in Rio Grande than in any other state. Instead of the estimated 200,000 votes for Vargas, Rio Grande gave him almost 300,000; Prestes got fewer than 1,000 votes, or three-tenths of 1 per cent of the total. Minas, as Vargas had predicted, failed to supply its quota. In the official count in May it gave Vargas fewer votes than did his home state. Even so, until congress whittled down the Mineiro total for Vargas, his margin in Minas appeared substantial enough to let *A Federação* claim a narrow nationwide victory for the Gaúcho candidate. Aranha, who was governing Rio Grande during the election, charged that fraud had vitiated the elections in many of the states where Prestes won heavily.[29]

Still, everyone realized that the Paulista-controlled congress would declare Prestes the winner. The specter of 1922 now appeared, and with the same problem: the only hope the states opposing Prestes had to withstand federal pressure was to remain united. Though Vargas had secretly gone a long way toward arranging a separate peace for Rio Grande, there were serious drawbacks to his plan, namely, the certainty of a rupture with the Liberators over the abandonment of the Paulista Democrats and the probability of serious dissension within the PRR itself over the abandonment of Minas; such eventualities would make it far easier for Washington Luís to punish the PRR, if he chose to do so. An alternative was a military revolt against the federal government, the course that Nilo and Borges had considered in the wake of the 1922 election.

In 1930 there was no "false letters" scandal to alienate the army from the President-elect. However, the economic situation made the post-election climate much more volatile than in 1922, and the leaders of the Aliança Liberal began to consider the prospect of revolution. The international coffee market had collapsed, following the American stock market crash of October 1929. In 1930 New York price quotations for coffee fell to half the 1929 figure. Brazil still earned some 70 per cent of its foreign exchange from coffee, and the contraction of the American economy, followed by repercussions in Europe, left millions of bags of coffee standing in Brazilian ports. Valorization, which kept the international price of coffee artificially high, had postponed and exacerbated the problem of excess stocks by attracting new entrants into coffee production. Speculative investment had almost doubled the size of the crop in São Paulo between 1925 and 1929. In the period of 1927–29 production had already outstripped international sales by one-third, and growers were borrowing funds at an interest rate of 2 per cent a month to open new plantations. With the crash and the international depression, many coffee planters were ruined, and wages on the fazendas of São Paulo fell by 40 per cent. By November 1930, 23.6 million bags of coffee had been stored in São Paulo—almost twice the amount of Brazil's annual exports.[30]

The federal government had a problem of its own. Washington Luís had come into office with a program of financial reform and currency stabilization designed to strengthen Brazil's precarious financial position. At the end of 1926, when he took charge, Brazil's foreign debt (federal, state, and local obligations) amounted to $900 million, and foreign private investment totaled $800 million. Interest payments alone on government debts amounted to $63 million a year, and funding loan amortization payments were scheduled to begin in 1927. In addition, profits remittances on foreign capital amounted to $175 million yearly. These problems had to be attacked in two ways, the President believed. First, monetary and financial reforms were essential to keep the foreign debt from rising even higher, and second, a huge export surplus was needed to offset debt servicing and profits remittances.

To limit the growth of Brazil's foreign debt, Washington Luís had tried to stabilize the exchange rate in order to avoid having to repay loans in ever more expensive "hard" currencies, and had adopted a program of financial austerity. He had achieved a budget surplus in 1927, the first president to do so since Afonso Pena in 1908. On the second requirement, Washington Luís believed expanding exports meant encouraging coffee sales; nevertheless, he had left that problem to the government of São Paulo, since federal price supports would have inevitably clashed with his financial austerity and stabilization programs.[31] The administration's stabilization plan depended on the steady accumulation of gold in a conversion fund to bring fiat money up to parity with specie-redeemable currency. But by the end of 1930 Brazil's inability to sell coffee and the flight of capital from foreign firms struggling for survival at home had completely exhausted the nation's gold reserves, which had stood at £31 million in September 1929.

Moreover, there was a conflict of interest between the government of São Paulo and the federal government. São Paulo had virtually assumed the responsibility for coffee protection in 1924, and a series of interstate agreements in the late 1920's still revolved around São Paulo. In 1930 the state government negotiated a foreign loan of £20 million to pay planters for stockpiled coffee, but the sum was far from adequate, and São Paulo turned to the federal treasury. Washington Luís, however, refused to place even greater demands on his dwindling gold reserves or to issue fiat currency. After October 1929 he had gambled that falling coffee prices would expand sales.[32] They did not—the demand for coffee proved inelastic. The impasse inevitably turned the Paulista planters against their President.

Of the half dozen most economically developed states, Rio Grande do Sul was the only one not primarily dependent on foreign markets (since it sold charque and rice principally to Brazilians); unlike most of the other states, it did not feel the effects of the depression immediately. The respite was brief, however. Many Riograndense banks soon experienced heavy withdrawals, and their directors appealed to the state government for aid. Yet if São Paulo could not float sufficient loans in foreign markets or obtain adequate help from the treasury, how much less likely that Rio Grande do Sul would succeed. The administration did respond to Vargas's request for a loan to assist the foundering Pelotense Bank, but this was nothing more than a palliative measure. Banks in Rio Grande began closing their doors, as banks were doing all over the nation, and the pastoral and agricultural industries began to feel the pinch as mortgages were called in.

The depression was bound to strengthen the position of those who advocated revolt in Rio Grande. Though Vargas continued to temporize, with the concurrence of Borges, the partisans of peace and war were unquestionably straining the unity of the Gaúcho party. Neves wanted to keep the opposition alive in congress; Aranha favored outright revolt, and Flôres soon joined him. Senator-elect Paim and some of the older congressmen wanted reconciliation. The Castilhista slogan—"neither unconditional support nor systematic opposition"—was cited by Borges and Vargas as a guiding principle. But when it came to specifics, Vargas allowed Paim and Neves to interpret the phrase in their own way. Meanwhile he alternately supported the "reconciliation" and "resistance" factions, and was in fact able to use the antagonistic groups to maintain good relations with both the Mineiros and the President, thus transforming the division in PRR ranks into an asset.

No one in the party knew where the state government stood with respect to the administration, both because of uncertainty about the chain of command and because of the vacillation of Borges and Vargas. On the first count, Vargas purposely referred tough decisions to Borges, the party chief. But no one was sure where real power lay, since Borges was at his ranch in the interior and not easily accessible. He could be contacted only by telegraph and therefore was unable to stay abreast of the day-to-day and hour-to-hour developments known to Vargas. On the question of the future of the Aliança Liberal, Borges equivocated. In an interview published in late March, he stated that the Aliança would expire with the final vote count by congress; at the same time he asserted it could be reshaped to defend Vargas's platform. In April Borges agreed to let Neves continue the parliamentary campaign.

Vargas meanwhile had not rejected the possibility of returning to the President's fold. "We have no grievances to avenge," he wrote Borges; "what we do have are important economic and administrative interests . . . dependent in great measure on the goodwill of the federal government." Ever distrustful of Antônio Carlos, Vargas believed the Mineiros were seeking to push Rio Grande into a break with the President; if successful they would force Prestes to work with the PRM, since he would need at least two of the big three machines to operate effectively in congress. Vargas told the PRR chief he though it best to abandon the struggle and to make peace with the President, but he left the decision to Borges.[33]

If Vargas seems to have been indecisive, it was not because he balked at contemplating drastic alternatives. He and Aranha had long been considering the idea of revolution, partly because they feared the vengeance of the outgoing administration. For the Governor, however, this was simply one of several contingency plans. Luís Carlos Prestes, who as leader of the famous rebel column in the mid-1920's had become the hero of middle-class reformers, secretly contacted Vargas in September 1929 to discuss plans for a revolt.[34] By December Aranha had concluded that revolution was the only way to stop the Paulista steamroller. Soon thereafter Vargas made him the coordinator of revolutionary planning—as an alternative to accommodation with the federal government. After the March elections, Minas and Paraíba agreed to enter the conspiracy, also on a contingency basis. The tenentes of 1922, 1924, and 1926 (many of whom had fought the Gaúcho Military Brigade and provisional corps) crossed the Argentine and Uruguayan frontiers, making frequent contact with Aranha in the first half of 1930. Using his position as state secretary of the interior as a cover, Aranha ordered arms from Czechoslovakia. The governments of Rio Grande, Minas, and Paraíba shared the cost for these weapons in proportion to their ability to pay and obtain credit.

To direct actual military operations, the Gaúchos preferred an officer with a command to tenentes with an uncertain following in the regular army. Lt. Col. Pedro Góes Monteiro, who led an infantry unit in the Missões District, took the job. Born in the northeast, Góes nevertheless considered himself a Gaúcho, having spent much of his life in Rio Grande do Sul.[35] While in military school in Pôrto Alegre, he had been a member of the Castilhista Student Bloc and had known both Vargas and Neves. He was much closer to Aranha, however; the two had become good friends in the western region of the state. Góes and Aranha set a date in June for the revolution, even though the support of Vargas and Borges was still in doubt.

While the plans for insurrection were maturing, Luís Carlos Prestes suddenly issued a manifesto that completely staggered his fellow conspirators. At the end of May he announced his conversion to revolutionary Marxism and dismissed the budding plot against Washington Luís as a design to put a new elite in power. The darling of the urban middle classes had presented his admirers with a stark alternative to the prevailing political and social system. Though he repudiated the coming bourgeois revolution, Prestes neglected to return the money he had received from Aranha for the purchase of weapons.

Vargas hastily produced a statement, announcing that he would consider the campaign of the Aliança Liberal terminated with the count by congress, but that he would still support the Aliança program. The combination of the Prestes defection and the Vargas double-talk was too much for Antônio Carlos, who began to hedge on his commitment to revolution. In Rio Grande, Vargas and Borges grew more timid as the Mineiro's coolness to the conspiracy increased,[36] and after months of detailed preparations, Aranha saw his edifice crumbling. Unlike Vargas, Aranha had risked his entire political future on the revolution; without it he was ruined, for the federal government was aware of some of his subversive activities. Informing the conspirators in Minas that he was "fed up," Aranha resigned his post in the Rio Grande government on June 28. Federal authorities exulted, believing the plot had collapsed.

Washington Luís in the meantime had made no attempt to conciliate the leaders of the defeated Aliança Liberal. His pliant congress not only certified Júlio Prestes as president-elect but also punished the incumbent parties of Paraíba and Minas Gerais. In the case of the smaller state, the credentials committees recognized all the pro-Prestes candidates, five nominees for the chamber and one for the senate—this despite the fact that Vargas had beaten Prestes by a margin of three to one in the simultaneous presidential election, according to congress's own tally![37] Melo Viana's pro-Prestes faction was awarded 14 of Minas's 37 seats. Rio Grande do Sul came through the congressional purge unscathed. Since the two Gaúcho parties had not contested each other's seats, there was no way to juggle the election results in favor of minority candidates. Moreover, the understanding Senator Paim had negotiated with the administration probably tempered the President's treatment of the Riograndense delegation.

The troubles of Vargas's running mate, Governor Pessôa, did not end with the complete victory of the pro-administration opposition in congress. In Princesa, a town in the interior of Paraíba, a coronel had taken up arms against the state government. The rebellion was a response to Pessôa's efforts to force the population of the backlands to trade through the state port of Cabedelo rather than through Recife, in the neighboring state of Pernambuco. To this end, he had instituted a tax on goods moving across the Paraíba-Pernambuco frontier. The revolt was thus rooted in a dispute over the Governor's taxation policies, made all the more bitter by his attempts to punish his rivals politically. But the leaders of the Aliança Liberal believed the federal government was encouraging the rebels in order to create an excuse for intervention. Aranha (at the time still secretary of the interior in Rio Grande) covertly dispatched arms to Pessôa's government to help contain the revolt. João Pessôa's inconclusive struggle with the rebels ended abruptly on July 26, when an assassin gunned him down during a visit to Recife. Pessôa had only reluctantly agreed to bring his government into the revolutionary planning; now, as a martyr, he was perhaps worth more to the plotters than he had been as a conspirator.

The Paraíbano legislature quickly changed the name of the state capital from Paraíba to João Pessôa. They also adopted a new state motto—*Nego!* (I refuse!)—Pessôa's alleged response when Washington Luís had requested his support for Prestes. In the chamber of deputies Collor exploited the emotional situation ("President of the Republic, what have you done to the Governor of Paraíba?"),[38] but Vargas himself made no public statement, to the relief of the administration. Federal troops meanwhile had intervened in Paraíba to protect rebel-held municípios against reprisals, though Pessôa's legal successor was allowed to take office. Vargas wired the new governor in deliberately equivocating and murky language: "I have faith that the [federal] forces will respect the state's autonomy, remaining loyal to the glorious traditions of the national army. If, however, the evils currently afflicting . . . Paraíba continue, we ought not doubt that the civic energies of the nation will awaken, transformed into a generalized protest, which will immediately receive the support of Rio Grande do Sul."[39]

Nor did the Pessôa assassination strengthen the resolve of Antônio Carlos who, according to a famous anecdote, said, "Let's make the revolution before the people do." These brave words suggest the governor of Minas Gerais had perceived where the long-range interests of the political elite lay—but his actions did not suit his putative words. After the Paraíba affair he decided to bequeath the awful decision on Minas's participation in the revolution to his successor; thus the conspirators had to delay their plans still further until the inauguration of the new governor on September 6.

During this period Getúlio still had not decided to commit Rio Grande to the revolution, though in August he allowed Aranha to resume his preparations. At the same time Paim was continuing to relay messages between Pôrto Alegre and Rio, and Vargas played the injured party over the outrages in Paraíba. Paim knew a plot was brewing, but Vargas denied its importance. What the Governor's real attitude was is in doubt; he informed Borges on August 24 that he was willing to fold up the whole conspiratorial operation. At the end of the month Borges seems finally to have given Aranha the crucial support he needed, apparently won over by the argument that order could not be maintained in the midst of economic chaos, and that revolution was inevitable. Vargas was ready to follow the lead of the party chief.[40]

Elsewhere in Latin America the deepening depression was taking its toll, even among the most politically stable states. On September 6 Argentina experienced its first coup d'état in 40 years, an upheaval that boded ill for Brazil, whose record of political stability was almost exactly as long as Argentina's. The day of the Argentine coup was also the day a new governor took charge in Minas Gerais. Left with the decision on his state's participation in the plot, Gov. Olegário Maciel quickly indicated his willingness to keep Minas in the conspiracy.

Góes Monteiro and Aranha moved swiftly ahead with their military plans. In September Aranha informed Vargas that he had enough arms and ammunition to outfit some 110,000 men. The Military Brigade was ready for combat, and its equipment compared favorably with that of the regular army.[41] Aranha and Góes secured the collusion of enough army officers across the state to ensure that the vast majority of the troops in the Third Military Region, representing more than a quarter of all the federal forces, would join the revolt.

But Vargas and Borges wanted top military commanders in Rio in on the plot as well, so that the revolt could be rapidly consummated in a coup d'état and civil war averted. To that end, they dispatched Collor to the capital to solicit the support of sympathetic generals.[42] Though he brought back no definite commitments, he believed military leaders in Rio would accept the ouster of Washington Luís. A personal plea from Borges to the commander of the garrison in the capital of Paraná neutralized the army all the way to the border of São Paulo, except for the garrisons in Pôrto Alegre and Florianópolis, the island capital of Santa Catarina. The plotters in Rio Grande decided to make their move on October 3 and synchronized their plans with fellow conspirators around the country. The revolt was to begin simultaneously in Rio Grande, Minas, and the states of the northeast. In Minas and Rio Grande the state governments were to assume responsibility for the military attack; in the northeast Juarez Távora, one of the tenente rebels of 1924, would direct operations. João Alberto Lins de Barros and Alcides Etchegoyen, tenente veterans of the 1924 and 1926 uprisings, were given important assignments in Rio Grande.

In the final weeks before the revolt, Vargas played the invaluable role of keeping the regime off balance. He had convinced Paim that the plotters were now beyond the party's control; all of them, he assured Paim, had ruined their careers in the PRR. Paim conveyed his impression of the Governor's sincerity to the President. The reputation of the PRR as a bastion of legality, an image projected by both Castilhos and Borges, was almost certainly of help to Vargas in maintaining this fiction. Getúlio was equally effective in dealing with the commander of the Third Region, Gen. Gil de Almeida. Staunchly loyal to Washington Luís, Almeida had gathered many clues about the Aranha group and its activities. Aranha, however, with the aid of talented amateurs, had broken the code the General used in his communications with the war ministry, and so could anticipate all troop movements.[43] Vargas dealt with General Almeida as he did with Paim, making him privy to inconsequential details about the conspiracy but dismissing the revolutionaries as ineffectual and isolated from party and government. João Simplício Alves, who had replaced Aranha as secretary of the interior, was charged with the task of assuring Almeida of Getúlio's good faith; his job was made easier by his ignorance of Vargas's real plans.

At 5 P.M. on October 3 the revolt began, as Flôres and Aranha led an assault on the headquarters of the Regional Command; 20 minutes later Almeida was a prisoner. From the governor's mansion, Interior Secretary Alves heard the gunfire and interrupted his conversation with Vargas to discover what it meant. "Don't go outside, Simplício," Vargas coolly said. "It's the revolution."[44] Twenty persons were killed in the fighting in Pôrto Alegre, but in general resistance was light. Within a day Rio Grande was completely in the hands of the revolutionaries, and spearhead units were moving north. The Riograndenses supported the revolution enthusiastically, and military mobilization brought some 50,000 Gaúchos under arms within a few days.[45]

On October 4 Vargas issued a statement justifying the revolt on the grounds of Washington Luís's political excesses and handling of the economic crisis. Vargas defined his goals as the "restoration" of liberal democracy and economic recovery. "We are beginning a counter-revolution [sic] to obtain freedom and to restore the purity of the republican system," he asserted; he failed to mention any social or economic goals other than "national reconstruction." His declaration ended with the appeal, "Stand up, Rio Grande, for Brazil! You cannot shirk your historic mission!"[46]

The manifesto of the Mineiro party, which termed the movement "conservative," placed even greater emphasis on restoring democracy than the Vargas statement did. Uncertain themselves what economic and social innovations would be necessary, the rebels wished to reassure conservative forces at home and abroad of their good intentions.* Characteristically, Vargas waited until the PRM organ had published the Mineiro manifesto before releasing his own declara-

---

* In particular it was important to win over Brazil's foreign investors. The foreign-held federal debt alone had climbed from US $215 million in 1901 to US $683 million in 1930. See Agnes Waddell, "The Revolution in Brazil," *Foreign Policy Association Information Service*, VI, 26 (March 4, 1931), 497; see also Caio Prado Júnior, *História econômica do Brasil* (6th ed., São Paulo, 1961), p. 217.

tion to *A Federação,* which printed it on the evening of the fourth. Paim hurriedly issued a statement of his own, exposing Vargas's deception of Washington Luís and the PRR's allies, but the other parties of the Aliança were too deeply committed to have second thoughts.

The loyalist forces were concentrated between Bahia and São Paulo. The Mineiros were not able to push much beyond their own frontiers. Távora met little resistance in the northeast, but the main insurgent force was in the south. On October 12 Getúlio Vargas assumed the nominal command of the revolutionary army (actually led by Góes) and left Pôrto Alegre for the front. By the time his troops met the first important resistance, on the southern border of São Paulo, Vargas claimed half the regular army in his ranks, in addition to a number of provisional corps and two of the three powerful state police forces. On October 24 the army executed a coup in Rio, ousting Washington Luís and installing in his stead a three-man military junta. Vargas, wary of an attempt at a last-minute compromise to keep him out of power, ordered Góes to radio the capital: the campaign would continue if Getúlio were not recognized as head of a provisional government. In Minas, Governor Maciel stood firmly with his fellow rebels. After extracting a pledge from Getúlio that there would be no purge of the army, the junta acceded to his demand, and hostilities ceased. Aranha, who had been directing the state government for the past two weeks, flew to Rio to arrange the transfer of power.

Getúlio made his triumphant entry into Rio on the last day of October, wearing a military uniform, a red bandana (a symbolic concession to the Liberators), and a broad-brimmed gaúcho hat. On November 3 he took office as "Chief of the Provisional Government." Eight days later he suspended the constitution and named interventors for all the states except Minas Gerais, governed by his ally Maciel. The Old Republic had fallen, and Brazil had its first dictator since Marshal Floriano Peixoto.

Economically, the Republic had never been hit so hard as in 1930, and the crisis might well have brought down any president in a country so dependent on the North Atlantic market. But the revolution of 1930 represented more than the fall of a government; it was the end of a political system. Presidential succession had always been a source of instability, and Rio Grande had often asserted an independent position in the politics of succession. The Gaúcho role was decisive, however, only when Minas and São Paulo could be separated—in 1910, 1919, and 1930. In 1922 the PRR had defied the bilateral entente and failed, though the campaign left President Bernardes a legacy of military revolts. In 1930 the Gaúchos were uniquely suited to lead a revolution against the government of Washington Luís: of the major political groups, the Riograndenses were the least dependent on the international economic system, and therefore the least discredited by its collapse.* The revolution of 1930 was a verdict on the viability of Brazilian federalism and the *café-com-leite* alliance on which it was predicated.

A major weakness of Brazilian republicanism was its identification with control by a political elite based on coronelismo. Even in the 1929–30 campaign the open discussion in congress of decisions already made by the elite,[47] as well as the President's publication of his correspondence with Vargas, makes it clear the Brazilian political oligarchy—including the Gaúchos—had little fear of a loss of legitimacy. In failing to develop broadly based parties that transcended state boundaries, the leaders of the Republic retained a primitive party system, or more precisely a system of interstate caucuses. As late as 1930 effective suffrage remained a privilege of a small sector of the population, even though registration and voting

---

* As early as 1934 a Marxist analyst of the revolution emphasized the importance of American capital in Rio Grande do Sul and concluded the Gaúchos paved the way for terminating British dominance and converting Brazil into a satellite of the United States. True enough, links between American capitalists and Gaúcho politicians dated back to the Farquhar–Pinheiro Machado friendship and, as indicated in Chapter 5, United States investment was undoubtedly proportionally greater in Rio Grande than in São Paulo and Minas. Yet I also showed in Chapter 5 that in 1920 a larger percentage of individually owned industrial firms were in Brazilian hands in Rio Grande than in any other state, and that Rio Grande was far less dependent on international sales than São Paulo. On balance, I believe the orientation toward the national market far outweighed the presence of American firms as a conditioning factor of Gaúcho political behavior in the revolution. For the other view, see Sinani [sic], in Fernando Lacerda, Luís Carlos Prestes, and Sinani, *A luta contra o prestismo e a revolução agraria e antiimperialista* (n.p., 1934), p. 89; quoted in Boris Fausto, *A revolução de 1930: Historiografia e história* (São Paulo, 1970), p. 16.

reached new peaks that year.* Ascendant urban groups could make no headway in the rural-based political system, as Luís Carlos Prestes's conversion to Marxism dramatically illustrated. In addition, the southern states' monopolization of power and perquisites had made federalism distasteful to the elites of the weaker states of the north.

Militarily, the revolution was a victory for state forces, in league with rebel army contingents, over loyalist federal forces in Rio; it was to be the last time the states could face down the federal government. The Gaúchos and Mineiros made a battle cry of "restoration"; but the victors also included a new element, the tenentes, who were clearly at odds with the *politica dos governadores*, a system they had tried to overthrow in 1922–26. A struggle between the tenentes (with whom Góes soon identified) and the civilian revolutionaries was inevitable. But Vargas had already proved his ability to survive factional battles. While still a student Getúlio had said to Pinheiro Machado, "In the politics of the Republic, your attitude has been to wait for the march of events, [then] to place yourself in front to guide them."[48] These words might well be applied to Getúlio himself. He had waited for the march of events; now he would guide them for 15 years.

* There were more than twice as many votes cast in the 1930 election as in the last contested election, in 1922. Though the percentage of voters relative to the total population was still small in 1930, the mobilization of so many new voters may have helped "overload" the system by making the electorate aware of its inability to affect the outcome of the contest.

# CHAPTER ELEVEN

# Forty Years Since

IN THE years since 1930 economic changes—and industrialization in particular—have introduced new political stresses in Brazil that have tended to weaken traditional state allegiances. Industrialization has provided an impetus to interstate migration, interregional communications and transportation, and the search for domestic instead of transatlantic markets. Regional rivalries are giving way to other cleavages, specifically between the industrial, urban, modern culture on the one hand and the agrarian, rural, traditional way of life on the other. The development of a literate urban labor force and its responsiveness to populist appeals have diminished the importance of coronelismo and caused a partial transformation of the political process. To be sure, the tempo of modernization has its regional disparities. In the simplest terms, a developed south faces a retarded north. Nonetheless, such a scheme subsumes the state rivalries of the Old Republic, in which the effective contenders for power were all political parties of the south.

Until recent decades the elements promoting national cohesion were not primarily economic. Obviously, a common language and culture have been unifying factors throughout Brazilian history; so were the political institutions during the colonial and Imperial eras. No less important were the values and experiences shared by the political and social elite, especially their matriculation at the same educational institutions and their extended families, which often transcended state boundaries. Yet in a vast country with a series of nonintegrated economies, the elite's own demand for local autonomy was as old as the Empire itself. After the suppression of the Farroupilha revolt in Rio Grande and the Praieira movement in Pernambuco (both in the 1840's), the quest for provincial autonomy— almost always associated with federalism—subsided until the promulgation of the Republican Manifesto of 1870. The constitution of 1891 incorporated the federalist principles of 1870; federalism corresponded to the economic particularism of the powerful states and reinforced their position. As in previous eras, the states in 1891 were linked to the Atlantic economy as suppliers of tropical goods. Domestic trade was largely limited to a coastwise traffic.

Federalism was only one expression of triumphant liberalism in the constituent assembly of 1890–91. Another was the extension of suffrage to all literate males. Expanding the electorate and allowing states to elect their own officials introduced the *politica dos governadores* and gave the coronéis a leading role in politics. A central factor in the political instability of the Old Republic was the intraparty competition for control of state governments that emerged once the governors were no longer named by an emperor in Rio de Janeiro. However, the attitude of the federal administration remained decisive for the 17 satellites. Since the president could intervene in the lesser states and determine the composition of their congressional delegations, Rio remained the real seat of power. The ultimate struggle for political power was thus the struggle for the presidency.

In determining the presidential succession, the political parties of São Paulo and Minas Gerais usually worked together, but by 1910 the PRR had also entered the contest. The three machines were able to dominate national politics because of the economic and electoral strength of their states; if necessary, they could also bring paramilitary forces to bear. The three parties were in a position to rally support by subsidizing newspapers, were able to deliver half the total vote in a presidential election, and could rely on their state armies to prevent presidential intervention. The leaders of the three autonomous parties, acting in concert, could avoid the crisis inherent in every presidential succession. Disagreement among the three could sometimes be resolved by compensating economic legislation; in São Paulo and Minas this usually meant the defense of coffee, in Rio Grande advantages for pastoral activities. Otherwise disagreement meant a contested election that imperiled the political system. This was true of all three seriously contested presidential races of the Old Republic, those of 1910, 1922, and 1930.

The PRR was outside the *café-com-leite* alliance, but unlike the parties of the satellite states, it did not have to fall into line with a Mineiro-Paulista decision. The Gaúchos had more than their share of members in the military, both in the Imperial era and after, and the events of the first six years of the Republic forged a bond between the army and the PRR. Sharply rising levels of political and military mobilization, governmental instability, economic crises, and the intransigence of Silveira Martins and especially of Castilhos led to the complete replacement of the Liberals by the Republicans in 1892, and to a civil war a year later. The conflict of 1893–95 brought untold suffering to the Gaúcho people; at the same time it enabled the PRR to consolidate its power and to play an independent role in the federation.

The Castilhista machine emerged from the war a highly disciplined organization that could marshal military and electoral power out of proportion to Rio Grande's demographic position in the nation. The war also convinced many military officers that the PRR, more than the non-ideological, brokerage-oriented parties of Minas and São Paulo, was the repository of Republican aspirations. Isolated from national politics under Castilhos, the Riograndenses supplied no ministers or presidents from 1894 to 1910, though they continued to maintain good connections with the army.

Between 1910 and 1930 three Gaúcho politicians attempted to gain control of the federal government when breaches occurred in the Paulista-Mineiro alliance. Pinheiro Machado, already influential in the succession of 1906, had made Rio Grande a "big" state by 1910. Yet his victory was short-lived. His method of domination required a weak president and the control of the political elite, a control that was exercised through the PRC and through the credentials committees in congress. When the Paulista-Mineiro alliance was reactivated in support of a strong president, Pinheiro's power began to decline, and the PRC disintegrated completely after his assassination. The Minas–São Paulo alliance was a logical outgrowth of the shared economic interests of the two coffee states; Pinheiro's coalition had no such cohesion.

Borges de Medeiros did not become personally involved in the contest for control of the presidency until after Pinheiro's death. Borges's intervention in the 1919 caucus came during a deadlock between Minas and São Paulo. In 1922, he initiated a unique experiment in presidential elections: he joined with Nilo Peçanha to mount a campaign against Minas and São Paulo at a time when the coffee giants were united. Pinheiro had worked out an alliance with the army; so did Borges and Nilo. Pinheiro, however, had also had the support of the Mineiro party and the "hip-pocket" votes of a delicately balanced but effective coalition of PRC satellites. In contrast, the Reação Republicana of 1922 was an attempt to unite three "semi-sovereign" states with Rio Grande and the military against São Paulo, Minas Gerais, and their clients.

Vargas's race in 1930 was the first direct bid by a Gaúcho civilian for the presidency, and victory depended on the unreserved support of Minas Gerais. The election—as interpreted by congress—demonstrated that an incumbent president could guide his candidate to victory even when the Mineiro-Paulista alliance was ruptured. However, 1930 was no ordinary election year, and economic stresses aggravated political discontent. The economic crisis, the fall of the Old Republic, and the rise of the tenentes as a political force led to new cleavages that crosscut state borders. The military's role in the decline of the old regime is well known from the facts and myths of *tenentismo*. The army, though ineffective against the police forces of the three powerful states, claimed to act as a national institution in a country where there was no political party that could stand for the "nation." Salvacionismo and tenentismo had their origins in a disenchantment with political liberalism; tenentismo was influenced as well by anti-imperialism. It is significant, however, that these movements made their appearance precisely when the elites of the three dominant machines were divided—in 1910 and 1922. In the years 1910–14 the salvacionistas failed to take over Hermes da Fonseca's government because of their preoccupation with state politics, their absorption into the state political elites, and their consequent dispersion and demoralization. The tenente rebellion of 1922 was the beginning of a division in military ranks that continued into the early 1930's.

The statesmen of the Old Republic failed to develop viable political institutions. In particular, they did not create political parties that traversed state lines, and they were unable to eliminate the crisis potential from presidential succession. Political mobilization (in terms of the percentage of population voting) remained low to the end of the era, even though more votes were cast in 1930 than ever before. The absence of broad political participation resulted in a caucus system (usually dominated by Minas and São Paulo) in which political elites made the major decisions. The conventions and elections that followed caucus decisions were normally formalities. The lack of popular participation in politics was related to the predominantly rural distribution of the Brazilian population and coronel rule in the município. Fraud extended from the local level to congress, where the credentials committees usually obeyed the president's orders on vote-counting in federal elections. The *politica dos governadores,* which tended to keep establishment groups at every level in power indefinitely, undermined the legitimacy of the political system among new urban groups, the reformist elements in the army, and the minority factions and parties of the political elite. The attempt of the three big southern states to monopolize federal power and patronage also tarnished the political system in the eyes of the elites of the north.

Regionalism declined as a pattern of political behavior after 1930 as new cleavage lines appeared in Brazilian politics. The "social question" became prominent in the 1930's, partly because of accelerating rates of urbanization and industrialization. New parties, based on social classes rather than geographic areas, surfaced as formidable organizations in this decade. Vocal communist, socialist, and fascist groups suddenly made Brazilian politics seem much more modern.

Vargas promoted and tried to control social mobilization under a quasi-corporativist aegis. One of the first steps in this direction was taken by Lindolfo Collor, the country's first minister of labor, who in March 1931 drew up a decree providing for government sponsorship of "qualified" labor unions. This meant the regime would exercise tutelage over union organization, membership, and financing. Collor emphasized that class cooperation rather than class struggle was the government's objective. Though no doubt influenced by corporativism, the bureaucratic apparatus for organizing and controlling unions (*sindicatos*) may have had a more direct source of inspiration in Rio Grande do Sul. The labor sindicato was analogous to the commodity syndicates of the late 1920's in the use of bargaining power. The union, having a monopoly on its service, could theoretically drive up prices (i.e. wages), just as the charque and rice syndicates did for their commodities.*

The government-directed organization of the working class was not accomplished in a single stroke, but proceeded apace with industrialization. By 1937 national industrial output was double the output of the mid-1920's, and the phenomena of industrialization and urbanization were facilitating, and indeed making mandatory, a modernization of the state. Both the national bureaucracy and the army were renovated. In 1936 Vargas introduced a civil service merit system in the bureaucracy; the army, which was enlarged repeatedly during the 1930's, was given better training and equipment. After some initial hesitation, Vargas also took the federal government deeper into the economy than it had ever been before. Government agencies were set up to improve the market position not only of coffee but of a variety of Brazilian exports, thereby realizing one of the demands of the Reação Republicana in 1922. Manufacturing also began to receive government support later in the Vargas era.

The states were no longer able to offer their industries financial aid in the 1930's as they had in the 1920's; the best illustration of this fact was the collapse of São Paulo's coffee institute in 1931. Indeed, far from providing economic assistance to their constituents, state governments were themselves besieging the national government with pleas for aid. The first step in the growth of the central government's authority was its assumption of state debts.

Political options were necessarily different in the 1930's, though this was not yet clear when Vargas took office as dictator. Six months after he had conquered Rio, his father, Manuel Vargas, counseled him to heed the adage of Floriano Peixoto: "have confidence while mistrusting." The most able Brazilian politician of the century hardly needed such advice. At the outset of his 15-year period in power, Getúlio relied on those he knew best, his fellow Gaúchos; he also let the Riograndenses scramble for the federal patronage that had previously been reserved for Mineiros and Paulistas.

---

* In practice, however, the system worked out differently. The unions did not have the opportunity to confront management directly but had to operate through government-controlled conciliation boards.

Gaúchos took over the federally licensed notarial offices and rushed into government jobs after appointees of earlier years were cashiered. Maurício Cardoso, who was more preoccupied with the moral tone of the revolution than Vargas and Aranha, noted with grave concern a case in which a federal employee with 40 years' service had been fired and replaced by an "illiterate."[1] Rio had become the prize of the victorious revolutionaries. Gilberto Amado, politician and litterateur of what was now called the First Republic, returned from Europe just after the revolution, and later described the "mood" in Rio under the provisional government:

The Jockey Club was filled with strange apparitions. Red bandanas colored the salons. On the hips of many new members, revolvers bulged like tumors. Straitlaced, peaceable men and high society ne'er-do-wells alike were transformed into "warriors." The free-spenders of the gaming tables moved about ponderously, also carrying weapons in their belts; some wore boots and army tunics strapped down with cartridge belts. An air of absurdity lightened the melodrama. At home during the evening, the only thing one heard on the radio was a lugubrious song about João Pessôa and his martyrdom; the singer's voice was maudlin.[2]

At the cabinet level, as in the bureaucracy, Vargas initially favored the Gaúchos. Aranha was Vargas's most powerful lieutenant in the early years, serving first as minister of justice and then as minister of the treasury. During Getúlio's first two years of office, Riograndenses headed the nonmilitary posts for a cumulative period equal to that of all the other states' representatives combined; this proportion held for the three most important posts, the ministries of treasury, transportation, and justice. Yet Vargas learned his job fast and soon freed himself from regionalism in his choice of personnel. By 1934 there was only one Gaúcho in the cabinet; at the same time there were two Paulistas and three Mineiros. Getúlio, however, was wary of naming men he knew only slightly to key positions, and two members of the Castilhista Bloc of 1907, Pedro Góes Monteiro and Eurico Gaspar Dutra, held top military posts during almost all of Vargas's decade and a half in power.

The first political challenge Getúlio faced in the 1930's was to strike some sort of balance between the demands of the tenentes, who sought fundamental social and economic changes, and those of the PRR and PRM politicians, who were content to achieve political reforms alone. The civilian forces were on the defensive in the years

1930–32. Establishment political parties in the 17 satellite states had collapsed, and in Minas a "Legion of October" replaced the PRM as the dominant political organization in 1931. As for Rio Grande, the PRR monopoly on power had been broken, and Liberators and Republicans governed in a "United Front" between 1930 and 1932.

Vargas's major political error in this period was turning São Paulo over to the tenentes, thereby alienating and uniting the Paulistas, who uniformly demanded home rule. Because Vargas would not entrust the interventorship of the state to the members of the Partido Democrático of São Paulo, who had supported him in the campaign of 1930, PD leaders joined forces with the PRP in a United Front of their own against outside intervention. Borges de Medeiros, seeing an erosion in the position of the civilian revolutionaries, feared the destruction of the machines that had been victorious in 1930. For him, as for Collor, Neves, Cardoso, Assis Brasil, and Raul Pilla (the de facto leader of the Partido Libertador after Assis became minister of agriculture in the provisional government), "reconstitutionalization" was the key to the success of the revolution. Vargas, assisted by Aranha, tried to prevent a split between the tenentes and the "constitutionalists"; he gave in to the latter's demands at the slowest rate possible as he continued to cope with the economic and financial crises that seemed to him to require the postponement of "politics."

But the Paulistas were unwilling to wait indefinitely for self-rule and reconstitutionalization, and on July 9, 1932, they rose against Vargas. They believed they could count on the support of Rio Grande, Minas, and anti-tenente elements in the army. As it turned out, the only important army support they got was from federal troops stationed in São Paulo itself. The response of Minas Gerais and Rio Grande do Sul was disastrous for the rebels. Flôres da Cunha, who had been appointed interventor in Rio Grande, controlled the Gaúcho Military Brigade, and despite earlier indications of sympathy for the Paulista movement, he chose to back Vargas. Pilla and Borges, the titular leaders of the Liberator and Republican parties, led a quixotic rebellion to honor a pact between the United Fronts of São Paulo and Rio Grande do Sul. Meanwhile Artur Bernardes unsuccessfully tried to foment a rebellion in Minas. Flôres and the commander of the Third Military Region opened a southern front against São Paulo, and at the same time easily quashed the rebellion in Rio Grande.[3]

At the beginning of October São Paulo sued for peace. Borges and Bernardes had already been taken prisoner, and Collor, Pilla, and Neves had been driven into exile. Cardoso and Assis Brasil had tried to mediate between the constitutionalists and Vargas even after the military conflict began, without success. The tenentes seemed to have emerged victorious—but Vargas and Flôres were also greatly strengthened. In November 1932 Aranha came to Pôrto Alegre to help Flôres set up a new party to replace the Liberator and Republican organizations, both badly riven by the Paulista revolt. The two parties of the First Republic lived on, as did their United Front— but in vestigial form. Flôres da Cunha was now the leader of Rio Grande. Borges had lost his authority, and the Generation of '07 had been split.

In order to pacify São Paulo, Vargas made good on a promise to hold a constituent assembly in 1933, and once Brazil returned to constitutional government, his dependence on the tenentes decreased. Under the constitution of 1934 Brazil remained a federal republic, but the federalism of 1891 was replaced by a diluted corporativism that gave more extensive powers to the government in Rio. In the new congress, delegates elected directly in geographic constituencies sat side by side with indirectly elected representatives of business and labor corporations. Since the deputies of the corporations supposedly represented occupational interests, regional (or state) cleavages were weakened.

In addition, there were extensive changes in the division of authority between the states and the central government. The federal government was given jurisdiction over subsoil rights, formerly reserved for the states. The states could no longer pass procedural law codes. States were still allowed to tax exports but were not permitted to exceed a 10 per cent ad valorem rate; import taxes were prohibited. Before a state could contract foreign debts it had to obtain special permission from the senate. Following the precedent of 1891, the constituent assembly chose the first new president, and gave Getúlio Vargas a four-year mandate; a direct election was to determine his successor in 1938.

In the mid-1930's Vargas faced a new threat from his old colleague Flôres da Cunha. Flôres cast himself in the role of upholding constitutional rule and preserving the federal system; at the same time he tried to act as a new Pinheiro Machado, attempting to control other state governments and to determine the presidential succession of 1938. In the meantime he bolstered his authority in Rio Grande, winning an indirect election as governor in 1935; he still controlled an important state police force and a number of provisional corps. But his struggle was a losing one. Vargas played off one group against another in Rio Grande and used the Gaúcho United Front to undermine Flôres's power; a move in the state legislature to impeach Flôres failed by only one vote. In Rio de Janeiro, meanwhile, Vargas and his military advisors were preparing a coup d'état to abolish the constitution of 1934 and establish a dictatorship amply supplied with the trappings of European corporativism. Flôres's government was in fact the last military obstacle to the coup.

The "parity" of state and federal forces of the Old Republic no longer existed, not only because of changes in arms technology, requiring expenditures for airplanes and armored tanks that were beyond the reach of the states, but also because of an increase in troop strength that made the federal army nearly double the size of all the state forces combined (see Figure 4). To finance the new military apparatus, the federal government allocated an increasingly large share of its budget to the army. In the years 1910–30 the military received, on the average, 12.2 per cent of the budget; by 1937 it was receiving 20.5 per cent.[4] One constant in the changing military picture, however, was Rio Grande's role as the leading supplier of top-ranking military officers.*

During the course of 1937 Vargas carried out successive measures to break the power of Flôres da Cunha. He appointed a general who was hostile to Flôres commander of the Third Region, ordered the Gaúcho provisional corps dissolved, and had his chief of staff, Góes Monteiro, position federal troops for an attack on Rio Grande do Sul. Finally, on October 14, the President "federalized" the Military Brigade. Outmaneuvered, Flôres fled to Uruguay two days later. Vargas made the regional commander, Gen. Manuel Daltro Filho, interventor; he was the first military ruler of the state since 1892.

---

* In 1937 there were more generals of division or brigade from Rio Grande than from any other state: 13 of Brazil's 40 generals were Gaúchos. Compiled from *Almanak do Ministerio da Guerra para o ano de 1937* (Rio, 1937), pp. 7–14.

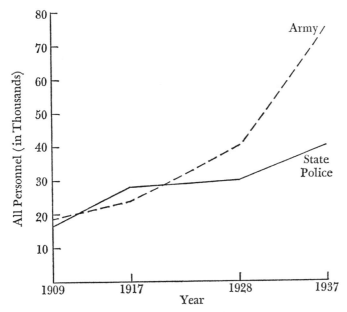

Fig. 4. Size of army (active) and all state police forces, 1909–37. Source: State police—See Table 1, p. 116; Instituto Brasileiro de Geografia e Estatística, *Anuário estatístico do Brasil: Ano V—1939/1940* ([Rio], n.d.), p. 1279 (figures exclude police of Federal District). Army—Computed from Directoria Geral de Estatistica, *Annuario estatistico do Brazil: 1° anno (1908–1912)* (n.p., 1917), II, 237; *Relatorio* (Rio, 1928), p. 98; *Relatorios* (Rio, 1930), p. 198; *Anuário estatístico: Ano IV—1938* (Rio, n.d.), p. 856.

On November 10, 1937, Vargas closed congress, proclaimed the existence of the Estado Nôvo (New State), and began to rule by decree. The Estado Nôvo constitution abolished interstate taxation and gave the president the authority to appoint state interventors at his discretion.* To underscore the centralization of the new regime and its nationalist aspirations, Vargas ordered the flags of the states burned in symbolic ceremonies; he also increasingly relied on military officers (whose allegiance was presumably to the nation rather than to their native states) to fill non-military posts. Getúlio Vargas, the regionalist who had defended liberal democracy

---

* Enforcement of the prohibition of interstate taxes was not total and immediate, however. Furthermore, the constitution technically never went into effect, since it called for a plebiscite that did not take place. Corporativist legislation, especially in the labor field, proceeded piecemeal—before, during, and after the Estado Nôvo.

and federalism in the late 1920's, had become an authoritarian centralist and nationalist. Birth on the frontier had undoubtedly made him aware of "Brazilianness" in a way no Carioca or Bahiano could understand, and perhaps Rio Grande's historic pattern of trading with other Brazilians rather than looking to foreign markets made him more disposed to nationalism in the 1930's.

After Vargas's fall from power in 1945, a new constitution brought back congressional representation on a geographic basis and dismantled some of the legal structures of the Estado Nôvo. Brazil, however, was clearly not going to return to the political system of the Old Republic. That possibility was ruled out on several grounds: the fiscal strength of the federal government, the relative weakness of the state police organizations, the development of national political parties, and the appeal of populist candidates in urban areas irrespective of state lines. Nevertheless, thanks to their wealth, population, and relatively high rates of literacy (which remained a voting requirement), the three big states retained their prominent positions in the federation. In addition, each provided a strong regional base for a national political party—namely, the Partido Trabalhista Brasileiro (Brazilian Labor Party) in Rio Grande, the Partido Social Democrático (Social Democratic Party) in Minas, and the Partido Social Progressista (Social Progressive Party) in São Paulo. Despite the development of new and fairly cohesive interest groups and the weakening of old allegiances, the military and the three dominant states of the Old Republic continued to supply every popularly elected president after 1945: Eurico Dutra (army, elected in 1945); Getúlio Vargas (Rio Grande do Sul, 1950); Juscelino Kubitschek (Minas Gerais, 1955); and Jânio Quadros (São Paulo, 1960).

In the years 1945–64 politics within Rio Grande tended to revolve around the populist PTB (Vargas's own creation) and an anti-PTB coalition. Populist and conservative forces were roughly balanced. PTB power was concentrated in Pôrto Alegre and a few other urban areas, and in a number of frontier municípios where estancieiros still determined how their dependents voted. The conservative opposition was found largely in the rest of the ranching community and in the colonial zone north and west of the state capital. The German- and Italian-Brazilians finally began to play an autonomous role following the Second World War and in general aligned themselves with the conservatives.[5] In large part this meant the Partido Libertador. When the PTB became the leading party in border municípios like Bagé, the center of Liberator strength moved to the Colonial Zone. The Church also was a conservative influence in the politics of the Colonial Zone, partly because of the large number of colonos in the priesthood.

In national politics Rio Grande do Sul remained a major state, and it continued to produce the third-largest vote totals in federal elections, though the state's voters were rarely united. Meanwhile other southern states, including São Paulo, passed Rio Grande in the percentage of population voting. Rio Grande still supplied leading national political figures, and members of the Generation of '07 were in and out of congress and the executive until the mid-1950's. Vargas returned to power on the PTB ticket in 1951; three-and-a-half years later, expecting to be deposed by the military, he committed suicide. The impression he tried to leave was that he was a martyr in the struggle between the Brazilian people and certain unspecified reactionary interests. João Neves served as foreign minister under both Dutra and Vargas, and Aranha headed the treasury in the early 1950's for Getúlio, as he had 20 years before. Flôres and Borges were among the founders of the anti-Vargas União Democrática Nacional (National Democratic Union) in Rio Grande in 1945; ten years later Flôres became acting president of the chamber of deputies, but the aged Borges had virtually withdrawn from political activity at the beginning of the postwar era. As for the other members of the Generation, Paim had stayed out of politics after 1945, and Collor and Cardoso had died during the Estado Nôvo period. Borges de Medeiros, the man Pinheiro had thought might be on the verge of death in 1915, outlived most of the Generation of '07. In his eighties he abandoned positivism for Catholicism; he received the last rites of the Church in 1961, at the age of ninety-seven.

A new generation of Gaúchos entered politics in the postwar years, and the most prominent were connected with Getúlio's PTB. One of these was a personal protégé of Vargas, a rancher from São Borja named João Goulart, who became labor minister and leader of the PTB, then vice president of Brazil, and finally, in 1961, president. His brother-in-law, Leonel Brizola, another urban-oriented estancieiro, won the governorship of Rio Grande in 1958. When his term expired in 1962, Brizola became a federal deputy from Guanabara (formerly the Federal District), and in that capacity began to radicalize the PTB.

The Gaúcho Military Brigade continued to provide a source of leverage against the national government. Governor Brizola managed to mobilize some 11,000 men in 1961 when military authorities in Brasília (the national capital after 1960) tried to keep his brother-in-law, then vice president, from assuming the presidency following the resignation of Jânio Quadros. More important to Brizola's success, however, was his alliance with the commander of the Third Region, Gen. José Machado Lopes. This became clear three years later when, during a military coup against Goulart, the Brigade initially supported the President but then made no attempt to resist the coup after the army in the Third Region joined the revolt.

The Goulart years (1961–64) had been characterized by administrative disorganization and increasing political polarization; in 1964 democratic political structures were closed down as conservative forces reacted against the efforts of Brizola and other radicals to transform the political and social system into a mass-based (authoritarian?) regime threatening foreign capital, the latifundium, and other traditional institutions. The army intervened in the political process on the side of the "revolutionaries," and the nation has remained under military tutelage since 1964. Two of Brazil's three military rulers since Goulart's fall have been Gaúchos—Artur Costa e Silva and Emílio Garrastazu Médici—but their loyalty was to the military corporation rather than to a Rio Grande–based political organization.

Despite rapid advances in industrialization after World War II, Brazil has remained an underdeveloped country, with all the maladies and weaknesses that the euphemism underdevelopment implies. Gaúcho society has been a relatively healthy specimen in the federation. Rio Grande do Sul has continued to industrialize, and has been outranked in manufacturing in the postwar years only by São Paulo, Guanabara, and Minas. In 1950 Rio Grande had the smallest percentage of underpaid and underfed farm workers among the states, chiefly because of the comparative egalitarianism of colono society. The small-farm pattern of the Colonial Zone (located principally in the Serra) has also demonstrated its economic superiority over the latifundia of the Campanha. The Colonial Zone has become the nation's foremost producer of wheat; mixed farming has also thrived there. Though this area accounted for only 27 per cent of the state's total farm acreage in 1960, it supplied 55 per cent of the overall crop production and a third of the livestock in that year. Yet the colonos have had their problems. Land has become increasingly difficult to obtain, since the colono population has continued to expand and the owners of latifundia in adjacent areas have refused to sell their properties. Many inhabitants of the Colonial Zone have therefore begun subdividing their holdings, increasing the number of subsistence farms.[6] Other Gaúchos, not only from this area but from others as well, have chosen to emigrate to other parts of Brazil, and in 1966 Paraná passed Rio Grande as the fourth most populous state. An outflow of capital has accompanied this migration.

Rio Grande do Sul today is a land of sharply differing life styles. In the rural area alone the contrast between the colono farmers north of the Jacuí-Ibicuí line and the gaúcho herdsmen of the Campanha estâncias is enormous. Pôrto Alegre, a city of one million inhabitants, provides still another cultural pattern; there the contrast between wealth and poverty is at its most striking, and grows more so as impoverished gaúchos drift into the city from the estâncias. Dusk is always melancholy in the state capital, and as the rag-pickers begin their patrol of the city streets, even the most casual observer must recognize the problems yet to be faced in Rio Grande—and indeed in Brazil at large.

# Notes

# Notes

The following abbreviations are used in the Notes:

| | | | |
|---|---|---|---|
| AAB | Archive of Assis Brasil | ARB | Archive of Rui Barbosa |
| ABM | Archive of Borges de Medeiros | AVB | Archive of Veríssimo de Bittencourt |
| ACF | Archive of Clodoaldo da Fonseca | DGE | Directoria Geral de Estatística |
| AFP | Archive of Floriano Peixoto | IBGE | Instituto Brasileiro de Geografia e Estatística |
| AGV | Archive of Getúlio Vargas | | |
| AOA | Archive of Osvaldo Aranha | RGS | Rio Grande do Sul |
| APM | Archive of Prudente de Morais | | |

CHAPTER ONE

1. Romero, *O castilhismo no Rio Grande do Sul* (Pôrto [Portugal], 1912), p. 2; José Verissimo, "Impressões do Sul," *Jornal do Commercio* (Rio), July 21, 1912, p. 4.

2. "Caudilhismo," *Anhembi*, VI, 71 (Oct. 1956), 224.

3. Moysés Vellinho, *Capitania d'El-Rei: Aspectos polêmicos da formação riograndense* (Pôrto Alegre, 1964), trans. by Linton Lomas Barrett and Marie McDavid Barrett as *Brazil South* (New York, 1968). Not all students of Gaúcho culture accept this viewpoint. For instance, Manoelito de Ornellas acknowledges the Spanish contribution to Riograndense society and culture, and treats the gaúcho of Rio Grande do Sul and the gaucho of the Plate as closely related types. See his *Gaúchos e beduínos (A origem étnica e a formação social do Rio Grande do Sul)* (2d ed., Rio, 1956).

4. [Francisco] Oliveira Vianna, *Populações meridionais do Brasil: História—Organização—Psicologia*, II: *O campeador riograndense* (Rio, 1952), 367; João Camillo de Oliveira Torres, *A formação do federalismo no Brasil* (São Paulo, 1961), p. 254; [Pedro] Góes Monteiro, *A revolução de 30 e a*

*finalidade politica do exercito* (Rio, n.d.), p. 68; [João] Pandiá Cologeras, *Problemas de administração* (São Paulo, 1933), p. 27.

5. Quoted from Samuel Putnam's translation *Rebellion in the Backlands* (Chicago, 1944), pp. 91–92.

6. Physiographic regions are discussed in Nilo Bernardes, "Bases geográficas do povoamento do Estado do Rio Grande do Sul," *Boletim Geográfico*, 171-172 (Nov.-Dec. 1962–Jan.-Feb. 1963), p. 6. The three-region division for social analysis is found in Thales de Azevedo, *Gaúchos: A fisionomia social do Rio Grande do Sul* (2d ed., Bahia, [1958]), pp. 26f; and Jean Roche, "As bases físicas da ocupação do solo no Rio Grande do Sul," in Roche and Aziz Nacib Ab'Saber, *Três estudos riograndenses* (Pôrto Alegre, 1966), pp. 54–57.

7. In 1809 a traveler noted that even in the southern Litoral (adjacent to the Campanha) estates were huge. The smallest were four leagues (more than 20,000 acres) and the largest 100 leagues (almost 600,000 acres). John Luccock, *Notes on Rio de Janeiro and the Southern Parts of Brazil; Taken During a Residence of Ten Years in That Country* (London, 1820). A scholarly treatment of the colonial era is Guilhermino Cesar, *História do Rio Grande do Sul: Período colonial* (Pôrto Alegre, 1970). For an introduction to the bibliography on colonial Rio Grande, see Cesar, pp. 287–96, and José Honório Rodrigues, *O continente do Rio Grande* (Rio, 1954), pp. 63–72.

8. Florêncio de Abreu, "O gado bovino e sua influência na antropogeografia do Rio Grande do Sul," in *Ensaios e estudos históricos* (Rio, 1964), p. 136.

9. Raymundo Faoro, "Rio Grande do Sul," manuscript for *Enciclopédia Delta-Larousse* (1968), p. 7.

10. In the same year, in Brazil as a whole, Negroes and mulattoes represented 56 per cent of the population. DGE, *Sexo, raça e estado civil, nacionalidade, filiação, culto e analphabetismo da população recenseada em 31 de dezembro de 1890* (Rio, 1898), pp. 2–3. Oliveira Vianna, among others, exaggerated the predominance of the white population among the gaúchos of Rio Grande, and even contended that the state had produced a "superior" racial type. *Populações meridionais*, II, 331. This view is also clearly implied in Domenico Bartolotti, *Il Brasile meridionale* (Roma, 1930), p. 416.

11. As noted above, Moysés Vellinho has argued that Riograndense gaúchos are distinct from their Platine cousins. See "O gaúcho riograndense e o gaúcho platino," in *Fundamentos da cultura riograndense: Segunda série* ([Pôrto Alegre], 1957), pp. 47–66. The differences he points to—that the Platine type was more nomadic, more subject to caudillismo in politics, and less European in racial background—are debatable, and reflect the author's desire to establish the "Brazilianness" of Rio Grande and its inhabitants. In any case, the alleged differences are matters of degree, and to the non-Ibero-American they appear less important than the similarities. Witness, for instance, the striking similarities in vocabulary of the two ranching societies: Port. *gaúcho,* Sp. *gaucho; estancieiro, estanciero; facão, facón; boleadeiras,*

*boleadoras; erva mate, yerba mate; bomba, bombilla; chimarrão, cimarrón; umbu, ombú; cochilha, cuchilla.* Identically spelled words include *pingo, chiripá, poncho, bombachas, charque,* and *churrasco.*

12. Johann Jacob von Tschudi, *Reisen durch Südamerika* (Leipzig, 1868), IV, 21.

13. The Farroupilha epoch has received more attention from Gaúcho historians than any other subject. Major studies include Alfredo Varela's massive but unreadable *Historia da grande revolução: O cyclo farroupilha no Brasil,* 6 vols. (Pôrto Alegre, 1933); Walter Spalding. *A revolução farroupilha* (São Paulo, 1939), containing numerous documents; and Dante de Laytano, *Historia da Republica Riograndense, 1835–1845* (Pôrto Alegre, 1936). Whereas the first stresses the rebels' ties with the Plate, the two later works, especially Spalding's, emphasize the essentially Brazilian quality of the Farroupilha movement.

14. Abreu, "Recursos financeiros da República de Piratini," in *Ensaios,* pp. 90–91, 98.

15. As late as 1844, Gonçalves proposed to the Barão de Caxias, then governor of Rio Grande do Sul, a federation that would include not only Rio Grande and the rest of Brazil but also Uruguay, Corrientes, and Entre Rios. Abreu, "A constituinte e o projeto da constituição da República Rio-grandense," in *ibid.,* p. 30.

16. Abreu, "O gado bovino," in *Ensaios,* p. 142; Faoro, p. 9.

17. Joaquim Luis Osorio and Fernando Luis Osorio Filho, *Historia do General Osorio* (Pelotas, 1915), II, 745; Ministerio da Guerra, *Relatorio apresentado a Assembléia Geral Legislativa pelo Ministro da Guerra Thomaz José Coelho d'Almeida* (Rio, 1889), Appendix B.

18. Computed from *Almanak do Ministerio da Guerra no anno de 1889* (Rio, 1889), Part 2, pp. 5–9. Of 25 generals born in Brazil, four were from Rio Grande. If two who were born in Uruguay but made their careers in Rio Grande are added to the list of Gaúchos, Rio Grande accounts for six in a total of 28.

19. *Annuario da Provincia do Rio Grande do Sul para o anno de 1889* (Pôrto Alegre, 1888), pp. 212–13.

20. Michael G. Mulhall, *Rio Grande do Sul and Its German Colonies* (London, 1873), p. 33; Alfredo Ferreira Rodrigues, *Almanak litterario e estatistico da Provincia do Rio Grande do Sul para 1890* (Pelotas [1889]), pp. 255f, 258f; Tschudi, IV, 81; Alfred Marc, *Le Brésil: Excursion à travers ses 20 provinces* (Paris, 1890), II, 454.

21. Sérgio da Costa Franco, *Júlio de Castilhos e sua época* (Pôrto Alegre, 1967), p. 18.

22. Ferreira Rodrigues, pp. 217, 224, 227.

23. M. Blanca París de Oddone et al., *Cronología comparada de la historia del Uruguay: 1830–1945* (Montevideo, n.d.), [p. 146].

24. Marc, II, 471. A traveler in the middle of the nineteenth century also commented on the large amount of smuggling across the Campanha fron-

tier, which could not be as easily patrolled as the areas along the Uruguay River and the Litoral. Roberto [sic] Avé-Lallement, *Viagem pelo sul do Brasil no ano de 1858: Primeira parte*, tr. Teodoro Cabral (Rio, 1953), p. 369.

25. M. F.-J. Santa-Anna Nery, *Le Brésil en 1889* (Paris, 1889), p. 446. As early as 1861–62 more than half the goods Rio Grande sent across her borders were destined for use in other parts of the nation. See William Scully, *Brazil; its provinces and chief cities; the manners & customs of the people; agricultural, commercial and other statistics, taken from the latest official documents; with useful and entertaining knowledge both for the merchant and the emigrant* (London, 1866), p. 247.

26. Faoro, p. 9; Rio Grande do Sul: Repartição de Estatistica, "Relatorio," manuscript [1899], p. 44.

27. Jean Roche, *La colonisation allemande et le Rio Grande do Sul* (Paris, 1959), pp. 232, 585; Stuart Clark Rothwell, *The Old Italian Colonial Zone of Rio Grande do Sul, Brazil* (Pôrto Alegre, 1959), p. 47.

28. Arsène Isabelle, *Voyage a Buénos-Ayres et a Porto-Alègre, par la Banda-Orientale, les missions d'Uruguay et la Province de Rio-Grande-do-Sul (de 1830 à 1834)* (Havre, 1835), p. 408; Nicolau [sic] Dreys, *Noticia descritiva da Provincia do Rio Grande do Sul* (Pôrto Alegre, 1961), p. 107.

29. *A Federação*, Sept. 19, 1884. The neglect of the Serra is stressed in Costa Franco, p. 2.

30. *Annuario* . . . 1889, p. 161; DGE, *Recenseamento da população do Imperio do Brazil a que se procedeu no dia 1º de agosto de 1872: Quadros estatisticos* (Rio, 1873–76), Part 17, p. 206 (microfilm). Figures for Pelotas are divided into three categories: Pelotas and two component parishes, Santo Antonio da Boa Vista and N.S. da Consolação do Boquete.

31. For a contemporary analysis, see Louis Couty, *Le maté et les conserves de viande: Rapport à son excellence Monsieur le Ministre de l'Agriculture et du Commerce* (Rio, 1880), pp. 132–49; for a modern treatment, see Fernando Henrique Cardoso, *Capitalismo e escravidão no Brasil meridional: O negro na sociedade escravocrata do Rio Grande do Sul* (São Paulo, 1962), especially pp. 174–88.

32. Isabelle, p. 485; *A Federação*, Feb. 10, 1885, Feb. 23, 1888, Dec. 11, 1884, March 22, 1889, and Dec. 6, 1891.

33. Most of my information on Osório is based on a flattering two-volume biography of the General by his son and grandsons: Fernando Luis Osorio, *Historia do General Osorio* (Rio, 1894), I, and Joaquim Luis Osorio and Fernando Luis Osorio Filho, *Historia*, II, cited in note 17 above.

34. Paulo José Pires Brandão, *Vultos do meu caminho* (São Paulo, 1935), p. 249.

35. Joaquim Nabuco, *Um estadista do Império: Nabuco de Araújo*, III (*Obras completas*, V) (São Paulo, 1949), 169. This famous work is one of the leading sources on politics in the time of Pedro II.

36. José Julio Silveira Martins, *Silveira Martins* (Rio, 1929), pp. 39–40.

Though not as good or as broad as Nabuco's study, this is one of the better exercises in filial piety. The other major biography is Osvaldo Orico, *Silveira Martins e sua época* (Pôrto Alegre, 1935).

37. Quoted in Silveira Martins, p. 53.

38. *Ibid.*, p. 53–55, 64.

39. Nabuco, III, 169.

40. [Egydio Barbosa Oliveira Itaquy], *Monarchia federal: Politica do augusto Senador Gaspar Silveira Martins; candidatura provincial: Porto Alegre, 18 de outubro de 1886* (Pôrto Alegre, 1886), p. 31.

41. Silveira Martins, p. 70.

42. For information on political fraud and violence in Rio Grande in the Imperial era, see, for example, Fernando Luis Osorio, p. 713; João Cezar Sampaio, *O coronel Sampaio e os "Apontamentos" do dr. Wenceslau Escobar (Sobre a revolução riograndense de 1893)* (Pôrto Alegre, 1920), p. 61; and *A Federação*, Feb. 14, 1885, Aug. 4, 1886.

CHAPTER TWO

1. Rio Grande had no professional schools before the establishment of the Republic; Brazil as a whole had no universities until the twentieth century, only autonomous professional schools. The country's only law schools were at São Paulo and Recife.

2. *Annuario da Provincia do Rio Grande do Sul para o anno de 1889.* (Pôrto Alegre, 1888), p. 161.

3. *Convenção republicana de 23 de Fevereiro* (Pôrto Alegre, 1882), p. 9.

4. Borges de Medeiros had completed his legal training in Recife, as had Silveira Martins.

5. Assis Brasil, *O opportunismo e a revolução: Conferencia publica do Club Republicano Academico: Realisada no dia 26 de junho de 1880* (São Paulo, 1880), p. 35.

6. *A Federação*, Sept. 28, 1886; Oct. 15, 1886.

7. Heitor Lyra, *História da queda do Império* (São Paulo, 1964), I, 132.

8. Alfred Funke, *Aus Deutsch-Brasilien: Bilder aus dem Leben der Deutschen im Staate Rio Grande do Sul* (Leipzig, 1902), p. 62.

9. Assis Brasil, *Dictadura, parlamentarismo, democracia* (Pôrto Alegre, 1908), p. 41.

10. Sérgio da Costa Franco, *Júlio de Castilhos e sua época* (Pôrto Alegre, 1967), p. 4. This is an excellent interpretative biography of Castilhos. An earlier treatment, detailed but uncritical, is Othelo Rosa, *Julio de Castilhos* (Pôrto Alegre, 1928). The second half of this work consists of selections from Castilhos' own writings.

11. João Daudt Filho, *Memórias de João Daudt Filho* (3d ed., Rio, 1949), p. 73.

12. *A Federação*, March 26–April 13, 1888. For other examples of his biting attacks on the rival parties, see *ibid.*, May 20, 1884; and Feb. 14, 1885.

13. *Ibid.*, Nov. 15, 1891; Castilhos to Bittencourt, Figueira (RGS), Sept. 24, 1896, AVB.

14. Castilhos to Bittencourt, Figueira (RGS), Dec. 8, 1902; Oct. 7, 1897; March 5, 1898, AVB; Castilhos to Borges, n.p., Aug. 28, 1898, ABM.

15. Some of Comte's Brazilian followers found support in his writings for federalism, though their logic was somewhat tortured, since the master believed a centralized state to be a progressive feature of modern times. See Comte, *Politique d'Auguste Comte: Textes choisis et présentés par Pierre Arnaud* (Paris, 1965), pp. 249–51; and João Cruz Costa, *A History of Ideas in Brazil: The Development of Philosophy in Brazil and the Evolution of National History*, tr. Suzette Macedo (Berkeley, Calif., 1964), p. 162.

Comte's major works were the *Cours de philosophie positive*, 6 vols. (Paris, 1830–42) and the *Système de politique positive*, 4 vols. (Paris, 1851–54.) A much briefer work but one of great importance in Brazil was his *Appel aux conservateurs* (Paris, 1855). The leading monographs on positivism in Brazil are Ivan Lins, *História do positivismo no Brasil* (São Paulo, 1964); João Camillo de Oliveira Torres, *O positivismo no Brasil* (2d ed., Petrópolis, 1957); the Cruz Costa work cited above, pp. 82–202; and Cruz Costa, *O positivismo na República: Notas sôbre a história do positivismo no Brasil* (São Paulo, 1956). A good monograph on positivism in Rio Grande is Florêncio de Abreu, "O movimento positivista no Rio Grande do Sul," in *Ensaios e estudos históricos* (Rio, 1964), pp. 223–36.

16. Rosa, Part 1, p. 250.

17. "Carta à Devoção do Menino Deus," in Rosa, Part 2, pp. 497–500. Comte's weird attempt to graft a liturgy derived from Catholicism onto a rationalist and evolutionary doctrine was a product of his final years, and the effort engendered a schism between those who were attracted by his metaphysics and those who accepted his ideas wholesale, embracing the religion as well. To the modern student, or at least to the Anglo-Saxon one, the elaborate rituals mapped out by Comte—such as the hierarchy of sacraments and the secular saints' calendar—seem of the same order of phenomena as Alfred Jarry's *Calendrier du Père Ubu*.

18. Castilhos to Assis, Pôrto Alegre, Aug. 14, 1887, AAB.

19. *Ibid.*

20. Rosa, Part 1, p. 236.

21. For a critical assessment of the historiography of the fall of the Empire, see George C. A. Boehrer, "The Brazilian Republican Revolution: Old and New Views," *Luso-Brazilian Review*, III, 2 (Winter 1966), 43–57.

22. Ernesto Senna, *Deodoro: Subsidios para a historia—Notas de um reporter* (Rio, 1913), p. 20. The best biography is R[aymundo] Magalhães Júnior, *Deodoro: A espada contra o Império* (São Paulo, 1957), 2 vols.

23. Osvaldo Orico, *Silveira Martins e sua época* (Pôrto Alegre, 1935), p. 311.

24. *A Federação*, Jan. 7, 1889.

25. Pelotas to Rui Barbosa, Pôrto Alegre, Feb. 12, 1890, ARB.

26. Ribeiro's peripheral role in the ministerial decisions is evident from the minutes of cabinet sessions. See Dunshee de Abranches, *Actas e actos do Governo Provisorio: Copias authenticas dos protocollos das sessões secretas do conselho de ministros desde a proclamação da Republica até a organisação do Gabinete Lucena, acompanhado de importantes revelações e documentos* (Rio, 1907), *passim*.

27. Pelotas to Barbosa, Pôrto Alegre, May 28, 1890, ARB. A good account of the principal political events in Rio Grande in the opening years of the Republic is Gustavo Moritz, *Acontecimentos politicos do Rio Grande do Sul 89-90-91* (Pôrto Alegre, 1939), I.

28. Costa Franco, pp. 79-80.

29. *Ibid.*, p. 155.

30. *Annaes da Assembleia dos Representantes do Estado do Rio Grande do Sul: Sessão extraordinaria de 1891* (Pôrto Alegre, 1891), p. 14.

31. Or so Castilhos claimed later. *A Federação*, Dec. 1, 1891.

32. *Annaes da Assembleia dos Representantes do Estado do Rio Grande do Sul: 1891: 1ª sessão ordinaria* (Pôrto Alegre, 1891), pp. 53-54. Seventeen of Brazil's 20 governors were more explicit in their support of the coup, and only one, an army officer ruling Pará, actually opposed the incipient dictatorship.

33. Castilhos to Piratinino de Almeida, [Pôrto Alegre], Nov. 13, 1891, in Fernando Luís Osório. *A cidade de Pelotas* (2d ed., Pôrto Alegre, 1962), p. 124; Alfredo Varela, *Remembranças* (2d ed., Rio, 1959), II, 99.

34. João de Deus Noronha Menna Barreto, *Os Menna Barreto: Seis gerações de soldados* (Rio, n.d.), p. 292.

35. Dunshee de Abranches, *O golpe de estado: Atas e atos do governo Lucena* (Rio, 1954), p. 98.

36. Vasques to Peixoto, Pôrto Alegre, April 24, 1892, AFP.

37. Caetano Faria to Peixoto, Pôrto Alegre, May 20, 1892; Castilhos et al. to Peixoto, Pôrto Alegre, June 3, 1892, AFP.

38. C. M. Delgado de Carvalho, *Le Brésil méridional: Etude économique sur les Etats du Sud: S. Paulo, Paraná, Santa-Catarina et Rio-Grande-do-Sul* (Rio, 1910), p. 504; *Annuario da Provincia ... 1889*, pp. 212-13; *Annaes da Assembleia ... 1891: 1ª sessão ordinaria*, p. 33.

39. Milton I. Vanger, *José Batlle y Ordoñez of Uruguay: The Creator of His Times* (Cambridge, Mass., 1963), p. 8.

40. Luis Leopoldo Flores, *Estado do Rio Grande do Sul: Apontamentos historicos, chorographicos, e estatisticos para o relatorio consular* (Lisboa, 1898), p. 22.

41. Raymundo Faoro, "Rio Grande do Sul," manuscript for *Enciclopédia Delta-Larousse* (1968), p. 10. Cf. the process in neighboring Uruguay, where shanty towns arose in the countryside and were contemptuously referred to as *pueblos de ratas* (rat towns). Vanger, p. 5.

42. Literacy figures computed from DGE, *Sexo, raça e estado civil, nacionalidade, filiação, culto e analphabetismo da população recenseada em 31 de*

*dezembro de 1890* (Rio, 1898), pp 426–29. Growth of population among regions computed from *ibid.*, pp. 426–29, and from *Recenseamento da população do Imperio do Brazil a que se procedeu no dia 1º de agosto de 1872: Quadros estatisticos* (Rio, 1873–76), part 17, pp. 205–6 (microfilm). Unfortunately, these data are only approximations and omit important information. No definition of literacy is supplied in either census, and no breakdown is made between urban and rural inhabitants within a given município. Parts of several municípios were omitted altogether from the total provincial figures in the 1872 census. Since most of these were located in the Campanha, its rate of growth between 1872 and 1890 is slightly overstated. I have classified municípios and parishes in the 1872 census as follows: *Serra.* Bento Gonçalves, Bom Jardim, Caxias, Cruz Alta, Dois Irmãos, Estrela, Itaqui, Lagoa Vermelha, Montenegro, Palmeira, Passo Fundo, Pinhal, Povo Nôvo, Rio dos Sinos, Santa Cruz, Santiago do Boqueirão, Santo Angelo, São Francisco de Assis, São Francisco de Borja, São Francisco de Paula, São José do Hortênsio, São Leopoldo, São Luís, São Martinho, São Sebastião do Caí, São Vicente, Soledade, Taquara, Taquari, and Vacaria. *Campanha.* Alegrete, Bagé, Caçapava, Cacequi, Cacimbinhas, Cangassu, Dom Pedrito, Encruzilhada, Erval, Lavras, Livramento, Patrocínio, Piratini, Quaraí, Rosário, Sant'Anna da Boa Vista, Santa Maria, São Gabriel, São Sepé, and Uruguaiana. *Litoral.* Arroio Grande, Belem, Cachoeira, Cerrito de Cangassu, Conceição do Arroio, Dôres de Camaquã, Estreito, Gravataí, Jaguarão, Mostardas, Pelotas (including Boa Vista and Boquete), Pôrto Alegre (including Anjos d'Aldeia; N. S. das Dôres; N. S. do Rosário; and Pedras Brancas), Rio Pardo, Rio Grande, Santa Isabel, Santa Vitória, Santo Amaro, Santo Antônio da Patrulha, São Jerônimo, São João de Camaquã, São José do Norte, São Lourenço, Torres, Triunfo, and Viamão. The division of municípios and changes of name were fairly frequent. A list of those extant in 1890 and 1920, organized into three regions, appears in note 28, Chapter 5.

CHAPTER THREE

1. Raúl Villa-Lobos [pseud. Epaminondas Villalba], *A revolução federalista no Rio Grande do Sul (Documentos e commentarios)* (Rio, 1897), fn, p. lvi. An indispensable source on the Gaúcho civil war.

2. Wenceslau Escobar, *Apontamentos para a historia da revolução riograndense de 1893* (Porto Alegre, 1920), pp. 139–45. For a Castilhista tract cataloging Federalist atrocities, see Mucio Teixeira, *A revolução do Rio Grande do Sul: Suas causas e seus effeitos* (Pôrto Alegre, 1893).

3. *A Federação*, Nov. 26, 1892. Both Evaristo and José Gabriel were eleventh-hour converts to republicanism, having left the Conservative Party soon after Francisco Tavares defected in July 1889.

4. Custódio José de Mello, *O governo provisório e a revolução de 1893* (São Paulo, 1938), I: *De 29 de novembro de 1889 a 5 de setembro de 1893,* book II, 101n. Many Federalists were allegedly killed in a reprisal for Evaristo's death. *Ibid.*, p. 101; Escobar, p. 136.

5. *A. Federação*, Nov. 26, 1892.

6. The military measures of Monteiro and Abbott are noted by Sérgio da Costa Franco in *Júlio de Castilhos e sua época* (Pôrto Alegre, 1967), pp. 111, 149. The count of executive orders is my own; data from *Leis, decretos, e actos do Governo do Estado do Rio Grande do Sul de 1891* (Pôrto Alegre, 1914), and *Leis . . . de 1892* (Pôrto Alegre, 1913), *passim*.

7. Francisco de Paula Alencastro, speech of July 11, 1891, in *Annaes do congresso constituente do Estado do Rio Grande do Sul: 1891* (Pôrto Alegre, 1891), p. 87.

8. Message to state legislature, Feb. 8, 1893, in Othelo Rosa, *Julio de Castilhos* (Pôrto Alegre, 1928), Part 2, p. 442.

9. Escobar, p. 111; *A Federação*, Dec. 16, 1899.

10. Angel Dourado, *Os voluntarios do martyrio: Factos e epizodios da guerra civil* (Pelotas, 1896), p. 164.

11. Villa-Lobos, p. lvii.

12. Alfredo Varela, *Remembranças* (2d ed., Rio, 1959), p. 94; Castilhos to Peixoto, Pôrto Alegre, March 21, 1893, AFP.

13. Escobar, p. 152.

14. For the Brazilian and Uruguayan claims, respectively, see L. F. de Castilhos Goycochea, *Gumercindo Saraiva na Guerra dos Maragatos* (Rio, 1943), p. 123; Manuel Fonseca, *Gumersindo Saravia: El general de la libertad* (Montevideo, 1957), pp. 53–79.

15. Fonseca, p. 74.

16. See, for example, [General] João Telles to Peixoto, Dom Pedrito (RGS), March 11, 1893, AFP.

17. José Maria Bello, *A History of Modern Brazil: 1889–1964*, tr. James L. Taylor with a new concluding chapter by Rollie E. Poppino (Stanford, Calif., 1966), pp. 114–15.

18. Eurico Jacinto Sales, *História de Bagé* (Pôrto Alegre, 1955), p. 278.

19. Mello, book I, 391.

20. June E. Hahner, *Civilian-Military Relations in Brazil, 1889–1898* (Columbia, S. C., 1969), p. 155.

21. Dourado, p. 25.

22. *Ibid.*, p. 334.

23. Escobar, p. 276; Germano Hasslocher, *A verdade sobre a revolução* (2d ed., Pelotas, 1894), p. 40.

24. The only other exception was São Paulo, where rapid economic growth brought some new names into the political elite.

25. Tavares to Morais, Bagé (RGS), Dec. 1, 1895, APM.

26. See, for example, Luis Leopoldo Flores, *Estado do Rio Grande do Sul: Apontamentos historicos, chorographicos, e estatisticos para o relatorio consular* (Lisboa, 1898), p. 23.

CHAPTER FOUR

1. Among those who comment on the low level of religiosity in Rio Grande are Jorge Salis Goulart, *A formação do Rio Grande do Sul* (2d ed., Pôrto Alegre, 1933), p. 211; and Florêncio de Abreu, "Silveira Martins, o

tribuno," in *Ensaios e estudos históricos* (Rio, 1964), p. 197. For statistical information on religion in the state, see note 1 for Chapter 5, below.

2. *A Federação*, Jan. 31, 1903. The only biography of Borges is both out of date and uncritical: see João Pio de Almeida, *Borges de Medeiros: Subsidios para o estudo de sua vida e de sua obra* (Pôrto Alegre, 1928).

3. The governors of Rio Grande intervened in local affairs 209 times between 1896 and 1923, according to one count. For a list of these interventions, see [Antonio] Baptista Pereira, *Pela redempção do Rio Grande* (São Paulo, 1923), pp. 245–53.

4. Art. 20, constitution of July 14, 1891, in *Constituições sul-riograndenses 1843–1947* (Pôrto Alegre, 1963), p. 58.

5. Homero Baptista to Prudente de Morais, Rio Grande, Aug. 23, 1897, APM.

6. Vivaldo Coaracy, *Encontros com a vida (Memórias)* (Rio, 1962), p. 45.

7. Rubens de Barcellos, "Reflexões sôbre a revolução de 23," in Mansueto Bernardi and Moysés Vellinho, eds., *Estudos riograndenses: Motivos de história e literatura* (2d ed., Pôrto Alegre, 1960), p. 58.

8. Quoted in Antonio Gomes Carmo [pseud. Simão de Mantua], "Borges de Medeiros: Pessoas e coisas," in *Figurões vistos por dentro* (São Paulo, 1921), II, 144. In addition to Petersen and Tubino, other PRR coronéis of modest social origins included Marcos Alencastro de Andrade, Antônio João Ferreira, Elias Amaro, Erico Ribeiro da Luz, Manuel Amaro, Pedro Ripoll, Virgílio Antonio da Silva, Pedro Pinto de Sousa, and Aquiles Taurino de Rezende. (Information supplied the author by Sérgio da Costa Franco, letter of Feb. 26, 1970.)

9. On the power of the subchiefs, see [Francisco] Antunes Maciel Junior, *O Rio Grande (Anotações esparças)* (São Paulo, 1912), pp. 56–57.

10. Castilhos to Borges, Figueira (RGS), Dec. 11, 1899, ABM.

11. Abreu, "O movimento positivista no Rio Grande do Sul," in *Ensaios*, p. 231.

12. José Antonio Flores da Cunha, *Perfidias de um bandido* (Rio, 1911), pp. 9, 15. The semi-literate João Francisco later defended himself in *Noventa e tres (Acontecimentos que engendraram a lucta de noventa e tres e as consequencias que acarretaram até o presente)* (Rio, 1934), I.

13. Dep. Diogo Fortuna to Borges, Rio, Nov. 5, 1903, ABM.

14. Mantua, II, 100.

15. Coaracy, p. 84.

16. For a brief biography, see Othelo Rosa, *Carlos Barbosa Gonçalves* (Pôrto Alegre, 1952).

17. *A Federação*, June 3, 1907. See also the Bloc's manifesto in the issue of April 27, 1907. Other information about the Generation of '07 can be found in *O Debate: Jornal Castilhista* (June–Dec. 1907); João Neves da Fontoura, *Memorias*, I: *Borges de Medeiros e seu tempo* (Pôrto Alegre, 1958), 79–86 and *passim*; André Carrazzoni, *Perfil do estudante Getúlio Vargas* (Rio, 1942); and Getúlio Vargas, "Saudação histórica—discurso feito

em 1906 pelo dr. Getúlio Vargas," in *Revista do Instituto Histórico e Geográfico do Rio Grande do Sul*, 90 (1943), 151–58. A good fictional account of pre–World War I student life is found in Erico Veríssimo, *O retrato* (Part 2 of *O Tempo e o vento*), (2d ed., Pôrto Alegre, 1963), *passim*.

18. João Camillo de Oliveira Torres, *O presidencialismo no Brasil* (Rio, 1962), p. 190. Assis Brasil's two works were *Democracia representativa* (Paris, 1893), and *Do governo presidencial na Republica brasileira* (Lisboa, 1896).

19. Joaquim Francisco Assis Brasil, *Dictadura, parlamentarismo, democracia* (Pôrto Alegre, 1908), pp. 7–9, 60.

20. Assis to Campos Sales, Lisbon, Oct. 25, 1897; Campos Sales to Assis, São Paulo, Nov. 24, 1897, AAB.

21. Assis to Morais, Ilha Grande (Amazonas), Oct. 27, 1901; Morais to Assis, Piracicaba (São Paulo), Nov. 15, 1901, AAB.

22. Castilhos to Bittencourt, Figueira, Aug. 15, 1902, AVB.

23. Castilhos to Bittencourt, Figueira, Dec. 7, 1896, AVB.

24. For an English translation, see Samuel Putnam, *Rebellion in the Backlands* (Chicago, 1944).

25. Castilhos to Bittencourt, Figueira, Oct. 6, 1897, AVB. See also Carlos Reverbel, "Os fanáticos de Entre Rios," *Correio do Povo*, Nov. 28, 1965.

26. Silveira Martins to Campos Sales, n.p., Aug. 7, 1897 (copy), APM.

27. See, for example, Pinheiro Machado's address on Oct. 26, 1898, in *Annaes do Senado Federal: Sessões de 1 de outubro a 30 de novembro de 1898* (Rio, 1899), III, 250.

28. Campos Sales to Assis, São Paulo, Nov. 24, 1897, AAB.

29. On the *politica dos governadores*, see [Manoel Ferraz de] Campos Salles, *Da propaganda à presidencia* (São Paulo, 1908), pp. 236–50. A good critique of the politics of Campos Sales is Francisco de Assis Barbosa, "A presidência Campos Sales," *Luso-Brazilian Review*, V, 1 (Summer 1968), 3–26. A semiofficial apology that is nonetheless informative is Alcindo Guanabara, *A presidencia Campos Salles* (Rio, 1902).

30. Campos Salles, pp. 236–78 *passim*, especially p. 250. The President was surprisingly candid on this matter (as on most others) in *Da propaganda à presidencia*.

31. Borges to Pinheiro, Pôrto Alegre, April 10, 1900; Castilhos to Borges, Vila Rica (RGS), April 14, 1900, ABM.

32. Pinheiro to Borges, Rio, April 11, 1900, ABM.

33. Campos Salles, *Da propaganda*, pp. 378–83.

34. *Ibid.*, pp. 370–84; Aurélio Veríssimo Bittencourt (Castilhos' secretary) to Pinheiro, Pôrto Alegre, Jan. 15, 1901, ABM.

35. Bittencourt to Pinheiro, Pôrto Alegre, Jan. 15, 1901, ABM.

36. Pinheiro to Borges, Rio, May 10, 1901, ABM.

37. Pinheiro to Borges, Rio, July 17, 1901, ABM.

38. Borges to Pinheiro, Pôrto Alegre, June 10, 1901; Pinheiro to Borges, Rio, June 27, 1901, ABM.

39. "Cartas de Júlio de Castilhos a João Francisco," *Província de São Pedro, 20* (1955), p. 17.

40. Dep. Cassiano do Nascimento to Borges, Rio, Sept. 18, 1901, ABM. The archival correspondence reveals that Assis Barbosa is wrong in asserting that the Gaúchos dropped Castilhos' candidacy in 1901 because of Pinheiro's desire to remain part of the "oligarchy of officialism" ("A presidência Campos Sales," p. 25). One factor was certainly Castilhos' reluctance to run. But the overriding reason for the Gaúchos' submission was concern for the security of their machine.

41. Pinheiro to Borges, Rio, July 30, 1901, ABM.

42. Castilhos to Bittencourt, Figueira, Sept. 13, 1897, AVB.

43. On Uruguay in this period, see Milton I. Vanger, *José Batlle y Ordóñez of Uruguay: The Creator of His Times 1902–1907* (Cambridge, Mass., 1963). In discussing João Francisco's support for Saraiva (pp. 139, 143, 220), Vanger incorrectly seems to imply that the Riograndense was acting on his own authority.

44. *A Federação*, Jan. 18, 1896.

45. Dep. Ildefonso Simões Lopes, speech in chamber of Dec. 14, 1906, as reported in *A Federação*, Jan. 3, 1907.

46. *A Federação*, Aug. 12, 1902, April 20, 1903; Pinheiro Machado, speech in senate of Dec. 22, 1904, as reported in *A Federação*, Jan. 9, 1905; Pinheiro to Borges, Rio, May 31, 1908, ABM.

47. *A Federação*, Oct. 11, 1904.

48. *Annaes da Assembleia dos Representantes do Estado do Rio Grande do Sul: 1914–1917. 23ª–27ª sessões ordinarias* (Pôrto Alegre, 1915–18), *passim* (projected figures). In 1919 the property tax slipped from first place, but it continued to be an important source of revenue throughout the Old Republic. Other new taxes were also introduced, but the export tax continued to be applied into the 1930's.

49. [João] Cruz Costa, *O positivismo na República: Notas sôbre a história do positivismo no Brasil* (São Paulo, 1956), p. 26.

50. José Verissimo, "Impressões do Sul," *Jornal do Commercio* (Rio), July 21, 1912, pp. 3–4.

51. Romero, *O castilhismo no Rio Grande do Sul* (Porto [Portugal], 1912), pp. xxi, 2, 8f, 13.

52. Mantua, pp. 105–7.

CHAPTER FIVE

1. The most useful work I have found for studying regional differences in political behavior is Juan J. Linz and Amando de Miguel, "Within-Nation Differences and Comparisons: The Eight Spains," in Richard L. Merritt and Stein Rokkan, eds., *Comparing Nations: The Use of Quantitative Data in Cross-National Research* (New Haven, Conn., 1966), pp. 267–319. The authors emphasize differences among regions in terms of ten

variables: economic development; social structure (stratification and urbanization); education at different levels; linguistic and cultural traditions; religious climate; social mobilization (voluntary organizations); political traditions; representation in the various national elites; values, norms, and basic personality; and family patterns. I have given only passing attention to cultural and social differences among the leading states because they had relatively homogeneous cultures and low levels of urbanization and industrialization, and because in some cases social and cultural data were not available. Regional or state cleavages based on language differences were of course nonexistent in Brazil. There were differences in "religiosity." In data collected for the Catholic population in 1910, Rio Grande ranked seventeenth of 21 units (20 states and the Federal District) in number of baptisms per thousand inhabitants, twentieth in church marriages per thousand population, and sixteenth in last rites (extreme unction) per thousand. In almost every case the states ranking lower than Rio Grande were in the thinly populated interior, where the relative lack of clergy probably affected the ranking. By these indicators, Minas Gerais and São Paulo—the only two states with ruling parties more powerful than Rio Grande's after 1910—clearly had higher degrees of religiosity than Rio Grande do Sul. There were disparities in education among the three leading states: in 1907, Rio Grande had 228 children in school per thousand school-age population, whereas São Paulo had 162 and Minas 141. I have no data on differences in family patterns. The other indicators of Linz and Miguel are treated in this and subsequent chapters. On religious differences, see DGE, *Annuario estatistico do Brazil: 1º anno (1908–1912)*, III: *Cultos, assistencia, repressão e instrucção* (Rio, 1927), 135f, 138. On differences in school enrollment, see DGE, *Estatistica da instrucção*, Part I: *Estatistica escolar* (Rio, 1916), I, ccviii.

2. João Lyra, *Cifras e notas (Economia e finanças do Brasil)* (Rio, 1925), p. 46. Unfortunately, these figures do not include the value of output in the tertiary sector (services). Lyra's data are from the 1920 census. In 1920, one milréis was worth U.S. $0.21.

3. Data on capital and workers from DGE, *Resumo de varias estatisticas economico-financeiras* (Rio, 1924), p. 38; and DGE, *Synopse do recenseamento realizado em 1 de setembro de 1920: População do Brazil* (Rio, 1926), pp. 88–89. For the number of workers I have relied on the second source, which uses broader criteria in defining the industrial labor force than the *Resumo*.

4. DGE, *Resumo*, pp. 11, 38, 142–43.

5. IBGE, *Anuário estatistico do Brasil: Ano V 1939 /1940* ([Rio], n.d.), p. 1380; Instituto de Expansão Commercial, *O Brasil actual* (Rio, 1930), p. 36. São Paulo had 46 per cent of the coffee trees in 1929 and Minas 24 per cent.

6. Lyra, pp. 85–88.

7. DGE, *Annuario estatistico do Brazil: 1º anno (1908–1912)*, I: *Territorio e população* (Rio, 1916), 66; *Diario do Congresso Nacional*, XLI, 16 (May 21, 1930), 545.

8. Maurice Duverger, *Political Parties: Their Organization and Activity in the Modern State*, tr. B. and R. North (New York, 1963), pp. 63, 67.

9. Directoria do Serviço de Estatistica, *Força policial militar: 1908–1912* (Rio, 1914), p. 28.

10. Eul-soo Pang, "The Politics of *Coronelismo* in Brazil: The Case of Bahia, 1889–1930" (University of California, Berkeley, unpub. Ph.D. diss., 1969), *passim*. Pang describes the Bahiano state police in 1919 as "a rag-tag army of underpaid and underfed men" (p. 171).

11. Data on officers and states of birth from *Almanak do Ministerio da Guerra para o anno de 1895* (Rio, 1895); *Almanak . . . 1930* (Rio, 1930); Theodorico Lopes and Gentil Torres, *Ministros da Guerra do Brasil: 1808–1946* (Rio, 1947), *passim*; Gerardo Majella Bijos, *O Clube Militar e seus presidentes* (n.p., n.d.), *passim*; and *fés de ofício*, Archive of the Ministério da Guerra.

12. Pedro Pinchas Geiger, *Evolução da rêde urbana brasileira* (Rio, 1963), p. 20. In official Brazilian statistics, urban and rural are distinguished by legal criteria alone, and Geiger follows this practice. Only *cidades* (the seats of municípios) and *vilas* (the seats of a município's districts) qualify as urban.

13. On coronelismo in the Old Republic, see Victor Nunes Leal, *Coronelismo, enxada e voto: O município e o regime representativo no Brasil* (Rio, 1948). This is undoubtedly the best general work on the subject, though now out of date. Another general treatment is Maria Isaura Pereira de Queiroz, *O mandonismo local na vida política brasileira (Da Colônia à Primeira República): Ensaio de sociologia política* (São Paulo, 1969). A major case study with broad implications is Pang (see note 10). Pang's seven-category typology emphasizes that coronéis were by no means all latifundium owners. Other studes of coronelismo in the Old Republic include Orlando M. Carvalho, *Política do município (Ensaio histórico)* (Rio, 1946); Walfrido Moraes, *Jagunços e heróis: A civilização do diamante nas lavras da Bahia* (Rio, 1963); Edilson Portela Santos, "Evolução da vida política no município de Picos, Piauí," *Revista Brasileira de Estudos Políticos*, 10 (Jan., 1961), 160–83; and João Camillo de Oliveira Torres, *Estratificação social no Brasil: Suas origens históricas e suas relações com a organisação política do país* (São Paulo, 1965), ch. 5. A collection of documents on coronelismo is in Edgard Carone, *A Primeira República (1889–1930): Texto e contexto* (São Paulo, 1969), pp. 67–95. For another discussion of coronelismo, see my article "Political Participation in Brazil, 1881–1969," in *Luso-Brazilian Review*, VII, 2 (Dec. 1970), pp. 3–24, in which I cite works on coronelismo in other periods and compare it with similar institutions in Spain and Italy.

14. Among those who have drawn this comparison are Daniel de Carvalho, *Capítulos de memórias, 1ª série* (Rio, 1957), p. 230; and João Camillo de Oliveira Torres, *O presidencialismo no Brasil* (Rio, 1962), p. 236.

15. On this point, see Love, "Political Participation in Brazil," pp. 7–10.

16. Computed from data in IBGE, *Anuário estatístico do Brasil: Ano V 1939/1940* ([Rio], n.d.), p. 1412.

17. Getúlio Vargas to Borges de Medeiros, Rio, July 14, 1925, ABM. Bernardes' pronounced nativism may have been a factor in his concern for the fate of Amazonas. Fear of foreign penetration in that sparsely settled state remains a preoccupation of Brazilian nationalists today.

18. See IBGE, *Anuário estatístico do Brasil: Ano V 1939/1940* ([Rio], n.d.), p. 1409.

19. For figures on São Paulo's interstate and foreign trade for 1911–18, see Warren Dean, *The Industrialization of São Paulo: 1880–1945* (Austin, Tex., 1969), p. 97. On Rio Grande's interstate trade, see Hercilio I. Domingues, *Notas sobre a evolução economica do Rio Grande do Sul: Estudo do commercio de exportação riograndense* (Pôrto Alegre, 1929), I, 36.

20. My statistical data in this paragraph are from Pires de Almeida, *L'agriculture et les industries au Brésil* (Rio, 1889), pp. 171–90; DGE, *Resumo,* pp. 11f; DGE, *Recenseamento do Brazil realizado em 1 de setembro de 1920: Synopse do censo da agricultura* (Rio, 1922), p. 59; Rio Grande do Sul: Departamento Estadual de Estatística, "Annuario: 1929 (Estatistica economica, 3ª secção)," manuscript (n.d.), p. 58; and DGE, *Synopse do recenseamento realizado em 1 de setembro de 1920: População pecuária* (Rio, 1922), p. 42.

21. Rio Grande do Sul: Departamento Estadual de Estatística, *Anuário estatístico da exportação 1920–1941* (Pôrto Alegre, 1942), pp. 51–68; Ministerio de Relações Exteriores, *O Brasil: Recursos possibilidades de desenvolvimento* (Rio, 1933), p. 169; *Annaes da Assembléa dos Representantes do Estado do Rio Grande do Sul: 1891. 1ª sessão ordinaria* (Pôrto Alegre, 1892), p. 33; Departamento Estadual de Estatistica, "Annuario: 1929," manuscript (n.d.), p. 139.

22. Decio Coimbra, *Aspectos da evolucão argentina* (Pôrto Alegre, 1926), p. 52; Fortunato Pimentel, *O Rio Grande do Sul e suas riquezas* (Pôrto Alegre, n.d.), p. 72; Amyr Borges Fortes, *Panorama econômico do Rio Grande do Sul* (Pôrto Alegre, 1959), p. 60.

23. Rio Grande do Sul: Departamento Estadual de Estatística, *Anuário estatístico da exportação 1920–1941* (Pôrto Alegre, 1942), pp. 51–68. The value of goods shipped out of state is a good indicator of the composition of the commercialized sector of the economy. Though in terms of total value, the corn produced in Rio Grande ranked higher than rice, corn was largely a subsistence and feed crop consumed in the state.

24. Large capital requirements for rice production are mentioned by Fortunato Pimentel in two works: *Aspectos gerais da cultura de arroz no Rio Grande do Sul* (Pôrto Alegre, 1949), p. 20, and *Aspectos gerais de Cachoeira* (Pôrto Alegre, 1941), p. 31. According to him, rice growing was dominated by the leading families of Pelotas and prominent families in a few other municípios. *Aspectos . . . de arroz,* pp. 20, 64.

25. DGE, *Synopse* . . . *1920: População do Brazil*, pp. 80–81; DGE, *Recenseamento realizado em 1 de setembro de 1920* (Rio, 1927), V (Part 1): *Industria*, lxii.

26. J. F. Normano, "Joint Stock Companies and Foreign Capital in the State of Rio Grande do Sul (Brazil)," *Harvard Business Review*, IX (Jan., 1931), 221; Consul C. R. Nasmith, "Confidential Report on the General Banking Situation in the Consular District of Porto Alegre, Brazil, with Particular Reference to the Stability of Local Banks as Collection Agencies. July 9, 1930," p. 4 (Dept. of State, Index Bureau 832.516/149 CRN/VR 851.6, National Archives of the United States).

27. Ministerio de Relações Exteriores, *O Brasil*, p. 62; T. de Souza Lobo, *São Paulo na Federação* (São Paulo, 1924), p. 202; Manoel Olympio Romeiro, *S. Paulo e Minas na economia nacional* (São Paulo, 1930), p. 79; Instituto Nacional de Estatística, *Anuário estatístico: Ano III 1937* (Rio, 1937), p. 439; IBGE, *Anuário estatístico do Brasil: Ano V 1939/1940* ([Rio], n.d.), p. 1320.

28. Some municípios that existed in 1890 did not exist in 1920, and vice versa. The following are those listed in either or both censuses: *Serra*. Alfredo Chaves, Antônio Prado, Bento Gonçalves, Bom Jesús, Caxias, Cruz Alta, Encantado, Erechim, Estrêla, Garibaldi, Guaporé, Ijuí, Itaqui, Júlio de Castilhos, Lageado, Lagoa Vermelha, Montenegro, Palmeira, Passo Fundo, Santa Cristina do Pinhal, Santa Cruz, Santiago do Boqueirão, Santo Angelo, São Francisco de Assis, São Francisco de Borja, São Francisco de Paula, São Leopoldo, São Luís, São Martinho, São Sebastião do Caí, São Vicente, Soledade, Taquara, Taquari, Vacaria, Venâncio Aires. *Campanha*. Alegrete, Bagé, Caçapava, Cangassu, Dom Pedrito, Encruzilhada, Erval, Lavras, Livramento, Pinheiro Machado (Cacimbinhas), Piratini, Quaraí, Rosário, Santa Maria, São Gabriel, São Sepé, Uruguaiana. *Litoral*. Arroio Grande, Cachoeira, Conceição do Arroio, Dores de Camaquã, Gravataí, Jaguarão, N. S. da Graça, Pelotas, Pôrto Alegre, Rio Pardo, Rio Grande, Santa Isabel, Santa Vitória, Santo Amaro, Santo Antônio da Patrulha, São Jerônimo, São João de Camaquã, São José do Norte, São Lourenço, Tôrres, Triunfo, Viamão.

29. Data in this paragraph from DGE, *Resumo*, p. 14; DGE, *Recenseamento . . . 1920: Synopse . . . da agricultura*, pp. 18–19; and Rio Grande do Sul: Directoria de Estatistica (Secçao demographica), *Boletim*, II: *1909* (Pôrto Alegre, 1911), p. 13.

30. Literacy figures by age groups are not available for 1890. In 1920 Brazil as a whole had a 35.1 per cent literacy rate among those fifteen years old and above; the rate for the same group in Rio Grande was 55.5 per cent. (In every census the Federal District, with virtually no rural education problem, had a higher percentage of literacy than any of the states.)

31. Computed from data in Rio Grande do Sul: Repartição de Estatistica, *Relatorio* (Pôrto Alegre, 1916), pp. 145–49. Another researcher using the same data but apparently different criteria found the Germans in first place.

See Jean Roche, *La colonisation allemande et le Rio Grande do Sul* (Paris, 1959), pp. 391–92. This work is a major study of the culture, geography, and history of the German-Brazilians in Rio Grande.

32. Roche, pp. 354–55, 391–92.

33. Compiled from Federação das Associações Ruraes do Estado do Rio Grande do Sul, *Annaes do Congresso de Criadores* (Pôrto Alegre, 1927), pp. 9–20; Borges de Medeiros, circular letter to local PRR leaders, Pôrto Alegre, Feb. 12, 1926, ABM.

34. Compiled from correspondence in ABM. I accept these allegations as generally accurate with respect to type and relative incidence of fraud. Presumably, many other instances were not reported because of Governor Borges's well-known partiality.

35. Leal, p. 29; Oliveira Torres, *O presidencialismo*, p. 235.

36. Pierre Denis, *Brazil*, tr. Bernard Miall (?4th ed., London, 1921), p. 311.

37. Roche, pp. 106, 553.

38. Data from *A Federação*, July 4, 1905; "Mappa demonstrativo do resultado da qualificação federal até 29 de janeiro de 1918," ABM.

39. Roche, p. 551.

CHAPTER SIX

1. For data, see *Diario do Congresso*, X, 7 (June 28, 1898), 68, and XVIII, 38 (June 20, 1906), 547–48, 553; DGE, *Annuario estatistico do Brazil: 1º anno (1908–1912)* (Rio, 1916), I: *Territorio e população*, 42–44, 66; IBGE, *Recenseamento geral do Brasil—1950, Série regional*, XX, Book 1: *Estado da Bahia: Censo demográfico* (Rio, 1955), 1; XXVIII, Book 1: *Estado do Rio Grande do Sul: Censo demográfico* (Rio, 1955), 1.

2. Gustavo Barroso, "Pinheiro Machado na intimidade—Evocações," in *Revista do Instituto Histórico e Geográfico Brasileiro*, 211 (April-June, 1951), 92; Daniel de Carvalho, *Capítulos de memórias: 1ª série* (Rio, 1957), p. 70. The best biography of Pinheiro is [João da] Costa Pôrto, *Pinheiro Machado e seu tempo: Tentativa de interpretação* (Rio, 1951). Also of some value are Hermes da Fonseca Filho, *Pinheiro Machado (Uma individualidade e uma época)* (Rio, n.d.); Othelo Rosa, *Pinheiro Machado* (Pôrto Alegre, 1951); Cid Pinheiro Cabral, *O senador de ferro* (Pôrto Alegre, 1969); and Cyro Silva, *Pinheiro Machado* (Rio, n.d.). An incisive and unflattering essay on Pinheiro's career is Antonio Gomes Carmo [pseud. Simão de Mantua], "General Pinheiro: José Gomes Pinheiro Machado," in his *Figurões vistos por dentro (Estudo de psychologia social brasileira)* (São Paulo, 1921), I, 151–89. Still another portrait, brief but vivid, is found in Érico Veríssimo's novel, *O Retrato* (Part 2 of *O tempo e o vento*) (2d ed., Pôrto Alegre, 1963), II, 369–75.

3. See, for example, Pinheiro Machado, speech in senate of July 12, 1915, in *Annaes do Senado Federal de 1 a 31 de julho de 1915* (Rio, 1918), IV, 153–54; Dep. Carlos Maximiliano Pereira dos Santos to Borges de Medeiros, Rio, Sept. 27, 1914, ABM.

4. Dep. Angelo Pinheiro Machado to Borges, n.p., June 21, 1905, ABM.

5. Pinheiro to Borges, Rio, July 15, 1905, ABM; *A Federação*, July 20, 1905; Pinheiro to Rui Barbosa, Rio, July 25, 1905, ARB.

6. Maria do Carmo Campello de Souza, "O processo político-partidário na Primeira República," in *Brasil em perspectiva* (São Paulo, 1968), p. 217. An excellent survey of politics in the Old Republic.

7. Dep. Manuel de Campos Cartier to Borges, Rio, Aug. 11, 1905, ABM.

8. *O Paiz* (Rio), June 26, 1905.

9. The best general study of coffee policy is Antônio Delfim Netto, *O problema do café no Brasil* (São Paulo, 1951). Other works include Afonso de E. Taunay, *Pequena história do café no Brasil (1727–1937)* (Rio, 1945), a summary of an excessively long multi-volume study; and Albert Mourier, *La valorisation du café* (Paris, 1938). A major study of financial and economic policy bearing heavily on coffee problems is José Maria dos Santos, *A politica geral do Brasil* (São Paulo, 1930).

10. In 1905 São Paulo's total revenue was 31,050 contos, of which 19,297 came from export duties. See Departamento Estadual de Estatística (São Paulo), *São Paulo: 1889–1939* (n.p., [1940]), pp. 13–14, 24.

11. Afonso Arinos de Melo Franco, *Um estadista da República (Afrânio de Melo Franco e seu tempo)* (Rio, 1955), II: *Fase nacional*, 585. Modeled after Joaquim Nabuco's *Um estadista do Império*, this work is an indispensable source on the political history of the Old Republic.

12. Pinheiro to Borges, Rio, May 19, May 21, and June 3, 1909, ABM.

13. *Annaes da Assembleia dos Representantes do Estado do Rio Grande do Sul, 1909* (Pôrto Alegre, 1910), pp. 24–25 (session of Sept. 24, 1909).

14. Barbara W. Tuchman, *The Proud Tower: A Portrait of the World Before the War, 1890–1914* (New York, 1966), p. 284. The standard biography of Rui is Luiz Viana Filho, *A vida de Rui Barbosa* (7th ed., São Paulo, 1965). For a different view, see R[aymundo] Magalhães Júnior, *Rui: O homem e o mito* (Rio, 1964). An excellent introduction to Rui's voluminous writings is Rui Barbosa, *Escritos e discursos seletos*, ed. Virgínia Cortes de Lacerda (2d ed., Rio, 1966).

15. Pinheiro to Borges, Rio, March 1, March 8, 1910, ABM.

16. Rui Barbosa, speech in senate of Nov. 13, 1914, in *Obras seletas* (Rio, 1955), IV, 17.

17. Fonseca to Borges, Petrópolis (Rio State), Sept. 15, 1915, in *A Federação*, Oct. 2, 1915.

18. Costa Pôrto, p. 114. See also Pinheiro to Borges, Rio, March 2, 1913, ABM; and José Vieira, *A Cadeia Velha (Memorias da Camara dos Deputados)* (Rio, n.d.), pp. 14–16, 197. Vieira's book is a frank account of the maneuvers of various congressional leaders in 1909.

19. Victor Nunes Leal, *Coronelismo, enxada, e voto: O municipio e o regime representativo no Brasil* (Rio, 1948), p. 166.

20. On Flôres, see José Antônio Flôres da Cunha to Borges, Rio, May 23, 1912, ABM; personal interview with José Bonifácio Flôres da Cunha, Pôrto Alegre, Dec. 5, 1964. For two of the many other instances where Pinheiro

chose candidates, see Elysio Couto to Ildefonso Fontoura, Rio, Jan. 11, 1915; and Pinheiro to Marcondes de Souza, Rio, Jan. 19, 1915, ABM.

21. *A Federação*, Dec. 14, 1910.

22. Gilberto Amado, *Mocidade no Rio e primeira viagem à Europa* (Rio, 1956), p. 123. An eyewitness account.

23. Charles A. Gauld, *The Last Titan: Percival Farquhar, American Entrepreneur in Latin America* (Stanford, Calif., 1964), pp. 253, 257, 273.

24. *A Federação*, May 20, 1905.

25. *O Paiz* (Rio), Oct. 30, 1910, p. 1.

26. Pinheiro to Borges, Rio, Oct. 22, 1910, ABM; Setembrino de Carvalho, *Memórias* (Rio, 1950), p. 110; Costa Pôrto, p. 174; Melo Franco, *Um estadista*, II, 603.

27. *Partido Republicano Conservador: Acto de convocação* (Rio, 1910), p. 43.

28. *Partido Republicano Federal: Preliminares de organisação: Discussão de programma, installação e deliberação da convenção provisoria, apresentação das candidaturas presidenciais, apuração e proclamação da eleição presidencial, instrucções* (Rio, 1895), p. 16.

29. *O Paiz*, Nov. 10, 1910, p. 2.

30. *Partido Republicano Conservador*, p. 25; *Partido Republicano Conservador do Ceará: Trabalhos da convenção convocada para o dia 1º de março de 1911* (Fortaleza, 1911), pp. 15–17, 43; Estado da Paraíba, *Incorporação do Partido Republicano, fundado em 1892, ao Partido Republicano Conservador* (Paraíba, 1911), pp. 3, 15, 30.

31. Borges to Pinheiro, Pôrto Alegre, June 26, 1911, ABM.

32. Borges, circular letter to local PRR leaders, Pôrto Alegre, Oct. 20, 1913; Borges to editor of *A Imprensa*, Pôrto Alegre, March 30, 1914; Armênio Jouvin to Borges, Rio, Sept. 8, 1912; Júlio de Medeiros to Borges, Rio, n.d.; Pinheiro to Borges, Rio, Oct. 22, 1910, ABM.

33. E.g., Borges to Pinheiro, Pôrto Alegre, Sept. 11, 1912, Dec. 15, Dec. 22, 1914; Pinheiro to Borges, Rio, Jan. 1, 1915, ABM.

34. E.g., Dep. João Simplício Alves de Carvalho to Borges, Rio, May 28, 1910; Pinheiro to Borges, Rio, Nov. 7, 1910; Borges to Pinheiro, Pôrto Alegre, Aug. 5, 1911; Borges to José Barbosa Gonçalves, Pôrto Alegre, May 28, 1912; Borges to Lima Brandão, Pôrto Alegre, July 20, 1912; Borges to J. S. Alves, Pôrto Alegre, May 30, 1912, ABM.

35. Borges to Pinheiro, Pôrto Alegre, Nov. 1, 1910, ABM.

36. Fonseca to Borges, Rio, Oct. 27, 1910; Pinheiro to Borges, Rio, Sept. 16, 1910; Borges to Pinheiro, Pôrto Alegre, Sept. 23, 1910, ABM.

37. Pinheiro to Borges, Rio, Sept. 16, 1910; Borges to Pinheiro, Pôrto Alegre, Sept. 23, 1910, ABM.

38. Pinheiro to Borges, Rio, Oct. 22, Oct. 26, 1910, ABM; *O Paiz*, Oct. 30, 1910, p. 1.

39. DGE, *Resumo de varias estatisticas economico-financeiras* (Rio, 1924), p. 131.

40. Pinheiro to Borges, Rio, April 9, 1913, ABM; see also correspon-

dence between Borges and Minister Barbosa Gonçalves in *A Federação,* Sept. 26, 1913.

41. E.g., Borges to Correia, Pôrto Alegre, Aug. 18, 1913; Borges to José Barbosa Gonçalves, Pôrto Alegre, May 28, 1912; Borges to Ildefonso Fontoura, Pôrto Alegre, May 30, 1912; Dep. J. S. Alves to Borges, Rio, April 29, 1912, ABM.

42. Melo Franco, II, 718.

43. Fonseca to Mena Barreto, Rio, Jan. 15, 1912, in João de Deus Menna Barreto, *Os Menna Barreto: Seis gerações de soldados* (Rio, n.d.), p. 312; Mena Barreto to Clodoaldo da Fonseca, Rio, April 28, 1913, ACF.

44. A. C. Correia Lopes to Borges, n.p., Jan. 10, 1911, ABM; Brígido Tinoco, *A vida de Nilo Peçanha* (Rio, 1962), pp. 164–65.

45. Costa Pôrto, pp. 168–69. Mena Barreto, then minister of war, later affirmed that Pinheiro planned intervention in São Paulo. Hermes da Fonseca Filho, *Marechal Hermes* (Rio, 1961), pp. 171–72. A work by a devoted son with some useful information.

46. Clodoaldo da Fonseca to João Severiano da Fonseca, Maceió (Alagoas), June 27, 1913, ACF.

47. A perceptive treatment of the political infighting in Ceará and its relation to national politics is found in Ralph della Cava, *Miracle at Joaseiro* (New York, 1970), pp. 81–176. For a harsher view of Padre Cícero, see Otacílio Anselmo, *Padre Cícero—Mito e realidade* (Rio, 1968).

48. Copy of Franco Rabelo's telegram to Hermes da Fonseca, in Rabelo to Borges, Fortaleza, Feb. 23, 1914, ABM.

49. Pinheiro to Borges, Rio, March 11, 1914, ABM.

50. *Ibid.;* Carvalho, p. 121.

51. [Emídio] Dantas Barreto, *Conspirações* (Rio, 1917), pp. 273, 277–78; Carvalho, p. 112; Costa Pôrto, pp. 195–96.

52. Pinheiro to Borges, Rio, Dec. 19, 1914, ABM.

53. Clodoaldo da Fonseca to João S. da Fonseca, Maceió, June 27, 1913, ACF.

54. Della Cava, p. 132. For a contemporary commentary in support of this idea, see Rodolpho Teophilo, *A sedição do Joaseiro* (São Paulo, 1922), pp. 10, 14, 25, 131, 136, 269. Salvacionismo has yet to be researched adequately, and the scant literature on the subject is a major impediment to a full understanding of the political process after 1910.

55. For example, both of Alberto Torres's most celebrated works were published in Rio in 1914—*A organisação nacional* and *O problema nacional brasileiro: Introducção a um programma de organisação nacional.* Lima Barreto's *Numa e a nympha* (cited in footnote, p. 136 above) appeared in 1915.

CHAPTER SEVEN

1. [Emídio] Dantas Barreto, *Conspirações* (Rio, 1917), pp. 212, 214; Clodoaldo da Fonseca to Borges, Maceió (Alagoas), March 4, 1913, ABM; Mena Barreto to C. Fonseca, Rio, April 28, 1913, ACF.

2. Dantas Barreto, p. 235. As late as June the President still supported Pinheiro's candidacy. Ildefonso Fontoura to Borges, Rio, June 27, 1913, ABM.

3. On the succession maneuvers in 1913, see Afonso Arinos de Melo Franco, *Um estadista da República (Afrânio de Melo Franco e seu tempo)* (Rio, 1955), II: *Fase nacional*, pp. 786–96; João Mangabeira, *Ruy: O estadista da República* (3d ed., São Paulo, 1960), pp. 176–84; [João da] Costa Pôrto, *Pinheiro Machado e seu tempo: Tentativa de interpretação* (Rio, 1951), pp. 180–89; Daniel de Carvalho, *Francisco Sales: Um político de outros tempos* (Rio, 1963), pp. 63–64; and Guerino Casasanta, *Correspondência de Bueno Brandão* (Belo Horizonte, 1958), pp. 32–58, 151–220. The last-named work is an important collection of documents for the study of national politics in the Old Republic.

4. Pinheiro to Borges, Rio, May 18, 1913, ABM.

5. Pinheiro to Borges, Rio, July 7, 1913, ABM; Melo Franco, II, 793; Hermes da Fonseca Filho, *Pinheiro Machado* (Rio, n.d.), p. 211.

6. Rui Barbosa, speech in senate of Nov. 13, 1914, in his *Obras seletas* ([Rio], 1955), IV, 10.

7. Pinheiro to Borges, Rio, July 22, 1913, ABM.

8. Pinheiro to Borges, Rio, Jan. 1, Jan. 8, 1915, ABM.

9. Pinheiro to Marcondes de Souza, Rio, Jan. 19, 1915 (copy), ABM; Pedro Cavalcanti, *A presidencia Wenceslau Braz 1914–1918* (Rio, 1918), pp. 54f, 57.

10. Borges to Marcos Andrade, Pôrto Alegre, July 22, 1915, ABM.

11. Dep. Vespúcio de Abreu et al. to Borges, Rio, Aug. 24, 1915, ABM.

12. Aníbal de Lemos to Borges, Dom Pedrito (RGS), March 9, 1917, ABM.

13. Barcelos to Longuinho da Costa, São Gabriel (RGS), July 20, 1915, ABM; Barcelos to Borges, n.p., June 3, 1915, in Barcelos [pseud. Amaro Juvenal], *Antônio Chimango: Poemeto campestre* (3d ed., Pôrto Alegre, 1961), p. 19.

14. Pinheiro to Borges, São Tomé (Rio State), July 26, 1915, ABM.

15. Barcelos, *Antônio Chimango*, p. 57.

16. Antonio Gomes Carmo [pseud. Simão de Mantua], *Figurões vistos por dentro (Estudo de psychologia social brasileira)* (São Paulo, 1921), I, 170.

17. *A Rua*, Jan. 9, 1915.

18. Quoted in *A Federação*, Sept. 29, 1915.

19. Mantua, I, 174. See Dep. Bueno de Andrada's eyewitness account of the assassination in *Correio da Manhã* (Rio), Sept. 9, 1915.

20. *Correio do Povo* (Pôrto Alegre), Sept. 11, 1915.

21. Borges to President Venceslau Brás, n.p., Sept. 13, 1915; Dep. Gumercindo Ribas to Borges, Rio, Sept. 30, 1915; Hermes da Fonseca to Borges, Petrópolis (Rio State), Sept. 9, 1915; Dep. Ildefonso Pinto to Borges, Rio, Sept. 28, 1915, ABM.

22. Ribas to Borges, Rio, Oct. 4, 1915, ABM.

23. Monteiro to Borges, Rio, Oct. 20, 1915, ABM; Costa Pôrto, p. 249.

24. Rosa to Borges, Teresina (Piauí), June 10, 1916, ABM.

25. Borges to Monteiro et al., n.p., Sept. 17, 1915, ABM.

26. Sen. Luís Soares dos Santos to Borges, Rio, March 15, 1917, ABM.

27. Azeredo to Borges, Rio, Sept. 19, 1915; Dep. Evaristo Amaral to Borges, Rio, May 10, 1916; Monteiro to Borges, Rio, March 19, 1916, ABM.

28. Gov. Bernardino Monteiro to Borges, Vitória (Espírito Santo), June 18, 1916; Gov. Caetano Albuquerque to Borges, Cuiabá (Mato Grosso), July 4, 1916; Marcondes Souza to Borges, Rio, June 12, 1917; Joaquim Pires to Borges, Rio, April 19, 1918; Fernandes Lima to Borges, n.p., May 5, 1918; Modesto Leal to Borges, Rio, May 16, 1918; Borges to Soares dos Santos, n.p., Oct. 28, 1915, and Feb. 24, 1916, ABM.

29. Soares dos Santos to Borges, Rio, Sept. 20, 1915; Borges to Soares, n.p., Sept. 22, 1915, ABM; Hermes da Fonseca to Borges, Petrópolis, Sept. 15, 1915, in *A Federação*, Oct. 2, 1915.

30. Borges to Farquhar, Pôrto Alegre, May 17, 1915; Borges to Dep. Joaquim Luís Osório, Pôrto Alegre, Sept. 30, 1916, ABM.

31. Borges to Dep. J. S. Alves de Carvalho, Pôrto Alegre, July 26, 1916; Osório to Borges, Rio, Oct. 21, 1916; S. M. C. Rough to Borges, Rio, Dec. 20, 1916; Abreu et al. to Borges, Rio, Dec. 28, 1916; Borges, circular letter to local PRR leaders, Pôrto Alegre, Aug. 23, 1916, ABM.

32. Monteiro to Borges, Rio, Dec. 24, 1915, Aug. 25, 1916; Alves de Carvalho to Borges, Rio, Aug. 10, 1916, ABM.

33. Thomas W. Palmer, Jr., "S. Paulo in the Brazilian Federation: A State Out of Balance" (Columbia University, unpub. Ph.D. diss., 1950), p. 99.

34. Borges to Soares dos Santos, Pôrto Alegre, Aug. 8, 1916, ABM.

35. Dep. Carlos Penafiel to Borges, Rio, Nov. 19, 1918, ABM.

36. Borges to Abreu, Pôrto Alegre, July 17, 1918, ABM.

37. Penafiel to Borges, Rio, Dec. 18, 1918, ABM.

38. Pereira dos Santos to Borges, Rio, Aug. 8, Nov. 22, 1916; Soares dos Santos to Borges, Rio, March 16, 1917; Pereira dos Santos to Borges, Rio, Oct. 16, 1916; Monteiro to Borges, Rio, March 17, 1917, ABM.

39. Amaral to Borges, Rio, April 12, 1917, ABM.

40. Borges to Rodrigues Alves, Pôrto Alegre, Nov. 9, 1918; Abreu to Borges, Rio, Nov. 11, 1918, ABM.

41. Pereira dos Santos to Borges, Rio, Jan. 29, Oct. 4, 1918; Abreu to Borges, Rio, Nov. 15, 1918; Soares dos Santos to Borges, Rio, Dec. 25, 1918, ABM.

CHAPTER EIGHT

1. Including the PRR. See *A Federação*, Feb. 4, 1919.

2. Borges, who was at his ranch in Cachoeira, relayed instructions to Dep. Vespúcio de Abreu through Lt. Gov. Protásio Alves. See Abreu to Alves, Rio, Jan. 6, Jan. 25, 1919; Alves to Abreu, Pôrto Alegre, Jan. 17, Jan. 21, 1919, ABM.

3. Abreu to Alves, Rio, Feb. 1, 1919, ABM; Joaquim Salles, *Se não me falha a memória (Políticos e jornalistas do meu tempo)* (Rio, n.d.), p. 136 (on Rui); Borges to Alves, n.p., Feb. 13, 1919; Sen. Vitorino Monteiro to Alves, Rio, Feb. 11, 1919; Abreu to Alves, Rio, Feb. 17, 1919; Borges to Alves, n.p., Feb. 17, 1919; Abreu to Alves, Rio, Feb. 20, 1919; Gov. Camilo Holanda to Borges, Cabedelo (Paraíba), Feb. 22, 1919, ABM.

Afonso Arinos de Melo Franco credits the Mineiros with Epitácio's triumph, in *Um estadista da República (Afrânio de Melo Franco e seu tempo)* (Rio, 1955), II, 938. But Epitácio and his biographer assert Gaúcho primacy. See Epitacio Pessoa, *Pela verdade* (Rio, 1925), p. 43; and Laurita Pessôa Raja Gabaglia, *Epitácio Pessôa (1865–1942)* (Rio, 1951), I, 322. Borges committed the Riograndenses to Epitácio at a time when the PRM leaders were still considering Arantes (February 17).

4. *Diario do Congresso Nacional*, XXX, 54 (July 10, 1919), 693. On Rui's program, see his *Campanha presidencial, 1919* (Bahia, 1919).

5. José Maria dos Santos, *A politica geral do Brasil* (São Paulo, 1930), p. 451; Melo Franco, II, 970.

6. Epitacio Pessoa, p. 183. The description of coffee policy is based on the sources listed in note 9, Chapter 6, above.

7. Epitacio Pessoa, p. 374.

8. Sen. Luís Soares dos Santos to Borges, Rio, June 4, 1920, ABM.

9. Abreu and Soares dos Santos to Borges, Rio, July 10, 1920; Abreu to Borges, Rio, Aug. 28, 1920; Dep. C. M. Santos to Borges, Rio, July 13, July 22, 1920; Borges to Abreu and Soares dos Santos, Pôrto Alegre, July 13, 1920; Abreu and Soares dos Santos to Borges, Rio, July 31, 1920; Bernardes to Borges, Belo Horizonte, Aug. 8, 1920, ABM.

10. C. M. Santos to Borges, Rio, Nov. 24, 1919; Supreme Court Justice Pedro Mibielli to Borges, Rio, May 5, 1920, ABM; Mozart Lago, *A convenção nacional de 1921: Factos e documentos* (Rio, 1921), p. 8; Abreu to Borges, Rio, April 22, 1921, ABM.

11. Melo Franco, II, 960; Vargas to Borges, Rio, July 29, 1925, ABM. A brief and laudatory biography is Paulo Amora, *Bernardes: O estadista de Minas na República* (São Paulo, 1964).

12. Borges to Sens. Raúl Soares and Bueno Brandão, Pôrto Alegre, May 24, 1921, ABM; Dep. Alvaro Baptista, quoted in Melo Franco, II, 993.

13. IBGE, *Anuário estatistico do Brasil: Ano V 1939/1940* ([Rio], n.d.), p. 1384; Borges to Abreu et al., Pôrto Alegre, June 6, 1921, ABM.

14. Borges to Abreu et al., Pôrto Alegre, June 20, 1921; Soares dos Santos to Borges, Rio, n.d., ABM; Lago, pp. 379–80.

15. Epitacio Pessoa, p. 475. Borges later implied he had been impressed, at least in the early stages of succession, by Epitácio's efforts to remain neutral. See Borges to Vargas, Irapuã (RGS), June 24, 1929, AGV.

16. Epitacio Pessoa, p. 480.

17. Borges to Abreu and Soares dos Santos, Pôrto Alegre, June 1, 1921, ABM.

18. C. M. Santos to Borges, Oct. 16, 1916; Abreu to Alves, Jan. 6, 1919, ABM.

19. Abreu et al. to Borges, Rio, June 18, 1921; Borges to Abreu et al., Pôrto Alegre, June 22, 1921, ABM; Nilo Peçanha, *Politica, economia e finanças: Campanha presidencial (1921–1922)* (Rio, 1922), pp. 108, 111f; Dep. Souza Filho (of Pernambuco), speech of Nov. 20, 1922, in *Annaes da Camara dos Deputados: Sessões de 13 a 22 de novembro de 1922*, XIII (Rio, 1927), 469. A modern and sympathetic biography of the candidate is Brígido Tinoco, *A vida de Nilo Peçanha* (Rio, 1962).

20. Lindolfo Collor, *A Reação Republicana* (Pôrto Alegre, 1921), p. 15.

21. The military did not run its "own" candidate in 1922 as stated in John J. Johnson, *Political Change in Latin America: The Emergence of the Middle Sectors* (Stanford, Calif., 1958), p. 160.

22. Mibielli to Borges, Rio, June 19, 1921, ABM; Francisco de Assis Barbosa, *Juscelino Kubitschek: Uma revisão na política brasileira* (Rio, 1960), I, 288.

23. Abreu to Borges, Rio, Nov. 22, 1921, ABM.

24. Text of resolution in Hélio Silva, *1922: Sangue na areia de Copacabana* (Rio, 1964), p. 72. See also José Honório Rodrigues, *Teoria da história do Brasil: Introdução metodológica* (3d ed., São Paulo, 1969), pp. 331–39.

25. C. M. Santos to Borges, Rio, April 1, 1922; Borges to Minister Luís Simões Lopes, Pôrto Alegre, May 3, 1922, ABM.

26. Raul Soares described the meeting in detail to Governor Bernardes. Soares to Bernardes, Rio, May 2, 1922, in Virgilio de Mello Franco, *Outubro, 1930* (n.p., 1931), pp. 53–67.

27. *Ibid.*, p. 53; Simões Lopes to Borges, Rio, May 16, 1922, ABM.

28. *Diario do Congresso Nacional*, XXXIII, 30 (June 8, 1922), 793, 804–78.

29. Mibielli to Borges, Rio, April 19, 1922; Abreu to Borges, Rio, April 12, 1922, ABM.

30. Abreu to Borges, Rio, June 7, June 12, 1922, ABM.

31. Borges to Abreu, Pôrto Alegre, April 24, 1922, ABM.

32. Abreu to Borges, Rio, July 27, 1922, ABM.

33. Peçanha to Borges, Rio, July 3, 1922, ABM.

34. *A Federação*, June 8, 1921. The debate took place on May 26.

CHAPTER NINE

1. Afonso Arinos de Melo Franco, *Um estadista da República (Afrânio de Melo Franco e seu tempo)* (Rio, 1955), II, 1072.

2. Laurita Pessôa Raja Gabaglia, *Epitácio Pessôa (1865–1942)* (Rio, 1951), I, 542; Clodoaldo da Fonseca, in Hélio Silva, *1922: Sangue na areia de Copacabana* (Rio, 1964), p. 502.

3. Gabaglia, I, 594.

4. Borges to Dep. Alvaro Baptista, Pôrto Alegre, April 13, 1922, ABM.

5. Although no Gaúcho served in the brief administrations of Nilo Pe-

çanha and Rodrigues Alves–Delfim Moreira, the PRR had been invited to participate in both.

6. "Quadro geral da votação na eleição presidencial [i.e. gubernatorial] no Estado a 25 de novembro de 1922," ABM.

7. Washington Luís Pereira de Sousa to Assis, Prata (São Paulo), Feb. 3, 1923, AAB; Lindolfo Collor, *A campanha presidencial do Rio Grande do Sul (1922-1923)* (Pôrto Alegre, 1923), p. 209.

8. Juarez Tavora, *A guisa de depoimento sobre a revolução brasileira de 1924* (São Paulo, 1927), I, 58.

9. Antero Marques, *Mensagem a poucos: 23* (Pôrto Alegre, 1964), pp. 56, 74.

10. Borges to Dep. J. S. Alves de Carvalho, Pôrto Alegre, March 30, March 31, 1923, ABM.

11. *O congresso do Partido Republicano* (Pôrto Alegre, 1924), p. 152; Borges to Sen. Vespúcio de Abreu, Pôrto Alegre, April 3, April 4, 1923; Lindolfo Collor to Borges, Rio, Dec. 15, 1923, ABM.

12. On the legal technicalities of the case and the supreme court's reversal of its decision in order to conform to the President's intervention, see Herman G. James, *The Constitutional System of Brazil* (Washington, D. C., 1923), pp. 138–39.

13. Alves to Borges, Rio, Jan. 8, 1923; Borges to Abreu et al., Pôrto Alegre, July 23, 1923, ABM.

14. Setembrino de Carvalho, *Memórias* (Rio, 1950), p. 209.

15. Dep. Getúlio Vargas to Borges, Rio, July 11, July 13, July 29, ABM.

16. Dep. Nabuco de Gouveia to Borges, Bagé (RGS), Nov. 30, 1923, ABM.

17. Borges to Col. José Franco Ferreira, Pôrto Alegre, Dec. 10, 1923, ABM.

18. For the text of the manifesto, dated Oct. 29, 1924, see Edgard Carone, *A Primeira República (1889-1930): Texto e contexto* (São Paulo, 1969), pp. 264–67; other documents on *tenentismo* are included in this collection. See also João Alberto Lins de Barros, *Memórias de um revolucionário* (Rio, 1954), pp. 24–67.

19. Assis to Batista Luzardo, Berachi (Uruguay), Dec. 15, 1924, in Lindolfo Collor, *As opposições sul-riograndenses e o movimento militar de São Paulo* (Rio, 1925), pp. 101–2.

20. Marques, p. 215.

21. See, for example, *A guisa*, cited in note 8 above; João Cabanas, *A columna da morte sob o commando do tenente Cabanas* (3d ed., Asunción, 1926); [Francisco] Assis Chateaubriand, *Terra deshumana (A vocação revolucionaria do Presidente Arthur Bernardes)* (Rio, n.d.); J[oaquim] Nunes de Carvalho, *A revolução no Brasil 1924–1925: Apontamentos para a historia* (Rio, 1927); and Mauricio de Lacerda, *Entre duas revoluções* (Rio, 1927). The last-named work is surprisingly modern in its perception of the plight of underdeveloped countries vis-à-vis imperial powers.

22. DGE, *Resumo de varias estatisticas economico-financeiras* (Rio, 1924), pp. 12, 38. The value of industrial output is for 1919, that of agriculture for 1920.

23. The thesis that tenentismo represented the urban middle class and the petite bourgeoisie in particular was first put forth in Virginio Santa Rosa, *O sentido do tenentismo* (Rio, 1933); reprinted as *Que foi o tenentismo?* (Rio, 1963).

24. He also made a bow to the demands of the industrial working class for retirement benefits and better working conditions. J. F. Assis Brasil, *A Alliança Libertadora do Rio Grande do Sul ao paiz* (n.p., 1925), pp. 5f, 10.

25. *Ibid.*, p. 10.

26. Bernardes to Borges, Petrópolis (Rio State), March 5, 1925; Borges to Gouveia, Pôrto Alegre, March 20, 1925, ABM.

27. Vargas to Borges, Rio, July 29, 1925, ABM. By this time Minas Gerais and São Paulo had already agreed on the succession. However, Rio Grande was still in a position to make trouble, as in 1921.

28. Vargas to Borges, Rio, Aug. 3, 1926, ABM.

29. Bernardes was more successful in defending the milréis in the international money market than in stabilizing domestic prices, and the latter endeavor was more important to Rio Grande's pastoral economy. In 1926 the milréis was worth U.S. $0.14, a full cent higher than in 1922; but in the same period (1922–26), the consumer price index rose from 188 to 266 (1912 = 100). On consumer prices for the city of Rio, see IBGE, *Anuário estatístico do Brasil: Ano V 1939/1940* ([Rio], n.d.), p. 1384; on the exchange rate, see Julian Smith Duncan, *Public and Private Operation of Railways in Brazil* (New York, 1932), p. 183.

30. Vargas to Borges, Rio, Oct. 8, 1926, ABM.

31. The story of Getúlio's reluctance to take the job and Borges's insistence that he do so has previously been treated as an anecdote, but it is not. The Borges papers confirm that the Governor made the decision for Getúlio. See Vargas to Borges, Rio, Oct. 10, 1926; Borges to Vargas, Pôrto Alegre, Oct. 13, 1926, ABM. On Getúlio's opinion of Washington Luís, see Vargas to Borges, Rio, July 29, 1925, ABM.

32. Alves to Borges, Rio, Dec. 8, 1923, ABM.

CHAPTER TEN

1. Agostinho Aquino et al. to Borges, São Borja (RGS), Jan. 13, 1919; Getúlio Vargas to Borges, São Borja, April 3, 1924, ABM.

2. For example, Gilberto Freyre, *Ordem e progresso: Processo de desintegração das sociedades patriarcal e semipatriarcal no Brasil sob o regime de trabalho livre: Aspectos de um quase meio século de transição do trabalho escravo para o trabalho livre; e da Monarquia para a República* (Rio, 1959), I, xxxiv (tr. and abridged by Rod W. Horton as *Order and Progress: Brazil from Monarchy to Republic* [New York, 1970]); and Paul Frischauer, *Presidente Vargas*, tr. Mário da Silva and Brutus Pedreira (São Paulo, 1943), p.

353. Both Ivan Lins and José Maria Bello exaggerate the degree to which Vargas was influenced by positivism. See Lins, *História do positivismo no Brasil* (São Paulo, 1964), pp. 200–201; and Bello, *A History of Modern Brazil: 1889–1964*, tr. James L. Taylor, with a new concluding chapter by Rollie E. Poppino (Stanford, Calif., 1966), p. 281.

3. *Religião da Humanidade, Edificio da sede pozitivista em Porto Alegre* (Pôrto Alegre, 1913), p. 4; *Homenagem da Brigada Militar ao emerito estadista rio-grandense Julio Prates de Castilhos no 30° dia de seu fallecimento (24 de novembro 1903)* (n.p., n.d.), pp. 110–12; *A Federação*, Sept. 24, 1908.

4. *A Federação*, April 24, 1907.

5. André Carrazzoni, *Perfil do estudante Getúlio Vargas* (Rio, 1942), pp. 28–29 and *passim*; "Saudação histórica—Discurso feito em 1906 pelo dr. Getúlio Vargas," *Revista do Instituto Histórico e Geográfico do Rio Grande do Sul*, 90 (1943), 154.

6. *Discurso pronunciado pelo dr. Getulio Vargas no banquete que a representação republicana do Rio Grande do Sul, no congresso nacional, lhe offereceu, por motivo de sua eleição para a presidencia do Estado, no "Jockey Club," do Rio de Janeiro, a 10 de dezembro de 1927* (Pôrto Alegre, 1928), p. 20.

7. Pinheiro to Borges, Rio, Jan. 8, 1915, ABM.

8. Marcos Azambuja to Borges, Uruguaiana (RGS), Aug. 21, 1920, ABM.

9. *A Federação*, Sept. 30, 1930. The rate of inflation was only 2.6 per cent between 1926 and 1927, and therefore was almost negligible as a factor in the higher value of sales in 1927. See IBGE, *Anuário estatístico do Brasil: Ano V 1939/1940* ([Rio], n.d.), p. 1384. On the development of the syndicate, see Sindicato Arrozeiro do Rio Grande do Sul, *A cultura do arroz no Rio Grande do Sul* (Pôrto Alegre, 1935).

10. On the lower costs in the Uruguayan charqueadas, see *A Federação*, Sept. 30, 1930; for comparative data on freight charges, see Federação das Associações Ruraes do Estado do Rio Grande do Sul (FARSUL), *Annaes do congresso de criadores, effectuado em Porto Alegre, de 24 a 29 de maio de 1927* (Pôrto Alegre, 1927), p. 44.

11. President Washington Luís Pereira de Sousa to Getúlio Vargas, Rio, Aug. 2, 1928, AGV.

12. *A Federação*, Oct. 1, 1929; FARSUL, *Annaes do IV congresso rural* (Pôrto Alegre, 1930), p. 14.

13. Computed from data in Rio Grande do Sul, Departamento Estadual de Estatistica, "Annuario: 1929 (Politica e moral, 2ª secção)" (manuscript, n.d.), p. 47.

14. Boris Fausto, "A revolução de 1930," in Manuel Nunes Dias et al., *Brasil em perspectiva* (São Paulo, 1968), p. 263; and Fausto, *A revolução de 1930: Historiografia e história* (São Paulo, 1970), pp. 32–38 (an important revisionist study using a Marxist framework). Fausto shows that the PD was decidedly agrarian in its orientation, and therefore more like the PL than previously believed. See also Paulo Nogueira Filho, *Ideais e lutas de um*

*burguês progressista: O Partido Democrático e a revolução de 1930* (2d ed., Rio, 1965), I, 154ff and *passim*.

15. Neves to Vargas, Rio, Nov. 11, 1928; Borges to Vargas, Irapuã (RGS), Dec. 20, 1928; João Pinto da Silva (Vargas's secretary) to João Daudt, Pôrto Alegre, Jan. 21, 1929, AGV. My account of the events of 1929 and 1930 is based on the archives of Getúlio Vargas, Borges de Medeiros, and Osvaldo Aranha, plus the following printed works: PRIMARY SOURCES (including memoirs). João Neves da Fontoura, *A jornada liberal* (Pôrto Alegre, 1932), 2 vols., and *Memórias, II: A Aliança Liberal e a revolução de 1930* (Pôrto Alegre, 1963); J[oaquim] F[rancisco] de Assis Brasil, *Attitude do Partido Democratico Nacional na crise da renovação presidencial para 1930–1934* (Pôrto Alegre, 1929); Firmino Paim Filho, *Ao Rio Grande do Sul e á nação* (n.p., n.d.); Lourival Coutinho, *O General Góes depõe . . .* (Rio, 1955), pp. 57–145; [Pedro] Góes Monteiro, *A revolução de 30 e a finalidade politica do exercito* (Rio de Janeiro, n.d.) pp. 1–102; Virgilio de Mello Franco, *Outubro, 1930* (n.p., 1931); Gil de Almeida, *Homens e factos de uma revolução* (Rio, n.d.); Paulo Nogueira Filho, *Ideais* (cited in note 14 above); *A successão presidencial: As cartas dos Snrs. Getulio Vargas e Antonio Carlos e as respostas do Snr. Washington Luiz* (n.p., n.d.); *Aliança Liberal: Documentos da campanha presidencial* (Rio, 1930); and *Revista do Globo (Edição especial): Revolução de outubro de 1930: Imagens e documentos* (Pôrto Alegre, 1931) (a good collection of documents and photographs for 1929–30). SECONDARY SOURCES. Afonso Arinos de Melo Franco, *Um estadista da República (Afrânio de Melo Franco e seu tempo),* III, 1273–1366; Boris Fausto, "A revolução" and *A revolução* (cited in note 14 above); John W. F. Dulles, *Vargas of Brazil: A Political Biography* (Austin, Tex., 1967), pp. 60–72; Agnes Waddell, "The Revolution in Brazil," *Foreign Policy Association Information Service,* VI, 26 (March 4, 1931), 489–506 (an excellent summary of financial and economic problems from 1926 to 1930); Antônio Delfim Netto, *O problema do café no Brasil* (São Paulo, 1959), pp. 123–26; Hélio Silva, *O ciclo de Vargas, II: 1926: A grande marcha* (Rio, 1965) and III: *1930: A revolução traída* (Rio, 1966) (works that contain many documents from the Aranha and Vargas papers, not all of them faithfully transcribed); and [Alexandre José] Barbosa Lima Sobrinho, *A verdade sôbre a revolução de outubro* (São Paulo, 1933) (which despite its early appearance remains the best general account). Other sources on specific events are indicated in the notes below.

16. Neves to Vargas, Rio, June 18, 1929, AGV.

17. Borges to Vargas, Irapuã, June 28, 1929 (copy); Vargas to Neves, Pôrto Alegre, June 15, 1929, AGV; Paulo Hasslocher to Vargas, Rio, July 9, 1929, in Silva, *1926,* p. 260.

18. Vargas to W. L. Pereira de Sousa, Pôrto Alegre, July 11, 1929; Pereira de Sousa to Vargas, Rio, July 25, 1929; Vargas to Pereira de Sousa, Pôrto Alegre, July 29, 1929, AGV.

19. Vargas to Neves, Pôrto Alegre, Aug. 14, 1929, AGV.

20. Neves to Vargas, Rio, July 6, 1929 (copy), ABM.

21. "Resumo da segunda conferencia entre o sr. dr. Getulio Vargas e Francisco Antunes Maciel, nesta data," Pôrto Alegre, July 26, 1929, AGV.

22. Vargas to Neves, Pôrto Alegre, July 1, 1929, AGV.

23. Vargas to Neves, Pôrto Alegre, May 16, Aug. 14, Sept. 2, 1929, AGV. Washington Luís did in fact strengthen the federal garrison at Juiz de Fora, Minas Gerais.

24. Vargas to Neves, Pôrto Alegre, July 12, 1929, in Neves, *Memórias*, II, appendix, pp. xix–xxii; Vargas to Aranha, Pôrto Alegre, Aug. 12, 1929, AOA; Vargas to Neves, Pôrto Alegre, Aug. 19, 1929, AGV.

25. Vargas to Borges, Pôrto Alegre, Oct. 24, 1929, ABM; "Notas informativas para uso particular," n.d., AGV.

26. Paim Filho, p. 6. This work is an exposé of Vargas's behavior written four days after the October 3 revolt. Paim's allegations are indirectly supported by the "Notas informativas" in the Vargas papers, cited in the note above.

27. Vargas to Neves, Pôrto Alegre, Aug. 23, 1929; Collor to Vargas, Rio, Aug. 12, 1929, AGV. Collor's interest in contemporary European politics may have been stimulated by his service on the foreign relations committee in the chamber and his knowledge of German.

28. Edigar Alencar, *Nosso Sinhô do samba* (Rio, 1968), p. 38.

29. Aranha to Pereira de Sousa, Pôrto Alegre, March 4, 1930, AOA.

30. Celso Furtado, *The Economic Growth of Brazil*, tr. Richard Aguiar and Eric Drysdale (Berkeley, Calif., 1963), p. 198; Nelson Werneck Sodré, *História da burguesia brasileira* (Rio, 1964), p. 288; Waddell, p. 501.

31. Waddell, pp. 498–500.

32. Delfim Netto, p. 130.

33. Vargas to Borges, Pôrto Alegre, April 15, 1930, ABM.

34. Vargas to Neves, Pôrto Alegre, Sept. 13, 1929, AGV.

35. Coutinho, p. 52.

36. Vargas to Borges, Pôrto Alegre, June 16, 1930; Borges to Vargas, Irapuã, June 19, 1930, ABM.

37. *Diario do Congresso Nacional*, XLI, 16 (May 21, 1930), 544.

38. Nogueira Filho, II, 481.

39. Vargas to Gov. Alvaro Carvalho, Pôrto Alegre, Aug. 15, 1930 (copy), ABM. The message was in the typically abbreviated language of a telegram, and I have supplied a half dozen connecting words.

40. Vargas to Paim, Pôrto Alegre, Aug. 8, 1930, AGV; Vargas to Borges, Pôrto Alegre, Aug. 24, 1930; Aranha to Borges, n.p., Aug. 30, 1930, ABM.

41. Aranha to Vargas, n.p., Sept. 13, 1930, AOA; Almeida, p. 278.

42. Dep. Francisco Flôres da Cunha to Borges, Livramento, Sept. 4, 1930; Vargas to Borges, Pôrto Alegre, Sept. 15, 1930, ABM; [Augusto] Tasso Fragoso, "A revolução de 1930," in *Revista do Instituto Histórico e Geográfico Brasileiro*, 211 (April-June, 1951), 27.

43. Virgilio de Mello Franco, pp. 313–14. General Almeida's intercepted messages are preserved in the Aranha papers.

44. Barbosa Lima Sobrinho, p. 288.

45. On popular support for the revolution, see Harrison to Secretary of State, Pôrto Alegre, Oct. 9 [1930] (Dept. of State, Index Bureau 832.00 Revolutions/30, National Archives of the United States). Estimates of the number of Gaúchos mobilized vary from 20,000 to 100,000; I have chosen what seems to be a plausible compromise.

46. The text of the manifesto is reproduced in Nogueira Filho, II, 725–27.

47. See, for example, Neves, *A jornada liberal*, I, 5–43.

48. *A Federação*, April 24, 1907.

CHAPTER ELEVEN

1. Osvaldo Aranha to Luís Aranha [Pôrto Alegre], March [?], 1932, AOA.

2. Gilberto Amado, *Depois da política* (Rio, 1960), p. 152.

3. On the period 1930–32, see Joseph L. Love, "Rio Grande do Sul as a Source of Political Instability in Brazil's Old Republic, 1909–1932" (Columbia University, unpub. Ph.D. diss., 1967), pp. 257–97. For a treatment of developments in Rio Grande since 1930, see Carlos E. Cortés, "The Role of Rio Grande do Sul in Brazilian Politics, 1930–1967" (University of New Mexico, unpub. Ph.D. diss., 1969). A general survey of national politics in the same period is Thomas E. Skidmore, *Politics in Brazil, 1930–1964: An Experiment in Democracy* (New York, 1967).

4. Computed from data in IBGE, *Anuário Estatístico do Brasil: Ano V 1939/1940* ([Rio], n.d.), p. 1412.

5. Cortés, pp. 15–16, 204, 218, and *passim*.

6. Pan American Union: Inter-American Committee for Agricultural Development (CIDA), *Land Tenure Conditions and Socioeconomic Development of the Agricultural Sector: Brazil* (Washington, D.C., 1966), pp. 136, 542.

Glossary
Note on Sources
Index

# Glossary

*Aliança Liberal* (Liberal Alliance). Coalition of the establishment parties of Minas Gerais, Rio Grande do Sul, and Paraíba, and the Partido Democrático Nacional, formed to support Getúlio Vargas in the presidential election of 1930.

*Aliança Libertadora* (Alliance of Liberation). Coalition of the Partido Democrático and the Partido Federalista in Rio Grande, formed to support Assis Brasil in the 1922 gubernatorial election; formally constituted as a party in 1924 and reorganized as the Partido Libertador in 1928.

*bacalhau.* Dried fish; consumed by lower-income and middle-income groups in Brazil as a substitute for charque. (In Portugal the word refers to codfish only, but it has a broader application in Brazil.)

*bacharel, bacharéis.* Law school graduate(s); more broadly, any humanistically educated university graduate.

*Bahiano.* Inhabitant of the State of Bahia.

*café-com-leite* (coffee with milk). Refers to entente between the Republican parties of the coffee-producing states of Minas Gerais and São Paulo; so named because Minas was also a dairy state.

*Campanha.* Hilly grassland region of Rio Grande do Sul, west of the Litoral and south of the Jacuí and Ibicuí rivers.

*capanga.* A henchman used to enforce a coronel's orders; often employed in electoral fraud.

*Carioca.* Inhabitant of the city of Rio de Janeiro.

*Catete.* Official residence of the president of Brazil in the Old Republic; located in city of Rio de Janeiro.

*caudillo.* A political leader who dominates his followers by the force of his personality.

*charque.* Dried (jerked) beef; the most important export of Rio Grande do Sul in the Old Republic.

*cochilha.* Rolling, grass-covered hill in Rio Grande; also, a series of such hills. Typical feature of the Campanha.

*colono.* Small farm owner of German or Italian origin; most frequently found in the Serra.

*coronel, coronéis.* Rural boss(es); typically a large landowner.

*coronelismo.* System of political control and manipulation of the rural vote by the coronéis.

*delegado.* A police officer with jurisdiction at the local (district) level.

*estância.* A rural estate used primarily for ranching.

*estancieiro.* Owner of an estância.

*faculdade.* A professional school or college, e.g., a law school.

*fazenda.* A plantation, ranch, or large farm. (A broader term than estância.)

*fazendeiro.* Owner of a fazenda.

*First Republic.* Same as Old Republic.

*Fluminense.* Inhabitant of the State of Rio de Janeiro.

*Gaúcho.* Originally the cowboy of Rio Grande do Sul, and later any inhabitant of the state; synonymous with Riograndense.

*Historical Republican.* One who agitated for a republic in Brazil before the fall of the Empire in 1889.

*Litoral.* Coastal portion of Rio Grande do Sul, containing alluvial areas of the Lagoa dos Patos and the Lagoa Mirim.

*Maragato.* Member of the Partido Federalista of Rio Grande do Sul; same as Federalist.

*Military Brigade.* The state police force of Rio Grande do Sul.

*Mineiro.* Inhabitant of the State of Minas Gerais.

*município.* A subdivision of a state equivalent in most respects to a county.

*Old Republic.* The first Republican regime in Brazil, which replaced the Empire in 1889 and fell with the revolution of 1930.

*Partido Democrático* (Democratic Party—PD). Opposition group in São Paulo State, founded in 1926; joined with the Aliança Libertadora to found the Partido Democrático Nacional in 1927.

*Partido Democrático [Republicano]* (Democratic [Republican] Party). Group of PRR dissidents organized by Assis Brasil in 1908; merged with the Partido Federalista in the Aliança Libertadora in 1922.

*Partido Democrático Nacional* (National Democratic Party—PDN). Loose grouping of state opposition parties, founded in 1927; the most important constituent groups were the Partido Democrático of São Paulo and the Aliança Libertadora.

*Partido Federalista* (Federalist Party). Opposition party in Rio Grande do Sul dedicated to introducing parliamentary government; organized by Silveira Martins in 1892 as the successor of the (Imperial) Liberal Party.

*Partido Libertador* (Liberator Party—PL). Successor to Assis Brasil's Aliança Libertadora, constituted in 1928.

*Partido Republicano Conservador* (Conservative Republican Party—PRC). Coalition of state parties that supported President Hermes da Fonseca; organized in 1910 and controlled by Pinheiro Machado until his death in 1915.

*Partido Republicano Federal* (Federal Republican Party—PRF). Coalition organized by Francisco Glicério to nominate Prudente de Morais for president and to support his programs; virtually destroyed by Prudente in 1897.

*Partido Republicano Mineiro* (Mineiro Republican Party—PRM). Establishment party in Minas Gerais during the Old Republic.

*Partido Republicano Paulista* (Paulista Republican Party—PRP). Establishment party in São Paulo during the Old Republic.

*Partido Republicano Riograndense* (Riograndense Republican Party— PRR). Establishment party in Rio Grande do Sul during the Old Republic; the organization of Castilhos, Borges de Medeiros, Pinheiro Machado, and Vargas.

*Paulista.* Inhabitant of the State of São Paulo.

*política dos governadores* (politics of the governors). Political system during the Old Republic that enabled the president and the governors of the major states to make the important decisions about federal policies and personnel; in a broader sense, the policy of establishment groups at all levels of government to maintain each other in power indefinitely.

*Reação Republicana* (Republican Resistance). Coalition of the establishment parties of Rio Grande do Sul, Rio de Janeiro, Bahia, and Pernambuco, formed to support Nilo Peçanha in the presidential election of 1922.

*Riograndense.* Inhabitant of the State of Rio Grande do Sul.

*salvacionistas (salvationists).* Reform-minded army officers who took over the governments of several northeastern states during the presidency of Hermes da Fonseca (1910–14) in order to "redeem" the states from entrenched political oligarchies.

*salvacionismo.* The collective activities of the salvacionistas; also, their program of "redemption."

*Sebastianism.* A millenarian cult based on the belief that Sebastian I, a king of Portugal killed in a battle against the Moors in 1578, would appear in Brazil to punish evildoers and reward the righteous.

*Serra.* Plateau north of Jacuí and Ibicuí rivers in Rio Grande do Sul, with both forests and rolling grasslands. Consists of three subregions: the Colonial Zone in the east, the Central Plateau, and the Missões (missions) District in the west.

*sertanejo.* An inhabitant of the sertão.

*sertão.* Backlands; brush country. Most often applied to the interior of the northeast.

*tenentes* (lieutenants). Nationalistic junior officers who rebelled against the federal government in the years 1922–26, and joined Vargas in the revolution of 1930.

*tenentismo.* The collective activities of the tenentes; also, their ill-defined revolutionary program.

# Note on Sources

Since I have furnished complete publication data in the Notes, with full citations for each chapter, it does not seem useful to reproduce the works cited in alphabetical order. Instead I have compiled a list of reference works of special importance for the study of both Rio Grande do Sul and the Old Republic, and have supplied further information on primary manuscript sources.

## 1. SELECTED REFERENCE WORKS NOT CITED IN TEXT

Abranches, Dunshee de. *Governos e congressos da Republica dos Estados Unidos do Brazil: 1889 a 1917*. 2 vols. São Paulo, 1918. (Good biographical source but sometimes inaccurate.)

Barreto, Abeillard. "Viajantes estrangeiros no Rio Grande do Sul," in *Fundamentos da cultura riograndense: Quinta série*. [Pôrto Alegre], 1962, pp. 15–48. (Critical essay on travel literature dating from the sixteenth century.)

Barros Paiva, Tancredo de. *Achegas a um diccionario de pseudonymos*. Rio de Janeiro, 1929.

Bernardi, Mansueto. "A bibliografia italiana referente ao Rio Grande do Sul," in *Fundamentos da cultura riograndense: Quinta série*. [Pôrto Alegre], 1962, pp. 159–76. (Critical essay on literature by Italian observers dating from the sixteenth century.)

Borges Fortes, Amyr, and João S. B. Wagner. *História administrativa, judiciária e eclesiástica do Rio Grande do Sul*. Pôrto Alegre, 1963. (An indispensable source on the details of administrative history.)

Carone, Edgard. *A República Velha (Instituições e classes sociais)*. São Paulo, 1970. (Appeared after the present book was in type. Though overly schematic, Carone's study is a major synthesis of the era of the Old Republic. Preceded by *A Primeira República (1889–1930): Texto e contexto*. São Paulo, 1969. The new volume will be complemented by a forthcoming study of the evolution of politics in the period.)

Cortés, Carlos E., and Richard Kornweibel. *Bibliografia da história do Rio Grande do Sul (Período republicano)*. Pôrto Alegre, 1967. (Especially useful for political history, but incomplete.)

*Enciclopédia rio-grandense*. 4 vols. Canoas, Rio Grande do Sul, 1957. (A general survey of Gaúcho culture.)

Ferreira, João Francisco. "Elementos para uma bibliografia sôbre o Rio Grande do Sul," in *Fundamentos da cultura riograndense: Primeira série*. [Pôrto Alegre], 1954, pp. 175–210; and "Ensaio para uma bibliografia do Rio Grande do Sul," in *Fundamentos . . . : Segunda série*. [Pôrto Alegre], 1957, pp. 139–79. (Uncritical general bibliographies, largely but not entirely overlapping.)

Ferreira Filho, Arthur. *História Geral do Rio Grande do Sul: 1503–1964*. 3d ed., Pôrto Alegre, 1965. (A brief survey of the sweep of Rio Grande's history.)

Fleuiss, Max. *Historia administrativa do Brasil*. São Paulo, 1922. (Contains lists of high-ranking federal personnel and important laws down to 1922.)

Instituto de Estudos Brasileiros and Divisão de Difusão Cultural, Universidade de São Paulo. *O Rio Grande do Sul: Curso de extensão universitária e de difusão cultural*. São Paulo, 1967. Mimeographed. (The best general bibliography on Rio Grande.)

Lacombe, Américo Jacobina. *Brasil: Período nacional*. México, 1956. (Contains a critical bibliography on the Old Republic, pp. 123–55.)

Love, Joseph L. "Indice cronológico dos papéis de Antônio Augusto Borges de Medeiros: 1909–1932," *Revista do Instituto Histórico e Geográfico Brasileiro*, 286 (Jan.–March 1970), pp. 223–76. (Contains excerpts from the most important letters and telegrams.)

———. "Pôrto Alegre: [Historical] Research Opportunities," in Robert M. Levine, ed., *Brazil: Field Research Guide in the Social Sciences*. New York, 1966, pp. 88–96.

Lyra, A. Tavares de. "O senado da República de 1890 a 1930," *Revista do Instituto Histórico e Geográfico Brasileiro*, 210 (Jan.–March 1951), pp. 3–102. (Brief biographies of all senators who served during the Old Republic; supplements Dunshee de Abranches.)

Villas-Bôas, Pedro. *Bibliografia do regionalismo gaúcho*. Pôrto Alegre, 1967, mimeo. (Catalog of Riograndense writers of poetry and prose.)

*Vocabulário sul-riograndense*. Pôrto Alegre, 1964. (Scholarly multi-author treatment of regional vocabulary.)

### 2. UNPUBLISHED PRIMARY SOURCES
#### A. Private Papers

*Collected papers*

Aranha, Osvaldo. Archive, Rio de Janeiro.

Assis Brasil, Joaquim Francisco de. Archive, Pedras Altas, Rio Grande do Sul.

Barbosa, Rui. Archive, Casa de Rui Barbosa, Rio de Janeiro.

Borges de Medeiros, Antônio Augusto. Archive, Instituto Histórico e Geográfico do Rio Grande do Sul, Pôrto Alegre.

Fonseca, Clodoaldo da. Archive, Rio de Janeiro.

Morais Barros, Prudente de. Archive, Instituto Histórico e Geográfico Brasileiro, Rio de Janeiro.

Vargas, Getúlio. Archive, Rio de Janeiro.

Veríssimo de Bittencourt, Aurélio. Archive, Pôrto Alegre.

*Miscellaneous manuscripts in possession of Walter Spalding, Pôrto Alegre.*

## B. Official Manuscript Collections

*Brazil*

Arquivo Nacional, Rio de Janeiro: Floriano Peixoto papers.

Ministério da Guerra, Arquivo, Rio de Janeiro: Miscellaneous *fés de ofício.*

Arquivo Público do Estado, Pôrto Alegre: Município de Cachoeira, Cartórios, 1902–1910.

Departamento Estadual de Estatística, Pôrto Alegre:

"Annuario: 1929." (Also includes data for 1930 and 1931.)

"Produção agrícola: Municípios 1946. Dados gerais—1920/1946."

"Relatorio: Elementos que se referem aos annos de 1897 a 1899 (Demographia, estatistica economica, eleitoral, agricola, pastoril, moral, etc.). Recenseamento federal de 1900."

*United States*

National Archives, Washington, D.C.: Department of State: Dispatches from United States Consuls in Rio de Janeiro, 1910–29 (Microcopy 519, roll 23); Index Bureau 832.00 Revolutions/30, 131; 832.516/149; 832.59 R471/34.

# Index

Abbott, Fernando, 29, 44, 59f, 66, 70, 74, 80, 84–86 *passim*
Abreu, Vespúcio de, 103–4
Acióli, José, 160
Acióli, Tomás, 150
Acióli family, 160f
Additional Act of 1834, 13
Aguiar, Eurípides, 175
Alagoas, 157–58, 159, 165, 167, 176
Albuquerque Lins, Manuel, 144f, 158, 172
Aliança Liberal, 228–38 *passim*, 242
Aliança Libertadora, 201, 203–7, 225. *See also* Libertadores
Almeida, Gil de, 240–41
Alves, João Simplício, 103, 241
Alves, Protásio, 82, 169
Amado, Gilberto, 251
Amaral, Evaristo, 50, 58–59, 81, 270
Amazonas, 125, 157ff, 174, 195, 277
Andrada, Antônio Carlos Ribeiro de, 168, 225–27, 230, 235–39 *passim*
Andrade Guimarães, Artur Oscar de, 53, 91
Andrade Neves, Eurico, 204, 214
*Antônio Chimango*, 29, 170–71
Aranha, Osvaldo, 205, 211, 230, 232, 251, 253, 257; character and biography, 216, 219–20; and revolution of 1930, 235–42 *passim*
Arantes, Altino, 178, 183f, 285
Argentina, 60, 66, 70, 100–101, 113f, 118, 127ff, 210f, 239
army: and PRR, 31, 74, 105, 110, 115–18 *passim*, 122–24, 137, 193, 247f; revolt against Deodoro da Fonseca, 47–48; and Gaúcho civil war, 61–62, 63, 68, 71f, 74; under Prudente de Morais, 93; and presidential successions (1910–30), 122–24, 144, 192–98 *passim*; under Afonso Pena, 142–43; and PRC,

150; under Hermes da Fonseca, 156–59 *passim*, 164; intervention in state politics, 157–63 *passim*; and revolution of 1923, 204f; and revolution of 1930, 239–44 *passim*; after 1930, 250–58 *passim*. *See also* salvacionistas; tenentes
Assis Brasil, Joaquim Francisco: early career, 28, 31, 32–33, 37ff, 43n, 44f, 48f, 64, 84–87 *passim*; background and character, 75n, 86; political theories of, 86, 212, 215, 225, 231, 288; as gubernatorial candidate (1922), 201–3; and revolution of 1923, 203–7; and tenentes' rebellions, 211; as founder of Partido Democrático Nacional, 225; 1930 and after, 229, 252f
Azeredo, Antônio, 139, 150, 176

*bacharelismo*, 136, 163, 171
Backer, Alfredo, 162
Bahia, 73, 90, 110, 115n, 167, 200; and presidential successions (1902–30), 97, 139–40, 144f, 180, 184, 190–91, 228; influence in national politics, 111, 137–38; state military power in, 116, 276; intervention in, 157ff; and revolution of 1930, 242
Bank of Rio Grande do Sul, 223
Barbosa, Rui, 147f, 149n, 157, 167, 198, 220; character and early career, 46, 145–46; and presidential successions (1906–22), 139f, 143–46 *passim*, 167, 181, 184f, 193
Barbosa Gonçalves, Carlos, 29, 83–85, 104, 146–47, 152, 217
Barbosa Gonçalves, José, 154f
Barcelos, Ramiro, 29, 31, 38, 43n, 45, 49, 170–71, 203
Barreto Leite, Domingos, 31n, 48, 51, 53
Barros Cassal, João, 42, 48, 53–54, 61

# BRAZIL
## the Old Republic